Just Ecological Integrity

Studies in Social, Political, and Legal Philosophy

Series Editor: James P. Sterba, University of Notre Dame

This series analyzes and evaluates critically the major political, social, and legal ideals, institutions, and practices of our time. The analysis may be historical or problem-centered; the evaluation may focus on theoretical underpinnings or practical implications. Among the recent titles in the series are:

Necessary Goods: Our Responsibilities to Meet Others' Needs
edited by Gillian Brock, University of Auckland

The Business of Consumption: Environmental Ethics and the Global Economy
edited by Laura Westra, University of Windsor, and Patricia H. Werhane, University of Virginia

Child versus Childmaker: Present Duties and Future Persons in Ethics and the Law
by Melinda A. Roberts, College of New Jersey

Gewirth: Critical Essays on Action, Rationality, and Community
edited by Michael Boylan, Marymount University

The Idea of a Political Liberalism: Essays on Rawls
edited by Victoria Davion and Clark Wolf, University of Georgia

Self-Management and the Crisis of Socialism: The Rose in the Fist of the Present
by Michael W. Howard, University of Maine

Ecofeminist Philosophy: A Western Perspective on What It Is and Why It Matters
by Karen J. Warren, Macalester College

Controversies in Feminism
edited by James P. Sterba, University of Notre Dame

Faces of Environmental Racism: Confronting Issues of of Global Justice, Second Edition
edited by Laura Westra, University of Windsor, and Bill E. Lawson, Michigan State University

Theorizing Backlash: PhilosophicalReflections on the Resistance to Feminism
by Anita M. Superson and Ann E. Cudd

Just Ecological Integrity: The Ethics of Maintaining Planetary Life
edited by Peter Miller and Laura Westra

American Heat: Ethical Problems with the United States' Response to Global Warming
by Donald A. Brown, Pennsylvania Department of Environmental Resources

Just Ecological Integrity

The Ethics of Maintaining Planetary Life

EDITED BY
PETER MILLER
AND
LAURA WESTRA

ROWMAN & LITTLEFIELD PUBLISHERS, INC.
Lanham • Boulder • New York • Oxford

ROWMAN & LITTLEFIELD PUBLISHERS, INC.

Published in the United States of America
by Rowman & Littlefield Publishers, Inc.
A Member of the Rowman & Littlefield Publishing Group
4720 Boston Way, Lanham, Maryland 20706
www.rowmanlittlefield.com

12 Hid's Copse Road
Cumnor Hill, Oxford OX2 9JJ, England

British Library Cataloguing in Publication Information Available

Library of Congress Cataloging-in-Publication Data

Just ecological integrity : the ethics of maintaining planetary life / edited by Peter Miller and Laura Westra.

p. cm.

Includes bibliographical references.

ISBN 0-7425-1285-1 (alk. paper) — ISBN 0-7425-1286-X (pbk. : alk. paper)

1. Ecological integrity. I. Miller, Peter, 1936– II. Westra, Laura.

QH541.15.E245 J87 2002

179'.1—dc21

Printed in the United States of America

™ The paper used in this publication meets the minimum requirements of American National Standard for Information Sciences—Permanence of Paper for Printed Library Materials, ANSI/NISO Z39.48-1992.

To planet Earth and all its inhabitants

and to

Carolyn Garlich
PM

and

Peter Westra
LW

Contents

Foreword

Steven C. Rockefeller

When the World Summit on Sustainable Development convenes in Johannesburg, South Africa, in 2002 it will be the thirtieth anniversary of the UN Stockholm Conference on the Human Environment, as well as the tenth anniversary of the Rio Earth Summit—the United Nations Conference on Environment and Development (UNCED). The Stockholm Conference marked that critical moment in global history when the international community came together to acknowledge its dependence on the natural environment and to recognize that human activity was degrading the environment at an alarming rate, posing a grave threat to the well-being of present and future generations. The nations gathered at Stockholm agreed that environmental protection should be added to the core agenda of the United Nations together with peace, human rights, and equitable social and economic development. Moreover, the Stockholm Declaration reveals an early awareness of the way these goals are interrelated.

In the three decades since Stockholm these issues have been addressed by international scientific panels, world commissions, summit meetings of heads of state, and special sessions of the UN General Assembly. The science of ecosystem conservation and the concept of sustainable development have been widely promoted. Over 180 international declarations and treaties (many of them regional) related to the environment and sustainability have been drafted and ratified. Many nations have adopted environmental standards, regulatory systems, and tax incentives. The annual rate of global population growth has slowed. Recycling is wide spread. Corporations are adopting energy efficient technologies and finding ways to eliminate waste and pollution. Wind and solar powered energy generation is increasing rapidly. Efforts at ecosystem restoration are being attempted in some regions. Much significant progress has been made. The transformation of our patterns of production, consumption, and population growth required to protect the integrity of Earth's ecological systems and the well-being of present and future generations has begun. In general, however, the efforts made to date have been very inadequate. They have failed to reverse the negative trends that are steadily destroying the health of the planet's ecological systems on which human life and the flourishing of civilization are dependent.

A few examples will illustrate the problem. Since 1972 the global population has risen more than 60 percent, dramatically increasing the pressure human beings place on ecosystems. Now over six billion, human numbers are expected to approach eight billion within the next twenty-five years. Most of the population growth is occurring in the developing world, and the number of people living in poverty has risen to 1.3 billion. Fossil fuel consumption has more than doubled, and the number of cars has almost tripled. Carbon emissions are 50 percent higher than they were in 1972, which is a major factor contributing to global warming. A massive extinction of species, on a scale not experienced by the planet in 65 million years, is being caused by human activities that involve habitat destruction, introduction of invasive species, pollution, and overharvesting. The loss of biodiversity has been greatest in fresh water ecosystems. Over 10,000 species, or 20 percent of the world's freshwater fish, have become extinct, endangered, or threatened. There has been mounting pressure on the world's marine fisheries, of which 25 percent are now depleted and 44 percent are being fished at their biological limit. Over half of the oceans' coral reefs are dying. Even though agricultural food production has more than doubled since 1972, roughly 40 percent of agricultural land has been seriously degraded by pollution, nutrient depletion, salinization, and erosion. The forests in developing countries have been reduced by over 10 percent, and the demand for firewood and lumber exceeds the sustainable yield. The water quality in these nations has declined significantly, and the over pumping of aquifers is causing the depletion of ground water supplies in many regions (Worldwatch Institute 2001).

A recent international report, *People and Ecosystems: The Fraying Web of Life*, which contains the initial findings of a comprehensive assessment of global ecosystems sponsored by the United Nations Development Programme, the United Nations Environment Programme, the World Resources Institute, and the World Bank (2000), provides a succinct summary of the situation:

> Earth's ecosystems and its peoples are bound together in a grand but tenuous symbiosis. We depend on ecosystems to sustain us, but the continued health of ecosystems depends, in turn, on our care. Ecosystems are the productive engines of the planet, providing us with everything from the water we drink to the food we eat and the fiber we use for clothing, paper, or lumber. Yet nearly every measure we use to assess the health of ecosystems tells us we are drawing on them more than ever and degrading them at an accelerating pace.

The report makes this further observation: "The current rate of decline in the long-term productive capacity of ecosystems could have devastating implications for human development and the welfare of all species." Here lies the challenge facing the World Summit on Sustainable Development. This situation provides the larger context for the essays contained in this book. They explore challenges and critical choices regarding the future of life on Earth that are fundamental to the Johannesburg Summit and to the ongoing debate that will take place in every nation following the Summit.

Major transformations of society require a shift in attitudes and values as well as institutional changes. This requires an examination of the ethics that govern human behavior and the reconstruction of old ways of thinking. This volume focuses special attention on the ethical dimension of the transition to sustainable ways of living. In this connection, many of the essays contain responses to the declaration of fundamental principles for building a just, sustainable, and peaceful global society found in the Earth Charter. The product of a decade long, worldwide, cross-cultural dialogue on shared values, the Earth Charter reflects an effort to build on and further develop the ethical visions in the Stockholm Declaration (1972), the World Charter for Nature (1982), the Rio Declaration (1992), and a variety of nongovernmental covenants and declarations.

When intergovernmental efforts to create an Earth Charter during the Rio Earth Summit proved unsuccessful, the project was reorganized in 1994 as a civil society initiative under the oversight of an international Earth Charter Commission. It has been the objective of the Earth Charter Initiative to clarify and set forth those fundamental ethical principles and strategies that government, business, and civil society must embrace in order to make the shift to sustainability. The document reflects the growing recognition of the need for world wide cooperation and a new global ethics in an increasingly interdependent world, and it gives expression to a consensus on shared values taking form in the emerging global civil society. Hundreds of international, national, and local organizations have endorsed the Charter and it is being widely used as an educational tool and guide to sustainable development.

At the heart of the Earth Charter is an ethic of respect and care for the community of life in all its diversity. Recognizing that people are interdependent members of the greater community of life, it affirms that all human beings have a shared moral responsibility to care for the larger living world. It takes the position that the needs and well-being of other life forms and ecosystems as well as of present and future human generations are worthy of moral consideration. In this way, the Earth Charter endeavors to expand and deepen the moral consciousness that will shape the policies and practices of industrial technological society in the decades ahead.

The Earth Charter recognizes that caring for Earth and caring for people are closely interconnected. Accordingly, it contains an inclusive ethical vision that emphasizes the eradication of poverty and the promotion of gender equality as well as the protection of ecosystems. It was drafted with the understanding that environmental protection and restoration, human rights, democracy, human development, and peace are interdependent and indivisible. Safeguarding the health and beauty of ecosystems, for example, cannot be achieved without eradicating poverty, promoting economic and social justice for all, strengthening democratic institutions, and creating cultures of tolerance and nonviolence. Holistic thinking and integrated problem solving are essential. The concept of "just ecological integrity" reflects these insights and considerations.

Technological innovation, private initiative, free market competition, and economic globalization are powerful forces shaping the contemporary world. They have a vital role to play in building a better future for all. However, when directed by the single-minded pursuit of economic growth these forces by themselves cannot be counted on to create a secure and promising future. If these forces are not governed and guided by institutions and leaders with a firm ethical commitment to a broad vision of justice and ecological well-being, there are abundant reasons to believe that environmental degradation and resource depletion will be ongoing, the gap between the rich and poor will continue to grow, parts of the world will remain outside the global market, aggravating problems of poverty and social breakdown, and the desperation and bitterness of the billions of excluded poor will lead to rising violence and spreading chaos. The developed nations will increasingly find themselves existing as heavily armed enclaves of threatened prosperity in a divided, dangerous, and declining world.

Some trends suggest that the world is already moving in this direction. However, there is an alternative possibility. Humanity is still able to choose a better way, but it will lose this opportunity if it fails to act decisively within the next two decades. The alternative involves recognizing that economic development, important as it is, is not an end in itself. It is a means. The twofold goal is human development—in the fullest sense—for all and the well-being of the greater community of life. The challenge is to harmonize the creative economic forces of free enterprise and global integration with the ideal of just ecological integrity and the spirit of the Earth Charter. The essays in this welcome volume explore the ethical dimensions of this and related critical issues.

References

United Nations Development Programme, United Nations Environment Programme, World Bank, and World Resources Institute. 2000. *World Resources 2000–2001: People and Ecosystems, The Fraying Web of Life*. Washington, D.C.: World Resources Institute.

The Worldwatch Institute. 2001. *Vital Signs 2001*. New York: W. W. Norton.

Introduction

Peter Miller and Laura Westra

This book is a cooperative venture of the Global Ecological Integrity Project and the Earth Charter Initiative. In June 2000, the Integrity Project convened an international conference on Connecting Environmental Ethics, Ecological Integrity, and Health in the Millennium in San José, Costa Rica, at which representatives of the Earth Charter Initiative took part. Many chapters in this volume originated from that memorable event, but we have also encouraged modifications and received new contributions to address our theme: *Just Ecological Integrity: The Ethics of Maintaining Planetary Life.*

A decade ago, when the Global Ecological Integrity Project initiated its multidisciplinary research, environmental issues had gained international recognition and the urgent need to address them was acknowledged. In June 1992 peoples and nations of the world met in Rio de Janeiro for an Earth Summit to set a course for ecologically sustainable development. A piece of unfinished business from that historic meeting was the negotiation and adoption of an Earth Charter, a set of principles, analogous to the Universal Declaration of Human Rights, to govern human conduct between peoples and with respect to nature.

Since Rio, the Earth Charter Initiative, headquartered in San José, Costa Rica, but operating globally, has pursued the task of bringing the Earth Charter to fruition. In the first section of this book we reproduce the Earth Charter along with several expositions of its history, meaning, and application. They tell the story of a remarkable process of global negotiations to develop a set of principles capable of eliciting meaningful commitments of people, organizations, and governments from a variety of cultural backgrounds. The authors of subsequent chapters further enrich this elucidation of the Earth Charter by seizing its concepts and incorporating them into their treatment of key issues for understanding and implementing a global ethic. The Earth Charter is a system of interlinked principles, an ecology of values. A keystone principle of the system is ecological integrity, the guiding concept for the Global Ecological Integrity Project. We here provide some background on the history and findings of the Integrity Project and an overview of the chapters that follow.

The Global Ecological Integrity Project

History

Around the time of the Earth Summit in Rio, Laura Westra convened the Global Ecological Integrity Project, a program of research supported by the Social Sciences and Humanities Research Council of Canada (SSHRCC) from 1992 to 1999 and by the NATO Advanced Research Workshop program in 1999. The project's first goal was to assemble an interdisciplinary team of scientists and philosophers to work on a definition of the concept of integrity. Although present in many regulatory documents since its first appearance in the U.S. Clean Water Act in 1972, the term has been widely used but consistently left undefined. This is surprising because integrity forms a part of many legal instruments, from Canada to Russia to Brazil. It also appears in the "mission statements" of many organizations, from the Union of Concerned Scientists to the Wildlands Project to the Earth Charter, ever since Aldo Leopold's famous claim that "a thing is right when it tends to preserve the integrity, stability, and beauty of the biotic community. It is wrong when it tends otherwise" (Leopold 1949).

The first interdisciplinary definition was reached in time to appear in Westra (1994), and that definition became a starting point for subsequent work by the Integrity Project. The project has produced a series of volumes on the interpretation of integrity and related concepts from a variety of disciplinary perspectives, drawing implications for human health and other sectors, such as urban areas, parks and protected areas, agriculture, fisheries, forestry, and other economic pursuits. In the final volume, Westra and her collaborators revisited the concept of integrity to review, expand, and clarify it (Westra 1994, 1998; Westra and Lemons 1995; Lemons, Westra, and Goodland 1998; Crabbé, Holland, Ryszkowski, and Westra 2000; Pimentel, Westra, and Noss 2000).

The work of the group received substantial recognition when the World Health Organization (WHO) convened a workshop involving their own scientists and members of the Integrity group in their Rome office. After serious consideration of the arguments and scientific evidence brought to the table by the Integrity group, coinvestigator Colin Soskolne and WHO Director (Rome Office) Roberto Bertollini produced a WHO document "Global Ecological Integrity and 'Sustainable Development': Cornerstones of Public Health" (1999).

But the emphasis of the group's work was not exclusively on scientific understanding, as the normative and public policy implications of our research were always at the forefront of our deliberations. As early as

October 1996, Westra convened a meeting in Montreal at the time of the IUCN meetings at which Steven Rockefeller presented a preliminary draft of the Earth Charter. From the beginning, Integrity Project philosophers and scientists alike have deliberated about the ethical dimensions and implications of our research, including such issues as biocentrism, anthropocentrism, and environmental justice. James Sterba, for example, addresses all these issues in Sterba 1998 and Westra the latter (Westra 1994; Westra 1998). Westra's 1998 book included a discussion of portions of the Earth Charter, and recognized that document in both its form and its goal, as a template of a desirable regulatory framework with global reach. For that reason, San José, Costa Rica was chosen as the most appropriate site for a final conference for the Integrity Project, as an ideal venue to explore common concerns with the Earth Charter Initiative and the University for Peace located there.

The Concept of Ecological Integrity

In Pimentel, Westra, and Noss (2000), the Integrity Group updated their understanding of ecological integrity, citing the newsworthy example of desert blooms in Chile following El Niño-induced rains after decades of dormancy. Ecological integrity, in common usage, is a broad "umbrella" that encompasses a variety of themes cutting across scientific and popular thought.

> 1. The example is drawn from *wild nature*, i.e., nature that is virtually unchanged by human presence or activities. Although the concept of integrity may be applied in other contexts, wild nature provides the paradigmatic examples for our reflection and research. Because of the extent of human exploitation of the planet, such examples are most often found in those places that, until recently, have been least hospitable to dense human occupancy and industrial development: deserts, the high arctic, high altitude mountain ranges, the ocean deep, and the less accessible reaches of forests. Wild nature is also found in locations whose capacity to evoke human admiration won their protection in natural parks.
>
> 2. The rapid bloom of desert organisms illustrates in a dramatic fashion some of the *autopoietic (self-creative) capacities* of life to organize, regenerate, reproduce, sustain, adapt, develop, and evolve.
>
> 3. These self-creative capacities are *dynamically temporal*. The present display of living forms and processes in the desert gains significance through its past and its future. Nature's rhythms are displayed over time; no momentary snapshot captures all of nature's potential. . . . [In relation to its past, the desert is part of *nature's legacy*, demonstrating capacities of organisms and systems for self-maintenance and evolution, past and future.]
>
> 4. Desert conditions, relieved by rains at rare intervals, are themselves the products of larger regional and global weather patterns. Indeed both the biological and geoclimatic processes that led to the blooming desert play them-

> selves out on a stage with much larger *spatial scope*. A major issue for conservation biology is the question of what spatial requirements are needed to maintain native ecosystems. . . .
>
> 5. Implicit in the above is the fact that biophysical phenomena constitute a system of interacting and interdependent components that can be analyzed as an *open hierarchy of systems*. Every organism in the desert comprises a system of organic subsystems and interacts with other organisms and abiotic elements to constitute larger ecological systems of progressively wider scope up to the ecosphere.
>
> 6. Note, finally, that ecological integrity is *valuable and valued*. . . . [T]he dramatic transformation of "barren" desert into a vital and diverse biotic community provoked wonder and appreciation. Other ecological communities, such as reefs and rainforests, display their prolific life in a more continuous, less seasonal or episodic fashion. More generally, the biological and physical processes at work in these instances gave rise to the totality of life on Earth, including ourselves, and maintain the conditions for the continuation of life as we know it. Thus natural ecosystems are valuable to themselves for their continuing support of life on Earth, as well as for the aesthetic value and the goods and services they provide to humankind. Indeed, ecological integrity is essential to the maintenance of ecological sustainability as a foundation for a sustainable society (Westra, Miller, Karr, Rees, and Ulanowicz 2000, 20–22).

The Integrity Group found to be particularly helpful definitions proposed by James Karr, which identify integrity with nature's evolutionary legacy as found primarily in wild nature:

> *Ecological integrity* is the sum of physical, chemical, and biological integrity (Karr and Dudley 1981; Karr 1996).
>
> *Biological integrity* is the ability to support and maintain a balanced, integrated, adaptive biological system having the full range of elements (genes, species, and assemblages) and processes (mutation, demography, biotic interactions, nutrient and energy dynamics, and metapopulation processes) expected in the natural habitat of a region (Karr and Chu 1995).

Karr's widely used *Index of Biotic Integrity* is calibrated from a baseline condition found "at a site with a biota that is the product of evolutionary and biogeographic processes in the relative absence of the effects of modern human activity" (Karr 1996), in other words, wild nature. It can measure the extent to which human impacts lead to a site deviating from the baseline condition of integrity.

Karr distinguishes ecological integrity from health. Whereas integrity points to the condition of wild nature, ecological health indicates sustainable land and water use:

> *Ecological health* describes the goal for the condition at a site that is cultivated for crops, managed for tree harvest, stocked for fish, urbanized, or otherwise intensively used" (Karr 1996).

A healthy site must meet two criteria: (1) its use does not degrade the place for future use (e.g., no loss of soil or groundwater), and (2) its use does not degrade any other areas beyond the site (e.g., no production of acid rain that degrades vegetation and lakes elsewhere). When these two conditions are met at a site, human activity is sustainable at that site. For a society to be ecologically sustainable, every site that it uses must be healthy in this sense and some areas must retain ecological integrity to maintain global biological functions, life support, biodiversity, and "nature's services" (Daily 1997; Karr 1996; Westra, Miller, Karr, Rees, and Ulanowicz 2000, 31–32).

Findings

As the above selections show, ecological integrity is both descriptively significant for scientific analysis and normatively significant for law, policy, economics, planning, management, and ethics. In its dual descriptive and normative roles, as a subject matter for a variety of different disciplines, and as a unifying theme for interdisciplinary analysis, ecological integrity functions much like the concept of human health. Health, disease, and dysfunction, like integrity and its loss, are at once categories of positive and negative value and empirically describable states of biological entities.

Among the basic conclusions emerging from the Integrity Project are these:

1. Despite apparent affluence in first world nations and global improvement in several health and well-being indicators, human "progress" has been mixed and precarious and, for significant numbers, nonexistent or lethal.
2. There is no way that current levels of population and consumption and modes of production can be sustained.
3. Although there are instances of ecological restoration, there are many signs of ecological deterioration around the globe.
4. Modern economies have a generic flaw: they fail to take into account, in an integrated way, the facts of human ecology. The Cartesian cultural split between people and nature is expressed in ecological sciences that study every creature except humans, and economic analysis that ignores the total dependence of human economies upon ecological processes.
5. Despite a growing body of policy, legislation, regulation, and international agreement that establish local, national, and international mandates to protect and restore ecological integrity, in most such policies, the fundamental notion of ecological integrity is left vague and unexamined.

In response to issues like these, the Global Integrity Project has created a multipronged response, which can be summarized by several linked elements.

(a) *Understanding*: Understand the global ecosphere in evolutionary context as a complex system of systems. Human economies are dependent subsystems of the ecosphere, which increasingly degrade the whole.
(b) *Values*: Adopt an ecological ethic that values natural systems and the multiple forms of life and gives more weight to global and intergenerational equity in humanistic ethics.
(c) *Measurement*: Develop indicators of human and ecological well-being consistent with the understanding and values in (a) and (b) and employ them in systems of measurement and reporting.
(d) *Prescriptions*: Develop prescriptions to guide conduct based on (a)–(c), including ecological principles for land-use zoning and sustainable exploitation of resources.
(e) *Social Measures*: Recommend effective social mechanisms and institutions for realizing the prescriptions in (d).

In previous publications, each of the above areas has been elaborated at some length in historical, philosophical, economic, political, and scientific ways and for a variety of sectors. In this volume, authors from the Integrity Project and others converge from a variety of perspectives on the values, rationales, and issues of implementation for a global ethic like the Earth Charter.

The Plan of This Book

Part 1 showcases the Earth Charter (chapter 1). The task of valuing the Earth is described in three sections: (1) An exposition (and critique) of the Earth Charter itself, its meaning, history, and uses (chapters 1–5); (2) Reflections connecting humanistic ethical systems with the Earth Charter (chapters 6–8); and (3) Systems of measurement to indicate progress and decline in achieving Earth Charter ideals (chapters 9 and 10). An introduction to part 1 relates these chapters to the tasks of ethical inquiry and negotiation.

Part 2 moves from principles to practice by exploring more concretely reciprocal impacts between humans and nature, with consequent responsibilities. Chapters 11–13 focus on our agricultural ties to nature, how these affect the human prospect, and the challenges of developing more sustainable practices. Chapters 14–17 look at human destructiveness in other spheres, with a case study of a major cyanide spill on the Tisza River in Eastern Europe, two theoretical pieces on destructive global production and consumption patterns, and the potential contributions of the Earth Charter to global warming issues. An introduction to part 2 identifies flawed valuations underlying industrial economies, which promote destruction by viewing nature as practically worthless apart from human industry.

Part 3 begins (chapters 18–20) by focusing on questions of justice that arise once nature is revalued to recognize intrinsic qualities, multiple benefits to humans, various kinds of environmental harms and limits, and our dependence on the natural systems of which we are a part. A series of case studies (chapters 21 25) examines issues of violence, risk, diverse perspectives, and the preservation of nature in local circumstances.

Acknowledgments

We gratefully acknowledge generous support for the Global Integrity Project by the Social Sciences and Humanities Council of Canada (1992–99) and NATO's Advanced Scientific Research Workshop program (1999). We have also received support in dollars or in kind for the June 2000 San José conference or this book from the Earth Charter Initiative, Sarah Lawrence College, the University of Winnipeg, and the University of Notre Dame. Ruth Lucier was particularly helpful in both conference organization and editorial suggestions for several book chapters. The International Society for Environmental Ethics, the North American Society for Social Philosophy, the International Society for Value Inquiry, the Society for Business Ethics, and the Society for the Philosophy of Technology also participated in the San José conference.

References

Crabbé, P., A. Holland, L. Ryszkowski, and L. Westra, eds. 2000. *Implementing Ecological Integrity: Restoring Regional and Global Environmental and Human Health.* NATO Scientific Publications. Dordrecht, Netherlands: Kluwer.

Daily, G. C., ed. 1997. *Nature's Services: Societal Dependence on Natural Ecosystems.* Washington, D.C.: Island Press.

Karr, J. R. 1996. "Ecological Integrity and Ecological Health Are Not the Same." Pp. 97–109 in P. Schulze, ed. *Engineering within Ecological Constraints.* Washington, D.C.: National Academy Press.

Karr, J. R., and E. W. Chu. 1995. "Ecological Integrity: Reclaiming Lost Connections." Pp. 34–48 in L. Westra and J. Lemons, eds. *Perspectives on Ecological Integrity.* Dordrecht, Netherlands: Kluwer.

Karr, J. R., and D. R. Dudley. 1981. "Ecological Perspective on Water Quality Goals." *Environmental Management* 5: 55–68.

Lemons, J., L. Westra, and R. Goodland, eds. 1998. *Ecological Sustainability and Integrity: Concepts and Approaches*. Dordrecht, Netherlands: Kluwer.

Leopold, A. 1949. *A Sand County Almanac and Sketches Here and There*. Oxford and New York: Oxford University Press.

Pimentel, D., L. Westra, and R. F. Noss, eds. 2000. *Ecological Integrity: Integrating Environment, Conservation, and Health.* Washington, D.C.: Island Press.

Soskolne, C. L., and R. Bertollini. 1999. "Global Ecological Integrity and 'Sustainable Development': Cornerstones of Public Health." WHO European Centre for Environment and Health. <http://www.who.it/Emissues/Globaleco/globaleco.htm> (17 July 2001).

Sterba, J. *Justice Here and Now*. 1998. Cambridge: Cambridge University Press.

Westra, L. 1994. *An Environmental Proposal for Ethics: The Principle of Integrity*. Lanham, Md.: Rowman & Littlefield.

———. 1998. *Living in Integrity*. Lanham, Md.: Rowman & Littlefield.

Westra, L., and J. Lemons, eds. 1995. *Perspectives on Ecological Integrity*. Dordrecht, Netherlands: Kluwer.

Westra, L., P. Miller, J. Karr, W. Rees, and R. Ulanowicz. 2000. "Ecological Integrity and the Aims of the Global Integrity Project." Pp. 19–41 in D. Pimentel, L. Westra, and R. Noss, eds. *Ecological Integrity: Integrating Environment, Conservation, and Health*. Washington, D.C.: Island Press.

Westra, L., and P. Wenz, eds. 1995. *Faces of Environmental Racism: Confronting Global Equity Issues*. Lanham, Md.: Rowman & Littlefield.

Part 1

Valuing the Earth

A New Global Covenant

Humanistic Values and the Earth Charter

Measuring Progress and Decline

Introduction to Part 1

A New Global Covenant

> We urgently need a shared vision of basic values to provide an ethical foundation for the emerging world community. Therefore, together in hope we affirm the following interdependent principles for a sustainable way of life as a common standard by which the conduct of all individuals, organizations, businesses, governments, and transnational institutions is to be guided and assessed.
>
> —Earth Charter 2002, Preamble

Ethical Inquiry and Negotiation

In the first section of part 1 we reproduce the Earth Charter (chapter 1) along with several expositions of its history, meaning, and application. These chapters tell the story of a remarkable process of global negotiations to develop a set of principles capable of eliciting meaningful commitments of people from a variety of cultural backgrounds.

On some accounts of ethics, such an achievement would be impossible. If, for example, an ethics is a completed revelation delivered in a past era on tablets of clay or by an authoritative teacher, followers might "Go . . . and make disciples of all nations . . . teaching them to observe [all that was commanded]" (Matthew 28: 19–20). But no discovery or negotiation of new principles could ensue.

Likewise, if ethics is primarily an expression of the power and interests of a ruling class, more imposed than taught, then it can have no legitimacy among the oppressed of the world.

If, on the other hand, in rejecting cultural imperialism one maintains that ethics can exist only parochially, within separate sociocultural groups, or privately, within individuals, then there could be no globally shared principles.

What we need is a view of ethics that permits mutual inquiry, debate, and negotiation of shared principles from different perspectives, as the Earth Charter requires. Ethics explores the nature, scope, content, and grounds of human responsibility. Our conceptions of responsibility rest in part on an understanding of who and what we are as human beings and how we relate to one another and to other beings. Thus, as our understandings of our place in the world change, we need periodically to rethink our ethical principles and responsibilities.

Ethics has many dimensions and starting points for reexamination. The broad injunction, *Do good and avoid evil or harm (insofar as possible),* makes implicit or explicit reference to (a) *moral agents* to whom the injunction is directed; (b) potential *beneficiaries or victims* of created goods and harms, i.e., the "stakeholders"; (c) *values* that define the kinds of good and harm that actions may cause; and (d) the *context* or *circumstances* in which the responsibility holds. For example, in the claim, "Parents are responsible for providing protection and nurture for their children," parents are the moral agents, their children the beneficiaries, protection and nurture the values, and the parent/child relationship the context. Together these specify the *content* of the responsibility.

Moral judgments also require *justification*, the provision of *reasons*, which make sense relative to one or more *value perspectives* or *worldviews*—fundamental beliefs about how the world works and what is of value (Miller 2000).

Together, these components of responsibility provide a framework for ethical inquiry, debate, and negotiation revolving around questions like: (1) *Who* is responsible?; (2) *To whom or what* are they responsible?; (3) What are the most serious *harms* to avoid and most important *benefits* (values) to pursue?; (4) What are the biophysical and human *circumstances* that are the *context* for responsibility?; and (5) What are *reasons* for recognizing these responsibilities and are the reasons credible from a variety of well-considered *perspectives*? The scheme thus encompasses both highly contextual particular moral judgments and broad philosophical, religious, cultural, and scientific foundations (*worldviews*) that provide a more global framework for ethical reflection.

Note that *religious* and *cultural* differences need not prevent agreement on a shared *content* for ethics, provided only that there is sufficient convergence to articulate responsibilities compatible with the different belief systems. This is particularly important for the prospect of negotiating a shared global ethic such as the Earth Charter. Although a global ethic does not require a global religion or government, it does require sufficient motivation and reason to seek common ground with others who have different starting points. Two basic sources of convergence are (1) a recognition of a threat to mutual interests and (2) love and care, not only for other humans, including future generations, but also other living things, "biophilia" (Wilson 1984). The Earth Charter Preamble invokes both. "The choice is ours: form a global partnership to care for Earth and one another or risk the destruction of ourselves and the diversity of life."

The Earth Charter

The Earth Charter (chapter 1) is a declaration of fundamental principles for building a just, sustainable, and peaceful global society in the twenty-first century. It is the ethical focus of this book. Other chapters expound (and critique) its origins, content, justification, and application.

Chapters 2–4 provide insiders' views of the Earth Charter Initiative. D'Evie and Glass (chapter 2) describe the reasons for creating the Earth Charter, the history of the consultative drafting process that created it, and the efforts to promote its adoption by individuals, governments, and other organizations. Adoption must be more than a formal resolution; the Charter must become "an ethical framework for sustainable living," which requires reflective education and the evaluation of practices. D'Evie and Glass also document the struggles to find common ground while respecting cultural differences.

Brenes (chapter 3) addresses the concept of universal responsibility, which pervades the Earth Charter. This demanding concept is universal with respect to both moral agents and beneficiaries, as expressed in the Charter's first paragraph: "[W]e, the peoples of Earth, declare our responsibility to one another, to the greater community of life, and to future generations."

Responsibility connects with other values. Brenes reports that Central American educators have developed an Integral Model of Education for Peace, Democracy, and Sustainable Development. Central to the model is a view of the self, having peace and universal responsibility at its core, surrounded by values signifying health within and healthy relations to human and living communities.

Engel (chapter 4) argues that the Earth Charter system of values rests on a democratic faith "that human beings have the rational and moral capacity to govern themselves for the common good of all under the uncertain evolutionary and historical circumstances of life on this planet." The Earth Charter, then, is a rewriting of the global covenant through deliberation about, and commitment to, comprehensive moral ends. It draws on a variety of historic undertakings pledging mutual respect and shared community, including a series of international summits since World War II. The Earth Charter goes farther than any of its predecessors in articulating a democratic faith, in the democratic consultative processes that produced it, and in the comprehensiveness of its moral vision. His account is a rich portrait of the ethical pedigree and content of the Earth Charter.

Davion (chapter 5) examines both the concept of integrity and the Earth Charter from an ecofeminist perspective. Ecofeminism sees close ties between the personal and political dimensions of life and between multiple forms of oppression, e.g., the oppression of people and of the environment exhibit the same basic "logic of domination" and often go hand in hand. While ecofeminists might agree that protection of ecological integrity is important, they have questioned its association with wilderness as a place "untouched by man," which may reflect a privileged androcentric perspective. They ask what distributions of power and privilege make it inconceivable or impossible for many to live according to an integrity ethic in the circumstances in which they find themselves. (See also Isla and Turner, chapter 25 of this volume.)

Davion finds points of harmony between ecofeminism and the Earth Charter because social, gender, and power issues are explicitly linked with environmental issues. On the other hand, the very features that Brenes and Engel find attractive about the Charter, the affirmation of universal responsibility and use of an inclusive "we" and "human family" to signify a covenantal undertaking, Davion views with suspicion. Families are often sites of patriarchal power, and universal responsibility is empty and insensitive when addressed to most people of the world, for whom oppressive social conditions leave little room for choice.

Davion's position raises the question: Is the negotiation of a true global ethic possible or desirable? In reply, we can ask, Is there a better alternative that can address our urgent global situation?

Humanistic Values and the Earth Charter

Although ethics is addressed to human *moral agents*, it doesn't follow that only they should be the *beneficiaries* of moral practice. Indeed the Earth Charter affirms that "every form of life has value regardless of its worth to human beings" (Principle 1a) and enjoins us to "treat all living beings with respect and consideration" (Principle 15). It is thus, in part, a *biocentric* ethic that departs from the dominant *anthropocentric* or *humanistic* ethics in the West, which holds that only human beneficiaries need to be taken into account in moral practice. Other things are important only insofar as they bear on the well-being of humans.

How, then, shall Western ethical traditions with well-developed concepts of rights and welfare for *humans* come to terms with the emergent environmentalism in the modern world? Chapters 6–8 provide three answers to that question.

Bartkowiak (chapter 6) argues that it would be a mistake to abandon anthropocentric ethics for environmental issues, even if you accept biocentric principles. Ethics has to be concerned with results, such as preventing real harms, and has to achieve those results by arguments with people and interventions in systems dominated by anthropocentric thinking. Because human welfare is closely linked with environmental conditions, many favorable environmental outcomes can be achieved on the basis of humanistic considerations, without trying to convert the world to biocentrism. For example, risk analysis used to justify incremental pollution should be rejected as a violation of human rights.

Zack (chapter 7), on the other hand, thinks that nothing short of rights for natural entities is likely to be able to protect nature from incremental destruction. She asks, "How can we Westerners bring intuitions, insights, and traditions concerning the intrinsic worth of natural systems and beings into the discourse of recognized practical reason or moral argument?" Only an approach based on rights and respect for persons affords strong moral protection. Thus individual organisms or species or populations or ecosystems should be classified as persons to gain the protection of our strongest moral principles. Acknowledging that such a move may appear extreme, Zack offers reasons to make it plausible.

In chapter 8, Braye and Lucier offer a third approach connecting humanistic values with global concerns: the virtues of leadership. They find the ideals of the Earth Charter inspiring and uplifting, but insufficient. Ideals require implementation, and implementation is often problematic because of tensions between the ideals. Focused leadership can help to achieve results. Braye and Lucier offer two models of leadership that complement one another, servant-leadership and philosophical leadership, which in combination can help people discover compassionate and reasonable ways to implement their adopted ideals.

Measuring Progress and Decline

The Earth Charter is a set of principles that aims to guide human conduct to better the world for people and nature. But we can know if things are better or worse only if we have some means to measure progress and decline. How can this be done? Chapters 9 and 10 address that question.

Anielski and Soskolne (chapter 9) comment on the paradox that, while signs of ecological deterioration abound, key economic and health measures, such as stock markets, the gross domestic product (GDP), and global life expectancies, have continued to rise. They argue that this picture is distorted because (1) in using up natural capital, such progress is not sustainable, and (2) the economic instruments fail to measure genuine progress in well-being. To address these defects, they propose the Genuine Progress Indicator (GPI) System of Sustainable Well-Being Accounts, which shows, e.g., that despite rising GDPs, both the United States and Alberta have declined in GPI since the 1970s.

Karr (chapter 10) notes that, although human success (like that of other organisms) depends upon the exploitation of Earth's ecosystems, we have only measured economic success, not the impacts of exploitation. A complete picture requires indicators that reflect the condition of ecological and economic systems as well as their interactions. For economic systems, we have the (defective) gross national product (like the GDP above) and improved measures, like the index of sustainable economic welfare (ISEW). For ecological systems we need measures of ecological condition, like Karr's Index of Biotic Integrity (IBI).

For ecology/economy interactions, estimates of the value of nature to the economy (a) define and classify the goods and services nature supplies, and (b) attach monetary valuations to these (by one estimate worth U.S. $33 trillion per year). Looking in the other direction, ecological footprint analysis estimates areas of productive land and water needed to sustain resource and waste assimilation requirements of economies. We are already in a deficit situation in relation to what the planet has to offer.

Conclusion

Thus a comprehensive valuing of the Earth requires a compelling set of ideals, such as the Earth Charter, and reflection on the meanings, connections, and implications for practice of those ideals, drawing upon our cultural resources and being sensitive to the effects of unequally distributed social power. It also requires personal, collective, and mutual commitments to the ideals, the human community, and the community of life, bringing to bear whatever capabilities and leadership skills we may possess or acquire. As the remainder of this book will make clear, valuing requires knowledge of the workings of human and natural systems, the sources of what we value, the harms and injustices created by our activities, and practical measures for reducing harm and injustice. Finally, valuing requires evaluations of the state of societies, economies, natural systems, and the interactions between these; and evaluation requires systems of measurement and reporting.

References

The Earth Charter Initiative. 2002. "The Earth Charter." San José, Costa Rica: Earth Council. <http://www.earthcharter.org/earthcharter/charter.htm> (January 12, 2002).

Miller, P. 2000. Approaches to Ecological Integrity: Divergence, Convergence, and Implementation. Pp. 57–73 in Philippe Crabbé, Alan Holland, Lech Ryszkowski, and Laura Westra, eds. *Implementing Ecological Integrity: Restoring Global Environmental and Human Health.* Dordrecht, Netherlands: Kluwer.

Wilson, E. O. 1984. *Biophilia*. Cambridge, Mass.: Harvard University Press.

A New Global Covenant

Chapter 1

The Earth Charter

Preamble

We stand at a critical moment in Earth's history, a time when humanity must choose its future. As the world becomes increasingly interdependent and fragile, the future at once holds great peril and great promise. To move forward we must recognize that in the midst of a magnificent diversity of cultures and life forms we are one human family and one Earth community with a common destiny. We must join together to bring forth a sustainable global society founded on respect for nature, universal human rights, economic justice, and a culture of peace. Towards this end, it is imperative that we, the peoples of Earth, declare our responsibility to one another, to the greater community of life, and to future generations.

Earth, Our Home

Humanity is part of a vast evolving universe. Earth, our home, is alive with a unique community of life. The forces of nature make existence a demanding and uncertain adventure, but Earth has provided the conditions essential to life's evolution. The resilience of the community of life and the well-being of humanity depend upon preserving a healthy biosphere with all its ecological systems, a rich variety of plants and animals, fertile soils, pure waters, and clean air. The global environment with its finite resources is a common concern of all peoples. The protection of Earth's vitality, diversity, and beauty is a sacred trust.

The Global Situation

The dominant patterns of production and consumption are causing environmental devastation, the depletion of resources, and a massive extinction of species. Communities are being undermined. The benefits of development are not shared equitably and the gap between rich and poor is widening. Injustice, poverty, ignorance, and violent conflict are widespread and the cause of great suffering. An unprecedented rise in human population has overburdened ecological and social systems. The foundations of global security are threatened. These trends are perilous—but not inevitable.

The Challenges Ahead

The choice is ours: form a global partnership to care for Earth and one another or risk the destruction of ourselves and the diversity of life. Fundamental changes are needed in our values, institutions, and ways of living. We must realize that when basic needs have been met, human development is primarily about being more, not having more. We have the knowledge and technology to provide for all and to reduce our impacts on the environment. The emergence of a global civil society is creating new opportunities to build a democratic and humane world. Our environmental, economic, political, social, and spiritual challenges are interconnected, and together we can forge inclusive solutions.

Universal Responsibility

To realize these aspirations, we must decide to live with a sense of universal responsibility, identifying ourselves with the whole Earth community as well as our local communities. We are at once citizens of different nations and of one world in which the local and global are linked. Everyone shares responsibility for the present and future well-being of the human family and the larger living world. The spirit of human solidarity and kinship with all life is strengthened when we live with reverence for the mystery of being, gratitude for the gift of life, and humility regarding the human place in nature.

We urgently need a shared vision of basic values to provide an ethical foundation for the emerging world community. Therefore, together in hope we affirm the following interdependent principles for a sustainable way of life as a common standard by which the conduct of all individuals, organizations, businesses, governments, and transnational institutions is to be guided and assessed.

Principles

I. Respect and Care for the Community of Life

1. *Respect Earth and life in all its diversity.*
   a. Recognize that all beings are interdependent and every form of life has value regardless of its worth to human beings.
   b. Affirm faith in the inherent dignity of all human beings and in the intellectual, artistic, ethical, and spiritual potential of humanity.

2. *Care for the community of life with understanding, compassion, and love.*
   a. Accept that with the right to own, manage, and use natural resources comes the duty to prevent environmental harm and to protect the rights of people.
   b. Affirm that with increased freedom, knowledge, and power comes increased responsibility to promote the common good.

3. *Build democratic societies that are just, participatory, sustainable, and peaceful.*
   a. Ensure that communities at all levels guarantee human rights and fundamental freedoms and provide everyone an opportunity to realize his or her full potential.
   b. Promote social and economic justice, enabling all to achieve a secure and meaningful livelihood that is ecologically responsible.

4. *Secure Earth's bounty and beauty for present and future generations.*
   a. Recognize that the freedom of action of each generation is qualified by the needs of future generations.
   b. Transmit to future generations values, traditions, and institutions that support the long-term flourishing of Earth's human and ecological communities.

In order to fulfill these four broad commitments, it is necessary to:

II. Ecological Integrity

5. *Protect and restore the integrity of Earth's ecological systems, with special concern for biological diversity and the natural processes that sustain life.*
   a. Adopt at all levels sustainable development plans and regulations that make environmental conservation and rehabilitation integral to all development initiatives.

   b. Establish and safeguard viable nature and biosphere reserves, including wild lands and marine areas, to protect Earth's life support systems, maintain biodiversity, and preserve our natural heritage.
   c. Promote the recovery of endangered species and ecosystems.
   d. Control and eradicate non-native or genetically modified organisms harmful to native species and the environment, and prevent introduction of such harmful organisms.
   e. Manage the use of renewable resources such as water, soil, forest products, and marine life in ways that do not exceed rates of regeneration and that protect the health of ecosystems.
   f. Manage the extraction and use of non-renewable resources such as minerals and fossil fuels in ways that minimize depletion and cause no serious environmental damage.

6. *Prevent harm as the best method of environmental protection and, when knowledge is limited, apply a precautionary approach.*
   a. Take action to avoid the possibility of serious or irreversible environmental harm even when scientific knowledge is incomplete or inconclusive.
   b. Place the burden of proof on those who argue that a proposed activity will not cause significant harm, and make the responsible parties liable for environmental harm.
   c. Ensure that decision making addresses the cumulative, long-term, indirect, long distance, and global consequences of human activities.
   d. Prevent pollution of any part of the environment and allow no build-up of radioactive, toxic, or other hazardous substances.
   e. Avoid military activities damaging to the environment.

7. *Adopt patterns of production, consumption, and reproduction that safeguard Earth's regenerative capacities, human rights, and community well-being.*
   a. Reduce, reuse, and recycle the materials used in production and consumption systems, and ensure that residual waste can be assimilated by ecological systems.
   b. Act with restraint and efficiency when using energy, and rely increasingly on renewable energy sources such as solar and wind.
   c. Promote the development, adoption, and equitable transfer of environmentally sound technologies.
   d. Internalize the full environmental and social costs of goods and services in the selling price, and enable consumers to identify products that meet the highest social and environmental standards.
   e. Ensure universal access to health care that fosters reproductive health and responsible reproduction.

f. Adopt lifestyles that emphasize the quality of life and material sufficiency in a finite world.

8. *Advance the study of ecological sustainability and promote the open exchange and wide application of the knowledge acquired.*
   a. Support international scientific and technical cooperation on sustainability, with special attention to the needs of developing nations.
   b. Recognize and preserve the traditional knowledge and spiritual wisdom in all cultures that contribute to environmental protection and human well-being.
   c. Ensure that information of vital importance to human health and environmental protection, including genetic information, remains available in the public domain.

III. Social and Economic Justice

9. *Eradicate poverty as an ethical, social, and environmental imperative.*
   a. Guarantee the right to potable water, clean air, food security, uncontaminated soil, shelter, and safe sanitation, allocating the national and international resources required.
   b. Empower every human being with the education and resources to secure a sustainable livelihood, and provide social security and safety nets for those who are unable to support themselves.
   c. Recognize the ignored, protect the vulnerable, serve those who suffer, and enable them to develop their capacities and to pursue their aspirations.

10. *Ensure that economic activities and institutions at all levels promote human development in an equitable and sustainable manner.*
   a. Promote the equitable distribution of wealth within nations and among nations.
   b. Enhance the intellectual, financial, technical, and social resources of developing nations, and relieve them of onerous international debt.
   c. Ensure that all trade supports sustainable resource use, environmental protection, and progressive labor standards.
   d. Require multinational corporations and international financial organizations to act transparently in the public good, and hold them accountable for the consequences of their activities.

11. *Affirm gender equality and equity as prerequisites to sustainable development and ensure universal access to education, health care, and economic opportunity.*
   a. Secure the human rights of women and girls and end all violence against them.

b. Promote the active participation of women in all aspects of economic, political, civil, social, and cultural life as full and equal partners, decision makers, leaders, and beneficiaries.
c. Strengthen families and ensure the safety and loving nurture of all family members.

12. *Uphold the right of all, without discrimination, to a natural and social environment supportive of human dignity, bodily health, and spiritual well-being, with special attention to the rights of indigenous peoples and minorities.*
   a. Eliminate discrimination in all its forms, such as that based on race, color, sex, sexual orientation, religion, language, and national, ethnic or social origin.
   b. Affirm the right of indigenous peoples to their spirituality, knowledge, lands, and resources and to their related practice of sustainable livelihoods.
   c. Honor and support the young people of our communities, enabling them to fulfill their essential role in creating sustainable societies.
   d. Protect and restore outstanding places of cultural and spiritual significance.

IV. Democracy, Nonviolence, and Peace

13. *Strengthen democratic institutions at all levels, and provide transparency and accountability in governance, inclusive participation in decision making, and access to justice.*
   a. Uphold the right of everyone to receive clear and timely information on environmental matters and all development plans and activities which are likely to affect them or in which they have an interest.
   b. Support local, regional and global civil society, and promote the meaningful participation of all interested individuals and organizations in decision making.
   c. Protect the rights to freedom of opinion, expression, peaceful assembly, association, and dissent.
   d. Institute effective and efficient access to administrative and independent judicial procedures, including remedies and redress for environmental harm and the threat of such harm.
   e. Eliminate corruption in all public and private institutions.
   f. Strengthen local communities, enabling them to care for their environments, and assign environmental responsibilities to the levels of government where they can be carried out most effectively.

14. *Integrate into formal education and life-long learning the knowledge, values, and skills needed for a sustainable way of life.*
    a. Provide all, especially children and youth, with educational opportunities that empower them to contribute actively to sustainable development.
    b. Promote the contribution of the arts and humanities as well as the sciences in sustainability education.
    c. Enhance the role of the mass media in raising awareness of ecological and social challenges.
    d. Recognize the importance of moral and spiritual education for sustainable living.

15. *Treat all living beings with respect and consideration.*
    a. Prevent cruelty to animals kept in human societies and protect them from suffering.
    b. Protect wild animals from methods of hunting, trapping, and fishing that cause extreme, prolonged, or avoidable suffering.
    c. Avoid or eliminate to the full extent possible the taking or destruction of non-targeted species.

16. *Promote a culture of tolerance, nonviolence, and peace.*
    a. Encourage and support mutual understanding, solidarity, and cooperation among all peoples and within and among nations.
    b. Implement comprehensive strategies to prevent violent conflict and use collaborative problem solving to manage and resolve environmental conflicts and other disputes.
    c. Demilitarize national security systems to the level of a non-provocative defense posture, and convert military resources to peaceful purposes, including ecological restoration.
    d. Eliminate nuclear, biological, and toxic weapons and other weapons of mass destruction.
    e. Ensure that the use of orbital and outer space supports environmental protection and peace.
    f. Recognize that peace is the wholeness created by right relationships with oneself, other persons, other cultures, other life, Earth, and the larger whole of which all are a part.

The Way Forward

As never before in history, common destiny beckons us to seek a new beginning. Such renewal is the promise of these Earth Charter principles. To fulfill this promise, we must commit ourselves to adopt and promote the values and objectives of the Charter.

This requires a change of mind and heart. It requires a new sense of global interdependence and universal responsibility. We must imaginatively develop and apply the vision of a sustainable way of life locally, nationally, regionally, and globally. Our cultural diversity is a precious heritage and different cultures will find their own distinctive ways to realize the vision. We must deepen and expand the global dialogue that generated the Earth Charter, for we have much to learn from the ongoing collaborative search for truth and wisdom.

Life often involves tensions between important values. This can mean difficult choices. However, we must find ways to harmonize diversity with unity, the exercise of freedom with the common good, short-term objectives with long-term goals. Every individual, family, organization, and community has a vital role to play. The arts, sciences, religions, educational institutions, media, businesses, nongovernmental organizations, and governments are all called to offer creative leadership. The partnership of government, civil society, and business is essential for effective governance.

In order to build a sustainable global community, the nations of the world must renew their commitment to the United Nations, fulfill their obligations under existing international agreements, and support the implementation of Earth Charter principles with an international legally binding instrument on environment and development.

Let ours be a time remembered for the awakening of a new reverence for life, the firm resolve to achieve sustainability, the quickening of the struggle for justice and peace, and the joyful celebration of life.

The Earth Charter can be found at http://www.earthcharter.org/earthcharter/charter.htm (12 January 2002). For more information please contact the Earth Charter International Secretariat, c/o Earth Council, P.O. Box 319-6100, San José, Costa Rica. Phone: (506) 205-1600; fax: (506) 249-3500; e-mail: info@earthcharter.org; website: http://www.earthcharter.org.

Chapter 2

The Earth Charter: An Ethical Framework for Sustainable Living

Fayen d'Evie and Steven M. Glass

The Earth Charter Initiative

The Earth Charter Initiative is a worldwide participatory process to promote the values and principles that can guide our behavior towards a sustainable way of life. The process consists of three main elements: the consultative drafting of the Earth Charter document; the building of intergovernmental support aimed at having the Earth Charter endorsed by the United Nations in 2002; and a valuing process, through which the principles of the Earth Charter are internalized and translated into people's daily lives and into the organizations and institutions to which they belong.

The Earth Charter reflects recognition of our interdependence, of the need for shared responsibility and a global partnership if we are to make the changes necessary for sustainable living. It also represents a code of conduct, which sets forth fundamental values and principles to guide individuals, organizations, businesses, communities, and nations towards ecological, social, and economic sustainability.

Why an Earth Charter?

The argument for a global Earth ethic can be explained as follows. We live in a world of rapid change and growing interdependence. The problems we face are complex and do not fit within the political boundaries, local or national, that attempt to address them. Our challenges must be addressed by a constituency equally broad, with common values and norms, derived from recognized common interest. The future of the human species and the larger community of life on Earth is in doubt if human beings cannot address war and proliferation of nuclear weapons, climate change, biodiversity loss, depletion of resources like soil and water, overpopulation, poverty, social violence, inequitable development, ignorance, and injustice. As the Earth Charter states, "We stand at a critical moment in Earth's history, a time when humanity must choose its future. . . . The choice is ours: form a global partnership to care for Earth and one another or risk the destruction of ourselves and the diversity of life."

Fundamental changes are needed in our values, institutions, and ways of living. We must learn and internalize the deepening scientific truths of our connectiveness, not only with one another, but also with the broader community of life. There must be understanding that what is human today has become so through evolution and relationship with all life over eons and that this evolution continues. Sustainability depends on the decisions we make—on the actions we take, though these must be infused with the awe of being. Our inner dialogues must include weighing our current levels of production and consumption with the words contained in the Preamble, "We must realize that when basic needs have been met, human development is primarily about being more, not having more." Thus, at the core of our inner dialogues needs to be recognition that "the spirit of human solidarity and kinship with all life is strengthened when we live with reverence for the mystery of being, gratitude for the gift of life, and humility regarding the human place in nature."

The challenges that confront us not only spread beyond our traditional borders—they interact with one another like a virus that forms new strains even as it is treated. The Earth Charter Preamble sets out that our environmental, economic, political, social, and spiritual challenges are interconnected. There are more environmental refugees than political ones in the world today. As environments erode, populations must shift, and conflicts are created; disease is able to proliferate and slums and political instability are created. One may start with corruption, lack of transparency, poverty, inequitable distribution of wealth, or any of the multitude of challenges and connect them like stacked dominos awaiting the removal of one.

We have lived through centuries in which the rights of individuals have been developed and codified. It is widely acknowledged today that transactions and communications transcending traditional boundaries have allowed the powerful input of transnational corporations and civil society into the process of governance, but there are not only few laws to govern our future; there is no collective value system to be a foundation for such laws nor a system of ethics to connect our multifarious activities. Inherent in the Earth Charter is recognition that new sets of international dilemmas give rise to the need to articulate and give life to an Earth community, not only a community of humans, but also a community with all life.

At the heart of our motivations for action are our ethical and value systems. These are motivations to which we respond individually and as organizations. The heterogeneous value systems can lead to conflictual, uncollaborative action.

Alternatively, by focusing on the "common good," moral synergies can be elicited, which can in turn lead to harmonious collective action. This is what the Earth Charter is about—finding a shared set of principles and values upon which we, within our diverse backgrounds and cultures, can unite to light a pathway of partnership toward a more just, sustainable, and peaceful future.

History of the Development of the Earth Charter

Earth Charter consultations have been going on for over a decade, since the late 1980s, following a recommendation by the Brundtland Commission. Representatives from both governmental and nongovernmental organizations (NGOs) tried to secure the adoption of an Earth Charter in 1992, at the Rio Earth Summit, but governments were not ready for it. In 1994, the Earth Charter initiative was reignited by Ruud Lubbers, prime minister of the Netherlands, Maurice Strong, chairman of the Earth Council and the secretary-general of the Earth Summit, Mikhael Gorbachev, chair of Green Cross International, and Jim MacNeil, who had been secretary-general of the Brundtland Commission.

During the years 1995 and 1996, extensive research was conducted in the fields of international law, science, religion, ethics, environmental conservation, and sustainable development in preparation for the drafting of the Earth Charter. The Earth Council and a number of partner organizations conducted Earth Charter consultations throughout the world in an effort to promote the global dialogue on common values and to clarify the emerging consensus regarding principles of environmental protection and sustainable living. The consultation process began with an international conference at the Peace Palace in the Hague in May of 1995. Representatives from thirty countries and over seventy organizations participated in the Hague meeting. A study of over 50 international law instruments was prepared and circulated as a resource for those contributing to the consultation process.

In addition to international law instruments and NGO declarations, the ideas and principles in the Earth Charter are drawn from a variety of sources. The Earth Charter is influenced by the new scientific worldview, including the discoveries of contemporary cosmology, physics, evolutionary biology, and ecology. It draws on the wisdom of the world's religions and philosophical traditions. It reflects the social movements associated with human rights, democracy, gender equality, civil society, disarmament, and peace. It builds on the seven UN summit conferences on children, the environment, human rights, population, women, social development, and the city, held during the 1990s.

As the consultation process progressed, a general agreement was reached on a set of criteria for the proposed Earth Charter. It was established that the Charter should be: a declaration of fundamental ethical principles for environmental conservation and sustainable development; composed of principles of enduring significance that are widely shared by people of all races, cultures, religions, and ideological traditions; relatively brief and concise; a document with a holistic perspective and an ethical and spiritual vision; and a declaration that adds significant new dimensions of value to what has already been articulated in relevant documents.

Early in 1997, the Earth Council and Green Cross International formed an Earth Charter Commission to give oversight to the process. Five cochairs (and the commission membership) were selected to represent the regions of the world: Kamla Chowdhry, Asia and the Pacific; Amadou Toumani Toure, Africa and the Middle East; Mercedes Sosa, Latin America and the Caribbean; Mikhail Gorbachev, Europe; and Maurice F. Strong, North America. A secretariat for the commission was established at the Earth Council. Steven Rockefeller, a professor of religion and ethics at Middlebury College in the United States who had prepared the 1996 Summary and Survey, was invited to head up the drafting process and an international drafting committee was created.

In March 1997, a Benchmark Draft of the Earth Charter was issued by the Commission at the conclusion of the Rio+5 Forum held in Rio de Janeiro. The Rio+5 Forum, which was organized by the Earth Council as part of a worldwide review of progress toward sustainable development since the Rio Earth Summit, brought together over 500 representatives of NGOs and National Councils of Sustainable Development. Intensive consultations on the text of the Earth Charter were held during the six days of the forum. The Benchmark Draft, which contained a short preamble, eighteen principles, and a conclusion, provided a new focus for the ongoing international dialogue on the Earth Charter. During the years 1997 and 1998, numerous conferences and meetings on common values and text of the Benchmark Draft were held in all regions of the world. The Earth Council created an Earth Charter internet website (www.earthcharter.org). Mikhail Gorbachev hosted a three-day meeting on the Earth Charter for representatives from Russia, Europe, and the drafting committee in March 1998. In April, Gorbachev participated in an Earth Charter forum for Pacific Rim countries in Kyoto, Japan. This same month a special conference on the Earth Charter and human rights was held at the Boston Research Center for the 21st Century in the United States. This was followed several months later by a conference on the scientific foundations of the Earth Charter, hosted by the Hastings Center, a U.S. organization specializing in bio-medical and environmental ethics. The Earth Charter was also presented and debated at a series of conferences on religion and ecology at the Center for the Study of World Religions at Harvard University. National Earth Charter committees were formed in over thirty-five different countries.

In December 1998, representatives from twenty-four national Earth Charter committees gathered for a six-day Earth Charter Continental Congress of the Americas in Cuiabá, Mato Grosso, Brazil. Some groups drafted national and regional Earth Charters as part of their contribution of the consultation process and the Earth Charter movement. Comments and recommendations on ways to improve the text of the Earth Charter were forwarded to the drafting committee, which circulated revised versions of the document for further comment during 1998. Gradually Benchmark Draft II took form.

Early in 1999, a special international drafting meeting was held at the Pocantico Conference Center of the Rockefeller Brothers Fund outside New York City to complete work on Benchmark Draft II. This meeting included representatives from Argentina, Australia, Brazil, Canada, Costa Rica, Germany, the Philippines, Pakistan, Russia, and the United States with contributing members in India, Kenya, and the Netherlands. In April, the Earth Charter Commission formally released Benchmark Draft II.

Over the next eleven months numerous translations of the Earth Charter text were completed and Earth Charter dialogues involving both experts in diverse fields and representatives from grassroots communities were conducted in many countries. During 1999, the Earth Council organized two on-line conferences on the new text in English (April) and Spanish (November). The April on-line conference was conducted over a two-week period and attracted participants from 78 countries and 300 universities. Multistakeholder national fora examining the text were held in a number of countries, for example, a national forum of 100 delegates was held in Canberra, Australia during February. Three regional Earth Charter conferences were held over 1998/99 to provide a synthesis of national level consultations: (1) Latin America: Mato Grosso, Brazil, December 1998; (2) Central Asia: Kyrgyzstan, June 1999; and (3) Africa and the Middle East: Cape Town, December 1999. Presentations and workshops on the Earth Charter were conducted at the Parliament of the World's Religions, which was also meeting at this time in Cape Town.

A team of international lawyers from the IUCN Commission on Environmental Law carefully reviewed the document and made recommendations. The number of national Earth Charter committees grew to forty-five. During October 1999, representatives from these national committees participated with the drafting committee in a ten-day on-line conference that focused on the text of the document.

In January 2000, another special international drafting meeting was held in an effort to finalize the document. Work continued on the text through February. The basic structure of Benchmark Draft II was preserved. However, extensive revisions were made in wording and in the ordering of the principles in an effort to make the document as concise and coherent as possible. Meeting at the UNESCO headquarters in Paris in mid-March, the Earth Charter Commission carefully reviewed and refined the text in the light of the international discussion. The final version of the Earth Charter was issued on March 24.

In drafting a document to reflect and represent the various cultures and belief systems to which it must apply required dialogue, accommodation, and at times vote taking within the drafting committee. There were specific instances in which beliefs clashed; for example, the contemplated phrase "compassion for all beings" was questioned by indigenous societies, for whom this precept may have precluded hunting, but for whom "Respect Earth and life in all its diversity" echoes thousands of years of connectivity with nature and animals taken with respect. The issue was resolved, though not for all societies and belief systems, by inserting "compassion" within Principle 2, which gives it higher weight, and including Principle 15, which specifically addresses the issues of expressed concern by indigenous societies.

The very term "sustainable development" is not found within the Earth Charter, though former drafts contained this term. After extended debate, the omission was finally assented to following comments from a university student on one of the on-line forums poignantly asserting it be a term, given its use since Rio, denoting that ongoing development is an assumed part of the definition.

Another example of cultural differences that arose had to do with women from Latin America preferring the term gender "equity" to gender "equality" as an expression of the differences in men and women that should be appreciated and acknowledged. Other women preferred the term "equal." The issue was resolved by use of both terms, and the "equality" was included as it had been an agreed upon declaration of the Beijing Conference on Women and it was felt that an internationally debated and decided issue should be carried forward.

The issue of reproductive health was resolved in similar fashion, as the language employed in 7e: "Ensure universal access to health care that fosters reproductive health and responsible reproduction" and in Principle 11: "Affirm gender equality and equity as prerequisites to sustainable development and ensure universal access to education, health care, and economic opportunity" affirms decisions reached at the Beijing Summit. The Earth Charter does not contain language that affirms or precludes abortion or birth control and letters to the Secretariat have questioned the Earth Charter as not being strong enough on either side of the issues. Different cultures and traditions will have to resolve what is contained within the Charter: "An unprecedented rise in human population has overburdened ecological and social systems" and it is hoped this wording will guide and frame deliberations on this challenge.

Earth Charter as an Ethical Framework in Practice

The valuing process catalyses people to translate the Earth Charter principles into their daily lives, for example through professional codes of conduct, ethical frameworks for local and national Agenda 21s, or through educational curricula.

The World Federation of Engineers has been examining the implications of the Earth Charter for engineering practice, and is recommending that engineers be expected to know and use the Earth Charter principles in their work. The International Council of Local Environmental Initiatives (ICLEI) has endorsed the Charter and is seeking its international municipal members to publicly debate and ratify the Earth Charter and use it in municipal planning and governance. In the Philippines, an Earth Scout program has been started, wherein the young people undertake a series of learning and experiential activities focused on the environment. The International Ombudsman Program, a collaborative effort of the Earth Council, IUCN, and the University for Peace in Costa Rica, will use the Earth Charter as a values framework in its work.

Education is one of the areas that feature some of the most innovative uses of the Earth Charter as an ethical framework. In Australia, the Earth Charter was used to develop curriculum material for primary and secondary schools that engages children to reflect on their individual and shared values. What is interesting about that material is that it brought reflection on ethics into every part of the curriculum—from mathematics to science to English to arts. For example, in math, younger children practiced basic math skills by counting and classifying the different types of rubbish left over from their lunches, and calculating how much waste this amounted to over a year. This led to discussions about personal consumption, conservation, and energy efficiency. The Earth Charter is an integral part of a new training program for teachers developed by UNESCO, which will be available on the web, freely reproducible, and on CD-ROM. Many groups around the world from Sokka Gakkai to the Paulo Freire Institute have been developing ways of incorporating Earth Charter principles into university courses, high school courses, kindergarten education, and nonformal training.

In other countries, people have drawn on the Earth Charter in theater, dance, songs, and storytelling to bring environmental ethics to life. In the Philippines, an Earth Charter theater troupe has been touring a play around rural indigenous villages. Using the allegory of a man's soul that is stolen by evil spirits, the play explores indigenous people's struggles for self-determination. After each performance, the villagers and performers discuss the ethical issues that have been brought up.

In such ways, the Earth Charter can provide a tool for bringing ethics to the forefront for all of us.

Differentiation and Commonality

The previous examples illustrated how the Earth Charter is being interpreted in the context of local cultures, in the context of the different sustainable development issues that different groups are experiencing. This leads to a key point: that using the Earth Charter as an ethical framework does not imply imposing standardized cultural norms. This was at times a contentious issue during the drafting of the Charter with various groups warning against any wording that implicitly promotes a homogenization of cultures. We must accept that there are differences in belief systems, in worldviews, in cultural practices and in morality. This is part of the reality and part of the resources of our Earth community. During the Earth Charter drafting process, it was clear that it is vital to respect cultural and spiritual identity and encourage people to use the Charter to elicit and clarify their own values and strengthen their identity.

The task is to respect these differences and yet move to identify common values, shared amongst cultures. This has not been an easy process.

It must be remembered that the Earth Charter does not define specific actions to be taken or refrained from. It asks that its principles and values be applied in specific instances, but this does not abnegate individual or group decision making and weighing of choices. Rather, it assures and deepens consideration. There are groups that have studied application of the Earth Charter and have decided to write their own charter. The city of San José, Costa Rica studied and trained over one thousand municipal employees who wrote their own Earth Charter, which is commemorated by a plaque at the entrance to the municipal building. There are countries, for example China, where a literal translation of the Earth Charter does not fit broadly within the youth culture. A Chinese writer has rewritten the Earth Charter, keeping the ideas of each principle, while making it more accessible to the Chinese community. In the dissemination of the Earth Charter, organizations are asked to endorse the Charter and use it in ways that are "appropriate given the circumstances." Interpretation and differences are anticipated. The drafters would hope that the Earth Charter becomes a springboard both for inner reflection and outer action. The inner work will create a distinct Earth Charter within each individual who contemplates its framework, but this framework will promote dialogue and resulting partnership toward common goals with a distinct Earth community aware of shared values and commonly avowed goals.

The values ultimately must become personal values that translate into joint actions; that is the valuing process referred to earlier, without which the Earth Charter will remain poetic words that do not effect change. The individual and joint valuing process is necessary so we can all take part in identifying our individual and collective contributions to the universal responsibility that we share for taking care of the global family and the global life processes of the Earth. As Steven Rockefeller has said, if society does not exercise its power of creating ethical vision and decision, then blind impulse, uncriticized habit, and drift will govern the course of events.

The Earth Charter can be seen as a dynamic process for clarifying values, a tool for highlighting ethics, and a framework for challenging practices and guiding the changes needed to achieve sustainable living. In one sense, the Earth Charter is simply words. However, the significance of the Earth Charter is the extent to which those words become activated to symbolize real values, real ideals, real commitment, real action, and real change.

Our values and our norms are a reflection of our environment and the survival of both species and individuals within that environment. It now becomes necessary to contemplate whether survival of the fittest, if it accurately described the human past, will change due to common threat into survival through shared responsibility for our interdependent destiny and through collaborative action to bring to fruition the fragile vision of a sustainable global community.

Note

The authors are both employees of the Earth Council and their perspectives expressed in this chapter are a result of the interpretive and internalization process that the Earth Charter promotes. The history of the Earth Charter is derived from a handbook that is currently being compiled by the Earth Charter Secretariat.

Chapter 3

The Earth Charter Principles: Source for an Ethics of Universal Responsibility

Abelardo Brenes

It is of paramount importance that a document such as the Earth Charter, which pretends to serve as a code of ethics by whose principles humans should orient our personal lives and organizations during the forthcoming century, should have a solid ethical foundation that is meaningful in diverse cultures.

The objective of this chapter is to share my personal understanding concerning the Charter's values and principles, as well as the reasons why I believe it has such a foundation and meaningfulness. I will also endeavor to share a pedagogical approach that we have been developing at the University for Peace, within the framework of the Central American Program for the Culture of Peace and Democracy. This program has been in existence since October 1994 and has designed for its diverse educational activities an Integral Model of Education for Peace, Democracy, and Sustainable Development.

This model is based on the Declaration of Human Responsibilities for Peace and Sustainable Development, which is a document that was jointly developed by the University for Peace and the foreign ministry of the Costa Rican government in 1989 as a working document for an international conference that took place during that year, entitled Seeking the True Meaning of Peace. In October of that same year, the government of Costa Rica, presided over by Dr. Oscar Arias, presented this document to the General Assembly of the United Nations and in May of 1990 decreed it as a document of public interest within Costa Rica. Dr. Steven Rockefeller, coordinator of the Earth Charter Drafting Committee, considered this document a valuable predecessor to the Earth Charter and for this reason he invited me to joint this committee in October 1998.

My main contribution to the Earth Charter has been the "Principle of Universal Responsibility," which was the central core ethical orientation of the 1989 document, inspired by the message of one of the key participants in that conference, His Holiness the XIV Dalai Lama of Tibet. "Universal responsibility" essentially implies that *each and every* human being is ethically responsible to live in accordance with the values and principles of environmental sustainability, peace, and observance of human rights. Moreover, given the global impact of all human actions, responsibility is also universal in relation to our ethical commitments.

Before going on to explain the pedagogical approach of the Integral Model and how it is attempting to contribute to the development of the Earth Charter as a pedagogical tool, I wish to explore the implications of assuming the principle of universal responsibility as its axiological pillar.

The Axiological Foundation of the Earth Charter

The axiological foundation of the Earth Charter is explicitly stated in the Preamble, in section 1 of the principles, entitled "Respect and Care for the Community of Life," and in the final section, entitled "The Way Forward." There are certain reiterations between these three sections, which contribute to a reinforcing effect of the fundamental values and principles.

One of the more interesting discussions within the drafting process concerned the value structure that should be the foundation of the Charter. The ordering of the four first principles, in chapter 1, reflect the predominant perspective that "respect" is the core value. From it the other three core values of "care," "build," and "secure" can be derived. I have argued against a hierarchical approach based on a single core value and instead proposed that the fundamental principle of the Charter is *responsibility*, which is a composite of these four values. This principle is first enunciated in paragraph 1 of the Preamble, thus:

> We stand at a critical moment in Earth's history, a time when humanity must choose its future. *As the world becomes increasingly interdependent and fragile*, the future at once holds great peril and great promise. To move forward we must recognize that in the midst of a magnificent diversity of cultures and life forms we are one human family and one Earth community with a common destiny. We must join together to bring forth a sustainable global society founded on respect for nature, universal human rights, economic justice, and a culture of peace. Towards this end, it is imperative that we, the peoples of Earth, declare our *responsibility* to one another, to the greater community of life, and to future generations (emphasis added).

In this passage, consciousness of responsibility arises from perception of the interdependent nature of our diverse world and is expressed in diverse basic contexts of interrelationship in which humans live. Each of us is responsible to one another, to the greater community of life, and to future generations.

It is also of significance the way in which it is posited that we should define our identities:

- As members of one human family
- As members of one Earth community with a common destiny.

This implies that the concept of "community" is fundamental as a qualification of the kind of relationship that we should cultivate in these spheres of belongingness. In the Integral Model of Education for Peace, Democracy, and Sustainable Development (which we shall consider in the next section), it is also assumed that living in peace is tantamount to living in accordance with the "spirit of community." Moreover, it is assumed that there are four key traits of an authentic human community:

- Membership in a community allows for the satisfaction of vital needs for all its members
- There is a commitment on the part of all its members towards the mutual protection, enhancement, and promotion of a common good of the community
- The idiosyncrasy of each member is valued and her/his contributions are synergistically integrated within the diversity of the group
- All members participate in the making of those decisions that affect common well-being.

The second paragraph of the Preamble, Earth, Our Home, derives the implications for action of an ethic based on the principle of *responsibility* by introducing the value of *protection* of the Earth's "vitality, diversity, and beauty" as a sacred duty. This is so, because if the integrity and sustainability of the biosphere are not assured, humanity cannot enjoy well-being, which depends upon a healthy state of the biosphere.

The third paragraph, The Global Situation, argues that globally we are in a critical moment of environmental destruction and depletion traceable to human impacts due to "dominant patterns of production and consumption" and an accelerated growth in human population. These environmental problems are interrelated with a host of social problems, such as communal breakdown, inequities and injustice, poverty, ignorance, and violence.

An ethics of responsibility assumes that humans have certain degrees of *freedom of choice* (implied when the previous paragraph concludes, "these trends are perilous—but not inevitable"). Thus the fourth paragraph of the Preamble states that we have a fundamental choice: to "form a global partnership to care for Earth and one another or risk the destruction of ourselves and the diversity of life." It is significant to note that it is not being affirmed that "life" itself will necessarily be destroyed, although we can reach a critical threshold of destruction of biodiversity which could render human existence untenable or without much meaning. The full paragraph is as follows:

> *The Challenges Ahead*
> The *choice* is ours: form a global partnership to care for Earth and one another or risk the destruction of ourselves and the diversity of life. Fundamental changes are needed in our values, institutions, and ways of living. *We must realize that when basic needs have been met, human development is primarily about being more, not having more.* We have the knowledge and technology to provide for all and to reduce our impacts on the environment. The emergence

> of a global civil society is creating new opportunities to build a democratic and humane world. Our environmental, economic, political, social, and spiritual challenges are interconnected, and together we can forge inclusive solutions (emphasis added).

This paragraph also introduces the idea that we need to define clearly that human development is about "beingness" over and above "havingness." This is one of the major challenges of our time, given that the process of economic globalization is motivated by an insatiable desire on the part of hegemonic groups to compulsively subordinate their sense of being to the existential dimensions of "having" and "doing." Thus, the universal scope of our shared responsibility needs to be brought to the fore.

This is done in paragraph 5 of the Preamble, which states:

> *Universal Responsibility*
> To realize these aspirations, we must decide to live with a sense of *universal responsibility*, identifying ourselves with the whole Earth community as well as our local communities. We are at once citizens of different nations and of one world in which the local and global are linked. Everyone shares responsibility for the present and future well-being of the human family and the larger living world. The spirit of human solidarity and kinship with all life is strengthened when we live with reverence for the mystery of being, gratitude for the gift of life, and humility regarding the human place in nature (emphasis added).

This "sense of universal responsibility" can be cultivated when we live "with reverence for the mystery of being, gratitude for the gift of life, and humility regarding the human place in nature." This points to one valuable element for a pedagogy to foster this kind of consciousness.

The principle of universal responsibility is developed in this paragraph with two distinct implications. On the one hand, each and every human is responsible. This is referred to in the phrase "everyone shares responsibility." On the other hand, according to subprinciple 2b, there is a differentiated responsibility: "with increased freedom, knowledge, and power comes increased responsibility to promote the common good." This caveat is absolutely essential in order for the principle of universal responsibility to have practical meaning in a world with such radical inequalities and power differentials.

The key to this distinction in the ethical implication of the principle of universal responsibility can be justified if one distinguishes between two different, yet interrelated meanings of the concept of "responsibility":

1. As *an ethical commitment* towards the consequences of one's actions. In this perspective, all humans should share the same framework of values and pursue the same general goals, particularly in relation to present and future generations. Nevertheless, it could be argued that to the degree that someone has undertaken actions that have caused harm to the natural environment or to society or has greater power due to ownership of natural resources, then one has a greater moral responsibility to correct the actions and compensate for the damage done. This implication is alluded to in sub-

principle 2a: "[W]ith the right to own, manage, and use natural resources comes the duty to prevent environmental harm and to protect the rights of people."

2. As a *capacity to respond.* This implies that to the degree that one has greater power, then one has a greater degree of freedom of choice to respond or not to respond and, therefore, a greater responsibility to pursue those common ethical ideals.

Some of the powers that we have are acknowledged in paragraph 4 of the Preamble, when it states that "We have the knowledge and technology to provide for all and to reduce our impacts on the environment." Thus science and technology must clearly be subsumed by ethics. Moreover, the power derived from living according to a sense of belonging to a global community is also recognized in the following sentences of that same paragraph: "The emergence of a global civil society is creating new opportunities to build a democratic and humane world. . . . [T]ogether we can forge inclusive solutions."

The choices that we have are articulated more clearly in the third paragraph of the epilogue, entitled "The Way Forward." It states the following:

> Life often involves tensions between important values. This can mean difficult choices. However, we must find ways to *harmonize diversity with unity, the exercise of freedom with the common good, short-term objectives with long-term goals*. Every individual, family, organization, and community has a vital role to play (emphasis added).

Given this reasoning, it is clearer how the four key verbs that start each of the four main principles are components of the principle of responsibility. Taken together, the infinitives "to respect," "to care for," "to build," and "to secure" assume an integral and interdependent set of values and attributes.

Thus, the first main principle, "Respect Earth and life in all its diversity," assumes a strong cognitive component, but also significant affective and aesthetic dimensions.

The second main principle, "Care for the community of life with understanding, compassion, and love," assumes that we should cultivate a higher level of knowledge, more akin to wisdom, as well as affective attributes and dispositions, such as "love" and "compassion."

The third main principle, "Build democratic societies that are just, participatory, sustainable, and peaceful," and the fourth main principle, "Secure Earth's bounty and beauty for present and future generations," imply action oriented values, which can be derived from and complement the previous values and attributes.

Taken together, these values jointly provide a strong foundation for an ethics of universal responsibility and also provide a promising framework for a pedagogy based on the Charter. If we assume that responsibility is based on a sense of respect, recognition of our interdependence, and an affective disposition to care (nurtured, in turn, by motivations based on love and compassion), then we should give attention to cultivating these attributes and dispositions through education.

The Integral Model of Education for Peace, Democracy, and Sustainable Development

An example of an approach to education that follows a similar rationale to the one just articulated for the Earth Charter is the Integral Model of Education for Peace, Democracy, and Sustainable Development. This model was developed within the context of the Culture of Peace and Democracy in Central America program, a project of the Central American governments which has been executed by the University for Peace since 1994. Its emphasis is on conflict prevention through a broad educational framework that links peace, human rights and duties, democracy, and sustainable human development for the development of a culture of peace. The educational strategy seeks to disseminate exemplary community-based experiences of cultural expressions of peaceful and democratic practices, with an emphasis on the responsibility that the various sectors of civil society and governments have in fulfilling these values and principles.

The Integral Model has been developed with contributions coming from both the cultures and processes within the region and the international academic community. The model comprises topics such as the global challenges expressed in the main UN world summits and conferences of the nineties; peace and development as human rights and their expression in Central America's official policy expressed in the Alliance for Sustainable Development; human needs, rights, and duties; the ethics of universal responsibility to live in peace, democratically and sustainably; peace among the genders and within the family; peace and interethnic relationships; the spirit of community; the culture of peace; active nonviolence and the lessons from Gandhi and other peace leaders; peaceful conflict resolution; integral democracy; peace with nature and sustainable development; mass communications and journalistic practices; and the culture of peace.

The core of this educational approach is a model of selfhood which was constructed in successive stages, incorporating diverse theoretical and empirical sources, particularly the response that people from varied sectors within Central America gave to the question, What does it mean for you to live in peace?

The model (figure 3.1) starts from the assumption that there are specific orientations that can guide life practices for building a culture of peace. Each person is assumed to be living in three contexts of interrelationship, which therefore constitute three dimensions of expression of either violent or peaceful relationships: with oneself, with others, and with nature. The model posits that we have internal representations of these three spheres of interrelationship and, moreover, that a culture of peace should be founded on an integrated consciousness that goes beyond dualisms such as inner/outer and mind/body. This implies a view of personhood as fully integrated in the world.

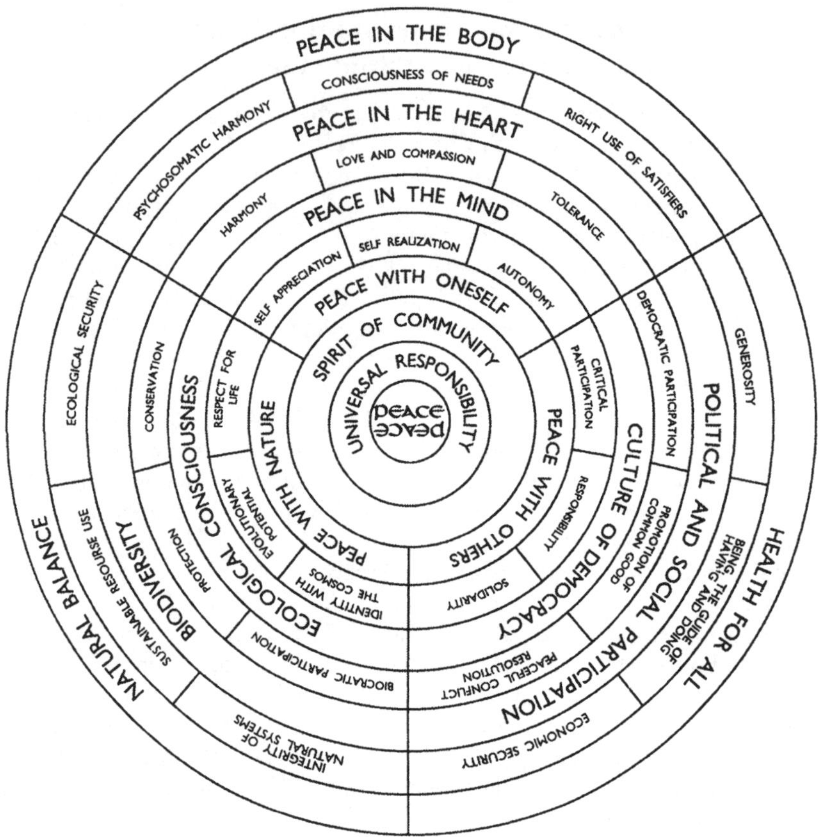

Figure 3.1. Fundamental Values and Themes of the Integral Model of Education for Peace, Democracy, and Sustainable Development

Within this perspective, the model posits three dimensions or levels of expression of peace within the "peace with oneself" domain, with corresponding values and traits for each: peace in the mind, peace in the heart, and peace in the body. These traits are as follows:

1. *Peace in the body* consists of bodily health based on psychosomatic harmony, which entails the development of a consciousness of our organism's needs for physical health and wise optimization of satisfiers for these needs. The optimization of satisfiers would reduce the impact that individual consumption has on the natural environment. The value orientation of "voluntary simplicity"

sums up this approach. This approach is supported by extensive psychological research (Cushman 1990) that suggests that the "consumer society" is driven by an "empty self" model of personhood, in which individuals seek to satisfy the need for participating in social and natural communities by a sense of belonging to pseudocommunities of consumers, which would be an example of pseudo need satisfaction.

2. *Peace in the heart* refers mainly to the satisfaction of psychological needs that generate a sense of basic security and trust. To achieve this, the model supposes that it is necessary to cultivate qualities such as love, compassion, and tolerance. These qualities, in turn, are related to liberation from those attachments and compulsions which cause negative emotions, such as anger, hate, and envy and which also sustain materialistic consumer lifestyles. True emotional gratification and security are met by identifying and obtaining satisfiers based of giving and receiving love and compassion. This psychological substratum is the foundation for the development of forms of relationship based on solidarity and generosity between humans.

3. *Peace in the mind* refers to the possibility of self-realization based on an ethical consciousness of universal responsibility. This entails that, firstly, one is responsible towards oneself to achieve inner peace and, moreover, to develop one's highest and most meaningful personal mission in life. This takes on meaning by appreciating one's place in natural and human history, understanding the interdependence of all beings in the universe, the nature of the present-day global challenges and the fulfillment of a life course geared by a global ethic. In this sense, peace in the mind is understood as the tranquillity of consciousness that one can experience when one's existence takes on its fullest meaning.

Based on Buddhist thinking, three shifts in consciousness are posited as crucial for such an orientation:

(1) *Equanimity,* the capacity to treat all human beings (and, on another dimension, all living beings) with an equal sense of benevolence, at the same time that one values the singularity of each being, as well as each person's inherent right to seek happiness and to express that singularity in a unique life mission that contributes to a common good. This kind of orientation is also fundamental for the development of *tolerance*, by realizing that there is essentially no difference between one's friends and one's enemies. The true enemy are those mental conditionings which gear us to react through fear/anger.

(2) The *equality of self and others*, that is, the shift from an egotistical orientation to a social and ecological orientation in which one realizes that life takes on its highest meaning when one orients one's freedom to serving the common good.

(3) The *commitment to altruistic life practices*. This requires autonomy, both autonomy of agency (external freedom or freedom to act) and critical autonomy, that is, the capacity to question social values and to formulate one's own values for a meaningful life. It manifests as a commitment to channeling

one's life policies towards a universal agenda of emancipation for all humans from life conditions that create suffering, oppression, subjugation, and alienation, through nonviolent means.

However, given that humans do not live in isolation and that our life projects are to a certain degree determined by collective decisions in our families, communities, nations, and the world as a whole, one needs to be able to participate critically in collective decisions at all these levels.

The foundation of such a capacity is *moral integrity*, that is, the coherence between one's life policy and the values that sustain it. Thus, by focusing on peace with others, critical autonomy will be expressed as political participation geared towards the common good.

In this perspective, the concept of power is not understood as power of domination of humans over humans or towards nature. Rather, a key assumption of the model is that a culture of peace is founded on the power that all human beings need to have in order to fully realize their potentials, which requires effective equality, respect, and mutual support between humans.

The main themes for the "peace with others" dimension are democratic culture, social and political participation, and health for all. For the "peace with nature" dimension, they are ecological consciousness, commitment towards biodiversity, and maintenance of a natural balance.

A rationale for the pedagogical application of the model is illustrated by a series of thirteen workshops that took place in Rincón Grande de Pavas, Costa Rica, in 1999. This is a very poor urban community of 60,000 people, many of whom have immigrated from other urban settings and from the countryside. The Culture of Peace program had been supporting the community leadership since 1997, in the design of a vision and plan for community development, including strategies for achieving effective support on the part of local and national government, by means of nonviolent action. Under the assumption that the community had accumulated significant experience, which had educational value, the workshops developed in 1999 were geared to supporting the leadership in valuing the cultural significance of their emancipatory struggle and to developing skills as peace culture promoters.

The flow of personal and group reflections and discussions took on the following order:

Preliminary Reflections

How is violence expressed in our personal lives, social relationships, and in our relationship to nature? How does this make me (us) feel?

What would a peaceful world be like? (What kinds of persons would be required, what kind of community, and what kind of relationship with nature?)

Once the group was introduced to the notions of direct and structural violence, attention was given to the forms of direct violence that were present in the community, in personal, social, and environmental contexts and the structural causes of these forms of violence. Structures could refer to psychological traits and processes, social relationships and organizations, and patterns of relating to the environment.

On the basis of this diagnosis of the nature and causes of violence, participants were introduced to the values and themes of the Integral Model of Education for Peace, to the perspective of common global challenges and the need to live according to a global ethic on the basis of a consciousness of universal responsibility. Within this broad framework, participants then reflected on the significance that these elements could have for the resolution of the causes of direct and structural violence in their lives. In this light, their community development plan was also reviewed for the purpose of identifying values and principles of a peaceful culture.

Challenges at Multiple Scales

The next phase consisted in examining the interrelationship between the local community challenges, national and regional challenges, and global challenges. The normative framework for this analysis was human rights and freedoms, particularly the Right to Peace and the Right to Development. The key questions raised were:

What do the inhabitants of Rincón Grande de Pavas have in common with people in the rest of the world? What implications do global processes and challenges have for them? What can Rincón Grande de Pavas teach the rest of the world by means of their emancipatory struggle and construction of a life politics based on an ethics of universal responsibility?

Ideals of Personal Development

In the next phase the participants meditated on their ideal personal development, on the basis of a transformation of consciousness guided by the values of equanimity, the equality of self and others, and a commitment to altruism. This led to the construction of a personal model of integral development, utilizing life-size silhouettes drawn on sheets of paper to indicate their needs and forms of satisfying them, as well as their powers and resources. Then the men and women separately shared their models for the purpose of identifying differences and commonalities. Finally, the group as a whole constructed a model of the ideal person that could promote a culture of peace, representing the commonalities of the male and female models.

Community Development

The following phase of the workshops was oriented to exploring how they could develop as a community in order to realize their model of ideal selfhood. A community was defined as a form of relationship in which individuals are aware of their commonalities and are committed to a common good; personal uniqueness is honored and is the basis for equal participation in those decisions that affect the life of the group.

Addressing Globalization

Finally, the process of globalization, in particular the structural adjustment policies, was examined in relation to its consequences for policies of development in Costa Rica, i.e., how transformations in governmental economic and social policies affect the life of impoverished communities. Within this perspective, strategies were developed to deal with and resist the negative consequences of globalization and to take advantage of potential opportunities, such as participating in international civil society networks of solidarity. These strategies were developed within the tradition of Gandhian models of nonviolent struggle for social justice, which are premised on the idea that empowering an emancipatory agenda of human development can have a broader educational impact, not only to those directly involved but to the broader society. A key component of these strategies is fostering alliances with significant cultural actors, such as schools and journalists. The lessons learned in this process of change, the models of selfhood, and the lifestyles constructed on the basis of an ethics of universal responsibility are transformed into radio, television, and printed media programs that are shared in the public opinion. In this light, the group was able to understand in what ways their model of personal and communal development could contribute to the global dialogue on what it means to live in accordance to universal values of a culture of peace.

Reference

Cushman, P. 1990. "Why the Self Is Empty: Toward a Historically Situated Psychology." *American Psychologist*, 45 no. 5 (May): 599–611.

Chapter 4

The Earth Charter as a New Covenant for Democracy

J. Ronald Engel

> The pressing question is therefore how the present system can be modified to become truly sustainable . . . . Are there democratic processes available, capable of bringing about a change of direction? Is it possible at all to find solutions within the framework of democratic structures? Is it possible to institute democratic control at the international level where today de facto the fundamental economic and political decisions are taken? Or do we have to resign ourselves to the fact that the development of society increasingly escapes democratic control? Has the dream of democracy in reality come to an end?
>
> —Lukas Vischer, "People's Participation in Building a Just and Sustainable Society" (2000, 3)

The Question of Politics in the Twenty-First Century

The defining question that we face at the beginning of the twenty-first century is no different than humans have faced since their emergence as self-conscious, relatively autonomous actors in the course of planetary evolution. This question is the central question of politics: "How might we so construct our lives together that all life flourishes?" (Sturm 1998b, 21).

In 2001 it is impossible to ask this question apart from the debate about the meaning, purpose, and prospects of democracy in world history. Since the end of World War II, the idea of democracy has been widely accepted—at least rhetorically—as the best answer history offers to the central question of politics and the de facto global ethic of our age (McKeon 1951, 522–23). More than this, however, it is a particular meaning of democracy, variously named procedural, minimalist, free market, representative, protective, liberal, or Western democracy, that has achieved widespread acceptance, especially in the latter part of the century following the end of the Cold War (Fukuyama 1992).

Compared with other political systems, this kind of democratic order has undeniable advantages. Procedural democracy guarantees the opportunity for public debate, free elections, protection of minorities, and other liberal constitutional rights (Dworkin 1977). The current debate is occasioned, however, by the failure of this type of democratic order to effectively engage the "global situation." As the Earth Charter describes it: global patterns of production, consumption, and reproduction are widening the gap between rich and poor, undermining communities, threatening global security, and destroying the life sustaining systems of the planet.

Two moral indictments lie at the core of this criticism: the failures of procedural democracy to provide either (1) effective opportunities for morally responsible citizenship locally, nationally, and globally, or (2) a commanding and defensible vision of the common good that can serve as a measure of human action (Westra 1998, 150). Procedural democracy fails on both these counts because it does not believe that democratic societies can or should exercise collective self-government for an explicit and shared idea of the common good. Procedural democracy tends to conceive the public world as an arena of competition between individuals and groups, each pursuing its own preferences, where the only ethical constraints are such principles of justice as give others the right or fair opportunity to pursue their interests. Questions of justice regarding the distribution of the goods of the society need to be separated from final questions of the good for individuals, society, or life as a whole, and the latter cannot be dealt with in the public realm. However, it is not merely an absence of a common good, but the implicit and uncritical assumption that society's most general purpose is to maximize those economic resources with which individuals may pursue their diverse interests, that is being called into question.

A number of efforts have appeared in recent years to offer alternatives to this dominant school of democratic public philosophy. Many of these have focused on the first indictment, the need for a more participatory and responsible understanding of democratic citizenship (Barber 1984; Kariel 1970). Others, primarily addressing the second indictment, have looked to the traditional religions of the world, to science-based natural law, to a new and more relational view of the self and world, or to a theistic metaphysical perspective to provide the vision of the common good necessary to motivate and direct the citizen initiatives required to solve the world's social and environmental problems (Oelschlaeger 1994; Callicott 1994; Mathews 1991; Gamwell 2000). Still others look to classic civic republican or pragmatist philosophies for clues to constructing a viable theory of contemporary democratic practice (Farrar 1988; Nussbaum 1990; Pangle 1992; Rockefeller 1991a; Selznick 1992).

The Earth Charter as a Reconstruction of the Democratic Faith

My argument is that whatever else the Earth Charter may symbolize, it stands squarely within this debate. Its grounding premise is the democratic faith that human beings have the rational and moral capacity to govern themselves for the common good of all under the uncertain evolutionary and historical circumstances of life on this planet. Its fundamental purpose is to articulate a universal, holistic, and transcendent vision of the democratic faith for our contemporary global situation, thus answering what Steven Rockefeller, chair of the Earth Charter drafting committee, calls the "most fundamental spiritual quest of our time, . . . a search for a faith and ways of living that at once liberate the self and the other, creating authentic community with nature as well as among people" (Rockefeller 1991b).

The Charter pursues this aim in a number of ways. It strongly affirms twentieth century doctrines of universal human rights. It retrieves strands within the democratic tradition that have been muted in recent years, in particular, our common humanity, the embeddedness of the human community within the order of nature, and the dependence of politics and ethics upon a substantive ontology or conception of the good. It draws extensively upon understandings of environmental ethics that have grown out of modern democratic moral traditions, such as the land ethic and responsible resource conservation. And it boldly sets forth the new and radical democratic claim that all citizens bear "a universal responsibility" for the perpetual flourishing of the whole of life on planet Earth.

The word "democracy" appears only three times in the Charter, and only the second usage, in Principle 3: "Build democratic societies that are just, participatory, sustainable, and peaceful" suggests such an alternative understanding of democracy. Nonetheless, a close reading of the text reveals it to be permeated with democratic vocabulary, principles, and assumptions, beginning with the opening declaration that humanity can and must collectively choose its future, and concluding with the assertion that as members of a common humanity with a common destiny we are beckoned "to seek a new beginning."

It is important that we read the Earth Charter in this way. Otherwise, we miss its power to challenge the dominant social consensus. This is true for several reasons. As the American civil rights movement suggests, reformers transform public attitudes through their ability to hold societies accountable to their highest ideals (Goulet 1985). In the final analysis, our present political arrangements are only retained because they are perceived to be legitimate, and their legitimacy rests on the perception that they are ethically justified. In spite of the fact that popular rhetoric identifies free trade and democracy, leaders the world over still must give lip service to larger and more substantive meanings of democracy to legitimate their regimes, as President George W. Bush's explicit appeal in his inaugural address to "our democratic faith" in the capacity of citizens to seek a common good beyond their comfort indicates.

General prescriptions for public policy, such as those of the Earth Charter, can only be effective if they are solidly grounded in concrete historical movements, in the sweat and blood struggles over many centuries for rationally, morally, and empirically defensible democratic ideals and institutions. There is far too much skepticism today regarding the nature and power of moral ideals to make it credible that goodwill, or agreement on abstract values, or changes in individual motivation can, by themselves, move us much closer to justice, peace, and ecological integrity. Real progress entails these things in combination with the hard work of democratic public debate and social change.

Only by assuming the full burden of the democratic inheritance—its vulnerabilities as well as its strengths—will we be able to transcend its current distortions. Democracy, like any other great moral and cultural tradition, is tragically flawed. The democratic idea of freedom emerged in the ancient West as a direct result of the social dialectics of slavery (Patterson 1991). Democracy has flourished in close association with commercial cultures, exclusive social bonds, imperial ambitions, and Promethian defiance of natural limits (Sagan 1991). Intrinsic to the democratic experience are constant temptations to escape the moral burdens of public life by the duplicitous substitution of bargaining for deliberation, paranoia, apathy, overindulging the appetites, or withdrawal into islands of sectarian self-righteousness. But the democratic inheritance also contains sources of its own criticism and renewal, a cumulative wisdom of hard-won institutional principles and public virtues to counter such tendencies and enable ordinary people to create self-governing communities that can limit ambition and corruption and serve justice and the common good (Farrar 1988).

I would like to expound this interpretation of the Earth Charter by showing how it expresses a more universal, holistic, and transcendent covenantal understanding of the democratic faith than any comparable aspirational international document so far written. Covenants are critical components in the maintenance of any social order. They establish obligations, regulate behavior between parties, introduce a measure of predictability into social life, and, most important of all, articulate a purposive and shared vision of the common good. Any effort to deliberately change the values of a social order involves an attempt to articulate a "new covenant" that challenges former implicit or explicit covenantal understandings. It is a tenet of the democratic faith that covenants need to be constantly criticized and renewed in light of new deliverances of human reason, experience, and conscience.

The difference between the Earth Charter's covenantal understanding of democracy and that of procedural democracy runs deep. It ultimately turns on the issue of whether human beings have the potential to make meaningful covenants for the common good across wide cultural, national, and religious differences. Advocates of procedural democracy believe such covenants may be possible for relatively homogeneous communities, or for voluntary organizations within civil society, but not for the political institutions that embrace such diverse constituencies as modern democratic societies, and certainly not for the international institutions that embrace world civilization as a whole. Today's diverse citizenry, it is presumed, cannot share a common vision of the good, or even a substantial conception of justice. As Ronald Dworkin puts it, "Political decisions must be, so far as possible, independent of any particular conception of the good life, of what gives value to life. Since the citizens of a society differ in their conceptions the government does not treat them as equals if it prefers one conception to another" (Dworkin 1977, 127). At best they can reach agreement on the neutral procedures by which the global market of economic and political competition is to be ordered. The covenantal democratic faith of the Earth Charter believes otherwise.

Rewriting the Global Compact

The Earth Charter may be viewed as a culminating product of repeated attempts since the founding of the United Nations in 1945 to rewrite the global social compact along more comprehensive covenantal lines. I refer here to the many hundred declarations, commission reports, and people's treaties relevant to environment, development, human rights, and peace adopted by international governmental and nongovernmental bodies over the past half-century (Burhenne and Irwin 1983; Commonweal Sustainable Futures Group 1992; Kung and Kuschel 1993; Rockefeller 1996; Weston, Falk, and D'Amato 1990). All of these efforts in one way or another have sought to challenge the capacity of procedural democracy and the corporate-dominated global free market system with which it is allied to adequately answer the political question. All offer some ingredient for an alternative vision of the democratic ideal, and many, such as the Stockholm Declaration in its call for "a common outlook and for common principles to inspire and guide the peoples of the world," explicitly call for a new global ethic. Taken as a body they reveal the trends in progressive international thinking that have led to the universal, holistic and transcendent covenantal vision of the Earth Charter. Especially significant precursors in this respect are the Universal Declaration of Human Rights (1948), the Stockholm Declaration on the Human Environment (1972), the World Charter for Nature (1982), Our Common Future (1987), Caring for the Earth (1991), the several declarations of the People's Earth Summit at Rio (1992), the declaration of the Parliament of World Religions, Toward a Global Ethic (1993), and the agreements and reports of the seven United Nations summit conferences held during the 1990s on children, the environment, human rights, population, social development, and women.

Behind these documents, of course, lies an even greater body of covenantal statements and understandings that have served as vehicles for the articulation of democratic aspirations and principles throughout human history. The covenants of many cultures and religions have contributed in this way to the Earth Charter. The Earth Charter draws extensively, for example, upon the universalistic democratic principles of the great eighteenth century revolutionary declarations and the philosophy of creative public action that underlies them (Ravitch and Thernstrom 1992). In this view the covenantal activities of promise making, promise keeping, and forgiveness of broken promises made by free and equal citizens in self-governing communities are an authentic exercise of the inherent human capacity for politics, and one of the chief means whereby democratic communities can control human selfishness, nurture public virtue, and achieve justice and the common good (Arendt 1958).

Although differences need to be noted, the Earth Charter covenant is also indebted to the covenantal thinking of the Hebrew prophets (Adams 1986; McCoy 1991). Like the biblical covenants, the Earth Charter entails an unconditional agreement of community, friendship, peace, and justice; it establishes the terms for an inclusive community of mutual respect and trust of indefinite duration—a community within which persons can grow to moral and spiritual maturity by assuming responsibilities for the continuing well being of all parties. Like the Hebrew prophets, the Earth Charter proclaims a covenant inclusive of the entire created order whose moral law is the law of the creative process itself and whose imperative is to "act so as to meet the conditions for the progressive creation of the world of humanity and of all being" (Sturm 1988, 128), or alternatively stated, as "the kind of human activity that nourishes and perpetuates the historical fulfillment of the whole community of life on Earth" (Engel 1990, 10).

The Earth Charter is written in the voice of the first person plural to make clear that it is a binding enactment of free individuals with the capacity to reach beyond ties of blood, religion, ethnicity, and nation to choose their future together, to mutually commit to enduring and comprehensive moral purposes. "Together in hope we affirm the following interdependent principles for a sustainable way of life. . . ." The Charter thus stands in the classic democratic tradition that assumes the sovereignty of the people as a whole to choose the purposes for which they live and the form of government that will best embody those purposes (Selznick 1992). It is the ultimate "consent of the governed," democracy in its radical root meaning of "the rule of the people." The agreement of the people precedes the formation of the state. But it is a covenantal rather than a contractual understanding of the agreement of the people.

The Earth Charter is even more explicit in this regard than its most important comparable predecessor, the Universal Declaration of Human Rights. The latter, although it is addressed to all peoples and nations, and constitutes a standard toward which "every individual and every organ of society" should "strive," was not conceived as an international agreement of this kind. However, the Universal Declaration did eventually come to serve as a "soft law" covenantal foundation for such "hard law" treaties as the International Covenant on Civil and Political Rights. In similar fashion, the Earth Charter has developed in tandem with the proposed International Covenant on Environment and Development—the text that is referred to in the conclusion of the Charter as "an international legally binding instrument on environment and development" (IUCN Commission on Environmental Law 1995).

A Universal Democratic Covenant

Those who join the covenant of the Earth Charter are pledging themselves to abide by moral understandings that are universal in two primary senses of the word: they are principles that are to be held universally, by all persons and peoples, and they constitute a moral standard that is to be applied universally—to all human relationships, both between humans and with the rest of life as well. The key concept of "universal responsibility" in the Charter encompasses both these meanings: "Everyone shares responsibility" for the "human family and the larger living world."

The concept of world citizenship took a quantum leap forward after the founding of the United Nations. Although the authors of earlier national declarations, such as the French Declaration of the Rights of Man and Citizen, assumed that they were speaking directly to and for universal humanity as well as their fellow nationals, only after 1945 did major international declarations appear that were the products of extensive deliberations among representatives of diverse nations, and that spoke in covenantal terms regarding the obligations pertaining between the peoples of the Earth. When the Preamble of the Earth Charter announces, therefore, that "it is imperative that we, the peoples of Earth, declare our responsibility to one another, to the greater community of life, and to future generations," it carries forward a movement that began with the Charter of the United Nations: "We the peoples of the United Nations, determined to save succeeding generations from the scourge of war, which twice in our lifetime has brought untold sorrow to mankind . . . ." However, no document written since the founding of the United Nations has entailed such extensive international consultations as the Earth Charter, and none is more explicit about the identity and vocation of world citizenship: "We are at once citizens of different nations and of one world in which the local and global are linked." Appropriately, the promoters of the Earth Charter are circulating it as a "people's treaty" and hope to achieve endorsement by the United Nations in 2002, the tenth anniversary of the epic gathering of NGOs and national government representatives that originated the Earth Charter process at the Rio Summit in 1992.

With regard to the first understanding of universality, therefore, the Earth Charter completely universalizes the community of human moral agents that are included in the covenant and accountable to it and in so doing eloquently expresses the emerging identity of cosmopolitan citizenship felt by many people throughout the world. The Earth Charter explicitly aims to express the rights and obligations of all individuals, the deprived and poor as well as privileged, and through individuals, all human institutions. All "organizations, businesses, governments, and transnational institutions" are now bearers of global moral responsibility and are to be impartially judged as such. (The Charter also recognizes in Principles 2a and b that universal responsibility entails differential obligations depending upon circumstances.) This radical universalization of the global covenant is based both on intrinsic moral grounds, and on the conviction that we have reached a point in the history of the world where the majority of persons and groups must take responsible citizenship seriously if the Earth is to continue to flourish. It is not an option, or mere ideal, but a universal imperative grounded in the very nature of the planetary condition. As Latin American liberation theologian Leonardo Boff declares, "We have come to such a point of interdependence that we are either all saved or all lost" (Boff 1997). World civilization will become a universal moral democracy, or perish. "The choice is ours: form a global partnership to care for Earth and one another or risk the destruction of ourselves and the diversity of life."

The Earth Charter covenant also involves a radical universalization of the spheres of human activity to which its moral standards apply. Signatories are asked to pledge themselves to principles of moral responsibility that apply to all beings, human and nonhuman, present and future—in effect, to principles that are truly and fully comprehensive principles of universal moral law. Principles 1 and 2, "Respect Earth and life in all its diversity," and "Care for the community of life with understanding, compassion, and love," are comprehensive universal principles in this sense. They constitute a thoroughgoing Gandhian or radically expanded Kantian moral imperative: every being must be considered an end in itself and not a means; and as an end is worthy of our respect and care.

A Holistic Democratic Covenant

The heart of the Earth Charter covenant is the affirmation that all citizens of the world must covenant to work together for the common good of the biosphere—for the flourishing of the whole community of life. The Earth Charter is profoundly holistic in its vision of the evolutionary passage of the "one Earth community" (repeatedly referenced as "community of life," "Earth and life in all its diversity," "whole Earth community," "greater community of life") whose well-being and destiny is the ultimate end or reference point on behalf of which responsible citizenship by all individuals and groups should be exercised. At no point does the Earth Charter depart more radically from the perspective of procedural democracy than in its assertion of the priority of the good conceived as the maximal flourishing of the unity in variety of the Earth community inclusive of humans and the rest of nature.

It is possible to see behind the Earth Charter the vision of the Greek polis that has inspired the democratic ideal throughout the course of history. The ontology that is presented here is the ontology of the polis, a relational whole in which the good of the whole is inseparable from the good of each of its members and the right ordering of mutual relationships between them (Sturm 2000). The Charter states this ontology most explicitly in Principle 1a: "Recognize that all beings are interdependent and every form of life has value regardless of its worth to human beings," and in the concluding subprinciple 16f, but the relational ontology of unity in diversity pervades the text (e.g., Principle 1: "Respect Earth and life in all its diversity").

Moreover, since the individuals and particular life-forms that compose the Earth community each have value (an "inherent dignity" in the case of persons, Principle 1b) the model of global community proposed is richly suggestive of what Aristotle in the *Politics* conceived as a polity or what we today would call participatory democracy. This may not be an adequate model for the biosphere apart from its human members. But for its human members, who can identify with the biosphere, and make free self-conscious moral decisions to respect and care for it as a whole, as well as for each of its individual members and life-forms in their uniqueness and diversity, the "one Earth community" can be conceived as a democracy and they should relate to it as such. This is congruent with what Herman Daly and John Cobb call the "biospheric vision": "Human beings can derive part of their identity from membership in the biosphere. They can participate in decisions it makes, and they can care for the whole, as well as for its individual members in their diversity. In this qualified sense, *for its human members*, the whole biosphere can and should be a community of communities" (Daly and Cobb 1989, 202). This is the holistic democratic covenant that the Earth Charter asks us to join.

According to Aristotle, the polis is a self-sufficient community because it is the community within which all the goods necessary to the good life may be found in proper relationship (O'Neill 1993). In today's globally interdependent world, the only self-sufficient community within which all the goods necessary to the good life may potentially be found in proper relationship to one another is the Earth as a whole. Some of these goods, such as the atmosphere, the oceans, the integrity of most ecosystems and the biosphere itself, are global common goods, and must therefore be governed in common. But in a global civilization, it takes global cooperation to achieve the proper conditions for the production, distribution, and consumption of most other important goods as well.

The Earth Charter conceives the Earth as a polis, at least for its human members, and the well-being of the one Earth community as a plural good. Indeed, it is a plural good in plural ways, each good and each way vital to the flourishing of the whole. This holistic quality of the Earth Charter is vividly captured by the remarks of Marcus Arruda at the People's Earth Summit in 1992: "People came here concerned not only with nature, but with every different aspect of human life on Earth. They came here to discuss human rights, nature rights, racism, forests, water, air, the foreign debt—everything that seems to be an isolated issue that has nothing to do with the rest until all of a sudden the pieces become part of a whole unified picture that is seen by people everywhere" (Commonweal Sustainable Futures Group 1992).

In addition to the diversity of the world's individual organisms, human and nonhuman, the Charter embraces a plurality of kinds of communities, so that its vision of the global polis might be best characterized as a community of communities and, potentially for humans, as a democracy of democracies. It acknowledges a diversity of ecological systems and cultures, scales of community (local, regional, global), types of natural processes and areas (nature reserves, wildlands, marine areas), and social organization (families, civic organizations, businesses, governments, international regimes). It highlights a long menu of moral concerns, from species extinction, resource depletion, pollution, and genetic engineering to poverty, gender inequality, international inequity, military violence, and ignorance. And it offers a plurality of principles of justice to address these moral concerns, both general and particular: respect and care for Earth in all its diversity, protection and restoration of ecosystem integrity, preservation of biodiversity, recycling, conservation of renewable resources; universal human rights, economic justice, a culture of peace; freedom, equality, equity, solidarity. And if this plurality is not sufficient, it proposes fifty-three distinct and specific policy prescriptions in its subprinciples!

There are multiple cultural layers to the Earth Charter. At one level, the Charter draws upon overlapping convergences among the diverse national and regional cultures of the world; at another level, upon the world's diverse religious, and philosophical traditions; and at still another level, upon the plurality of democratic moral traditions that have emerged from these diverse national, religious and philosophical cultures and, ecologically reconstructed, now provide the primary moral frameworks in which contending moral concerns and principles are to be sorted out.

Democratic humanism inspires the Charter's strong emphasis on the "inherent dignity of all human beings and in the intellectual, artistic, ethical, and spiritual potential of humanity" (1b), on beauty, the natural and cultural heritage, scientific knowledge, art, tradition, education, and the importance of being rather than having. *Democratic liberalism* informs the Charter's insistence upon fundamental freedoms, including transparency and accountability in governance, an independent judiciary, and the rights to freedom of opinion, expression, peaceful assembly, association, and dissent. *Participatory democracy* informs the Charter's repeated support for meaningful participation in decision making, strengthening local communities and civil society, awareness and knowledge of the commons and its ecosystemic relationships, and holding multinational corporations and governments accountable to the citizenry. *Democratic socialism* informs the Charter's emphasis on social, economic, and environmental rights such as rights to potable water, clean air, food security, education, sustainable livelihood, and on the equitable sharing of wealth. *Civic republicanism* inspires the Charter's strong conception of the common good, self-sacrifice, and public virtue, including the virtues of prudence and restraint, such as the precautionary approach, the assumption of those responsibilities befitting one's freedom, power, and capacities, and stewardship of Earth's resources for future generations. *Democratic humanitarianism* undergirds the Charter's principles of care and compassion for all living things, protecting the vulnerable and serving those who suffer, preventing cruelty to domestic and wild animals, and pursuing a life of nonviolence. Finally, the claims of various contemporary *liberation movements* are evident in the special attention the Charter gives to the needs of women, minorities, indigenous peoples, and youth.

In the global polis all of these goods and contending democratic philosophies are present and in various complex interdependent relationships. What kind of overarching moral and practical priorities does the Earth Charter establish between them?

A good case can be made that Principle 5, "Protect and restore the integrity of Earth's ecological systems, with special concern for biological diversity and the natural processes that sustain life," has a certain moral and practical priority. Not only does it have pride of place, as the first policy prescription within the first set of policy prescriptions, "II. Ecological Integrity," but it sets the ultimate biological context within which all other concerns must be addressed, as the Preamble states, the "conditions essential to life's evolution." The Charter exists first and foremost for the sake of the community of life in its wholeness and therefore its unity in diversity or integrity as a functioning system.

But an equally good case can be made for the moral and practical priority of humanity's well-being. Three of the four pillars of a sustainable global society are matters of social ethics: universal human rights, economic justice, and a culture of peace. The global situation is described largely in terms of human suffering, and most of the policy prescriptions involve changes in social institutions and attitudes. Moreover, the Earth Charter repeatedly drives home the message that not only are human well-being and social justice priorities in their own right, but only through the elimination of poverty and other human deprivations, and the establishment of just and nonviolent social and economic relationships, will the citizens of the world be in a position to protect and restore the integrity of Earth's ecological systems.

The single most significant development that may be traced through the long line of international declarations that paved the way to the Earth Charter was the recognition, beginning at Stockholm, that the most urgent environmental issues are inseparable from the most urgent social issues of the world. Growing awareness of these relationships fueled the discussion of "sustainable development" in the 1980s and "just and sustainable communities" in the 1990s (Engel 1995). Principle 7 vividly expresses this need to integrate a wide range of competing ecological and social values: "Adopt patterns of production, consumption, and reproduction that safeguard Earth's regenerative capacities, human rights, and community well-being."

The Earth Charter thus embraces what has come to be called an "eco-justice" ethic—a comprehensive and holistic moral approach in which ecological and social (including economic and cultural) well-being are considered both dependent and independent variables (Bakken, Engel, and Engel 1995, 5). It is not possible to adequately address one without also addressing the other; yet each also needs to be addressed on its own terms. Eco-justice ethics include, but are broader than, "environmental justice," the concern for the disproportionate burden of environmental degradation borne by poor and minority communities. Systematic expositions of eco-justice ethical approaches based on one or more democratic moral traditions may be found in the philosophical and theological literature. Peter Bakken uses both philosophical and theological resources to explicate how the great triad of democratic justice, freedom, equality, and community, may be creatively reformulated when placed in the context of a holistic vision of the Earth community with its immense constraints as well as opportunities for novel ethical relationships (Bakken 2000). The Earth Charter does not adopt any of these ethical systems in particular, nor settle any of the tensions that exist between them and the principles they espouse, but provides a comprehensive eco-justice agenda (replete with such basic eco-justice principles as freedom, equality, community; participation, solidarity, sufficiency, sustainability) to guide citizen deliberation and choice (Hessel 1996). These ethical systems can provide moral clarification and guidance to these deliberations.

If there is one overarching moral and practical priority for the Earth Charter it is the radical democratic imperative of forming a global compact among all citizens to engage in individual and collective moral deliberation for the sake of the flourishing of all life. Only through such a covenant will they be empowered to take responsibility for the integrity of the biosphere; to redress global injustice; to establish peace. Only through such a covenant will they have reason to think that success in restoring ecological systems and building just human communities in specific places and situations can be sustained under conditions of global interdependence. Again and again, the Earth Charter insists that the way forward is through local, national, and international relationships that have the qualities of partnership, mutual respect and care, cooperation, dialogue, a collaborative search for truth and wisdom, participatory decision making, and shared commitment to serve the common good—precisely the kind of holistic covenantal relationships that are intrinsic to the democratic ideal of free and equal citizens engaging in mutual deliberation and choice in a polis.

A Transcendent Democratic Covenant

As leader of the worldwide consultative process that led to the decision to make a "world ethic for living sustainably" the foundation for *Caring for the Earth* in 1990, and as a participant in the subsequent drafting of the Earth Charter text, I can attest to the authenticity of the covenant-making process that culminated in these texts. They give cause for hope that people can indeed govern themselves for the good of the whole. Most especially, they show how the moral and spiritual imaginations and good faith commitments of many thousands of misnamed "ordinary citizens" can outrun the thinking of democratic theorists who insist that ethics are relative and that people of diverse cultures cannot agree on a vision and standard of the common good. But they also show something else: the shared sense that such ultimate commitments involve a relation to the transcendent.

The sense of transcendence in human experience—of ideals, purposes, meanings, laws, potentialities, loyalties, affections, gifts that outrun what we can see or understand—is expressed in the Earth Charter in a number of ways. Each points to an embracing creativity in the nature of things that presents itself as the source, ground, and end of our shared existence. The experience of transcendence has been thematized in a wide diversity of religious and secular traditions throughout human history. The Earth Charter takes the radical democratic posture that underneath all these different interpretations there is a natural religious piety we all can share and a common covenant we can all make with the ultimately reliable powers of life.

It may come as a shock to recognize that in the last analysis the Earth Charter is built upon trust in the transcendent. Everything that it prescribes is the result of decades of the most rigorous scientific, legal, and moral argument and debate; moreover, it takes an entirely this-worldly evolutionary and historical worldview. Why then do I make this claim?

In part it is simply a matter of hearing what the Charter literally says. The Earth Charter confesses that the beauty and vitality of life we joyfully celebrate and wish to protect, restore, and enrich, is a "gift" not of our making; that an attitude of "reverence for the mystery of being" and "humility regarding the human place in nature" is required if we are to feel "human solidarity and kinship with all life"; that the responsibility of citizenship we are asked to assume is a "sacred trust"; that the peace we may hope to find after all our striving is a matter of right relationship to a greater whole than the Earth itself, "the larger whole of which all are a part."

For the rest it is simply a matter of recognizing what the Charter logically implies. The pledges it asks us to make with one another on behalf of Earth and the community of life are not provisional or qualified, but indefinite, open-ended pledges to and for all present as well as future human generations, and pledges not to this nation alone, or this belief system, or even humanity alone, but to and for the whole community of life in which we are to stand in a new relationship of unwavering respect and care. They lead at every point to our need to reach out towards more than we can ever experience, do, or know. Citizenship becomes an ethical union within the context of a spiritual vocation. What we are pledging to do is beyond what we have any assurance we can actually achieve; and the success of the work we are being asked to take up is out of our hands. We cannot, simply by willing it, make ourselves feel love and compassion for the community of life; we cannot force the "change of heart and mind" that will enable us to commit ourselves to the values of the Charter; we cannot see the present and future generations we are asked to take responsibility for, much less can we know how to truly secure Earth's bounty and beauty for them; we cannot deliberately achieve right relationships with the universe. Everywhere we turn we encounter our dependence upon sources, purposes, meanings, and consequences beyond the bounds of our intentionality.

The more one ponders the Earth Charter the larger loom hope, trust, commitment, and faith. They are not sufficient to save us. Scientific knowledge, good institutions, hard work, informed moral choices, the fifty-three policy prescriptions, and much more, are all necessary. But without the democratic faith that a greater creativity than we command is being mediated to us through the evolutionary process and our cooperative efforts for the common good, and that there is that in existence that will not betray our trust, we have no adequate foundation for the covenant we are asked to join.

References

Adams, James Luther. 1986. *Voluntary Associations: Socio-Cultural Analyses and Theological Interpretation.* Ed. J. Ronald Engel. Chicago: Exploration Press.

Arendt, Hannah. 1958. *The Human Condition.* Chicago: University of Chicago Press.

Bakken, Peter W. 2000. "Freedom, Equality, and Community in the Eco-justice Literature." *The Journal of Liberal Religion* 1(April): 2.

Bakken, Peter W., Joan Gibb Engel, and J. Ronald Engel, eds. 1995. *Ecology, Justice, and Christian Faith: A Guide to the Literature.* Westport, Conn.: Greenwood Press.

Barber, Benjamin. 1984. *Strong Democracy: Participatory Politics for a New Age.* Berkeley: University of California.

Boff, Leonardo. 1997. *Cry of the Earth, Cry of the Poor.* Marynoll, N.Y.: Orbis Press.

Burhenne, Wolfgang E. and Will A. Irwin. 1983. *The World Charter for Nature: A Background Paper.* Berlin: Erich Schmidt Verlag.

Caldwell, Lynton Keith. 1984. *International Environmental Policy: Emergence and Dimensions.* Durham: Duke University Press.

Callicott, J. Baird. 1994. *Earth's Insights: A Survey of Ecological Ethics from the Mediterranean Basin to the Australian Outback.* Berkeley: University of California Press.

Commonweal Sustainable Futures Group. 1992. *The Peoples Treaties from the Earth Summit.* Bolinas, Calif.: Common Knowledge Press.

Daly, Herman and John Cobb. 1989. *For the Common Good: Redirecting the Economy toward Community, the Environment, and a Sustainable Future.* Boston: Beacon Press.

Dworkin, Ronald. 1977. *Taking Rights Seriously.* Cambridge: Harvard University Press.

Engel, J. Ronald. 1990. "Ethics of Susainable Development." P. 10 in J. Ronald Engel and Joan G. Engel, eds. *Ethics of Environment and Development: Global Challenge, International Response.* London: Belhaven.

Engel, J. Ronald. 1995. "Sustainable Development." Pp. 2456–62 in Warren T. Reich, ed. *Encyclopedia of Bioethics*, Volume 4. New York: The Free Press.

Farrar, Cynthia. 1988. *The Origins of Democratic Thinking: The Invention of Politics in Classical Athens.* New York: Cambridge University Press.

Fukuyama, Francis. 1992. *The End of History and the Last Man.* New York: Avon Books.

Gamwell, Franklin. 2000. *Democracy on Purpose: Justice and the Reality of God.* Washington, D.C.: Georgetown University Press.

Glendon, Mary Ann. 2001. *A World Made New: Eleanor Roosevelt and the Universal Declaration of Human Rights*. New York: Random House.

Goulet, Denis. 1985. "The Ethics of Power and the Power of Ethics" in *The Cruel Choice: A New Concept in the Theory of Development*. New York: University Press of America.

Hessel, Dieter. 1996. "Ecumenical Ethics for Earth Community." *Theology & Public Policy* 8: 17-29.

IUCN Commission on Environmental Law. 1995. *Draft International Covenant on Environment and Development.* Prepared in cooperation with the International Council of Environmental Law. Gland, Switzerland: World Conservation Union.

Kariel, Henry, ed. 1970. *Frontiers of Democratic Theory.* New York: Random House.

Kung, Hans, and Karl-Josef Kuschel, ed. 1993. *A Global Ethic: the Declaration of the Parliament of the World's Religions.* New York: Continuum.

Mathews, Freya. 1991. *The Ecological Self.* London: Routledge.

McCoy, Charles S. 1991. "Creation and Covenant: A Comprehensive Vision for Environmental Ethics" in Carol S. Robb and Casebolt, Carl J., ed. *Covenant for a New Creation.* Maryknoll, N.Y.: Orbis Books.

McKeon, Richard, ed. 1951. *Democracy in a World of Tensions: A Symposium Prepared by UNESCO.* Chicago: University of Chicago Press.

Nussbaum, Martha. 1990. "Aristotelian Social Democracy" in R. Bruce Douglass, Gerald M. Mara, and Henry S. Richardson, eds. *Liberalism and the Good.* New York: Routledge.

O'Neill, John. 1993. *Ecology, Policy and Politics: Human Well-Being and the Natural World.* New York: Routledge, 1993.

Oelschlaeger, Max. 1994. *Caring for Creation: An Ecumenical Approach to the Environmental Crisis.* New Haven, Conn.: Yale University Press.

Pangle, Thomas L. 1992. *The Ennobling of Democracy: The Challenge of the Postmodern Age.* Baltimore, Md.: Johns Hopkins Press.

Patterson, Orlando. 1991. *Freedom in the Making of Western Culture.* New York: Basic Books.

Ravitch, Diane, and Abigail Thernstrom, eds. 1992. *The Democracy Reader: Classic and Modern Speeches, Essays, Poems, Declarations and Documents on Freedom and Human Rights Worldwide.* New York: Harper Perennial.

Rockefeller, Steven C. 1991a. *John Dewey: Religious Faith and Democratic Humanism.* New York: Columbia University Press.

Rockefeller, Steven C. 1991b. "Convergence: Reflections on Religious Life, Democracy, and Ecology." *Union Seminary Quarterly Review* 45: 238.

Rockefeller, Steven C. 1996. *Principles of Environmental Conservation and Sustainable Development: Summary and Survey.*

Sagan, Eli. 1991. *The Honey and the Hemlock: Democracy and Paranoia in Ancient Athens and Modern America.* Princeton: Princeton University Press.

Selznick, Philip. 1992. *The Moral Commonwealth.* Berkeley: University of California Press.

Sturm, Douglas. 1988. *Community and Alienation: Essays on Process thought and Public Life.* Notre Dame: University of Notre Dame Press.

Sturm, Douglas. 1998. *Solidarity and Suffering: Toward a Politics of Relationality.* Albany: State University Press of New York.

Sturm, Douglas. 2000. "Identity and Alterity: Summons to a New Axial Age." *Journal of Liberal Religion* 1(April). < http://www.meadville.edu/sturm_1_2.html> (February 8, 2002).

Vischer, Lukas. 2000. "People's Participation in Building a Just and Sustainable Society" in *Democratic Contracts for Sustainable and Caring Societies.* ed. Lewis S. Mudge and Thomas Wieser. Geneva: WCC Publications.

Weston, Burns H., Richard A. Falk, and Anthony D'Amato, eds. 1990. *Basic Documents in International Law and World Order.* St. Paul, Minn.: West Publishing Co.

Westra, Laura. 1998. *Living in Integrity: A Global Ethic to Restore a Fragmented Earth.* Lanham, Md.: Rowman & Littlefield.

World Conservation Union, the United Nations Environment Programme, and the World Wide Fund for Nature. 1991. *Caring for the Earth: A Strategy for Sustainable Living.* Gland, Switzerland.

Chapter 5

Ecofeminism, Integrity, and the Earth Charter: A Critical Analysis

Victoria Davion

The concept of ecological integrity has received quite a lot of attention in the field of environmental philosophy, but little attention within ecological feminism, a constellation of theoretical positions linking forms of human oppression with environmental exploitation. The concept of ecological integrity and several core ecofeminist ideas are present in the Earth Charter (2002), a document which will be presented to the United Nations as a formal charter in 2002. The purpose of this chapter is to present important ecological feminist insights, and to examine both the concept of ecological integrity and the Earth Charter document through an ecological feminist lens. I shall argue that a focus on ecological integrity is consistent with ecological feminist concerns, provided that questions of ecological integrity are always seen as political in addition to scientific. I shall also argue that portions of the Charter are consistent with core ideas of ecological feminism, while others are problematic. I begin with a discussion of ecological feminism.

Ecological Feminism: Some Key Ideas

Ecological feminism refers to a constellation of positions bringing feminist insights to environmental philosophy. Feminists began to formulate theories about connections between abuses of nature and human oppression, such as sexism and racism, in the early 1970s. Although there are a wide variety of ecofeminist positions, a core position held by all is that there are important conceptual, epistemological, political, ethical, and theoretical links between abuses of nature and a variety of human oppressions. Ecological feminists agree that any environmental ethic failing to examine such links is conceptually and practically lacking (Warren 1990).

Analysis of value dualisms has been central in ecological feminist discussions of Western patriarchal culture. A value dualism is a pair of disjuncts in which each is seen as radically different from the other, and one is ranked above the other in a hierarchy of value. Ecological feminists such as Val Plumwood (1993) argue that a reason/nature dualism serves as a fault line underlying the conceptual framework of Western patriarchal cultures. This forms the basis for a series of related dualisms where whatever is associated with nature is seen as radically different and inferior to whatever is associated with reason. Examples commonly discussed in ecological feminist literature include civilized/primitive, masculine/feminine, mental/manual, and human/nature. These pairs legitimate a number of oppressions, including oppressions based on class, race, and sex.

Karen Warren (1990) distills the point about both conceptual and historical connections justifying dominations of women and nature within dominant Western frameworks. She argues that both rely on a "logic of domination," which asserts that certain differences constitute moral superiority, and uses alleged moral superiority to justify domination of the inferior group by the superior one. Warren provides the following as a typical argument using the logic of domination to justify human moral superiority over "nature."

(A1) Humans do, plants do not, have the conscious capacity to consciously change the community in which they live.

(A2) Whatever has this capacity is morally superior to whatever doesn't have it.

(A3) Humans are morally superior to plants and rocks.

(A4) For any X and Y, if X is morally superior to Y, then X is morally justified in subordinating Y.

(A5) Humans are morally justified in subordinating plants and rocks. (129)

Warren argues that the same kind of logic allows for the sexist domination of women in Western patriarchy due to the historical association of women with nature. She suggests that arguments of the following form are typical in justifying sexism.

(B1) Women are identified with nature and the realm of the physical; men are identified with the "human" and the realm of the mental.

(B2) Whatever is identified with nature and the realm of the physical is inferior to ("below") whatever is identified with the "human" and the realm of the mental.

(B3) Thus, women are inferior to men.

(B4) For any X and Y, if X is superior to Y, then X is morally justified in subordinating Y.

(B5) Men are justified in subordinating women. (130)

According to Warren, arguments A and B are conceptually connected because both use the logic of domination to justify subordination of one group by another. They are historically connected because premise (B2) relies on the acceptance of some version of argument A justifying the devaluation of nature presupposed in B. Warren and many other ecological feminists maintain that the justification for many oppressive institutions, such as American slavery, has relied on associating certain groups of humans with "nature." Because of these connections, fighting against the oppression of humans and the exploitation of nature are part of the same battle. Those working for social justice and those working for environmental protection should therefore be allies.

Concern for animals has also been a major theme in ecological feminist thought. Carol Adams (1991) suggests that concern for animals is part of the ecological feminist project, because acknowledging their value is part of disengaging the logic of domination, and because the exploitation of the Earth in general is part of much animal agriculture. Adams connects the exploitation of animals with the exploitation of black women, who as "lung runners" in U.S. poultry processing plants must scrape the lungs out of 5,000 chicken chest cavities per hour. According to Adams, "Both women workers and the chickens themselves are the means to the end of consumption, but because consumption has been disembodied, their oppressions as worker and consumable body are invisible" (131). Some ecological feminists have argued for universal vegetarianism except in cases where meat is required for survival. Others have argued for a more contextual approach, avoiding practices that are cruel and disrespectful to animals when possible, such as factory farming. The strategy of locating sites of multiple oppressions, such as poultry processing plants, has been a central one within ecological feminism.

The strategy of locating multiple oppressions is also evident in ecological feminist discussions of environmental racism. Ecological feminist analysis helps raise questions of how ethical, economic, and aesthetic discourses serve to justify environmental racism, and how lack of power and alienation make it especially difficult for certain communities to fight back. Other issues include ways in which racist conceptions of people and urban areas as dirty and hopeless justify mistreatment, and how in male-dominated societies women may be disproportionately affected by toxins. As always, ecological feminism focuses on the fact that toxic dumping affects not only humans, but nonhumans as well (Cuomo 1998).

Another concern central to ecological feminism has been the politics of "development." In the ecological feminist classic *Staying Alive* (1989), Vandana Shiva claims that in India, Western-style development has been highly problematic, and while both sexes have been affected, it is often women who lose most. Shiva refers to Western-style development as Western patriarchy. She argues that the devaluation of nature and women within Western patriarchy is imported in Western-style development projects. Hence, she argues that such development is often worse for women than for men. As in the West, knowledge associated with women is seen as unscientific and becomes discredited. "Scientific knowledge," mainly under the control of men, is considered real. Using India as an example, Shiva documents how, as these new "scientific methods" are employed, women—the primary providers of food, water, and fuel—are displaced. Because new methods tend to ignore nature's cycles and the interconnections between natural processes, results fail over time. They are unsustainable. Chapters on water, food, and forests document in impressive detail how and why many modern scientific techniques have been unsuccessful, destroying more sustainable ways of living.

The present discussion can provide only a glimpse of the highly textured and complex discussions often referred to by the umbrella term "ecological feminism." The key ideas that I shall be working with in my analysis of both ecological integrity and of the Earth Charter are as follows: Investigations into concrete environmental issues such as pollution, waste disposal, radiation, and extinction of wild species are always about more than they appear to be because they are in part results of destructive and inaccurate conceptions of reality (Cuomo 2001). We must address how power operates in areas pinpointed as environmental issues/problems. As Warren, Cuomo, Shiva, Plumwood, and others have pointed out, we need to examine underlying value systems that justify exploitation, and these have something to say not only about the value of nature, but about the value of various human beings as well. While looking at environmental problems, we must identify historically embedded assumptions lying beneath the surface of these problems, and look for the relationships between them. Ecofeminist critique of dualistic thinking reminds us that "the personal is political, the ecological is social, and culture is never completely separate from nature" (Cuomo 2001). Environmental issues are deeply political—and never separate from other issues of social justice.

Ecological Integrity

Among concerned environmentalists, some philosophers, scientists, and others have focused on the concept of ecological integrity in formulating an environmental ethic. According to Allan Holland, "Reduced to its simplest, integrity is wildness" (in Westra 1994, xii). In *The Principle of Integrity* (1994), Laura Westra suggests that in order for an ecosystem to have integrity, it must (a) retain the ability to deal with outside interference and, if necessary, regenerate itself; (b) its optimum capacity for the greatest ongoing possible development options within its time and location must be undiminished; (c) it must retain its ability to continue its ongoing change and development, unconstrained by human interruptions past or present. On this approach, questions of whether ecosystems possess integrity are largely scientific.

Using a biocentric approach, Westra and others argue that because human and nonhuman well-being depend on the existence of at least some ecosystems possessing integrity, protecting intact ecosystems must be a foundational concern of any environmental ethic. Therefore, Westra advocates for a general moral injunction to respect the integrity of ecological and biological processes, except in self-defense.

From ecological feminist standpoints, the need to preserve at least some level of ecological integrity is clear, and approaches such as Westra's are basically consistent with most ecological feminist thought. For example, Vandana Shiva's critique of development discussed above focuses on how development projects disrupt ecological integrity, although she does not use those exact words.

Ecological feminists have raised crucial questions about what it means to be "wild." And the idea that, in order to be wild, an area must have been free from both past and present human "interference" or "modification" requires analysis. It is important from ecological feminist perspectives to avoid dualistic thinking. Humans are part of "nature," even if this has been basically denied within much of the Western tradition. And, if humans are part of "nature," mere presence is not necessarily a threat to integrity. Ecofeminists have pointed out how the idea of wilderness as a place "untouched by man" has often been presented in an androcentric and ethnocentric manner in standard wilderness protection literature. Ecological feminists have argued that traditional approaches to environmentalism in the United States have focused on wilderness from privileged, white, middle-class perspectives in which concerns of working-class or racial minorities have been seen as marginal or as competing with wilderness preservation (Gaard 1997). While certain forms of human interference are clearly threats to ecosystem integrity, questions of what forms of interaction count as "interruption," as well as who benefits from various ways of construing "interruption" would all be interesting ecological feminist projects.

Ecological feminist analysis would examine how distributions of power and privilege might make it impossible for most people to live with integrity, as well as why living with integrity might simply be unattractive for those with the resources to make such choices. For example, what specific social/institutional configurations make it such that in developing and developed countries, many do not have resources to attempt to "live in integrity"—just surviving takes up more than all the time available. Unfortunately, in many situations, the ability to even conceive of "living in integrity" reflects power and privilege. And, ecological feminist analysis would ask about specific power distributions forcing many people into lifestyles that are clearly unsustainable in the long run, for the sake of short-term survival. A focus on the structural aspects of the distribution of power and privilege that make individual *choices* to live in integrity either inconceivable, impossible, or both, within particular concrete situations, is crucial for ecological feminist analysis. In addition, ecological feminist analysis would question why political, economic, and social structures make choices to live with integrity concretely, in particular times and places, unattractive or difficult even for people with fair amounts of power and privilege (such as whether choosing to live with integrity would require significant losses of both).

The Earth Charter

The Earth Charter (2002) contains much that is consistent with ecological feminist thinking. The Charter's basic aim is respect and care for the community of life. This is said to involve the following four broad commitments:

1. Respect Earth and life in all its diversity.
2. Care for the community of life with understanding, compassion, and love.
3. Build democratic societies that are just, participatory, sustainable, and peaceful.
4. Secure Earth's bounty and beauty for present and future generations. (2)

According to the Charter, fulfilling these broad commitments will require paying attention to maintaining ecological integrity, issues of social and economic justice, and the promotion of democracy, nonviolence, and peace.

From an ecological feminist perspective, all of these are worthy goals. And, it is important that the Charter seems to realize that preserving ecological integrity and promoting economic and social justice are highly interconnected enterprises. From this standpoint, the Charter is consistent with ecological feminism's commitment to seek connections between various environmental issues and other issues less obviously connected to environmental protection. The Charter specifies the importance of promoting human equality and minimizing animal suffering, central ecofeminist projects. In addition, the Charter does not merely imply the importance of eradicating sexism by speaking of the need for equality of all peoples. It has a specific subprinciple in the section on social and economic justice that calls for the affirmation of gender equality and equity as prerequisites to sustainable development and the ensuring of universal access to education, health care, and economic opportunity for women. This is clearly a key part of any ecological feminist vision. Finally, the Charter recognizes that the needed changes will require changes in dominant value systems and in particular, the notion of what it means to be human, which is again central in ecological feminist thought.

Although the broad goals of the Charter are consistent with some key insights of ecological feminism, there are several problems with the Charter from ecofeminist perspectives. The Preamble is troubling. The use of the word "we" for "humanity" raises critical issues. The Preamble begins "We stand at a critical moment in Earth's history, a time when humanity must choose its future." And "To move forward we must recognize that in the midst of magnificent diversity of cultures and life forms we are one human family and one Earth community with a common destiny" (1). Although there is a recognition that "the gap between rich and poor is widening," the Preamble asserts that "the choice is ours: form a global partnership to care for Earth and one another or risk the destruction of ourselves and the diversity of life" (1). Finally there is a call for the acceptance of "universal responsibility."

> To realize these aspirations, we must decide to live with a sense of universal responsibility, identifying ourselves with the whole Earth community as well as

> local communities. . . . Everyone shares responsibility for the present and future well-being of the human family and the larger living world. The spirit of human solidarity and kinship with all life is strengthened when we live with reverence for the mystery of being, gratitude for the gift of life, and humility regarding the human place in nature (2).

The Preamble ends by stating that the Charter is meant to be a standard for the conduct of all individuals, organizations, businesses, governments, and transnational institutions.

Most obviously, the uncritical use the term "family" is troubling. Ecological feminists and other feminists have paid a great deal of attention to the ways in which women have been abused within patriarchal families. Hence, the uncritical adoption of the notion of "family" with no discussion of questions of power within a family is highly problematic. Questions of leadership and authority are always loaded within ecological feminist discourse. Simply adopting this term as if it is friendly and unproblematic is deeply disturbing from an ecological feminist perspective.

The document has the tone of a message from those with political authority to "the people." Although framers claim to have sought input from a variety of people, the document speaks consistently of "empowering people," rather than helping people empower themselves. So, I am left wondering just who is the intended audience for this document. It is hard to believe that the "we" being addressed includes people whose only next concern is short-term survival.

The notion of "universal responsibility" is also troubling. "We" (all humans) are not responsible for the current situation, nor can "we" (all humans) make choices in favor of change. As I stated above, ecological feminism is more interested in why institutional structures make certain so-called "choices" either impossible, inconceivable, or both. Stating that every human has "universal responsibility" is at best empty, and at worst insensitive to the situation of many (most?) people on the planet. While there are subprinciples stating "we" must (a) "accept that with the right to own, manage, and use natural resources comes the duty to prevent environmental harm and to protect the rights of people," and (b) affirm that with increased freedom, knowledge, and power comes increased responsibility to promote "the common good" (2), nothing is stated about whether private ownership of natural resources is appropriate, or whether the differences in freedom assumed are fair. Hence, the implication that certain changes in patterns of ownership and distribution of resources are "unthinkable" seems implicit, an implication that is highly troubling from an ecological feminist perspective. While there is a subprinciple that calls for the promotion of equitable distribution of wealth within and among nations (4), this appears later in the document, and nothing about the tensions between this goal and the assumptions in (a) and (b) above is specifically mentioned. In closing, the Charter mentions the "common destiny" (5) of human beings. However, ecological feminists are committed to noticing key differences in the destinies of various human beings and in examining the power structures that make many such destinies intolerable.

In conclusion, the Earth Charter is a mixed bag from an ecological feminist perspective. On the positive side, it recognizes the link between environmental and other social issues, including the need for areas manifesting ecological integrity. It sees environmental issues *as* social, which is crucial. It also specifically calls for the eradication of sexism and other forms of oppression and of just distribution of wealth and resources, although as noted above, these calls seem to be in tension with certain other portions of the document. However, it calls for "choice" and "universal responsibility" for all, when responsibility is *clearly* not universal, and where choice of the sort called for is often (usually) impossible for most individuals living in the world. Hence, the document contains some significant flaws. In addition, from an ecological feminist standpoint, it is necessary not only to call for change but to examine the concrete conditions which make much of what the Charter calls for impossible, rather than simply calling for such changes.

References

Adams, Carol J. 1991. "Ecofeminism and the Eating of Animals."*Hypatia: A Special Issue, Ecological Feminism* 6 (1): 125–145. An article discussing the connections between ecological feminism and vegetarianism.

Cuomo, Chris J. 1998. *Feminism and Ecological Communities: An Ethic of Flourishing.* London: Routledge. The concept of flourishing is used to ground an ecological feminist ethic.

———. 2001. Unpublished manuscript.

The Earth Charter Initiative. 2002. "The Earth Charter." San José, Costa Rica: Earth Council. <http://www.earthcharter.org/earthcharter/charter.htm> (January 12, 2002).

Gaard, Greta. 1997. "Ecofeminism and Wilderness." *Environmental Ethics* 19 (1): 5–24.

Holland, Alan. 1998. "Foreword," in Laura Westra, *Living in Integrity.* Lanham, Md.: Rowman & Littlefield, xi–xvi.

Plumwood, Val. 1993. *Feminism and the Mastery of Nature.* London: Routledge. An analysis of the logic of dualistic thinking within Western patriarchies and some suggested alternatives.

Shiva, Vandana. 1989. *Staying Alive: Women, Ecology and Development.* London: Zed Books. A discussion of the negative impact of patriarchal style Western development in India.

Warren, Karen J. 1990. "The Power and Promise of Ecological Feminism." *Environmental Ethics* 12 (2): 125–146. A discussion of the conceptual connections between environmentalism and feminism.

Westra, Laura. 1994. *An Environmental Proposal for Ethics: The Principle of Integrity.* Lanham, Md.: Roman & Littlefield.

———. 1998. *Living in Integrity.* Lanham, Md.: Rowman & Littlefield.

Humanistic Values and the Earth Charter

Chapter 6

A Pragmatic Focus on Humans

Julia J. Bartkowiak

A recent trend in environmental ethics is the rejection of anthropocentric or human-centered views for much broader biocentric positions. Part of the rationale behind this movement is the belief that the more narrow human-centered perspective cannot protect the natural environment, especially in those cases in which human interests seem to be contrary to the protection effort. Although I am not rejecting a biocentric approach, this paper argues that a refusal to make use of anthropocentric views is problematic. An anthropocentric approach is also consistent with much of the Earth Charter. For example, the Preamble mentions that: "The resilience of the community of life and well-being of humanity depend upon preserving a health biosphere with all its ecological systems, a rich variety of plants and animals, fertile soils, pure waters, and clean air." In fact, human-centered approaches, such as a human rights approach, can still provide an effective tool for protecting the Earth and all its inhabitants in certain cases. Indeed the Preamble of the Earth Charter identifies universal human rights as one of the foundations of a sustainable global society. At the present time, biocentrism does not connect with many fields that remain primarily focused on impacts experienced by human beings. By accepting certain anthropocentric views, environmental ethics will be able to interact with diverse fields of study within a variety of cultures. If environmental ethics completely rejects a human-centered approach, it is unlikely that ethicists will be able to contribute either to policy discussions concerning many current environmental issues or the resolution of specific problems which require immediate action. Thus, certain anthropocentric approaches can be useful as an integral part of an environmental pragmatism which makes use of a variety of ethical theories to address global environmental issues.

It is important to recognize that anthropocentrism can be a valuable approach for a number of reasons. First, there are practical reasons for maintaining anthropocentric views within environmental ethics. One important consequence of such an approach is that it does not require its proponents to convince other people to accept a completely foreign point of view, a problem faced by proponents of certain biocentric views. For example, deep ecology requires a "conversion" that is similar to a religious conversion. As many of its proponents point out (e.g., Naess 1998), deep ecology is considered to be a spiritual commitment that is typically accepted after a deeply moving personal experience or insight. In fact, many deep ecologists either speak of their own conversion experiences, which resulted in a major change in their attitudes and lifestyle, or discuss experiential methods for getting other people to understand and accept the principles of this Earth-centered view (e.g., Devall and Sessions 1995).

As is the case with missionary religions, I see no possibility of getting everyone to either have a conversion experience or accept the faith. Some people simply will retain commitments or perspectives other than the ones that the missionaries would prefer that they have. Thus, deep ecology is doomed to fail if its goal is to convert everyone. Even with a more moderate goal of converting the majority of people or enough people to impact social policy, deep ecologists are not likely to accomplish this task in the near future. Such major attitude changes are the result of introducing new ideas that conflict with many predominant views in the world today. Since the shaping of attitudes towards the environment is a part of socialization, each of us is influenced by environmental socialization. This influence plays a role in how we see ourselves, other people, nonhuman life, and the Earth itself. As many biocentrists point out, a careful exploration of this relationship between ourselves and the rest of the universe provides a basis for knowledge of our moral responsibilities and a more complete understanding of ourselves. This exploration, although an important task, is time consuming. Consequently, if ethicists refuse to engage in anthropocentric discussions of the environment at the present time they will isolate themselves and lessen the impact they could have on current environmental policies and practices.

Because of the consequences of environmental practices, environmental ethics is also more complex than many other social issues. One single person, business, or nation can have an enormous impact on others who either are not involved in the decision making for that action or are not geographically close to the agent. For example, a decision to dump toxic chemicals into a body of water or an accidental chemical spill can impact every living thing that is connected to that body of water. As scientists have pointed out, the changes produced from one environmental practice can be complicated and are not entirely predictable. When pollution causes climate changes, there are not only immediate consequences but also significant long-term consequences. Additionally, environmental practices affect everything on the planet and recently have begun to reach into space. Since our understanding of the world has changed over time and will continue to do so, there is no good reason to believe that the solutions that seem best today will be the ones that are accepted in the future. Consequently, a multifaceted approach that includes anthropocentric methods seems best able to deal with actual environmental issues.

Biocentrism is problematic in another important way. It either introduces new terms or new understandings of terms in order to create a conceptual revolution. In other words, the analysis or introduction of terms is the first step in getting other people to see that they must *change* their understanding and ultimately alter their views and lifestyles. Since such work has been critical in initiating most social revolutions, I don't intend to discount its importance. Yet, in the area of environmental ethics there is an urgency. The natural environment is being damaged at an incredible rate and immediate actions must be taken to prevent certain obvious harms, for example, the pollution of the sole source of drinking water for a particular region. By advocating an anthropocentric approach for specific cases, I am asserting that we have good reason to believe that there is no single answer to existing and future environmental problems. Instead, as with any inductive reasoning task, we must attempt to utilize several diverse environmental ethics to fit the cases that we are addressing. Without such an approach, environmental problems cannot be adequately resolved.

An advantage to anthropocentrism is that it will, in certain cases, provide short term solutions. For example, a human rights based approach, while clearly a human-centered approach, can provide a more immediate means of addressing environmental issues and policies for certain cases. Since a human rights approach focuses on moral concepts that are prominent in national and international decision making and policy setting, it can provide a generally accepted means for solving environmental problems by utilizing existing international agreements. Rights concepts, even if they are not entirely clear, have become an important part of national and international dialogue, policies, and laws. An environmental ethics which makes use of human rights language—a language that is common to many individuals and governments—is more likely to result in general agreement in important cases in which immediate action is required. Additionally, human rights language can bridge the gaps between very different fields of study within countries that have adopted the Universal Declaration of Human Rights or one of the other United Nations documents pertaining to human rights.

I will provide one detailed example to demonstrate how a human rights approach could be used to resolve current environmental issues. Since 1987, with its issuance of the report *Unfinished Business*, the environmental Protection Agency (EPA) of the United States has used environmental risk analysis to determine its environmental policies and practices. At the present time, risk analysis has been accepted by the majority of businesses and rejected by the majority of environmental groups (Anderson 1996, 72). Environmental groups have a number of reasons for opposing the use of risk analysis by the EPA, including concerns that risk analysis is unjust because its methods ensure that poor people are exposed to more environmental risks than the wealthy (Eilbergeld 1993). In fact, some advocates of environmental justice within the United States have already successfully used anthropocentric views to accomplish some changes in environmental practices. These advocates have pointed out that policies that result in greater exposure of the poor to environmental risks violate equal protection clauses of U.S. law. More importantly, many risk analysis methods assume that environmental degradation is necessary for economic progress. This assumption is neither obviously true nor reflective of the Earth Charter, especially "Section II. Ecological Integrity." Additionally, since risk analysis most often measures the effects of environmental practices on humans, biocentric views will have little or no impact on these analyses. More changes will occur by using a human rights approach.

If a convincing case can be made for the claim that risk analysis violates international human rights agreements, then the United States cannot justify its use of risk analysis for determining environmental policy and practice. Relying on risk analysis would result in violations of human rights, and the United States has signed documents and regularly pledged a strong commitment to policies that uphold these rights. I intend to demonstrate that such a case can be made; the adoption of risk analysis methods by the EPA violates both the Universal Declaration of Human Rights and the International Covenant on Civil and Political Rights. Because of these rights violations, environmentalists are correct to reject the use of risk analysis. The EPA should develop alternative methods for determining policies and practices. Additionally, this conclusion is not just one that is relevant to the United States. Any nation that has signed one of the United Nations human rights agreements should not be using risk analysis to determine environmental policy or practice.

Briefly, risk analysis is considered to be a scientific method of determining the costs and benefits of adopting particular environmental policies, deciding whether to build new industries, setting priorities for reclaiming areas that have already been polluted, and so on. Advocates of risk analysis believe that, once the degree of risk has been determined or assessed, these risks can be compared with assessments of risk from other actions and ultimately used to effectively manage environmental risks. Although the scope of environmental risks can extend beyond human beings, in practice the focus is primarily on the health impacts for humans. Notice that risk analysis assumes that some risk is inescapable and the goal is to minimize the risk or costs while maximizing the benefits (which are primarily economic ones). Even if we simply accept the assumption that some risk is inevitable, a human rights approach provides good reason to reject the use of risk analysis as it is currently practiced. Human rights violations will inevitably result from risk analysis because the analysis must use environmental risk assessment (ERA) to calculate the risks involved. This calculation, similar in many respects to a utilitarian calculation, is claimed to form the scientific basis for determining the short- and long-term environmental risks. However, several assumptions that must be used in order to perform the calculations violate human rights.

First, when we accept that humans have rights, we are accepting a belief in the inherent value of human life. This is apparent in the prefaces of both the Universal Declaration of Human Rights and the International Covenant on Civil and Political Rights, which state that the "recognition of the inherent dignity and of the equal and inalienable rights of all members of the human family is the foundation of freedom, justice, and peace in the world." If we recognize this inherent dignity, then it is difficult to argue that a risk to human health or life is acceptable or can accurately be quantified and used to determine total costs and benefits of each environmental decision. In other words, if we accept the belief that all humans have inherent dignity, human beings cannot be sacrificed for economic benefits through the use of ERA. This is especially true since those calculating the risk are rarely exposed to the hazard(s) (Bartkowiak 2000).

More specifically, environmental risk assessment typically involves some method of estimating a monetary value for human illness and death. Each of the commonly used methods for estimating this value ensures that human rights violations will occur. According to one method of evaluating environmental risks, The human capital approach, an individual's value is based on the earnings lost if their exposure to pollution causes poor health or premature death. Thus, rather than having inherent value, the human capital approach claims that any person's value is determined by their ability to produce goods and services. Using this approach, the value of a U.S. citizen in 1992 was lowest for someone 65 years old or older ($22,977) and highest for someone 15–24 years old ($873,096) (*Pollution Prevention and Abatement Handbook* 1997, 3–4). These "values" for human life are used to determine whether the costs, of pollution prevention, for example, outweigh the benefits for any particular course of action. Not only does this method of placing monetary value on people's lives ignore the multiple ways in which human beings are valuable, it also guarantees unequal treatment of individuals based on age, income, job skills, and the country in which they live. Since this unequal treatment involves a denial of the equal value of all humans, any nation with a commitment to human rights has no reason to adopt the human capital approach.

Another common method of assessing risks is the contingent valuation approach. This approach uses a survey to ask individuals what they are willing to pay to reduce their chances of dying prematurely. The people surveyed are asked what dollar amount they would be willing to surrender in order to avoid a particular environmental hazard. These surveys determined that, in 1990, the value of the life of a U.S. citizen ranged from $1.2 to $9.7 million (*Pollution Prevention and Abatement Handbook* 1997, (4). Notice that this monetary amount is significantly higher than the human capital approach. However, there is no reason to believe that even these figures provide an accurate representation of the value of human life. On the contrary, these figures seem arbitrary and are likely to differ from survey to survey. Additionally, assigning this monetary value does not reflect the position of inherent value that is present in human rights documents.

Since there are a number of other methods for assessing risks, a common response to problems with a particular ERA approach is to suggest that another approach is much better and avoids the problems inherent in the criticized approach. Other approaches mentioned include the wage differential approach, the cost of illness approach, and an approach based on disability-adjusted life years (DALYs). However, no method of placing monetary values on human life can avoid the fact that such an enterprise is based on assumptions that violate human rights. With each model, the view that human life is inherently valuable has been rejected for the belief that each human life has a specific value that can be accurately stated. Because the various risk assessment methods also assume that the value of life varies greatly from individual to individual, they involve a denial of the equal rights of all human beings. Additionally, because these models calculate different values for human life depending on the geographic location of that life (because of differences in the cost of living, wages, and so on within each area), risk analysis denies the belief that each human life, regardless of its location, has equal value. Most importantly, risk analysis includes the assumption that human life can be sacrificed in those circumstances in which ERA determines that other benefits outweigh the calculated value for human life. No nation that is seriously committed to the inherent dignity of human life and equal treatment for all individuals should accept these assumptions. A commitment to human rights requires us to accept that there are no circumstances under which degradation in someone's health or their death from exposure to environmental hazards can be balanced against economic gains to other individuals (who are typically not exposed to these risks). In other words, human life would always come out as more important than any economic benefit.

Risk analysis is an established part of EPA decisions within the United States and has also become important internationally. Many multinational corporations and the World Bank have embraced risk analysis. In fact, the World Bank now requires risk assessments for many of its loans. Within the body of literature that comprises the World Bank policies and guidelines for risk assessments, it is relatively easy to find assumptions that undermine human rights. The World Bank assumes that some level of risk to human health and life is acceptable, and its risk assessment practices have included the relocation of Dhanora Village (population 3,750) to expand a petrochemical plant in India (Environmental Hazard and Risk Assessment 1997, 5). The acceptance of such risky, "Category A" projects is detrimental to human health and the biosphere. A human rights focus could be especially helpful in altering World Bank policy because the World Bank must take into account any international agreements that are in effect in the project area. Thus, any nation that has signed human rights agreements could argue that, for example, the relocation of entire villages of people is a violation of human rights. In fact, "Category A" projects are the ones that are most likely to violate human rights. Since these projects are also the ones that are most harmful to the environment, a human rights approach could be used to limit or deny approval of these projects.

Thus, although it is a human-centered focus, a human rights approach is able to accomplish some of the goals of environmentalists. Environmentalists have advocated replacing risk analysis with a policy of reducing and eliminating toxins. Since toxins cause poor health and death, the promotion of human rights does require the reduction and elimination of toxins. Even if the primary reason given for reducing or eliminating toxins is to benefit human beings, such a policy will have effects that reach beyond humans. Toxin reduction and elimination is conducive to both human flourishing and the flourishing of other living things within that area. This is especially true when people within that area have adopted attitudes that do not separate humans from their surroundings (biocentric attitudes, for example).

Certainly, some people will continue to believe that human interests require the degradation of nonhumans and the environment. In such circumstances, a human rights approach will not provide the needed level of environmental protection. This paper is not suggesting that a human rights approach will accomplish all environmental goals. The social change that is necessary for survival and, more importantly, flourishing in a technological world cannot be accomplished solely through a human rights approach. Thus, proponents of an Earth-entered ethics must continue with their attempts to convince others to adopt a deep respect for the Earth. Additionally, the conceptual analysis of terms used in environmental ethics is crucial. Conceptual analyses accomplish the important tasks both of developing a better understanding of current environmental terms and creating new terms that carry the specific meanings needed for contemporary discussions of the environment. More importantly, these analyses also provide the ideals or standards which environmental policies and attitudes can then strive to achieve.

However, the current trend in environmental ethics which involves a rejection of anthropocentric attitudes results in a refusal to use approaches, like human rights, that are internationally recognized and established. In the short term, anthropocentric approaches can be effective because such approaches are more likely to result in action in some cases of environmental degradation that require immediate attention. Consequently, to meet all the various challenges presented by environmental concerns and to adhere to the Earth Charter, environmental ethics cannot afford to reject anthropocentric approaches.

References

Anderson, Frederick R. 1996. "CRA and Its Stakeholders: Advice to the Executive Office," in *Comparing Environmental Risks: Tools for Setting Government Priorities,* edited by J. Clarence Davies. Washington, D.C.: Resources for the Future.

Bartkowiak, Julia. 2000. "Calculating the Value of Human Health and Life." Presented at the 28th Conference on Value Inquiry, Lamar University, Beaumont, Texas, April 14.

Devall, Bill and George Sessions. 1995. "Deep Ecology," in *Earth Ethics: Environmental Ethics, Animal Rights, and Practical Applications*, edited by James Sterba. Englewood Cliffs, N.J.: Prentice Hall.

Eilbergeld, Ellen K. 1993. "Risk Assessment: The Perspective and Experience of U.S. Environmentalists." *Environmental Health Perspectives* 101(2) (June): 100–104.

"Environmental Hazard and Risk Assessment." 1997. *Environmental Assessment Sourcebook Update*, The World Bank, No. 21(December).

Environmental Protection Agency (EPA). 1987. *Unfinished Business*.

Naess, Arne. 1998. "The Deep Ecological Movement: Some Philosophical Perspectives," in *Environmental Ethics: Divergence and Convergence*, 2nd edition, edited by Richard G. Botzler and Susan J. Armstrong. Boston: McGraw-Hill.

Pollution Prevention and Abatement Handbook. 1997. Washington, D.C.: World Bank.

Chapter 7

Human Values as a Source for Sustaining the Environment

Naomi Zack

> Every form of life has value regardless of its worth to human beings.
> —Earth Charter, Principle 1a

Due to the overwhelming dominance of homo sapiens, natural environments are no longer self-sustaining, and their continued existence will depend on human agreement to sustain them. Given present commercial historical realities, such agreement will require new kinds of moral reasoning about the relationship between human beings and ecological systems.

The preservation of natural environments is obviously of great human utility as a source of valued things. But the sustenance of natural ecosystems and their inhabitants, on the basis of their intrinsic worth, does not yet have an effective theoretical defense against human speciesism, the continual expansion of capitalistic systems, and the present dependence of humans on human-made physical and social environments. The intrinsic worth of natural ecosystems has been explained by proponents of deep ecology and maintained within traditional indigenous cultures, but such advocacy seems thus far to operate in a cognitive dimension separate from the rest of Western (i.e., "Northern/Euro-American/secular-technological") moral reasoning. So the question is, How can we Westerners bring intuitions, insights, and traditions concerning the intrinsic worth of natural systems and beings into the discourse of recognized practical reason, or moral argument?

The three dominant moral theories of utilitarianism or consequentialism, virtue ethics, and deontology are each plausible systems to apply to natural systems and beings. However, I shall argue that only deontology is capable of accomplishing the required theoretical goals, because only deontology could confer personhood on natural systems and beings.

Jeremy Bentham (1823) was the first to note that the test for inclusion in the domain of those whose well-being counts is not the capacity for rational thought, but the ability to suffer. ("The question is not, Can they reason? Nor, Can they talk? But, Can they suffer?") So, we could extend a utilitarian calculus to natural subjects. But, utilitarian insights do not tell us how to weigh the beneficial consequences to natural subjects, or what to do when human goods are maximized to a greater extent than nonhumans are harmed. Utilitarianism yields a model of humane treatment of nonhuman life, which could result in the extinction of such life whenever humans believe that the pain suffered by nonhumans is too great. If nonhuman absence of pain is not sufficient for calculating maximal results for nonhumans, it is not clear how humans could define nonhuman flourishing. For example, do animals flourish if they are forced to subsist in the margins of their ecosystems, or, do they flourish if new ecosystems are artificially created for them? But even if something like John Stuart Mill's concept of "higher pleasures" is applied to animals or ecosystems as a standard for sustainable conditions under which they flourish, the flourishing of nonhuman beings is still likely to be judged not as important as the flourishing of human beings. This would be particularly true when the nonhuman being is an entire ecosystem likely to be jeopardized by development that will enhance human livelihood and happiness.

Virtue ethics looks more promising because the moral ground is higher and provides a perspective from which we can value natural beings in a way totally apart from their use to us. We can value them and teach our children to value them as an expression and extension of what is best in our character. Indeed, our own flourishing may require an appreciation of, and respect for, natural beings in ways that treat such beings with the utmost moral and aesthetic seriousness. Thus, Thomas Hill (1983) explains how our behavior toward natural beings reveals the presence or absence of human traits such as sensitivity, humility, and gratitude.

The problem with the virtue ethics approach is that it seems to relegate the sustenance of natural environments and beings to the province of manners and sensibility. This aspect of human life is personally and socially important only after pressing problems of survival have been solved, and it is not usually a priority in the face of human need and suffering. More problematic, the sustenance of natural beings as part of the development of human virtue remains an enterprise in which humans, and not those natural beings, are central. On a good day, when I am not too pressured by concerns directly affecting my livelihood, I may make a contribution to the preservation of rain forests. And why, as a matter of virtue? Because it will reflect well on me in contexts where I have to account for myself, and more important, will strengthen my virtue of generosity. Something stronger than this kind of rationale would seem to be necessary if sustenance of natural environments is a serious moral issue.

I now turn to deontology. I want to examine the radical view that we need to assent to a general principle which will admit natural beings to what Kant called "the kingdom of ends." This can be accomplished only if natural beings are granted the status of persons, in the same ways in which human beings are persons. Such recognition will require competent, adult human representatives, similar to the ways in which the human personhood of children and adults of diminished capacity is represented by parents and guardians. Mere stewardship or trusteeship over ecosystems and their inhabitants will not succeed in protecting them from depredation and eventual destruction because that kind of representation is at best defensive. Once the defense is overcome, for example, once the land is wrested into the commercial domain, there is at present nothing illegal or broadly immoral about its destruction. By contrast, the parental rights or guardianship of children and adults of diminished capacity can only be abrogated if children and wards grow up or acquire full capacity. Children and wards are not "adventured" to the fortunes of the marketplace if one particular guardianship comes to an end, because their need of guardianship is absolute.

If an ecosystem had the status of a person, then depriving it of life or assaulting its inhabitants would be in principle no different from crimes of murder or assault committed against human beings. One can imagine a situation in which killing members of an endangered species would be a far more serious crime than it is in most places at present, but this does not capture what is distinctive about personhood. Even if deliberately killing natural beings were a capital crime, as things now stand, so long as such beings are not persons, the reason for the punishment would rest on something different from their inherent rights.

I once heard Winona LaDuke, a North American spokesperson for indigenist concerns, talk about a hydroelectric project that had required extensive flooding of land, so that, among other ecological results, 10,000 elk were drowned. "Who gave them the right," she asked, "to drown 10,000 elk?" (See also LaDuke 1999.) I think that is the kind of question which has to be addressed in moral reasoning that is relevant to the sustenance of natural environments.

In a secular capitalistic society, the rights of ecosystems and their inhabitants would have to be constructed. This could be done by basing such rights on the same kinds of moral sentiments and intuitions that motivate doctrines of universal human rights. The twentieth century has not provided good reason to be optimistic about such doctrines, but their worth as ideals remains indisputable. Thus, even if there were not universal agreement and compliance about including ecosystems and their inhabitants in the "kingdom of ends," the consensual and practical limits of the theoretical inclusion would not detract from its value as an ideal. (Human secular morality is an ongoing project.)

The grounds for human secular morality are ultimately unreasoned in the deontological sense. I cannot "prove" that it is wrong to drown 10,000 elk or to allow twelve million children to starve to death. Unfortunately, either you "see" the wrongness of one or both of these things, or you do not. Similarly, there are reasons short of proof which can be given for granting the status of persons to nonhuman beings and I will now suggest five. (It should be noted that I am not proposing fictitious personhood, as in the case of corporations, but real personhood.)

1. Ecosystems and their inhabitants are living beings, like human beings, and they are entitled to the same rights that human beings are supposed to have. (I am simply asserting the consequent here, not claiming that it follows from the antecedent.)

2. As living beings, it is possible to say that some states of affairs, primarily their ongoing life, or their sickness and death, are better or worse for natural beings. It follows from this that natural beings have positive interests as do human beings.

3. The interests of natural beings, while dependent on the forbearance and assistance of humans, are not in particular cases dependent on particular human beings. This independence of natural beings is analogous to the independence of a human child, in distinction from the dependence of fetuses, who require the support of particular individuals.

4. Many human beings have compassionate sentiments for natural beings, as they do for other humans. They suffer when natural beings are injured and are satisfied and pleased when they flourish. If compassion as a motive is also a reason to curtail the suffering, and promote the flourishing, of humans, then the same holds for natural beings.

5. There is good reason to believe that natural beings suffer when they are injured or destroyed and this similarity to human life is an important qualification for admission to the realm of persons because the one secular basis for universal human rights is the capacity to suffer.

What would be the consequences of person status for nonhuman beings? First, they would have a fundamental right to life. They would also have political rights, expressed through their human representatives, as well as rights to "free speech," expressed in the same way, and other rights, such as freedom of association. There would be a presumption of their liberties, chief of which would be the negative right not to be bought or sold. This last right is perhaps the key benefit of personhood for vast numbers of extant nonhuman beings.

One confusion in the view I am proposing is that it is not clear what the individual unit would be if nonhuman beings were persons. In the case of ecosystems, size and density might be variables. In the case of so-called lower lifeforms, swarms, schools, and flocks might be single persons. I am not sure that a dog would qualify as a person (I know that many would disagree here) although I am quite certain that a single elephant, dolphin, or chimpanzee would.

I have presented an extreme view which many would consider absurd and utopian. My hope is that reasoned objections to such a view will pinpoint the kinds of reasons which underly present legal policies and moral oblivion concerning natural beings.

I anticipate three main lines of objection to including nonhuman beings in the domain of persons: religious, commercial, and speciesist. The religious objection sanctifies human dominance over the land, its resources and animals, on the grounds that a (for the most part, Christian) God created human beings to subdue and rule the Earth. There is no empirical foundation for this objection. The commercial objection is an unfortunate result of the historical ways in which the Western technological project seems to have acquired the capacity to monetize everything on the planet. This project appears to have no bounds and it even has a poor record for the sustenance of human life in situations of conflict with market values. The speciesist objection is difficult to sustain on secular grounds, as a moral position, and it is theoretically weak in the face of genetic engineering and cyborg technologies which are now on the horizon, that is, both hereditary and morphological material from other species may become ordinary components of human beings. Furthermore, should there ever be encounters with extraterrestrial intelligent life, human speciesism will be even more difficult to defend.

The most general values of human development and flourishing would be served by granting personhood to ecosystems and natural beings. It would make us all more virtuous and, in the long run, the quality of human life would be better. But these utilities to humans would be secondary gains, so to speak, and not primary reasons for including natural beings in the domain of persons.

References

Bentham, Jeremy. 1823. "Value of a Lot of Pleasure or Pain, How to be Measured," XVII, *An Introduction to the Principles of Morals and Legislation*. London: W. Pickering.

The Earth Charter Initiative. 2002. "The Earth Charter." San José, Costa Rica: Earth Council. <http://www.earthcharter.org/earthcharter/charter.htm> (January 12, 2002).

Hill, Thomas E. 1983. "Ideals of Human Excellence and Preserving Natural Environments," *Environmental Ethics* 5: 211-24.

LaDuke, Winona. 1999. *All Our Relations: Native Struggles for Land and Life*. Cambridge, Mass.: South End Press.

Chapter 8

The Earth Charter, Servant-Leadership, and Philosophy: Valuing the Earth by Implementing Ideals

Rubye Howard Braye and Ruth Miller Lucier

Introduction

The Earth Charter provides us with ideals that lift our spirits and rally us to the cause of protecting natural environments. The Charter reminds us that we are to "recognize that in the midst of a magnificent diversity of cultures and life forms we are one human family." We are invited by the Charter to "join together to bring forth a sustainable global society founded on respect for nature, universal human rights, economic justice, and a culture of peace." The Charter strongly recommends that "we, the peoples of Earth, declare our responsibility to one another, to the greater community of life, and to future generations" (Earth Council 2000).

True valuing of Earth, however, must go beyond giving lip service to these beautifully articulated ideals; implementation is essential. And implementation requires focused effort, since the ideals themselves embody the possibility for gridlock and potential conflict. For example, the Earth Charter's call for equitable distribution of wealth within and among nations appears at odds with its support for community rights and personal freedoms; its call for an open-ended meeting of basic human needs coexists uneasily with its concerns about overburdened ecological and social systems; its call for unified global action is tenuous in relation to its endorsement of cultural diversity, local democratic choice, and the protection of vulnerable minorities. Hence the mix presents deeply rooted challenge. By lifting up two sets of principles and two distinct but compatible strategies based on servant-leadership and philosophical leadership, the authors of this essay intend to encourage the adoption of consensual and conceptually sound solutions.

The Contribution of Servant-Leadership to Environmental Decisions: The Strategy of Enlightened Application

A promising option for clearing the way for concrete, consensual applications, and hence for implementation of the Earth Charter's ideals, is found in the concept of servant-leadership. This concept introduced by Robert K. Greenleaf in the early 1970s suggests that social dilemmas can be most effectively resolved by assuming and acting in accordance with a carefully articulated leadership model. Greenleaf's model requires that the leader endorse the following proactive aspects of involvement: listening, empathy, healing, persuasion, awareness, foresight, conceptualization, and commitment to the growth of others, to stewardship, and to community.

Naturally, commitments to stewardship and community include the care and management of the environment, locally, nationally, and globally. It is thus appropriate that the servant-leader be actively engaged in caring for the environment in the widest sense, namely, as the whole Earth setting in which we live and work.

The servant-leadership perspective suggests powerful ways of motivating all involved in dynamic global interaction, holding that the facilitation of this motivational process is what genuine leaders should aspire to. As Greenleaf (1991) urges, each of us as a potential leader must begin with the natural feeling that we want to serve, and to serve first. Once conscious choice prompts one to lead, this motivational difference manifests itself in the care taken by the servant-leader to make certain that other people's highest priorities and genuine needs are being addressed (Greenleaf 1991, 7).

The servant-leader must gauge the integrity of her or his motivation by asking whether the proactive aspects of leadership (given in the initial paragraph of this section) are applied wisely. Wise application will enable those served to grow as persons even as they are being served, and grow in the sense of becoming "healthier, wiser, freer, more autonomous, and more likely to become servant-leaders themselves." The servant-leader will, in addition, be measured by whether (while she or he serves) the least privileged in society will benefit. The servant-leader fails to reach appropriate goals if, during the leader's term of service, the most vulnerable become "further deprived" (Greenleaf 1991).

Target Areas for Global Servant-Leadership

Any who internalize the servant-leadership perspective in the area of global environmental activism must consider the value and impact of their decisions in comprehensive ways, noting that in the home, at work, and in the community actions have consequences that ripple beyond us. It is crucial that leaders listen to the experts and acknowledge that leadership involves first acquiring as full an understanding as possible of the total situation and then acting in ways that reflect stewardship.

Leadership at the family level is essential. Families are tremendous consumers. Given the growing world population and the associated consumption rate, resource deficiency, and decreasing sustainability, we must use less and take better care of the fragile environment. Parents must teach youth to conserve. Focus on the environment at the elementary and high school levels is important; however, college level students must also be engaged. It is they who will soon assume positions in the workforce and it is they who in that capacity must communicate to coworkers the importance of being good stewards.

Problems of air quality and water quality must be addressed. These disproportionately affect children and are life threatening to those with emphysema, lung problems, and weak immune systems. The air quality problem is especially acute for developing countries. In China, for example, the use of coal has so polluted the air that not long ago, the Chinese Environmental Bureau admitted that Beijing had not only become the smoggiest city in China but that at certain times, had air pollution that even exceeded that of Mexico City, long considered the world's most contaminated city. This has not only made respiratory illness a top killer of Beijing residents, but has required that trees only fifteen years old be cut down (Pan 1999). The pollution could eventually reach other nations' shores and affect us all.

Near the top of the agenda must be the education of children and youth. Educators must, in concert with parents, instruct and teach by example. Both must share the benefits of responsible environmental stewardship and management. The consequences of environmental management, good and bad, must be articulated in ways that help the next generation understand the effects these will have on themselves and their children for years to come.

Media responsibilities need to be emphasized. As servant-leaders, those who control the media—newspapers, radio, television, and film—anywhere are obligated to communicate the importance of environmental stewardship. Any who fail to do so (or worse, any who communicate an antithetical message) should be appropriately penalized. Media's behavior has consequences; media must share the burdens and benefits of responsible activism. For example, we patronize companies that advertise on television and radio in support of various programs that we enjoy. When these companies and stations support practices that we disagree with, we should no longer buy the products. Such withdrawal of support directly affects the company and indirectly affects the station. As consumers, we are not powerless.

The press might also be kept responsible through oversight by citizen groups that have a "watchdog" function. These might be volunteer, nongovernmental organizations such as the Haw River Assembly (HRA) of North Carolina. This grassroots group monitors press reports about river quality and demands accuracy. The HRA provides the press with carefully collected data concerning the state of the environment as well as scientific opinions about possible negative effects of land use proposals. The power of the press is thus enlisted in a positive way in the effort to protect and restore a river at risk and becomes, in the process, an effective advocate for sound environmental policy. All-community meetings, such as the Bennett Environmental Forum, reinforce this result.

Transformation of Current Regulations

As societies become increasingly complex, governmental roles need to be clarified in ways that facilitate the settling of land use issues. Where possible, governmentally sanctioned entitlements to land need to be honored so that large numbers of people will be secure in their ability to freely own and manage land in beneficial ways. For the good of all, there are flora and fauna that should be left pristine and untouched. Where property is privately owned, and alteration is prohibited by the government on behalf of the citizenry, the government should have a legal obligation to provide some type of compensation to the owners. The compensation should be comparable to the amount the owners would have received had the property been altered for personal use.

Citizen action groups might also serve as a check on exploitative use of land where exploitation is defined as use that would greatly decrease and/or destroy the diverse life sustaining and aesthetic value of the land either immediately or in the long term. Private citizens need to think of themselves as stewards who own the land jointly with future generations.

When land use is debated, servant-leaders must encourage and help all parties to understand the global commitment which the Earth Charter encourages, a commitment which places upon us all an overriding duty to prevent environmental harm. To this end governments around the world should intervene and assist where appropriate.

Philosophical Leadership: The Strategy of Integrative Reflection

A second and vitally strategic area of leadership involves leadership that provides for a linking and prioritizing of foundational concepts. Such conceptual activity is crucial for setting appropriate goals, even though it may make tasks (as Søren Kierkegaard points out) not easier but more complex (Kierkegaard 1956, 84ff.).

The role of philosophy is to encourage reflection and to seek out areas of inconsistency that arise even in the most sincerely intended leadership initiatives. While working to implement the Earth Charter ideals, for example, the philosophical leader will immediately detect the potential for paradox generated by linking (1) calls for the protection of politically mandated individual rights (including property rights) with (2) appeals for communal sharing. Embedded in this gestalt is the basic question of natural versus political entitlement.

The paradox about property arises because within a world where resources are controlled in practice by governments through the use of armed force, legal entitlements can conflict with intuitive requirements of distributive justice (including natural entitlements based on concepts of fairness). For example, owners of land in Cuba immediately before Castro's revolution had received legal entitlement primarily through inheritance from ancestors, who had, through military force, simply declared entitlement and forced the indigenous peoples to work the land in the conquering culture's style. Many landowners in the United States of America have land due both to broken U.S. government treaties and to their own forebears' access to metal armaments that were more efficient at the time than those available to the indigenous peoples. In the democratic Peru of today, 90 percent of the wealth is still owned by 1 percent of the people, mostly those who inherited the legal entitlement to the nation's land and its resources from conquistadors. It is worth noting that Peru is only one of a large number of countries of the world in which the national wealth is possessed by very few. So fairness would seem to require some rethinking of the idea of private property to determine what is owed to those whose ancient ancestors sustained and nurtured their homelands' environments well, but nevertheless lost access to land through foreign invasion.

In the above cases, and in similar cases throughout the world, the Lockean suggestion that property is a natural result of a person's (or a person's ancestors') simple act of appropriating resources from contexts in which there was always "enough, and as good left in common for others" (Locke 1963, 176), is a suggestion that has never been totally or uniformly true. Moreover Locke's suggestions about the legitimacy of entitlements received from forebears' initial or ongoing use of land also falters if the forebears took the property by force, or used the involuntary bondage of others as the means for accomplishing its fruitful production.

Since it is possible that all peoples have had ancestors who have been victimized, the call for justice concerning land use is muted by the need to acknowledge that not all of history can be known, and that no absolute assessment of private entitlements may ever be possible. Still (1) respect for legitimate expectations, and (2) the need for fairness (especially when fulfillment of basic needs is in question), must be taken into account. Even the most benevolent leadership cannot be effective if deep and pervasive levels of unfairness remain unreflected upon and unaddressed.

Philosophical leadership strategies that encourage reflection about fairness have a salient role to play in persuading both the public and the private sectors to contribute to the promotion of the well-being of the most vulnerable members of human and nonhuman populations. Philosophical principles that could plausibly guide altruistic, voluntary contributions might include these:

- The principle that opportunities for the receiving of available aid should be preferentially directed to the most severe cases of need (especially cases of severe shortages of food, health care, etc.) so that the most disadvantaged may receive prioritized assistance with the meeting of basic needs—at least until they can be reasonably judged to be able to meet these needs by their own efforts alone
- The principle that those who have been injured or deprived of resources by policies established and enforced by those with wealth to give should be preferentially helped before help is given to those who have not been so injured
- The principle that governments that share the ideals of fairness to all, compassion, truthfulness, and so on, should be preferentially helped before help is given to political units that do not share these ideals

Of these principles only the first and second would imply rights on the part of recipients. The justification we intuit for the first principle is based on the inculcation or cultivation of trust; for the promotion of trust in others generates protective rights. The rights implied by the second principle are intuited in connection with our duty to compensate (that is, to pay reparation to) those whom we have harmed.

Donors who value virtue for its own sake should endorse the third principle. A modified version might justify giving to those with moral promise and to those whose own actions are motivated by virtuous intentions, namely, those who have what Kant calls "a good will" (Kant 1964, 61ff.).

The application of these principles would have definite practical consequences. The first principle, if applied, would justify the giving of a disproportionately large share of available aid to a needy country with which a donor country had worked closely and cooperatively, especially if the donor country had established and encouraged a relationship of trust. If the second principle were utilized, then, if a donor country had intervened in the affairs of the constituency in ways that upset the environmental support systems that had enabled the meeting of basic needs (e.g., through the offering of medicine in isolation from population control options, causing the population to outstrip its material base), then targeted aid would be warranted. Application of the third principle would require that if there were evidence that a country were attempting to organize in ways that would make it a morally better social unit (say, by adopting policies that would enable the people within it to be morally better persons), then that country could be judged to be an especially appropriate recipient of whatever help the donor country was able to give.

Protecting the Vulnerable: Aiding Women and Children

As principles to guide giving are reflected upon, it becomes obvious that a clear global priority needs to be placed on the aiding of impoverished women and children. Children are by definition innocent of their plight (they were not present when their social and material prospects were degraded), and are also the most malleable among us and hence carry the most potential for moral perfection. Women farmers in traditional cultures who work the land to provide food for children and the extended families around them also become clear candidates for life-sustaining donation.

In applying principles to protect the vulnerable, we tacitly accept the social ideal of an interconnected human community, one that suggests that a good life for humans necessarily involves mutual support of deserving others.

Comprehensive Caring

As we welcome the place of animals as sharers of Earth, their vulnerabilities and our reflective responses to them also come into focus. If, in the shared environment, animals befriend humans, display virtues, or offer an aesthetic dimension of innocence, mystery, and significance to other creatures' lives, their ability to flourish becomes clearly relevant to the quality of human life, as the Earth Charter suggests. The first and second principles would support their entitlement to targeted aid.

Toward Paradox Resolution

While paradoxes concerning private property and compelling obligations to share will inevitably arise, they may be rationally addressed through a deepening of human understanding and enlightened persuasion. Private property may be voluntarily given. Those who have rights may call attention to them; those in need may, with dignity, seek and accept the help.

Paradoxes may also be managed through the recognition of hierarchies of rights and an acknowledgment that there may be multiple, legitimate, uses of land. The rights of all to enjoy the Earth may be voluntarily respected by those with legal entitlements to the land; activists may purchase land in order to protect and preserve it.

However, where blatant disrespect of privately or publicly owned land is shown, governments should offer their support to those who defend the preservation of the integrity of that land. For the land, as a continuing source of beauty, inspiration, and diversity of life-forms, is profoundly important to the quality of life of current residents of the planet, as well as a priceless legacy to pass on to future generations. A presently living individual's rights are important, but these may be overridden by the collective rights of countless others not yet born. The requirement of fair use and rational sharing of resources must include the sharing of resources over time, taking into account the basic needs of all who will inhabit planet Earth.

Once both the hierarchies of rights and the fair use requirement are acknowledged, governments will have grounds for intervention in cases of abuse. For just as an individual's rights to raise her or his offspring can be overridden in cases where the well-being of the child is clearly at stake (on the grounds that the overarching right of the collective human family to prevent harm to the innocent, and to protect its citizens' lives, outweighs the right of the abusive parent), so too a government may override rights to the use of one's private land, when the use is clearly abuse. In clear cases of environmental abuse (as identified by responsible citizen groups of the sort mentioned earlier), societal standards for the rational protection of land may be the only available means of preventing the degradation of the most threatened portions of our globally interconnected ecosystem.

By (1) adopting servant-leadership strategies to aid and direct the persuasive process, and by (2) offering leadership that is grounded in appropriately sensitive philosophical reflection, we can encourage one another to discover and to put into place compassionate, reasonable methodologies for instantiating agreed-upon ideals.

Note

This essay includes material from two papers presented at a conference on "Connecting Environmental Ethics, Ecological Integrity, and Health in the New Millennium" held in San José, Costa Rica, June 24–29, 2000: (1) "Servant-Leadership: Managing Resources in the Global Environment," by Rubye Howard Braye, and (2) "Environmental Preservation and Preferential Rewards: Toward an Ethic of Accountability and Choice," by Ruth Miller Lucier.

References

The Earth Charter Initiative. 2002. "The Earth Charter." San José, Costa Rica: Earth Council. <http://www.earthcharter.org/earthcharter/charter.htm> (January 12, 2002).

Greenleaf, Robert K. 1991. *The Servant as Leader.* Indianapolis: The Robert K. Greenleaf Center.

Kant, Immanuel. 1964. *Groundwork of the Metaphysic of Morals,* edited and translated by H. J. Paton. New York: Harper and Row.

Kierkegaard, Søren. 1956. "Concluding Scientific Postscript: On His Mission," in *Existentialism from Dostoevsky to Sartre,* edited by Walter Kaufmann. Cleveland and New York: World Publishing Company.

Locke, John. 1963. "Two Treatises of Government," second treatise, in *Social and Political Philosophy*, edited by John Somerville and Ronald E. Santoni. Garden City, N.Y.: Doubleday.

Pan, H. 1999. "Air Pollution Blocks Beijing's Blue Sky." Environment News Service. <http://ens.lycos.com/ens/sep99/1999L-09-01-02html> (28 December 2000).

Measuring Progress and Decline

Chapter 9

Genuine Progress Indicator (GPI) Accounting: Relating Ecological Integrity to Human Health and Well-Being

Mark Anielski and Colin L. Soskolne

Introduction

Indicators are critical for monitoring the health of humans. They also are critical for monitoring the health of ecological systems, society, and the economy. Indicators provide vital signs to citizens and decisionmakers about trends in the condition of human, social, and natural capital. Indicators of health can be used as an early warning system of risks to human health and hence of the sustainability of current trends in health. With the development of robust quantitative databases and information systems providing indicators of human, ecological, economic, and societal health, it is now possible to conduct more integrative analyses of the overall condition of societies, taking several determinants of human health into account.

Many researchers have provided evidence that ecological integrity (EI) is rapidly declining. Some functional measures of EI have been developed (e.g., the Index of Mean Functional Integrity [Loucks et al. 1999] and the Index of Biological Integrity [Karr and Chu 1999]), but these have not yet been sufficiently widely implemented to be of use epidemiologically. McMichael's (1993) overview, given its health-based approach, is most useful for the epidemiologist. More recently, the Organization for Economic Cooperation and Development (OECD) (1998), the World Bank (1993), World Resources Institute (1999, 1997), and the World Health Organization (WHO) (1992) have recognized the possible human health consequences of declining EI. Some authors (Smith 1994; Mason 1992) have suggested that humanity has as little as two generations remaining before EI has diminished to the point where adaptive strategies will not be optional, but necessary for survival.

Despite these supposed threats to human health, the classic indicators of human health have been showing improvements for several decades. In addition, the traditional economic indicators, like rising gross domestic product (GDP) and stock market indices, suggest growing prosperity in the United States of America and elsewhere (Anielski 2000). Concern about present and future possible negative human health impacts from the degradation of environmental life-support systems justifies further work among epidemiologists because epidemiology is a public health science that informs policy.

If the role of epidemiology is to prevent epidemics, then a great challenge lies before this field to avert the potentially catastrophic consequences from environmental collapse. The human, social and environmental indicators and trends shown in this paper provide a starting point for assessing what long-term impacts to human health may result from declining social and ecological well-being. Interdisciplinarity between epidemiology and ecological economics may provide the motivating information to justify the driving of policies toward sustainability.

The explosion of quality of life, economic, social, and environmental indicators as a result of expanded data management capacity has enhanced our capacity to explore complex interrelationships among the variables that impact human health and EI. However, no comprehensive or unified analytical framework that integrates the complex interplay of human, ecological, and economic health has emerged. Indeed, the social cohesion factors of well-being have yet to emerge.

The 1998–99 edition of the biennial World Resources report by the World Resources Institute (WRI) (1999) focused on linking environmental change and human health data. However, no specific framework was specified as a theoretical basis for the choice of indicators. The WRI report provided new indicators that attempt to summarize some of the specific characteristics of the environment (such as air quality and access to clean water).

Other examples of environmental indicators that attempt to measure ecological and environmental conditions and sustainable development include: (1) the World Wildlife Fund's (2001) Living Planet Index (LPI), and (2) Ecological Footprint (EF) analysis by Wackernagel and Rees (1996). EF is a measure of how much ecological capital is required to sustain current consumption levels in relation to the average global carrying capacity of the Earth.

Alternative measures of economic well-being that might replace the GDP have also emerged. These include the Genuine Progress Indicator (GPI) (Cobb et al. 1995) and its predecessor, the Index for Sustainable Economic Welfare (Daly and Cobb 1994). These represent efforts to correct for the shortcomings of GDP as an economic measure of well-being; it tends to either ignore or confound environmental and social costs associated with economic output and consumption. For example, the more the environment is polluted and natural resource stocks are depleted, the more the GDP grows.

Measuring Ecological Integrity and Human Health

In a study by Sieswerda et al. (2001), the EI concept was used to unify environmental health indicators and transcend the usual piecemeal approach to environmental threats, thereby focusing on broader issues to clarify the paradoxical inverse relationship between declining EI and improving human health. Available aggregate data were used to explore possible relations between life expectancy and the large-scale deterioration of EI. In addition to indicators of EI as putative determinants, GDP per capita was used as a surrogate for socioeconomic confounding.

Sieswerda et al. considered that "development" would be an important confounder of any EI-health relation. Because richer countries are healthier than poorer countries as measured by traditional health indicators—life expectancy, percent low birth weight babies, and infant mortality—they had wanted to isolate the positive influence of development on health from the negative influences of concurrent environmental degradation. Toward this end, they used GDP per capita (standardized by purchasing power parity [PPP] to 1985 international dollars) as a surrogate variable to control for potential socioeconomic confounding. PPP is the number of units of a country's currency required to buy the same amount as $1 would buy in the "average country" (World Resources Institute et al. 1999). Thus, this variable takes cost of living into account. Once socioeconomic status was controlled, as represented by GDP per capita, the relation between EI and life expectancy all but disappeared in their analysis.

The result of Sieswerda et al.'s attempt to relate traditional health indicators to declining EI produced the finding that health is improving while EI is declining. This apparent paradox is explained by Sieswerda et al. as being attributable to international trade that permits wealthy nations to import the resources needed to maintain both their high levels of consumption and their corresponding high levels of health, while disposing of their wastes elsewhere. Wealthy nations thus impose ecological deficits on the developing regions of the world. Meanwhile, the drawdown of the world's ecological capital continues, forcing accelerating declines in and collapses of the world's ecological life-support systems. Technology and trade thus insulate rich populations from the ill effects of local ecological disintegrity, thus blinding them to their de facto continued dependence on EI somewhere else.

The relation between declining EI and human health is undoubtedly highly complex, and mediated by many interrelated social, political, and economic factors that Sieswerda et al. were unable to consider. Second, it is likely that their measures of EI were insufficiently representative of the true ecological situation. The concept of EI is relatively new, and measures of EI are still being formulated and are very much in the "trial and error" phase.

For GDP per capita to be a confounder, it has to be causally related to the outcome in question and be unaffected by the other covariates in the model. If the other covariates in the model are causally related to GDP per capita, however, then it may be inappropriate to control for GDP per capita, because if GDP per capita is in the causal pathway, controlling it will adjust away part of the effect under study and may create confounding (Sieswerda et al. 2001). It is most likely, however, that there are multiple causal pathways from covariates to outcomes. Some pathways probably go through GDP per capita and others not.

Fundamental Flaws in Measuring Economic Progress

Paradoxically, the word "economy" comes from the Greek *"oikonomia,"* meaning the careful management or stewardship of the household. "Ecology" is comprised of the words *"oikos"* (household) and *"logia"* (knowledge or logic). Anielski (2000) argues that modern economics has lost its soul by focusing almost exclusively on monetary (chrematistic) measures of well-being to the exclusion of measuring the physical condition and welfare of individuals, households, communities, and the environment.

For example, the United Nation's System of National Accounts (UNSNA) and the GDP, derived from the national accounts, simply account for the monetary value of the goods and services produced in an economy while ignoring the physical realities of the "living capital" (human, social, natural) which contributed to this production (Anielski 2000).

Indeed, Simon Küznets (1965), the original architect of the United States' GDP and System of National Accounts and 1971 winner of the Nobel Prize in economics, warned the U.S. Congress that: "The welfare of a nation can scarcely be inferred from a measurement of national income as defined (by the GDP). Goals for more growth should specify of what and for what." Robert Kennedy once remarked that the "Gross National Product [GNP or GDP] measures everything, in short, except that which makes life worthwhile" (Kennedy 1993).

The GDP ignores, for example, the value of many important activities, such as unpaid work (housework, parenting, eldercare, volunteerism) and the value of ecosystem services in providing society with clean air, water, and waste assimilation. Neither does the GDP distinguish between expenditures in the economy that contribute to genuine improvements in human, social, and environmental "health" or well-being, and those that were made to mitigate or repair damage to or erosion of human health (e.g., disease), social cohesion (e.g., crime), or EI. Indeed, the greater the level of production and the more money changing hands, the greater the GDP grows.

The GDP also does not distinguish between health care expenditures that contribute to improved human health and those made to mitigate against disease, injury, or other human health outcomes that are impacted by various determinants of health (socioeconomic, environmental, genetic, and others). When decisionmakers use the GDP and other economic variables to guide decision making, they are diagnosing the health of the patient "economy" through a very narrow lens.

Genuine Progress Indicator Well-Being Accounting

In order to measure the total health and well-being of the economy, society, and the environment, a more comprehensive system of accounting for the physical conditions of total well-being or total wealth is needed. The Genuine Progress Indicator (GPI) System of Sustainable Well-Being Accounts has been developed by Anielski et al. (2001) to address this challenge, providing a more holistic diagnostic tool for measuring the overall health and well-being of nations. The new GPI accounting system has been applied for the first time to the province of Alberta, Canada (Anielski et al. 2001).

GPI accounting takes an interdisciplinary, integrated approach to assessing the condition of overall well-being and thus is ideally suited to measuring the overall conditions of and risks to human health, social cohesion, and EI. However, GPI accounts do not provide a definitive answer to discerning where epidemiological and EI thresholds may exist. Rather, they provide evidence of long-term trends in the condition of all "living capital."

GPI accounts allow decisionmakers to diagnose the total health and well-being at the individual, household, societal (community), and the environmental scale. GPI accounts provide meaningful indicators of the condition and sustainability of "living capital" (human, social, and natural-environmental) and produced capital (manufactured and financial).

One of the strengths of the GPI accounting system is that it takes a traditional accounting approach. Using both physical and qualitative inventories or assessments of all capital, and monetary values of production, the data can be presented in the form of a GPI balance sheet and net sustainable income statement. The GPI balance sheet, for example, shows the current and historical physical conditions of all assets and liabilities related to human, social, natural, and produced capital. The GPI balance sheet provides an early warning system of emerging risks to sustainable well-being. The GPI income statement accounts for the full costs and benefits associated with economic production (GDP) in an economy. These include accounting for the total costs and benefits associated with consuming human, social, and natural-environmental capital in the production of goods and services. The structure of the GPI income statement is drawn from the original U.S. GPI model by Cobb, Halstead, and Rowe (1995) at Redefining Progress and updated by Anielski and Rowe (1999) for measuring sustainable economic welfare.

From the data contained in the GPI accounts, indicators of well-being (genuine progress indicators) can show longitudinal trends. For example, the Alberta GPI accounts developed by Anielski et al. (2001) include some 51 indicators of well-being (table 9.1). The breadth of the database and the GPI's open architecture lends itself to analyzing the interrelationships of variables that determine human health and ecological well-being outcomes. For example, changes in human health conditions can be compared with trends in the condition of ecosystems, natural resource stocks, or socioeconomic conditions. The accounts can also be used to show liabilities or risks to well-being that may be emerging in areas of social cohesion (e.g., poverty, income inequality), ecosystem fragmentation, toxic waste production, and other risk factors.

Table 9.1. The Alberta Genuine Progress Indicators of Sustainable Well-Being

GPI Economic Well-Being Indicators	GPI Social-Human Well-Being Indicators	GPI Environmental Well-Being Indicators
• Economic growth	• Poverty	• Oil and gas reserve life
• Economic diversity	• Income distribution	• Oil sands reserve life
• Trade	• Unemployment	• Energy use intensity
• Disposable income	• Underemployment	• Agriculture sustainability
• Weekly wage rate	• Paid work time	• Timber sustainability
• Personal expenditures	• Household work	• Forest fragmentation (ecological integrity)
• Transportation expenditures	• Parenting and eldercare	• Fish and wildlife
• Taxes	• Free time	• Parks and wilderness
• Savings rate	• Volunteerism	• Wetland
• Household debt	• Commuting time	• Peat land
• Public infrastructure	• Life expectancy	• Water quality
• Household infrastructure	• Premature mortality	• Air quality related emissions
	• Infant mortality	• Greenhouse gas emissions
	• Obesity	• Carbon budget deficit
	• Suicide	• Hazardous waste
	• Drug use	• Landfill waste
	• Auto crashes	• Ecological footprint
	• Divorce	
	• Crime	
	• Problem gambling	
	• Voter participation	
	• Educational attainment	

GPI accounts yield a longitudinal time series of: (1) the physical-qualitative inventory of stocks and flows of living and produced capital, and (2) monetary accounts or full cost-benefit accounts related to the consumption of living and produced capital. From this inventory, any number or combination of indicators and composite indicators of genuine well-being, sustainability, or quality of life can be derived. These could include indicators of EI.

There are limitations to the GPI accounts, including lack of data and incompatible data time-series. Nor do the indicators themselves reveal causality between a driver or multiple drivers and health or ecological outcomes. The indicators provide only a rough portrait of overall well-being. GPI accounts do, however, allow decisionmakers to assess the trade-offs, relationships, and common trends between variables. For example, the GDP can be compared with trends in human health (e.g., disease, premature mortality, suicide), environmental degradation, natural resource depletion, and social costs (e.g., crime).

Living Capital Declines While the Economy Booms

The Alberta GPI accounts by Anielski et al. (2001) show that economic growth (GDP) from 1961 to 1999 has been mirrored by a dramatic loss of EI (fragmentation) of Alberta's forests. The Alberta GPI accounts also reveal declines in the stock and quality of other natural capital, including forests, agricultural soils, and groundwater and wildlife habitat.

Prior to this study, Anielski (2000) illustrated the potential utility of GPI accounting for assessing overall changes in the conditions of human, societal, and environmental well-being vis-à-vis economic prosperity. Anielski (2000) compared the U.S. GPI cost-benefit analysis (Anielski and Rowe 1999) results with traditional measures of economic prosperity, like the GDP and stock market indicators. In addition, Anielski compared measures like the U.S. GPI against other measures of human development, ecosystem integrity, and sustainability, including the UNDP Human Development Index (2000), the World Wildlife Fund's (2001) Living Planet Index, the Ecological Footprint analysis (Wackernagel and Rees 1996), and Miringoff and Miringoff's (1999) Index for Social Health.

The U.S. GPI (Cobb et al. 1995) and its predecessor, the Index for Sustainable Economic Welfare (ISEW) by Daly and Cobb (1994), were updated in 1999 by Anielski and Rowe (1999). The U.S. GPI is an account of sustainable economic welfare, measured in monetary terms. It is constructed by taking GDP (personal consumption expenditures) and adjusting for unaccounted benefits (e.g., unpaid work) and netting out estimated costs of environmental and social degradation associated with economic production. For example, the monetary value of unpaid work is added while the regrettable expenditure (costs) to correct against the decline in the condition of environmental, human, and social capital are deducted.

The U.S. GPI results for 1999 show that U.S. GDP per capita rose steadily from 1950 to 1999, yet the GPI, a wider account of economic well-being, rose with GDP up until the mid-1970s, then has declined since its peak (figure 9.1). The key determinants of this decline in sustainable economic well-being (GPI) are rising income inequality, declining stocks of nonrenewable energy resources (oil and gas), loss of wetlands and old-growth forest ecosystems, and the growing environmental costs associated with greenhouse gas emissions and the accumulated costs of ozone-depleting substances (e.g., CFCs). In addition, there have been rising levels of the cost of crime, family breakdown, and a net loss of quality leisure time.

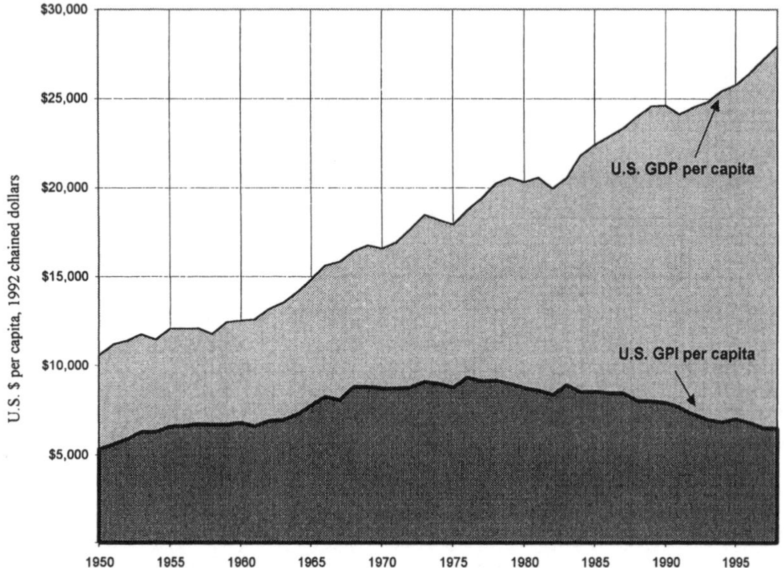

Source: Data derived from spreadsheets from the U.S. Genuine Progress Indicator (GPI) for 1999. Redefining Progress, Oakland, Calif.

Figure 9.1. U.S. GDP Growth (Per Capita) Versus GPI (Per Capita), 1950 to 1999

Evidence of Declining Living Capital

Using the detailed cost and benefit analysis contained in the 1999 U.S. GPI accounting system of data spreadsheets (Anielski and Rowe 1999) and analysis by Anielski (2000), a comprehensive "report card" of the changes (trends) in key indicators of well-being in the United States was developed (see table 9.2, appended to this chapter). This total "well-being diagnostic report card" shows where the United States is better or worse off in 1999, relative to 1950, or after almost 50 years of economic progress. Of the 28 indicators examined, 7 showed improvements, 18 showed declines, and 3 showed no discernable change. While many of the proxies for the condition of human, social, and environmental capital are based on monetary estimates of costs or benefits, they nevertheless provide a common denominator for comparison with monetary metrics of economic prosperity. Ideally, we would like to compare real physical or qualitative conditions in these "living capital" assets and identify emerging "liabilities" to sustainable well-being.

The results are sobering. Virtually every indicator of human, social, and environmental well-being has declined in the United States since 1950. Yet, virtually every measure of financial and economic prosperity (GDP and stock markets) has shown dramatic increases. For example, the market value of all stocks traded on U.S. stock exchanges has increased 6,060 percent (in current dollars per capita) from 1950 to 1999. The U.S. GDP per capita increased 1,529 percent (in current dollars). And, levels of financial debt (personal, business, and government debt) have risen 3,262 percent (current dollars per capita) since 1950, to in excess of U.S. $26 trillion, eclipsing all other market values, including the GDP and stock markets.

Some of the more important declines in living capital include the growing disparity between the incomes of the rich and poor in the United States that may lead to the erosion of social cohesion. Such signs of poverty are likely to have long-term human health impacts. The social fabric of households and communities also appears to be fraying, as evidenced by increases in divorce and family breakdown as well as by high levels of crime and the world's second highest level of incarceration rates after Russia.

The United States' GPI results also suggest rising ecological liabilities or deficits, with the loss of wetlands and old growth forest ecosystems, as well as the increasing ecological liability associated with the extraction and burning of fossil fuels. Agricultural sustainability may also be a question with soil erosion impacts. Ozone depletion caused by accumulated chlorofluorocarbons (CFCs) in the atmosphere also poses a long-term human health risk. The only exceptions to declining ecological health have been improvements in air quality that began following the introduction of stringent environmental standards in the 1970s.

While the results suggest declining stocks and flows of living capital, they do not necessarily provide definitive evidence that these losses in EI are having any measurable impact on long-term human health. In fact, the continual increase in U.S. life expectancy suggests that the metameasure of human health is improving. Neither does the evidence provide any sense of where potential unsustainable thresholds might exist for ecological or human health, given the continuation of the trends we observe. The problem is that the indicators of both human health and ecosystem health conditions may simply not be sensitive enough to emerging risks to sustainable well-being and thus need to be refined and expanded. This is where epidemiological studies and detailed EI studies could assist in shedding light on why declining living capital is relevant to long-term well-being. For example, more detailed analysis of the incidence of disease by age-sex cohorts, associated with various ecosystem regions across the United States, could provide useful information about these complex relationships.

Another perspective on living capital conditions is to compare other international indicators of human development, social health, and ecological health relative to the GPI, the GDP, and other measures of economic well-being (see table 9.2 [chapter appendix], and figure 9.2). Figure 9.2 compares the key monetary expression of economic well-being (the GDP per capita) with several indices of social, human, and ecological well-being indicators. By converting raw data to an index we can compare trends in the GDP per capita against the UN Human Development Index (for the United States), the GPI per capita (converted to an index), the Index for Social Health (Miringoff and Miringoff 1999), the Living Planet Index (World Wildlife Fund 2001) and a measure of the U.S. EF deficit.

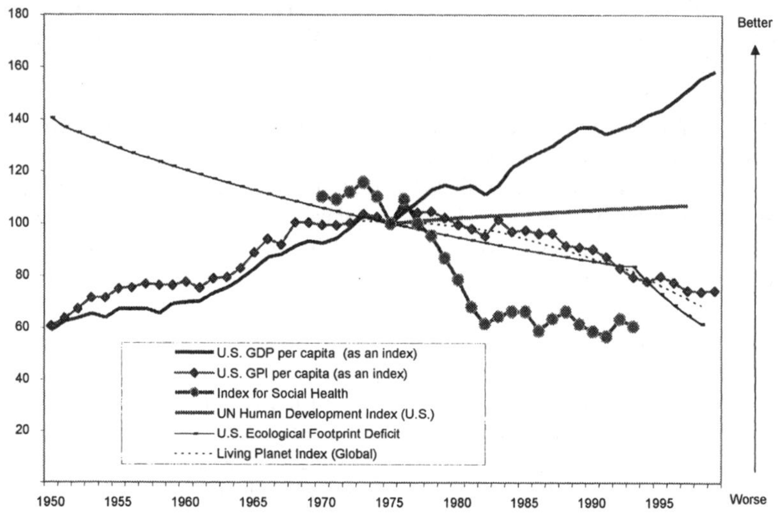

Sources: 1. U.S. GDP: U.S. Bureau of Economic Analysis. 2. U.S. GPI: Redefining Progress (www.rprogress.org). 3. Index for Social Health: Miringoff (found in Brink and Zeesman [1997]). 4. UN HDI: *Human Development Report 1999*. 5. U.S. Ecological Footprint: derived from sources: Wackernagel and Rees (1996) and www.rprogress.org. 6. Living Planet Index: World Wildlife Fund (2001).

Figure 9.2. Living Capital Indicators versus Economic Growth (GDP): The U.S. GPI, GDP, Index for Social Health, WWF Living Planet Index, and UN Human Development Index (U.S.) 1950 to 1999, 1975 as Benchmark Year.

The results show that while the United States' GDP has continued to increase over the past 50 years, virtually every measure of human, societal, and environmental well-being has declined. The only exception is the UNDP Human Development Index (HDI) that has risen slightly. However, this is not surprising given that the HDI is composed of only five key indicators which includes GDP per capita and life expectancy, both of which have increased. Again, while the GDP, stock markets, and debt have risen substantially in 50 years, three composite indices of living capital all show declines.

Anielski (2000) shows that since 1970, U.S. financial wealth indicators grew dramatically. For example, a composite index of U.S. stock market values and total credit market debt reached heights of 1,688 basis points by 1999 from the 1970 benchmark year of 100 basis points; an increase of some 16.9 times the 1970 value. At the same time, the Index of Social Health (ISH) had fallen by almost half (55 percent) by 1993, compared to 1970. The global Living Planet

Index, a broad measure of global ecological health, fell 68 percent by 1995 since 1970. So, as financial assets have shown torrid growth, real or living capital has been eroding.

The World Wildlife Fund's (2001) LPI—a composite index of the health of the world's forests, fresh waters, and oceans—shows that between 1970 and 1999, the world's ecosystems have declined by 33 percent. This ranged from declines of 12 percent for forests, 50 percent for fresh waters, and 35 percent for oceans (World Wildlife Fund 2001). The study also found that human pressure on nature has increased about 50 percent over the study period and concluded that "the natural wealth of the world's forests, freshwater ecosystems, oceans and coasts has declined rapidly, particularly in freshwater and marine ecosystems." The authors concluded that sometime in the 1970s, humanity passed the point at which it lived within the global regenerative capacity of the Earth. These findings are supported by the independent work of Loucks et al. (1999) and Karr and Chu (1999), who found that between 1982 and 1997, in the ecosystems that they have monitored, there has been an approximately 50 percent decline in their ecological and biological integrity, respectively.

The conclusion that the Earth's carrying capacity has been breached is based on the EF analysis of humanity by each nation. The EF analysis is used as the basis for calculating the overshoot of global ecosystem carrying capacity. The EF is a measure of the land area, resources, and ecosystem services (e.g., to assimilate waste) required to meet current levels of human consumption of food, materials, and energy. While some historical EF data points are available for the United States, the LPI for the United States is not. We have assumed that the global LPI can serve as a proxy for EI for the United States, given the significant EF that Americans impose on both North American and global ecosystems from their lifestyles. Future analysis should consider an LPI or similar index for the United States that could be compared with other U.S. indicators of economic, social, and human development and environmental well-being.

The UN Human Development Index (HDI) for the United States (using only the five data points: 1975, 1980, 1985, 1990, and 1997 and interpolating between years) suggests rising quality of life in the United States since 1975. However, this may be misleading because the HDI includes only GDP per capita (as a proxy for income and economic prosperity), life expectancy, literacy, and educational attainment. Since both GDP and life expectancy have risen for the United States and most nations along with rising levels of educational attainment, it is not surprising that this narrow measure of human well-being is improving.

The Miringoff and Miringoff (1999) Index of Social Health (ISH), which includes a composite index of 17 social and human health indicators, has shown a steady decline since the benchmark year of 1971, including indicators such as suicide rates, teen pregnancy, income inequality, life expectancy, and other intuitive social and human health indicators. Many of these are also used in the GPI accounting framework.

Discussion

The GPI accounting provides a framework for well-being measurement that until now has not existed. Important progress is being made in measuring economic welfare, human development, and ecological integrity, including the UN Human Development Index, the Living Planet Index, the total wealth accounting (monetary) by the World Bank, Index for Sustainable Economic Welfare/Genuine Progress Indicator, and the Index for Social Health. However, no holistic, integrated, and unified framework for assessing the well-being of human, social, produced (built), and natural capital (or total wealth) has emerged.

The GPI accounting framework provides an important starting point towards a more holistic and unified analytic framework for assessing the physical, qualitative, and monetary conditions or expressions of living capital. With an abundance of publicly available statistical data, the construction of longitudinal GPI accounts is achievable for most jurisdictions.

The GPI system of well-being accounts provides a powerful tool for policy analysis, allowing decisionmakers to examine the interrelationships between economic, social, human health, and environmental variables as contributors to well-being. The relationships among these variables and their impact on human health and EI can be examined through a holistic, integrated analytical framework. GPI accounts also provide important longitudinal information necessary to assess trends in the condition of the real wealth (living capital) of a nation, region, or community, and to use this information for examining "what if" scenarios for the future. Further work is needed to address the question of equal weighting of individual indicators in the construction of the GPI well-being composite indices, indicator selection bias, and researching other methods of selecting and combining meaningful measures of sustainable well-being.

The examples of GPI accounting presented in this paper provide a glimpse of what is possible for future well-being accounting. Even more detailed and comprehensive GPI accounts of well-being are desirable; accounts capable of demonstrating the full impact on human health and well-being of ecological degradation. Only then will epidemiology be able to fulfill its role as the science for rational policy formulation in this critical area.

References

Anielski, Mark. 2000. "Fertile Obfuscation: Making Money Whilst Eroding Living Capital." Paper presented to the 34th Annual Conference of the Canadian Economics Association, University of British Columbia, Vancouver, B.C. <www.pembina.org> (22 May 2001).

Anielski, Mark, Mary Griffiths, David Pollock, Amy Taylor, Jeff Wilson, and Sara Wilson. 2001. *Alberta Sustainability Trends 2000: The Genuine Progress Indicators Report 1961 to 1999.* The Pembina Institute for Appropriate Development. <www.pembina.org> (22 May 2001).

Anielski, Mark, and Jonathan Rowe. 1999. *The Genuine Progress Indicator—1998 Update.* San Francisco: Redefining Progress. <www.rprogress.org> (22 May 2001).

Brink, Satya, and Allen Zeesman. 1997. "Measuring Social Well-Being: An Index of Social Health for Canada." R-97-9E. Applied Research Branch, Strategic Policy, Human Resources Development Canada.

Cobb, Clifford, Ted Halstead, and Jonathan Rowe. 1995. *The Genuine Progress Indicator: Summary of Data and Methodology*. San Francisco: Redefining Progress.

Daly, Herman, and John B. Cobb. 1994. *For the Common Good: Redirecting the Economy toward Community, the Environment, and a Sustainable Future*, 2nd edition. Boston: Beacon Press.

Karr, J. R., and E. W, Chu. 1999. *Restoring Life in Running Waters: Better Biological Monitoring*. Washington, D.C.: Island Press.

Kennedy, Robert. 1993. "Recapturing America's Moral Vision," in *RFK: Collected Speeches.* New York: Viking Press. Speech delivered March 18, 1968.

Küznets, Simon. 1965. "Economic Growth and Structure," in *Towards a Theory of Economic Growth.* New York: W.W. Norton.

Loucks, O., O. H. Ereksen, J. W. Bol, R. F. Gorman, P. C. Johnson, and T. C. Krehbiel. 1999. *Sustainability Perspectives for Resources and Business.* Boca Raton, Fla.: Lewis Publishers.

Mason, J. 1992. "The Greenhouse Effect and Global Warming." Pp. 55–92 in *Monitoring the Environment,* edited by B. Cartledge. Oxford: Oxford University Press.

McMichael, A. J. 1993. *Planetary Overload: Global Environmental Change and the Health of the Human Species*. Cambridge: Cambridge University Press.

Miringoff, Marc, and Marque-Luisa Miringoff. 1999. *The Social Health of the Nation.* New York: Oxford University Press.

Organization for Economic Cooperation and Development (OECD). 1998. *Towards Sustainable Development: Environmental Indicators*. Paris: OECD Publications.

Sieswerda, L. E., C.L. Soskolne, S. C. Newman, D. Schopflocher, K. E. Smoyer. 2001. "Toward Measuring the Impact of Ecological Disintegrity on Human Health." *Epidemiology* 12: 28–32.

Smith, D. 1994. "How will it all end?" In *Health and the Environment,* edited by B. Cartledge. Oxford: Oxford University Press.

The United Nations Development Program. 2000. *Human Development Index 1999.* New York.

Wackernagel, M., and W. E. Rees. 1996. *Our Ecological Footprint: Reducing Human Impact on the Earth.* Gabriola Island, B.C.: New Society Publishers.

World Bank. 1993. *World Development Report 1993: Investing in Health.* New York: Oxford University Press.

World Health Organization (WHO). 1992. *Our Planet, Our Health: Report of the WHO Commission on Health and the Environment*. Geneva: WHO.

World Resources Institute, United Nations Environment Programme, United Nations Development Programme, World Bank (joint publication). 1999. *World Resources 1998–99.* New York: Oxford University Press.

World Resources Institute, United Nations Environment Programme, United Nations Development Programme, World Bank (joint publication). 1997. *World Resources 1996–97.* New York: Oxford University Press.

World Wildlife Fund. 2001. *The Living Planet Report 2000.* <www.wwf.org> (22 May 2001).

Appendix

Table 9.2. Is the United States (U.S.) Better Off or Worse Off in 1999 Compared to 1950?

	Better Off or Worse Off than in 1950?	% Change in Cost/Value Per Capita since 1950 (or Benchmark Year)	Absolute Quantitative Change
What we want more of...			
Longer life (life expectancy)	▲Better	Up 8.5% since 1970	Average life expectancy has increased 6.0 years between 1970 and 1997
More sustainable and genuine progress (GPI)	▼ Worse	Down 29% since 1978 peak	
Higher Quality of Life (UN Human Development Index and Index for Social Health, Miringoff)	▲▼ Better and Worse	U.S. HDI improved 7.2% between 1975 and 1999; the ISH declined 45% between 1970 and 1993	
More economic growth (GDP)	▲Better	Up 164% (1992 $) Up 1,529% (current $)	
More U.S. stock market growth (total stock market capitalization value)	▲Better	Up 6,060% (current $)	
More personal consumption (expenditures)	▲Better	Up 181%	
Higher quality and more household durables	▼Worse	Down 245%	
More leisure and family time	▼Worse	Down 1,428%	19% less leisure time per worker; 58% increase in hours of TV viewing per household
More productive farmland	▼Worse	Down 248%	
More volunteerism	▲Better	Up 128%	169% increase in average hours volunteered per cap.
More renewable energy use	▲Better		3% of total energy consumption from less than 2/10th of 1% in 1950
What we want less of...			
Less debt (total market credit)	▼Worse	Up 3,262% (current dollars per capita)	20,410% increase in margin debt
Less foreign borrowing	▼Worse	Up 400% (since 1983 peak of net foreign lending).	
Less inequality (income and wealth)	▼Worse	Up 18% (since 1968 low)	In 1995 the richest 0.5% of families claimed 28% of net worth, almost as much as the bottom 90% of the population (32%)

Continued on next page

Table 9.2—Continued

	Better Off or Worse Off than in 1950	% Change in Cost/ Value Per Capita since 1950 (or Benchmark Year)	Absolute Quantitative Change
What we want less of (continued) . . .			
Less poverty			19% of U.S. citizens still live in poverty
Less family breakdown	▼Worse	Up 121%	195% increase in number of divorces; 238% increase in number of kids impacted by divorce
Less hours of work	▼Worse		7% more hours worked per annum per worker
Less commuting time	▼Worse	Up 89%	30% increase in times commuting to work
Less underemployment	▼Worse	Up 375%	125% increase in the number of constrained hours per worker
Less automobile accidents	▼Worse	Up 200%	
Smaller Ecological Footprint	▼Worse	Up 152%	The U.S. has the third-highest EF in the world; each American consumes over 5 times the global carrying capacity
Less depletion of nonrenewable resources	▼Worse	Up 389%	14% increase in nonrenewable energy produced per capita from U.S. sources
Less long-term environmental damage	▼Worse	Up 142%	73% increase in barrels of oil equivalent of nonrenewable energy consumed per capita
No net loss of wetlands	▼Worse	Up 358%	6% decrease in the area of total wetlands
No net loss of old growth forests	▼Worse	Up 6%	69% less old growth forest
Less ozone depletion	▼Worse	Up 5,109%	9,247% increase in global CFC production
Less air pollution	▲Better	Down 67%	42% improvement in ambient air quality; but emissions of CO are down 13%, NO_2 up 132%, VOCs down 9%, SO_2 down 15%, and particulate matter up 83%
Less water pollution	▼Worse	Up 33%	
Less noise pollution	▼Worse	Up 43%	

Source: The analysis is based on Anielski 2000.

Chapter 10

Understanding the Consequences of Human Actions: Indicators from GNP to IBI

James R. Karr

Humans depend on an astounding variety of indicators to assess their situation. We monitor and evaluate trends in biological (body temperature, cholesterol, death rates), economic (income, expenditures, stock market profit, inflation rate), and social (numerous crime statistics, adult literacy) terms. Many, although not enough, of us buy cars based on gas mileage. We use weather reports to guide decisions about weekend activities. Some still seek guidance on how to live their lives from the study of planetary alignments. In all dimensions of life, we use scores of indicators to guide individual and collective decision making.

Indicators provide useful information when science and experience show that they are reliably connected (through cause or correlation) to the course of events. But indicators are irrelevant when they are not connected with the way events unfold. Still other presumed indicators are downright misleading when they ignore or overlook important information.

One major class of indicators—ecological indicators—has been ignored for most of the last century. Economic analysis and economic indicators have been used to guide society as if living systems were of no consequence to human success. Contaminated air, overworked soils, extinction of species, declining fish populations, human conflicts based on resource shortages, and inner-city and rural poor relegated to lives that limit their achievement are the result.

Few in leadership roles have asked the fundamental question: what is left out with our current indicators? Arguably, this modern array of environmental and social challenges is in a very real sense a result of our dependence on indicators that leave something out (Chu and Karr 2001). I begin with a simple illustration of the interpretation of indicators tied to the effects of climate on human society. I then briefly explore recent efforts to develop indicators that may help to protect us from leaving things out.

Alternate Interpretations of Climate Indicators

Weather, the march of seasons, and climate influence modern society as they influenced medieval society. Both societies "understood," at least from *their* knowledge base, how human actions "determine" climate. Peasants and lords in the medieval Warm Period of the thirteenth century saw their bountiful harvests as an indicator (or sign) that God was smiling on them (Fagan 2000). That situation changed abruptly in the fourteenth century as Europe moved into the Little Ice Age, the period from 1300 to 1850 when Europe was subject to abrupt climatic shifts. "Cycles of excessive cold and unusual rainfall could last a decade, a few years, or just a single season. The pendulum of climate change rarely paused for more than a generation" during this period (48). Arctic winters followed blazing summers and catastrophic droughts alternated unpredictably with torrential rains. Deteriorating climatic conditions resulted in crop failures; cattle perished, famines brought epidemics, and "bread riots and general disorder brought fear and distrust" (91). Glaciers advanced and withdrew, devastating villages. The weather brought unprecedented and unpredictable levels of human misery. Alarmed villagers agreed to do penance, to do good Christian works to counteract the forces creating havoc on their lives. To them, failed crops and the weather that caused harvest collapse were indicators of the wrath of God.

Although that perspective has not entirely disappeared in modern times, understanding of the forces responsible for shifting climate patterns has improved. The common theme in both medieval and modern views is that humans are responsible for climate trends. But few modern humans expect doing penance to alter current trends. Most understand that controlling human-induced increases in "greenhouse gases" may slow and even reverse human-induced warming trends. Most also recognize that long-term climate trends responsible for the Medieval Warm Period, the Little Ice Age, and the relatively benign climate since the Little Ice Age cannot be controlled. At best, society can, with careful planning and reasonable levels of administrative plasticity, improve its ability to withstand inevitable climate changes (Fagan 1999).

Indicators in the Modern World

Advances in science and technology provide modern society with a mind-numbing array of measurements. At the same time, recognition that twentieth century indicators are not adequate to twenty-first century challenges has stimulated a cottage industry. From local citizen groups to national and international agencies efforts are being made to select indicators that will meet twenty-first century needs: cities (Sustainable Seattle 1998), states and provinces (Oregon Progress Board 2000; Minnesota Planning 1998; British Columbia 1998; Ohio Lake Erie Commission 1998), nations (Sykes and Lane 1996; NRC 1999; EPA 2000; NIC 2000; Stabb 2000), and international organizations (IJC 1996; UNDP 2000; Hayward 2001). Most such efforts recognize that the narrowly conceived economic indicators of the past are inadequate and that we can no longer ignore ecological indicators. As Klaus Toepfer (2001), executive director of UNEP, recently noted, "The challenge of this new century is to extend the economic progress of the last 50 years, while halting the ecological decline—a sick planet will, sooner or later, lead to a faltering economy."

Accomplishing that task in economically, socially, and environmentally responsible ways is the central goal of the Earth Charter (2002). The Earth Charter is a global declaration based on the sense that: (1) the present economic mode is no longer viable; (2) an increasing gap between "haves" and "have nots" is no longer acceptable; and (3) the mindless ravaging of resources and abuse of human rights is no longer tenable.

The Earth Charter builds on more than a century of societal evolution, an evolution that sees the global human community inextricably linked as never before. The first stages of that evolution came early in the twentieth century; it was especially rapid after World War II with widespread recognition of global economic and military interdependence. In the last decades of the twentieth century recognition of social and ecological interdependence spread (Thiele 1999). This evolution ties together three converging and interdependent quests that are the core of Earth Charter: (a) quest for environmental sustainability recognizes intergenerational interdependence; (b) quest for environmental justice recognizes social and geographic interdependence; and (c) quest for environmental integrity recognizes ecological interdependence.

But current indicators, especially widespread economic indicators, are ineffective at recognizing and communicating these interdependencies because they implicitly endorse unsustainable values and lifestyles. Those indicators, in effect, give people permission to escape responsibility for their actions. We need a new generation of indicators that will improve understanding of the consequences of human actions and stimulate revisions in our values and lifestyles. With changes in values and lifestyles, we can hope that improved decision making will follow and the important goals of the Earth Charter can be attained.

Human Economic Success Derives from Exploitation of Earth's Ecosystems

Human development has always depended on what could be taken from Earth's ecosystems; humans continue to extract commodities from (or use the absorptive capacities of) those systems. Their capacity to supply our needs seemed without limit. Our economic (accounting) systems have long tracked with great fanfare the growth in wealth that derives from that extraction, seducing us into believing there are no limits. Unfortunately, humans have given relatively little attention either to their impacts on ecosystems or to the boomerang effects back onto society itself.

Humans are like many other organisms in all these respects. Like other ecosystem engineers (crown-of-thorns starfish, beavers, and elephants), human ecosystem engineers alter their environments. But humans too are unique among ecosystem engineers. They have the capacity to understand the consequences of their actions and avoid those that may threaten the human future. To do that, however, humans need to account for the myriad effects of human actions on economic and ecological systems.

Hierarchy of Indicators

A carefully selected hierarchy of indicators will facilitate our efforts to account for our actions and protect our long-term interests. Those indicators must reflect the condition of ecological and economic systems as well as the consequences of their interactions with human society (figure 10.1). For simplicity, figure 10.1 emphasizes two distinct systems—economic and ecological—as if they were not integrally connected to each other. They are, of course; the economic system is a wholly owned subsidiary of the ecological system. (Note that, for the present, I am ignoring social systems.)

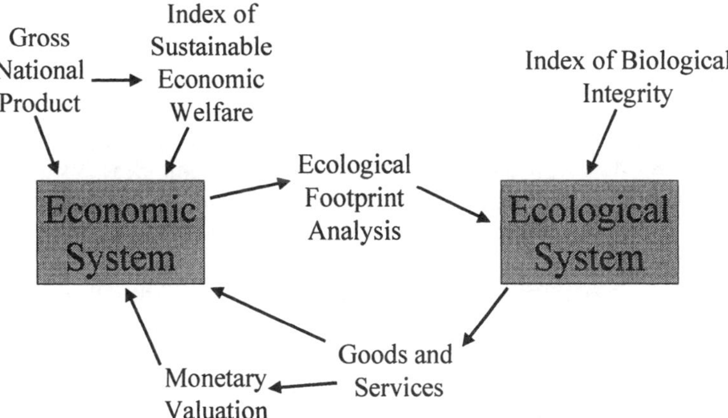

Figure 10.1. Two systems crucial to the success of human society and examples of indicators used to track those systems and their interactions.

The Economic System

Although early economists such as Adam Smith, David Ricardo, and John Stuart Mill regarded long-run growth as unlikely because limits would eventually retard and stop growth (Prugh et al. 1995), mainstream economics starting in the 1870s fostered a different worldview, a worldview that has driven neoclassical economics to abstraction. Economics emphasized theory over observation and ignored data that could not be easily reconciled to theory. (A similar problem plagues modern ecology as well [Sagoff 1997, 2000; Karr 2001].) According to Prugh et al. (1995) this led to several assumptions: (1) The environment is a subset of the human economy. (2) Because materials and services provided by the environment are not indispensable, human-made capital can be substituted for natural resources. (3) The doctrine of substitutability makes it possible to reject natural limits, and thus accept continued economic and population growth as logical extensions of past trends. (4) Human welfare is best served by a view of people as "human molecules" who benefit the general good by pursuing their own interests through the market (the "invisible hand"). These views developed in an era when the Earth was relatively empty of human beings, their artifacts, and their wastes, but we now live in a different era. Assuming operation of the invisible hand ignores the "invisible foot" of the modern human economy (Rees 2000).

Economists use the value of all products and services created and traded for money in the economy, GNP or gross national product, as an indicator of well-being. But calculation, even discussion, of GNP inevitably centers on the extent to which GNP is meant to aggregate market activity or, alternatively, to judge improvements in welfare (Costanza et al. 1997a). Because of these and other ambiguities, a number of other measures have been proposed, some involving corrections to GNP, others more original (see chapter 3, Costanza et al. 1997a). My intent here is not to review those complexities but to note that debates continue in the economics community. Perhaps the most relevant indicator to the present discussion is the index of sustainable economic welfare (ISEW), originally developed by Daly and Cobb (1989). Although it still measures how much is being produced and consumed, ISEW, among other things, adjusts for the sustainability of consumption, its negative impacts on natural capital, and its distribution across income classes (Costanza et al. 1997a). ISEW improves on common measures of economic growth to reflect additional health costs of toxic waste dumps, water quality reduction, loss of soil fertility, and so forth. By correcting for pollution effects, depletion of renewable and nonrenewable resources, and other long-term environmental damage, we get a more accurate assessment of economic welfare produced by the economy. This pioneering effort demonstrates that an economy is not at its healthiest when its size is maximized (higher GNP). Rather, a healthy economy provides for the well-being of its citizens without widening social inequities or speeding environmental degradation. In the end, the true test of economics will be its ability to develop a measure of total human welfare to replace a dominant focus on economic throughput. (See also the discussion of the Genuine Progress Indicator [GPI] system, a successor to ISEW, in Anielski and Soskolne [2002], chapter 9 of this volume.)

The Ecological System

Human interactions with ecological systems are primarily efforts to maximize through our engineering prowess the harvest of some valued commodity. A variety of disciplines (agriculture, forestry, fisheries, wildlife biology, water resources) developed specifically to apply ecological and engineering principles to achieve that goal. Twentieth-century supplies of grains, fruits, livestock, wood fiber, and fish are a testament to the success of humans behaving as ecosystem engineers.

Paralleling the development of these commodity-focused disciplines has been the proliferation of government agencies with mandates to maximize "their" individual commodities. Unfortunately, there has been minimal interest in the effects of their actions on the commodity mandate of other agencies, or on broader questions of ecological health. Biological targets have been too narrow (more wood, ducks, or salmon; hardier and more productive corn and potatoes); ecological thinking has been rare (Karr 2001).

Thirty years ago a broader mandate was created with passage of the 1972 amendments to the Water Pollution Control Act by the U.S. Congress, over the veto of then President Richard M. Nixon. Now called the Clean Water Act, this bill (PL 92-500) called for the restoration and maintenance of "the chemical, physical, and biological integrity of the Nation's waters" (Section 101(a)). The word integrity was "intended to convey a concept that refers to a condition in which the natural structure and function of ecosystems is maintained" (GPO 1973, 76). The use of integrity in this context establishes a goal based on *natural* condition. It also provides a scientific foundation and framework to the definition and measurement of that condition. Finally, it establishes a normative concept, the suggestion about how things should (or should not) be. It specifically notes that "any change induced by man which overtaxes the ability of nature to restore conditions to 'natural' or 'original' is an unacceptable perturbation" (77). Since then, a powerful Endangered Species Act calling for protection of species and their habitats and rhetoric of "ecosystem management" illustrate the continuing turn toward a broader conceptual goal.

Despite these clear statements of lofty goals, national and international assessments of the condition of the nation's biological resources, "the basis of much of our current prosperity and an essential part of the wealth that we will pass on to future generations" (Pulliam 1995), are in their infancy (LaRoe et al. 1995; Mac et al. 1998; UNDP 2000). A global "millennium ecosystem assessment" is being initiated this year (Daily 2001). These recent activities are a major step forward. They are likely to improve our understanding of the status and trends of livings systems. They will also inevitably provide the knowledge necessary to identify and use sophisticated indicators of the condition of Earth's living resources. Those indicators will provide a view through a biological lens that was ignored through most of the twentieth century. With those indicators we may be more successful in efforts to halt the pervasive and complex problem of biotic impoverishment caused by the activities of human society (Woodwell 1990; Chu and Karr 2001).

Efforts to protect ecological systems have much in common with efforts over the past three centuries to eradicate human diseases. A healthy river, lake, or landscape sustains the supply of goods and services needed by both human and nonhuman dependents. Applying the concept of health to rivers and landscapes is a natural outgrowth of scientific principles, legal mandates, and changing societal values (Karr and Rossano 2001).

We can learn much from the experience of health professionals as we strive to protect our life support systems. Health professionals recognize and respond to changing health challenges, strive to avoid unintended consequences (iatrogenic or doctor-caused disease), employ both cure and prevention, and take a systematic approach. We can make major strides forward in the protection of ecological systems by using those lessons.

But to do that we must develop more systematic approaches to the measurement of system condition. Like competent medical practitioners, ecologists can deduce landscape condition through standardized "health evaluation" procedures. Sampling the biota of a place with standard protocols, followed by appropriate data analysis, is a robust way to both measure the condition of ecological systems and identify likely causes of degradation. The process combines biological monitoring (sampling the biota of a place) and biological assessment (using the samples to evaluate the condition of the sampled place). By applying biological monitoring and assessment in the context of relevant environmental factors (the kind and extent of human actions influencing the sample site), managers can improve their ability to protect (prevent "disease") and restore (cure "disease") ecological health. Biological monitoring and assessment are central to this activity because "ecosystem integrity is primarily a biological concern" (Reynoldson et al. 1995, 215).

Biological monitoring and assessment in North America has spread rapidly since the development, widespread testing, and application of multimetric biological indexes (Karr 1981, 1991; Davis and Simon 1995; Simon 1999; Karr and Chu 1999; Jungwirth et al. 2000). Multimetric biological indexes are modeled after econometric indexes such as the index of leading economic indicators or the consumer price index. A properly constructed multimetric index, an index of biological integrity or IBI, incorporates metrics that span ecological levels from individual through population to community, ecosystem, and landscape. Metrics also incorporate indicators of living systems with differential sensitivities to various human activities.

Interactions of Economic and Ecological Systems

As these examples clearly indicate, both economists and biologists have worked effectively in the past two decades to improve their ability to measure the condition of systems crucial to human welfare. Progress has also been made in the study of the interactions and interdependencies of these two systems.

Defining Goods and Services

For several decades, scientists and citizens have expressed concern about the loss of wetlands in North America and throughout the world. Partly to convince those who saw wetlands as wastelands, wetland advocates stressed the importance of wetland functions and their value to society. Specialists defined varying numbers of classes of functions and values, usually including hydrological, chemical, biological, and socioeconomic (Tiner 1984; Williams 1990; Brinson 1996).

The language and concepts have evolved in the last decade to extend beyond wetlands to virtually all environments. We now recognize and are busy cataloging the many ways that ecosystems provide basic necessities (the *goods*)—food, fiber, and water—and *services*—pollination, climate control, soil production (Daily 1997). In effect, ecosystems do "The Work of Nature" (Baskin 1997) that sustains life, including humans. The systematic documentation of the rich variety of goods and services as well as recognition of how dependent humans are on these systems provides very powerful arguments about the importance of indicators that reflect the status of ecosystems.

Monetary Valuation

Preparation of detailed listings of goods and services provided by ecosystems to human society opened the door for biologists and economists to calculate the monetary value of those goods and services. Costanza et al. (1997b), for example, estimated that the current economic value of 17 ecosystem services for 16 biomes average U.S.$33,000 billion per year (Costanza et al. 1997b), an amount about twice the global gross national product. Pimentel et al. (1997), focusing on vital services the biota provides (e.g., soil formation, crop breeding, pollination), estimated the total economic benefits of biodiversity for the United States ($319 billion) and the world ($2,928 billion)—5 percent and 11 percent of their respective gross domestic products.

Translating goods and services to aggregate economic value, even if the numbers themselves are at best an approximation, demonstrates that we can no longer pretend these values are zero. The studies are instructive because they stimulate discussion; they work less well for defining actions, identifying ecological limits, or describing competing uses of nature (Wackernagel et al. 1999).

Ecological Footprints

Humans are large animals with hefty demands for energy and materials (Rees 2000). By one estimate, the global human population in 1986 consumed the equivalent of nearly 40 percent of the net annual production of the Earth's terrestrial ecosystems (25 percent of marine and terrestrial systems combined; Vitousek et al. 1986). With 40 percent of the Earth's plant productivity going to support only one of the biosphere's tens of millions of living species, little wonder that the rest of those species and the ecosystems that support them are threatened.

Vitousek's study was an antecedent of ecological footprint analysis, a tool developed by Rees and colleagues (Rees and Wackernagel 1994; Wackernagel and Rees 1996). Footprint analysis uses the methods of trophic ecology to quantify the material and energy flows required to support a population of humans. A powerful accounting tool, footprint analysis estimates the area of land and water required to produce consumed resources and to absorb the wastes generated by a human community (Rees 1996, 2000). Demand and supply (based on the productive or absorptive capacity of natural systems) are combined to yield an estimate of the area "occupied"—in other words, taken over, or appropriated—by the population.

Footprint analyses have been completed at scales ranging from cities to nations. These analyses show that sustainable city or sustainable nation initiatives must understand the demands placed on a geographically wider ecological resource base. It also seems obvious that life for the inhabitants of modern cities will soon become intolerable if actions are not taken to protect the supply of goods and services that derive from living systems outside the boundaries of those cities. Cities too must do more to reflect on the ethical and moral responsibilities involved when they usurp the resources of people and cultures in regions occupied by their footprint.

By aggregating consumption in an ecologically meaningful way, and thus supplementing conventional measures of gross domestic product, ecological footprint analysis offers us something never before available to human society. It shows us the ecological deficits we are accumulating and clearly outlines the global sustainability gap we face (Rees 1996).

Conclusions

Catalogs of goods and services provided by natural systems and conversion of those benefits through monetary valuation to demonstrate the new economic benefits derived from natural systems provide critical information on flows from ecological to economic systems. Footprint analysis looks the other way, asking how much area is used by the collective activity of humans. These analyses look through a window but in opposite directions. Each offers a clearer view than ever before of humans' dominion over and dependence on Earth and the biosphere. But both approaches still use a human-centered accounting system. Both still consider living systems as providers of so many commodities. Neither directly measures the condition of the biosphere itself. Adding measures that track the condition of living systems, such as IBI, to the array of indicators used by society is central to the goal of making sure that we do not leave anything out.

Until we have comprehensive biological assessment to measure the health of ecological systems, our public policy decisions will lack a crucial foundation stone for informed decision making. It is simply not enough to know that we derive benefits from those systems. We must also understand their status and trends, how human actions influence those trends, and how we can avoid trends that threaten the well-being of human and nonhuman inhabitants of Earth.

Acknowledgments

This chapter was prepared with support from the Consortium for Risk Evaluation with Stakeholder Participation (CRESP) by Department of Energy Cooperative Agreements #DE-FCO1-95EW55084 and #DE-FG26-00NT40938.

References

Anielski, M., and C. L. Soskolne. 2002. "Genuine Progress Indicator (GPI) Accounting: Relating Ecological Integrity to Human Health and Well-Being." Chapter 9 in P. Miller, and L. Westra, eds. *Just Ecological Integrity: The Ethics of Maintaining Planetary Life*. Lanham, Md.: Rowman & Littlefield.

Baskin, Y. 1997. *The Work of Nature: How Diversity of Life Sustains Us*. Washington, D.C.: Island Press.

Brinson, M. M. 1996. "Assessing Wetland Functions Using HGM." *National Wetlands Newsletter* 18: 10–16.

British Columbia. 1998. *Environmental Trends in British Columbia 1998*. Ministry of Environment, Lands and Parks, Victoria, British Columbia.

Chu, E. W., and J. R. Karr. 2001. "Environmental Impact, Concept and Measurement of." Pp. 557–77 in S. A. Levin, ed. *Encyclopedia of Biodiversity*, Vol. 2. Orlando, Fla.: Academic Press.

Costanza, R., J. Cumberland, H. Daly, R. Goodland, and R. Norgaard. 1997a. *An Introduction to Ecological Economics*. Boca Raton, Fla.: St. Lucie Press.

Costanza, R., R. d'Arge, R. de Groot, S. Farber, M. Grasso, B. Hannon, K. Limburg, S. Naeem, R. V. O'Neill, J. Paruelo, R. G. Raskin, P. Sutton, and M. van den Belt. 1997b. "The Value of the World's Ecosystem Services and Natural Capital." *Nature* 387: 253–60.

Daily, G. C., ed. 1997. *Nature's Services: Societal Dependence on Natural Ecosystems*. Washington, D.C.: Island Press.

Daily, G. C. 2001. "Ecological Forecasts." *Nature* 411: 245. <http://www.millennium assessment.org> (5 July 2001).

Daly, H. E., and J. B. Cobb, Jr. 1989. *For the Common Good: Redirecting the Economy towards Community, Environment, and a Sustainable Future*. Boston: Beacon Press.

Davis, W. S., and T. P. Simon, eds. 1995. *Biological Assessment and Criteria: Tools for Water Resource Planning and Decision Making*. Boca Raton, Fla.: Lewis.

The Earth Charter Initiative. 2002. "The Earth Charter." San José, Costa Rica: Earth Council. <http://www.earthcharter.org/earthcharter/charter.htm> (January 12, 2002).

EPA (Environmental Protection Agency). 2000. *America's Children and the Environment: A First View of Available Measures*. EPA 240-R-00-006. Washington, D.C.: Office of Children's Health Protection, U.S. Environmental Protection Agency.

Fagan, B. 1999. *Floods, Famines, and Emperors: El Niño and the Fate of Civilizations*. New York: Basic Books.

Fagan, B. 2000. *The Little Ice Age: How Climate Made History 1300–1850.* New York: Basic Books.

GPO (Government Printing Office). 1973. *Legislative History of WPCA of 1972*. Washington, D.C.: GPO.

Hayward, S. 2001. *Index of Leading Environmental Indicators 2001*. San Francisco: Pacific Research Institute for Public Policy. <www.pacificresearch.org>.

IJC (International Joint Commission). 1996. *Indicators to Evaluate Progress under the Great Lakes Water Quality Agreement.* Windsor, Ontario: International Joint Commission.

Jungwirth, M., Muhar, S., and Schmutz, S., eds. 2000. "Assessing the Ecological Integrity of Running Waters." *Hydrobiologia* 422/423: 1–487.

Karr, J. R. 1981. "Assessment of Biotic Integrity Using Fish Communities." *Fisheries* 6(6): 21–27.

Karr, J. R. 1991. "Biological Integrity: A Long-Neglected Aspect of Water Resource Management." *Ecological Applications* 1: 66–84.

Karr, J. R. 2001. "What from Ecology Is Relevant to Design and Planning?" Chapter 6 in B. Johnson and K. Hill, eds. *Ecology and Design: Frameworks for Learning.* Washington, D.C.: Island Press. (in press).

Karr, J. R., and E. W. Chu. 1999. *Restoring Life in Running Waters: Better Biological Monitoring*. Washington, D.C.: Island Press.

Karr, J. R., and E. M. Rossano. 2001. "Applying the Lessons of Public Health to Protect River Health." *Ecology and Civil Engineering* 4: 3–18.

LaRoe, E. T., G. S. Farris, C. E. Puckett, P. D. Doran, and M. J. Mac, eds. 1995. *Our Living Resources: A Report to the Nation on the Distribution, Abundance, and Health of U.S. Plants, Animals, and Ecosystems*. Washington, D.C.: U.S. Department of the Interior, National Biological Service.

Mac, M. J., P. A. Opler, C. E. Puckett Haecker, and P. D. Doran. 1998. *Status and Trends of the Nation's Biological Resources*. 2 vols. Reston, Va.: U.S. Department of Interior, U.S. Geological Survey.

Minnesota Planning. 1998. *Minnesota Milestones 1998*. St. Paul, Minn.: Minnesota Planning.

NIC (National Intelligence Council). 2000. *Global Trends 2015: A Dialogue about the Future with Nongovernment Experts*. NIC 2000-02. Washington, D.C.: National Intelligence Council.

NRC (National Research Council). 1999. *Our Common Future: A Transition toward Sustainability.* Washington, D.C.: National Research Council.

Ohio Lake Erie Commission. 1998. *State of Ohio 1998: State of the Lake Report*. Columbus, Ohio: Ohio Lake Erie Commission.

Oregon Progress Board. 2000. *Oregon State of the Environment Report 2000: Statewide Summary*. Salem, Ore.: Oregon Progress Board.

Pimentel, D., C. Wilson, C. McCullum, R. Huang, P. Dwen, J. Flack, Q. Tran, T. Saltman, and B. Cliff. 1997. "Economic and Environmental Benefits of Biodiversity." *BioScience* 47: 747–57.

Prugh, T., R. Costanza, J. H. Cumberland, H. Daly, R. Goodland, and R. Norgaard. 1995. *Natural Capital and Human Economic Survival.* Solomons, Md.: International Society for Ecological Economics.

Pulliam, H. R. 1995. "Foreword." P. v in E. T. LaRoe, G. S. Farris, C. E. Puckett, P. D. Doran, and M. J. Mac, eds. *Our Living Resources: A Report to the Nation on the*

Distribution, Abundance, and Health of U.S. Plants, Animals, and Ecosystems. Washington, D.C.: U.S. Department of the Interior, National Biological Service.

Rees, W. E. 1996. "Revisiting Carrying Capacity: Area-Based Indicators of Sustainability." *Population and Environment* 17: 195–215.

Rees, W. E. 2000. "Patch Disturbance, Ecofootprints, and Biological Integrity: Revisiting the Limits to Growth (or Why Industrial Society Is Inherently Unsustainable)." Pp. 139–56 in D. Pimentel, L. Westra, and R. F. Noss, eds. *Ecological Integrity: Integrating Environment, Conservation, and Health.* Washington, D.C.: Island Press.

Rees, W. E., and M. Wackernagel. 1994. "Ecological Footprints and Appropriated Carrying Capacity: Measuring the Natural Capital Requirements of the Human Economy." Pp. 362–90 in A.–M. Jansson, M. Hammer, C. Folke, and R. Costanza, eds. *Investing in Natural Capital: The Ecological Economic Approach to Sustainability.* Washington, D.C.: Island Press.

Reynoldson, T. B., R. C. Bailey, K. E. Day, and R. H. Norris. 1995. "Biological Guidelines for Freshwater Sediment Based on Benthic Assessment of SedimenT (the BEAST) Using a Multivariate Approach for Predicting Biological State." *Australian Journal of Ecology* 20: 198–219.

Sagoff, M. 1997. "Muddle or Muddle Through? Takings Jurisprudence Meets the Endangered Species Act." *College of William and Mary Law Review* 38: 825–993.

Sagoff, M. 2000. "Ecosystem Design in Historical and Philosophical Context." Pp. 61–78 in D. Pimentel, L. Westra, and R. F. Noss, eds. *Ecological Integrity: Integrating Environment, Conservation, and Health.* Washington, D.C.: Island Press.

Simon, T. P., ed. 1999. *Assessing the Sustainability and Biological Integrity of Water Resources Using Fish Communities.* Boca Raton, Fla.: CRC Press.

Stabb, M. 2000. "When It Comes to the Environment, the Ecological Monitoring and Assessment Network Is Designed to Help Canadians see the Big Picture." *Nature Canada* 29(2): 24–28.

Sustainable Seattle. 1998. *Indicators of Sustainable Community 1998.* Seattle, Wash.: Sustainable Seattle.

Sykes, J. M., and A. M. J. Lane, eds. 1996. *The United Kingdom Environmental Change Network. Protocols for Standard Measurements at Terrestrial Sites.* London: Centre for Ecology and Hydrology, Natural Environment Research Council.

Thiele, L. P. 1999. *Environmentalism for a New Millennium: The Challenge of Coevolution.* New York: Oxford University Press.

Tiner, R. W. 1984. *Wetlands of the United States: Current Status and Recent Trends.* Washington, D.C.: U.S. Fish and Wildlife Service.

Toepfer, K. 2001. "Connect with the World Wide Web of Life." UNEP News Release 10/47. 5 June. Nairobi, Kenya: United Nations Environment Program.

UNDP (United Nations Development Programme, United Nations Environment Programme, World Bank, and World Resources Institute). 2000. *World Resources 2000–2001: People and Ecosystems, The Fraying Web of Life.* Washington, D.C.: World Resources Institute.

Vitousek, P. M., P. R. Ehrlich, A. H. Ehrlich, and P. A. Matson. 1986. "Human Appropriation of the Products of Photosynthesis." *BioScience* 36: 368–73.

Wackernagel, M., and W. E. Rees. 1996. *Our Ecological Footprint: Reducing Human Impact on the Earth.* Gabriola Island, British Columbia: New Society.

Wackernagel, M., L. Onisto, P. Bello, A. C. Linares, I. S. L. Falfan, J. M. Garcia, A. I. S. Guerrero, and C. S. Guerrero. 1999. "Natural Capital Accounting with the Ecological Footprint Concept." *Ecological Economics* 29: 375–90.

Williams, M. 1990. "Understanding Wetlands." Pp. 1–41 in M. Williams, ed. *Wetlands: A Threatened Landscape*. Oxford, England: Blackwell.

Woodwell, G. M. 1990. *The Earth in Transition: Patterns and Processes of Biotic Impoverishment.* New York: Cambridge University Press.

Part 2

People in Ecosystems: Reciprocal Impacts and Human Responsibilities

---

Sustainable Agriculture and the Human Prospect

Addressing the Destruction in Production

Introduction to Part 2

Part 1 presented the Earth Charter as an ethical framework for sustainable living, a new covenant that values the Earth as well as its human inhabitants. Part 2 moves from principles to practice by exploring more concretely reciprocal impacts of humans in nature and responsibilities that arise therefrom.

Sustainable Agriculture and the Human Prospect

If we are what we eat, then our extended human selves are rooted in soil like any tree. Agriculture tends this primary tie to Earth and presents some of the greatest challenges imaginable to sustainability. Chapters 11–13 examine this vital link.

Edwards and Pimentel (chapter 11) provide a wide-ranging review of human requirements for and availability of our most essential resources: food, water, and energy. Their neo-Malthusian conclusion is that standard estimates of population increase in the twenty-first century are unrealistically high. Population may peak at seven or eight billion in the shorter term, but the long-term carrying capacity for the planet may be only two to three billion individuals. Even this result will require extensive conservation measures and substitutions for fossil fuels. Given that half the world is already malnourished and degradation continues, a healthy and peaceful transition to a sustainable future is difficult to imagine.

The Edwards and Pimentel estimate of carrying capacity is based upon everyone globally enjoying a European standard of living with animal products in the diet. Should this dietary assumption be questioned? Goodland (chapter 12) documents ecological and health consequences of dairy products and meat in the diet. An unfortunate trend is that, with affluence, meat consumption increases. While small-scale domestic livestock may have some role in recycling cellulose and other wastes and utilizing rangeland, intensive livestock and dairy operations exact terrible ecological, animal welfare, and health costs and should not be encouraged or subsidized. With no compensating nutritional benefits from meat and dairy products, the Earth Charter principles rule against the promotion of intensive livestock and dairy operations.

What would an ecologically sound system of agriculture look like? Ryszkowski (chapter 13) notes that humans have colonized most of the productive lands of the world and created drastic transformations and numerous problems. Hence one strategy advocated for the protection of integrity is to create a network of protected wild areas (i.e., tracts of nature relatively unimpacted by humans). As Ryszkowski observes, however, that option is not available in many parts of the world and in any case is insufficient. We cannot write off agricultural lands, but should rather apply ecological science to policy, regulation, and practice so as to create agroecosystems with greater integrity. Ryszkowski identifies sound practices at the farm level (e.g., crop rotation, organic fertilizers, conserving soil moisture, integrated pest control), which need to be supplemented by diversification of the landscape structure with shelterbelts, hedges, meadows, midfield reservoirs and wetlands, riparian vegetation, and so on. Such practices can restore ecological functions and structures otherwise lost and address many of the ills of modern agriculture.

Addressing the Destruction in Production

Western agriculture, industry, and economics have emerged from an era that reduced the value of nature to almost nothing. According to Locke (1694, Second Treatise, sec. 42–43):

> Land that is left wholly to Nature, that hath no improvement of Pasturage, Tillage, or Planting, is called, as indeed it is, *waste*, and we shall find the benefit of it amount to little more than nothing.

Locke further calculated that improved land derives 99 to 99.9 percent of its value from cultivation rather than from the land itself. This valuation, which still permeates our economic system (e.g., in relying on the nature-blind gross domestic product as a primary index), may help to explain why we have treated nature so carelessly and brutally. Nor is agriculture the only destructive interface between humans and the rest of nature.

With the Earth Charter, we can see multiple errors in Locke's valuation of nature. He ignores (a) values apart from human utility, (b) the "psycho-spiritual utilities" of nature engaging thought and feeling, (c) nature's ability to create material goods (e.g., oxygenated air, clean water, natural edibles, and solar warmth) independently of our productive efforts, (d) the fact that our own productivity is part of nature's, uses complex natural ingredients, and is a coproduction with other natural processes. By ignoring these multiple kinds of value in nature, Locke therefore ignores our enormous potential for destruction in the course of our "improvements" on nature (Miller 1997). Chapters 14–17 all address the destructive side of our activities.

Lázár and Kiss (chapter 14) document the greatest ecological disaster in central Europe since Chernobyl, the January 2000 discharge of cyanide and heavy metals into the Tisza River (and a lesser spill in March of the same year). Their story has the bioregional backdrop of the Carpathian Basin, with its human and ecological history. Although carved into multiple jurisdictions after World War I, it is still united physically by the Tisza, which flows through it, and symbolically by its romantic past celebrated in art, literature, and political memories. Now the spill, which passed from Romania through parts of the Ukraine and Slovakia to Hungary, and new interjurisdictional environmental management initiatives also unite the region. In contrast to the spirit of Locke, Lázár and Kiss make evident the economic, social, cultural, and health links to the ecology of the region and how such links provide a basis for people of different nations to cooperate in protecting the land and waters that sustain them.

The authors also look at flaws in the design, operation, and permitting of the effluent impoundments that gave way as failures in responsibility, traceable, perhaps, to the earlier political deconstruction of the region.

The Tisza spill presents a striking entrance into the web of ecological/human connections through a destructive incident. That incident, however, is one of a long list of major polluting incidents by the mining industry, and mining is but one sector of many having similar or greater levels of impact, which together add up to a global ecocide. Why do we tolerate such levels of ecoviolence? To answer that question, McMurtry (chapter 15) offers a theoretical account of a structural flaw in society that drives planetary destruction. He proposes, as a generalization, but not a law, that parts of nature degenerate in direct proportion to corporate for-profit use of those resources. This need not be, but is the case because of an institutionalized blindness or refusal to see that for-profit resource exploitation unconstrained by "life-protective law" is destroying the planet. Some means of profit-making enhance life, while others do not. Profits made from life-enhancing means are legitimate, but society has to engage in self-protection by regulating or prohibiting life-diminishing enterprises.

According to McMurtry, we have become beholden to a corporate philosophy that systematically obscures the difference between life-enhancement and profitmaking. Moreover, he thinks the media, academics, and NGOs are complicit in keeping the public ignorant by failing to name the life-destroying for-profit sequences and philosophy that are the root cause of planetary destruction. He attributes the reluctance of analysts to examine and expose the causes of destruction to increasingly direct financial ties to corporations. As a consequence we now have "ethically bizarre" trade regimes in which corporate rights are supreme over societal and environmental interests. Yet these same trade regimes provide the opportunity for a solution. All that is required is that we incorporate basic standards of life protection into international trade agreements and enforce them with the same vigor as the other provisions.

As an aside we note that "The Way Forward" at the end of the Earth Charter calls for "the implementation of Earth Charter principles with an international legally binding instrument on environment and development." There is an unfortunate disconnect between the international moral and legal systems promoted by UN-related negotiations and international trade negotiations. Only the former is working towards a global ethic. Is there any way to bring the latter under the wing of the former?

McMurtry looks for solutions to destructive economic practices by regulation from without. Werhane and Hamilton (chapter 16) look for solutions by reform from within. They trace the destructiveness of the global economic system to its inherent mental models of free enterprise and consumption as a source of prosperity for all. On the positive side, those models have helped to raise the standard of living of the West. The authors think that "the multinational corporation is probably the most viable and creative social institution today" and could improve lives elsewhere, but only with a shift in mental models.

Werhane and Hamilton discuss several changes they would like to see. The most fundamental one is a shift to systems thinking, including social and environmental "value added" as equally important as economic gain. Another is to develop cultural sensitivity and flexibility to define value as it is found in the cultures where they operate. A third is to reconceive consumption, not as using up, but (consistent with systems theory) as exchanging goods and services. Ideally, nothing would get used up; everything would be reused or recycled in some fashion. However, since the law of entropy means that useful energy does get used up, energy will have to be derived from inexhaustible sources like sun and wind. Unilever is a multinational corporation operating globally, which has developed crosscultural sensitivity and adopted a triple-bottom-line philosophy. Shareholders, consumers, host countries, and citizens alike can approve of corporate activity that improves local social and environmental conditions while earning profits. Other corporations will have to develop a similar philosophy to become sustainable.

In the final chapter of part 2, Brown (chapter 17) turns attention to global warming, which threatens destructive changes in the world's climate. He asks what practical difference the adoption of the Earth Charter would make for this issue. In some respects he thinks it would make little difference, since there are already international agreements in place and it is currently U.S. recalcitrance, not absence of relevant principles, which stands in the way of progress. The United States bolsters its position by referring to outstanding issues, such as scientific uncertainty; whether developed countries should undertake greenhouse gas (GHG) emission reduction without developing countries doing so; the levels at which GHGs should be stabilized; and the weighing of costs and benefits of global warming programs.

On the first two issues, the Earth Charter is redundant. The UN Framework Convention on Climate Change (UNFCCC) and the Rio Declaration already enshrine the precautionary principle, which should guide the application of uncertain science, and the UNFCCC includes the recognition and agreement that developed countries must take the lead. However, the adoption of the Earth Charter with its biocentric/ecocentric stance would provide grounds for lowering GHGs as much and as quickly as possible, because of harmful effects to which many nonhuman life forms cannot adapt. For the same reason, cost-benefit analysis, employing standard, human-centered methodologies, would also be inappropriate to determine the extent of GHG reduction.

References

Hargrove, E. 1983. "Anglo-American Land Use Attitudes." Pp. 96–113 in *Ethics and the Environment*, edited by D. Scherer and T. Attig. Englewood Cliffs, N.J.: Prentice-Hall.

Locke, J. 1694. *Two Treatises of Government*. London: A. and J. Churchill at the Black Swan. Cited in Hargrove 1983, 109.

Miller, P. 1997. "Environmental Ethics and Canadian Forest Policy: From Locke to Gaia." Pp. 50–66 in *Canadian Issues in Applied Environmental Ethics*, edited by A. Wellington, A. Greenbaum, and W. Cragg. Peterborough, Ontario: Broadview Press.

Sustainable Agriculture and the Human Prospect

Chapter 11

The Future of Human Populations: Energy, Food, and Water Availability in the Twenty-First Century

Clive A. Edwards and David Pimentel

Introduction

The world population reached 6 billion in October 1999, which is more than a doubling of the 2.5 billion human beings that existed 50 years ago in 1950. This increase is greater than all population increases during the four million years of human existence. It raises the critical issue of how large a human population the globe can support on a long-term basis if current rates of multiplication continue.

This is not a new question. In 1798, Thomas Malthus, a British clergyman and intellectual, warned in his "Essay on the Principle of Population" of the tendency he saw for human populations to grow exponentially while food supplies increased only arithmetically. The inevitable consequence, if he were correct, would be that at some point human population increases would be limited by food availability. However, it proved to be the case that neither did the world population continue to increase exponentially as he predicted, nor was food production limited to arithmetical increases, so that during the nineteenth and early twentieth century his predictions were to some extent discredited and dismissed. Nevertheless population growth was rapid and the annual rate of world population growth peaked in 1964 at 2.2 percent per annum, but since then it has declined steadily, dropping to 1.4 percent per annum in 1998. The reasons for this fall in population growth rates are complex, ranging through regional food and water shortages, increases in infectious diseases, wars, and deliberate policies of birth control. Concomitantly food production has increased dramatically in industrialized countries particularly over the last 50 years (e.g., yields per acre have trebled in the United States since 1950). However, although increases in food production kept up with population growth for many years, yields per capita have decreased steadily since 1980, with the result that up to a third of the current global population is malnourished.

This raises the key questions of what is the maximum human population the planet Earth can support on a sustainable basis, and what are the most important factors limiting populations. Our hypothesis in this chapter is that the key factors influencing population growth are the availability of energy, food, and water. Closely associated with these factors are: arable land availability (including losses of productive land to urbanization), disposal or utilization of organic wastes, and the possible impacts of global climatic changes which have been predicted by the UN to increase by 2.4°C to 11.2°C.

We plan to review these various issues, in terms of realistic estimates of the human populations that the planet can eventually support on available natural resources, and still maintain a reasonable standard of life, and how our diminishing natural resources may be conserved, reclaimed, and utilized to maximum effect to provide the essentials for a satisfying human existence. Unless the issue is faced and resolved intelligently, the ultimate choice may be between governments controlling human numbers voluntarily or letting natural forces do this, probably with considerable suffering and even starvation to many members of the global population.

Human Populations

The current world human population of more than 6 billion was reached in October 1999 (Edwards and Pimentel 2000). Based on the present population growth rate of 1.4 percent per year, the population has been predicted by some people to double to 12 billion in approximately 50 years (PRB 1998). There have been even higher predictions based on past human population growth patterns and models that suggest that peak populations could increase to as much as 14 billion (Kapitza 2000). The United Nations in 2000 predicted population increases to 7.7 to 11.2 billion, and Edwards and Pimentel (2000) have suggested that such populations are unsustainable in the long-term.

Moreover, even with our present human global population of six billion, up to three billion people are malnourished (FAO 1992a; Nesheim 1993; McMichael 1993; Maberly 1994; WHO 1996; Brown et al. 1998). Rapidly increasing human population concentrations, especially in urban areas, which are associated with increasing food, water, air, and soil pollution by pathogenic organisms and chemicals, are causing rapid increases in the prevalence of disease and numbers of human deaths (WHO 1992, 1995; Pimentel and Edwards 2000). An estimated 40,000 children die each day due to malnutrition and other diseases (WHO 1995).

A critical issue in the sustainability of populations is the strongly regionalized distribution of human populations, which are very much larger in developing countries, such as China, India, and Pakistan, than in most developed countries in Europe and North America. Moreover, these are the countries where the rates of multiplication are greatest and which have the greatest potential for population growth, whereas in many industrialized countries populations are leveling off, and even in some countries such as Italy, decreasing. Although overall food production may continue to increase globally over the short term, the amounts of food produced regionally are probably inversely related to regional food needs, since those nations that multiply slowest are those that produce the most food. Worldwide there has been a strong movement of people from the land to cities and this is predicted to increase. The urban share of the total population has increased from 30 percent in 1950 to a predicted 69 percent in 2050.

Most forecasts of peak human global populations have been based on simulation models related to past population growth and using these to make population predictions without taking natural resource distribution and limitations into account. Such methods have resulted in widely varying figures, ranging through 14 billion (Kapitza 2000), 12 billion (PRB 1996), to a high of 11.2 billion, a medium of 9.4 billion, and a low of 7.7 billion.

However, when full account is taken of rapidly dwindling global fossil fuel energy reserves, diminishing productive cropland areas, food shortages, decreasing water availability, and increasing environmental degradation and pollution, such figures can be seen to be unrealistic. For instance, since 1950, although populations have doubled, lumber use has doubled, grain consumption has tripled, water use has tripled, fossil fuel use has increased fourfold, and paper use has grown six times. Such increasing use of resources per capita as populations continue to enlarge is clearly unsustainable and exacerbates the problem.

We suggest that although human populations may increase to seven or eight billion globally in the shorter term, the ultimate long-term carrying capacity for the planet Earth may be only two to three billion individuals. This conclusion is based on maintaining a European-style standard of living for everyone in the world associated with sustainable use of natural resources. For land resources, we suggest a need of 0.5 ha of cropland per capita using relatively inexpensive agricultural production systems (~8 million kcal/ha) and a diverse plant and animal diet for the people. The mean area 0.5 ha of cropland per capita is the level that existed in 1960. Since that time nearly one-third of the world's productive arable land has been lost due to urbanization, highways, soil erosion, salinization, and water-logging of the soil (WRI 1994; Pimentel et al. 1998). Additionally, approximately 1.5 ha of land per capita would be required to provide renewable energy after fossil fuels are exhausted. At the same time, a desirable goal would be to keep approximately 1 ha per capita of land for forest and pasture production. To achieve such figures, which total 2.5 ha per capita of productive land, it would also be essential to slow down or stop current land degradation associated with soil erosion and pollution (Pimentel et al. 1995). Many sustainable technologies for soil conservation, in agricultural and forest production, are currently available; they only need to be adapted generally on a global basis (Troeh and Thompson 1993).

Worldwide, balancing the population-resource equation will be very difficult, because current regional overpopulation, poor distribution of resources, and environmental degradation are already causing serious malnutrition, sickness, and poverty throughout the world, especially in developing countries (Gleick 1993; WHO 1995; Brown 1997; Pimentel and Pimentel 1996; Postel 1997). Based on the estimate that 0.5 ha of land per capita is necessary for an adequate and diverse food supply, it would be possible to sustain a global population of approximately two to three billion humans using renewable energy sources. However, arable land is currently being degraded and lost at a rate of more than 12 million ha per year (Pimentel et al. 1995). At this rate of loss, based on figures given above, in just 42 years there would be sufficient arable land to support a population of only two to three billion people. Thus it is critical even to sustain these populations that we find and adopt soil and water conservation techniques that will protect the remaining soil resources that currently produce more than 99 percent of the world's food (Pimentel et al. 1995; Pimentel et al. 1997b).

To maintain a world population of two to three billion, in addition to providing adequate food supplies, sufficient renewable energy, and enough forest products to support a reasonable lifestyle, it is also necessary to provide adequate freshwater resources for drinking water, agricultural, and industrial needs (Postel 1999). For agricultural and industrial production, as well as public needs, we suggest that approximately 1.2 million liters of water are needed per person each year. Hence, water resources will have to be conserved to the maximum extent and kept free of pollution. A range of technologies is currently available for the effective management and protection of water resources (Postel 1997) and these will be discussed later.

An eventual reduction in the world's population to approximately two or even three billion, in addition to using a reduced per capita water consumption rate, would help to decrease the current severe pressure on surface and groundwater resources and water pollution, especially in countries where it is predicted that water shortages will intensify with population growth (Postel 1997; Pimentel et al. 1997a).

A global adjustment of the world population from the current more than six billion to two to three billion could occur over approximately a century if the majority of the people of the world concurred that protecting human health, welfare, and living standards was vital. Although a rapid reduction in human population numbers to two to three billion would cause social, economic, and political problems, continued rapid growth to as many as 12 billion people would result in an even more disastrous situation. In such a situation, in addition to worldwide catastrophic nutrition, health, and environmental problems, political and economic tensions would be likely to increase dramatically as fossil fuel production starts to decline after about the year 2020.

Food Availability

Although Malthus predicted in 1798 that food production could not keep up with the growth in human populations, in the period since his forecasts, efficiency in food production increased dramatically, particularly over the last 50 years. For instance, crop yields in the United States trebled between 1945 and 1995. Up to 1980, global increases in food production were able to keep up with population increases, although the land areas available for crops have decreased dramatically. However, these increases in yields did not prevent widespread malnutrition or starvation, because they occurred mostly in the more industrialized countries. Many developing countries could not provide enough food to support their populations, and international trade and movement was inadequate. Moreover, since 1980 food production per capita has decreased considerably due to available land and soil loss and degradation.

There were global increases in food production of up to 3 percent annually in the last century, while increases in human population peaked at 2.2 percent per annum in 1964 and declined steadily to 1.4 percent per annum in 1998. The increases in food production have been achieved mainly in both industrial countries, and in the "Green Revolution" in India, by use of large quantities of inorganic fertilizers and synthetic pesticides which are produced basically from fossil fuels. Global use of fertilizers peaked in the 1980s and has been decreasing since then, although the use of pesticides is still increasing at a moderate rate, particularly in the United States. Such food production increases based on chemical inputs cannot be sustained in the long term. For instance, in the United States, the Council for Agricultural Science and Technology, a group of agricultural-based scientific societies, forecast in 1990 that the time scale for sources of inorganic fertilizers in United States were 51 years for nitrogen, 41 years for phosphorus, and 107 years for potassium. Similar calculations can be made for pesticides, most of which are also manufactured from fossil fuels. Additionally many insects, nematodes, mites, and plant disease organisms are rapidly developing cross-linked resistance to pesticides, which are becoming increasingly expensive and which limit the choices available.

The main limitations to food production are (1) loss of productive croplands, (2) loss of soils through wind and water erosion, (3) inadequate nutrient supplies in many poor soils, linked to long periods needed for nutrient regeneration, (4) enormous losses due to pests and diseases on crops both pre- and post-harvest, and (5) energy shortages to provide nutrients, pest control, cultivation, and irrigation needs.

More than 99 percent of human food comes from the terrestrial environment (FAO 1991; Pimentel and Edwards 2000). Currently, global food and fiber crops are grown on only 11 percent of the Earth's total land area of 13 billion ha. Annual losses of land to urbanization and highways range from 10 to 35 million ha (approximately 1 percent per annum) and half of this lost land is cropland (Doeoes 1994). Most of the remaining land area (23 percent) is unsuitable for crops or pasture, because the soil is too infertile or shallow to support plant growth, or the climate is too dry, wet, or cold, or the land is too steep or stony (Buringh 1989). Rates of loss of productive land from both erosion and poor management are very high. Globally more than 7 million ha of cropland is rendered unusable and 26 million ha, or an area the size of Kansas, is made unproductive annually.

In 1960, approximately 0.5 ha of cropland was available per capita to maintain life worldwide. Such an area of cropland per capita is needed to provide a diverse, healthy, nutritious diet of plant and animal products such as that available in the United States and Europe (Lal 1989; Giampietro and Pimentel 1994). However the current average per capita of world cropland is only 0.27 ha, or about half the amount needed to provide amounts of food to industrial nation standards. The shortage of productive cropland in 1999 is the principal underlying cause of current worldwide food shortages, malnutrition, sickness, and poverty (Leach 1995; Pimentel and Edwards 2000). More than 38 percent of the global cultivated area has already been damaged by different kinds of agricultural mismanagement (Gardner 1997).

Currently, a total of 1,481 kg/yr per capita of agricultural products is produced to feed Americans, compared with the Chinese food supply, which averages only 785 kg/yr per capita. By all resource criteria, the Chinese have reached or exceeded the limits of productivity of their agricultural system (Brown 1997). Their reliance on large inputs of fossil-fuel-based fertilizers, and pesticides, to compensate for shortages of arable land and their poor and severely eroded soils, indicates severe future problems for them (Wen and Pimentel 1992). The Chinese already import large amounts of grain from the United States and other nations, and inevitably will have to increase these imports in the future (Alexandratos 1995).

Intensive cropping, particularly with crops such as maize, that leave large areas of bare soil uncovered, can lead to extensive wind and water soil erosion. In the United States one third of the topsoil has already been lost and soil is still being lost at 18 times the rate it can be regenerated (Pimentel et al. 1995). The national average for soil losses in the United States is 18 metric tons per ha per year (18.3 tons per acre per year) and some states such as Iowa and Missouri have double that rate of loss. Rates of regeneration are about 0.5 metric tons per ha per year or 0.20 tons per acre. Globally, as much as 7 million ha of productive land is rendered unusable annually and 26 million ha of land (about the area of Kansas) is made at least temporarily unusable for crop production.

The current high rates of soil erosion throughout the world are of particular concern because of the slow rate of topsoil renewal; it takes approximately 500 years for 2.5 cm (1 inch) of topsoil to form under agricultural conditions (OTA 1982; Elwell, 1985; Troeh et al. 1991; Pimentel et al. 1995). Approximately

3,000 years are needed for natural reformation of topsoil to the 150 mm depth needed for satisfactory crop production.

The need for crop nutrients is also exacerbated by the wasteful disposal of organic wastes, which in many ways are a lost resource (Gardner 1997). In industrialized countries as much as 65 percent of the waste produced in urban situations is currently disposed of in landfills, where not only are the nutrients they contain lost, but they also may contribute to environmental pollution and emissions. These organic wastes could be used profitably for soil structure improvement or as a source of nutrient supplies in agricultural soils. The main obstacle to such use is claimed to be the financial and energetic costs of transport from the urban to the agricultural situation. Additionally some organic wastes, such as animal manure, are applied to soils simply to get rid of them, without realizing the nutrient they add to soil and the improvements in soil structure and function that result. Organic matter should be considered not as disposable garbage but as a soil-building natural resource to be used in fertilization regimes.

The Availability of Fossil Fuel and Renewable Energy

Currently, the world, and particularly the industrialized countries, depend mainly on fossil fuels such as oil, natural gas, and coal as their energy sources. The major global issue associated with the use of fossil fuels is that they have a limited future availability. For instance, in October 2000 the American Petroleum Institute predicted that at present rates of consumption, the remaining known oil reserves would last 63 years, but long before that they would be progressively more expensive to recover. The Institute forecast that the flow of oil would peak by 2010 and then drop off permanently unless previously unsuspected oil reserves were discovered.

Other predictions of future supplies of oil are even more pessimistic with suggestions that the world supply of oil will last only up to 44 years (BP 1994; Ivanhoe 1995; Campbell 1997; Duncan 1997; Youngquist 1997). Worldwide, the natural gas supply is adequate for about 50 years and that of coal for about 100 years (BP 1994; Bartlett and Ristinen 1995; Youngquist 1997). These estimates, however, are based on current consumption rates and current population numbers and these resources could well last for shorter periods if rates of consumption continue to increase, as seems likely.

Youngquist (1997) reported that current oil and gas exploration drilling has not borne out earlier optimistic estimates of the amount of these resources yet to be found in the United States. Both United States production and proven oil and gas reserves have continued to decline. It seems obvious, from current knowledge of global and United States fossil fuel resources, that however many new drilling sites are developed, domestic oil and natural gas production in the United States will be substantially less in 20 years than it is today. Current production is insufficient for domestic needs, and oil supplies are imported in increasing annual amounts (US DOE 1991; BP 1994; Youngquist 1997). Surveys suggest that the United States has consumed as much as three-quarters of the recoverable oil that was ever in its ground, and is currently consuming the last 25 percent of its oil reserves (Bartlett 1998). The United States is now importing about 62 percent of its oil, which puts the United States economy at considerable risk, due to fluctuating oil prices and difficult political situations, such as the 1973 oil crisis and the 1991 Gulf War (U.S. Congressional Record 1997). There are many current signs that the cost of fossil fuels will continue to escalate in the next few years.

Such predictions are complicated even further by the continuing increases in the use of oil, natural gas, and to a lesser extent, coal, particularly in industrialized nations. These increases in consumption involve not only their use as fuel but also in production of synthetic chemicals such as fertilizers and pesticides. Fossil fuel sources, which currently are readily available and relatively inexpensive in the United States, improve the general quality of life in many ways, but are taxed heavily in many other countries, particularly in the European Union. However, the gaseous emissions the utilization of fossil fuels produces cause considerable environmental pollution and contribute significantly to potential future climate changes (Pimentel and Pimentel 1996).

About 395 quads (1 quad = 10^{15} BTU or 383 x 10^{18} joules), from all energy sources, are used worldwide per year and about 345 quads of this come from fossil fuels. About one-quarter of the global consumption of fossil fuels is by the United States (US DOE 1995 a, b). Current energy expenditure is related to many factors, including population growth, urbanization, and high consumption rates for production and transport of food and other industrial commodities. Energy use has been growing even faster than world population growth. From 1970 to 1995, energy use was increasing at a rate of 2.5 percent (doubling every 30 years) whereas the worldwide population only grew at 1.7 percent (doubling about 40 years). Energy use is projected to increase at a rate of 2.2 percent (doubling every 32 years) compared with a population growth rate of 1.4 percent (doubling every 47 years) (PRB 1996; US DOE 1995b). Per capita use of fossil fuel energy in the United States is 8,740 liters of oil equivalents per year, more than 12 times the per capita use of oil in China, where most fossil fuel energy is used by industry, although about 25 percent is used for agriculture and food production (Wen and Pimentel 1992).

Industrialized nations consume about 70 percent of the total fossil energy used worldwide annually, while the developing nations, which have about 75 percent of the world population, use only 30 percent (International Energy Annual 1995). The United States, with only 4 percent of the world's population, consumes about one-quarter of the world's fossil energy annual production (Pimentel and Pimentel 1996). Fossil energy use in the different United States economic sectors has increased 20- to 1,000-fold in the past three to four decades, attesting to America's reliance on fossil fuels to support their affluent lifestyle (Pimentel and Pimentel 1996).

Developing nations that have high rates of population growth are increasing their fossil fuel use to augment their agricultural production of food and fiber. In China, since 1955, there has been a 100-fold increase in fossil energy use in agriculture to produce fertilizers, pesticides, and for irrigation used to increase grain and rice production (Wen and Pimentel 1992). In India, the Green Revolution was based on using fertilizers and pesticides produced from fossil fuels, which have to be imported at considerable costs.

However, global fertilizer production has declined by more than 23 percent since 1988, from its peak production of nearly 150 million tons per annum. This has occurred especially in the developing countries, due to fossil fuel shortages, currency problems, and high prices. In addition, the overall projections of the availability of fossil energy resources for fertilizers and all other purposes are discouraging because of the limited global resources of fossil fuels, which have been predicted to run out during the next 50 to 60 years (B.P. 1994; Youngquist 1997).

Since the Second World War, from the 1960s and 1970s, many nuclear power stations have been built, and these make significant contributions to electricity production. The main drawbacks to nuclear energy are associated with possible environmental hazards, in terms of accidents, and the disposal of nuclear wastes, which remain radioactive indefinitely. Clearly, there will have to be a global movement from dependency on fossil fuels as main sources of energy to renewable energy sources, if human populations are to be sustained and their quality of life maintained in the long term. Currently, various renewable energy technologies provide about 14 percent of the world energy needs and about 8 percent of United States needs. Biomass will continue to be an important source of energy globally as will the production of methane from organic wastes. Some of the renewable energy technologies, such as hydroelectric power, are well-established and the use of solar cells and ponds and wind power is increasing steadily, and ethanol production is quite common. Additionally photovoltaic systems (utilizing sunlight), hydrogen and fuel, and geothermal systems are innovative sources of renewable energy.

Using all of the currently available renewable energy technologies, such as hydroelectric power, biomass, solar and wind power, an estimated 200 quads of renewable energy could be produced worldwide on 20 percent to 26 percent of the land area (Pimentel and Pimentel 1996). Such a system would provide energy for about two to three billion people, i.e., provide each person with 5,000 liters of oil equivalents per year (half of America's current consumption per year but an increase for most people of the world) (Pimentel et al. 1998). However, the appropriation of over 20 percent of the global land area for renewable energy production would limit further the productivity of the vital ecosystems that humanity depends on for food.

Global Availability of Water

Water is essential to human existence, firstly for clean drinking water for the global population, secondly for a range of industrial purposes, but most importantly for irrigation of crops. Currently, about 93 percent of the world's available freshwater is used for crop irrigation (Postel 1999). The provision of adequate supplies of freshwater for human and agricultural needs is already critical in many regions, such as the Middle East (Postel 1997). Rapid human population growth and the resulting increased total water consumption is depleting the overall availability of water worldwide rapidly. Between 1960 and 1997, the per capita availability of freshwater worldwide decreased by about 60 percent (Hinrichsen 1998). A further 50 percent decrease in per capita water supply is projected by the year 2025. Irrigation currently contributes to production of a disproportionate amount of global food production: the 237 million ha of irrigated land is only 16 percent of the total global cropland but supplies more than a third of global food (Postel 1994).

Water resources and human population densities are extremely unevenly distributed worldwide. Although the *total* global amount of water available is enough to provide the world's current population with adequate amounts of freshwater, according to their *minimum* requirements, most of this water is concentrated in specific regions, leaving other areas moderately or extremely water-deficient. Even areas with good water supplies such as the United States and Canada suffer from serious drought and water shortages in some years. Currently, Texas is suffering major water shortages after several drought years. Water demands are already considerably above available supplies in nearly 80 nations of the world (Gleick 1993). In China more than 300 cities suffer from inadequate water supplies, and the problem is intensifying as the Chinese population increases (WRI 1994; Brown 1995). In arid regions, such as the Middle East and parts of North Africa, where yearly rainfall is low and irrigation is expensive, the future of agricultural production is grim and becoming even more so as populations continue to grow. Political conflicts over water in some areas, particularly the Middle East, have even strained international relations between severely water-starved nations (Gleick 1993).

The greatest threat to maintaining freshwater supplies is the progressive depletion of surface and groundwater resources that are needed to supply the needs of the rapidly growing human population. Surface water is not always managed effectively, often resulting in regional water shortages and pollution that threaten both humans and the aquatic biota that depend on water supplies. High rates of human consumption of surface and groundwater resources, in addition to increasing usage costs, are beginning to limit the option of crop irrigation in many arid regions. Furthermore, salinized and waterlogged soils can become unproductive from continued irrigation (Postel 1999), decreasing the area on which irrigation is possible, so that the global crop irrigated area per capita has been falling off rapidly since 1990.

Groundwater resources are also commonly mismanaged and over-tapped. Because of their slow recharge rate, which on average is usually between 0.1 percent to 0.3 percent per year (Covich 1993), groundwater resources must be managed carefully to prevent depletion. In many regions, human societies are not conserving groundwater resources effectively. In Beijing, China, the groundwater level is falling at a rate of about 1 m/yr; whereas in Tianjin, China, it is dropping 4.4 m/yr (Postel 1997). In the United States, aquifer overdrafts commonly average 25 percent more than their replacement rates (USWRC 1979).

The World Resources Institute reported in 2001 that by 2050 at least half the world's population will live in areas with water scarcity. In March 2001 a report issued on World Water Day entitled "Running on Empty" (Flesher 2001) predicted an even worse situation with two out of every three people in the world facing water shortages. The report further forecast that by 2025 millions of people would have to leave their homes in search of clean water.

Impacts of Global Climate Change

There is progressive agreement amongst scientists that emissions of carbon dioxide and effluent gases, such as nitrous oxide (N_2O) from industrial sources and automobiles, and methane (CH_4) emissions from various sources are having significant impacts on the ozone layer (Parry 1990). The carbon dioxide (CO_2) emissions arise from fossil fuel combustion, soil cultivation, biomass burning, and deforestation. Until the 1970s, more carbon was emitted annually from soils and land use conversion than from fossil fuel combustion. Currently about 25 percent of global CO_2 emissions result from agricultural activities. These emissions are believed to be exerting considerable influences on the global climate and this may increase unless managed. Until recently, the topic of climate change was still controversial, but there is now increasing consensus among most scientists that these gaseous emissions are already having significant effects on global temperatures. Over the past century there has been an average increase in temperature of nearly 1°C (Parry 1990). By October 2000, a full-scale United Nations sponsored review by hundreds of scientists concluded that if gaseous emissions are not curtailed, the Earth's surface temperatures might increase from as little as 2.7°C to as much as 11°C over the next century, depending on the degree of restrictions on emissions that are implemented worldwide. The potential implications of such large temperature changes, on landmasses and agricultural production, are enormous. As the polar icecaps melt, ocean levels will rise, flooding many low-lying areas across the world. Examples of areas at risk include Bangladesh, the Netherlands, and Florida in the United States, but also many other regions distributed worldwide. There is also agreement among scientists that temperature increases will be greater at higher latitudes. This could increase the potential for food production in northern parts of North America, Europe, and Asia. However, this would probably be more than balanced by losses in production at milder and lower latitudes. It is extremely difficult to predict the overall effects of global warming on rainfall patterns, but it is possible that monsoon rain in Africa and Asia might penetrate further northward, in the form of more intense rain over a shorter period, leading to shorter growing seasons and decreased agricultural production. A major effect of global warming would be increased evapotranspiration from plants and soils, which could also have adverse effects on food production. It seems probable that the overall effect of increases in temperatures globally would be to decrease the availability of water for crop irrigation. It also seems very likely that losses of crops to pests and diseases might increase since pests tend to multiply faster at higher temperatures. Thus, in balance, food production would probably fall.

A critical issue is that global warming would probably exert its greatest adverse effects on tropical developing countries, which are already net importers of food. The best illustration of the enormous potential impacts of global climate change on agriculture are the large changes in food availability regionally that have occurred after several drought years in the past. There have been many international efforts to integrate measures to control and decrease gaseous emissions such as through the Kyoto Protocol in 1989, in which many countries agreed to make efforts to decrease their gaseous emissions by 5 percent by 1912. However, actual attempts to implement even these modest aims have fallen short of the objectives, which even if achieved, would only have had modest effects on potential global climatic changes. There is a general consensus that climate changes due to greenhouse gases will affect agricultural production in major ways, but it is likely that the impacts will vary regionally, with many areas suffering decreased productivity, although a few regions could possibly benefit and increase production. Without a clear knowledge of the probable extent of global warming, changes in agricultural practices, changed cropping patterns and other issues that could be caused by climate change, we are still not in a position to make any accurate predictions as to what gaseous emissions will do to global food availability or regional distribution. However, it seems likely that they may gradually decrease per capita food production, putting even greater pressures on increasing human populations.

Potential Partial Solutions to Human Population Pressures on Natural Resources

Clearly, ever-increasing human populations exert progressively greater pressures on food and land availability, energy resources, and supplies of freshwater, which are finite resources. Hence, inevitably, there is some absolute limit on the human populations that planet Earth can support and still maintain reasonable life standards. However, human ingenuity still offers many possibilities that new resources may be found and available resources renewed, managed better, and supplemented by innovative technologies, but even in these conditions there must still be a finite limit to human populations.

Inputs to Food Production

Retardation of Soil Losses

If human populations are to be maintained in the long term, even if population increases level off, the efficiency of food production must be enhanced. First, global losses of productive land must be slowed dramatically. There must be increased awareness of the imperative need for good management of productive soils to minimize soil erosion. We have many well-tested methods of decreasing soil losses, but they are still utilized only poorly. Industrialized farming based on agrochemicals can produce impressive short-term increases in crop yields, but many of the agricultural practices involved lead to gradual degradation of the soils involved. For example, the increasing tendency in the United States and elsewhere to grow crops such as maize continually in monoculture or biculture accentuates adverse effects on soils. Much better cropping patterns and rotations are needed to ensure soil preservation. Currently, the basic need is to reverse the loss of productive soils by slowing urbanization of such land, avoiding current mismanagement practices thereby effectively slowing soil erosion significantly. Basically, this involves keeping land protected from the effects of wind and rainfall by maintaining some form of vegetative or other cover over the soil surface. On sloping land this usually involves terracing or the use of barrier crops. On shallower slopes and on flatter land it needs modifications to types of cultivations used, such as no-till, ridge tillage or conservation tillage, in place of deep plowing. It can also be assisted by use of live or dead surface mulches, strip-cropping, intercropping, rotations, and creation of barriers between fields. Often combinations of several of these methods are needed to ensure the maintenance of soil structure and fertility. Above all, overcropping with few rest periods or fallows has to be avoided.

Biological Inputs to Soil Fertility

Since inorganic fertilizers are dependent on fossil fuels for their manufacture, and forecasts of fossil fuel availability are on the order of less than 50 years, there is an urgent need to develop and use biological or cultural methods as alternatives to fertilizers to provide the essential nutrients for crop growth. Techniques used in the United States prior to 1945 involved planting legumes, such as vetch or clover, which can add about 100 kg per ha of nitrogen to the soil. There seems enormous potential to utilize legumes as nitrogen sources much more, particularly in developing tropical countries. There is also the untested potential to transfer the genes for nitrogen fixation to other crops using genetic modification technology.

Another practice that has been used to add nitrogen to soil and increase crop yields in Central America and other tropical countries is the use of agroforestry or mixtures of crops and woody perennials. Planting two rows of a leguminous tree *(Leaucea leaucea)* and then two rows of corn can reduce the area planted with corn by half, but has been found to produce double the yield of corn, compared to traditional corn production. The legume can be cut down to about 8 cm before the planting of the corn to reduce its competition with the corn crop. The maize crop has to be planted at twice the density in the rows, compared with traditional maize growing. Because about 60 kg of nitrogen can be added to the soil, the yields of corn can be very high. In addition to adding nitrogen to the soil, the legume trees can provide additional biomass to the soil and reduce soil erosion from about 30 t/ha/yr in a traditional corn system to only about 1 t/ha/yr in an agroforestry system.

There is an urgent need for much better utilization of the nutrients contained in agricultural and urban organic wastes, much of which are disposed of either in lagoons for animal wastes or landfills for urban wastes at considerable environmental and financial cost, in both North America and Europe. As much as 60 percent of the wastes that are put into landfills in many parts of the United States are organic. Not only would the utilization of these organic wastes go a long way towards minimizing the need for inorganic fertilizers, but they would also do much to improve soil structure, conservation, and pest and disease control. There needs to be greatly improved links between urban communities and the farmers in the surrounding countryside.

Biological Pest, Disease, and Weed Management

Global yield losses to pests of 40 percent are common and losses as great as 75 percent have been reported from some regions when both pre- and postharvest losses are considered (Pimentel and Lehman 1993). The use of synthetic pesticides since the Second World War has not been very effective in reducing these losses significantly. Many opportunities exist to reduce pesticide use through the use of nonchemical, biological alternatives, and it has been estimated that pesticide use in the United States could be reduced by more than 50 percent through the use of such nonchemical control measures. Many alternative biological control technologies exist today; we simply need to utilize the most appropriate of the wide array of nonchemical alternatives that are available.

Nonchemical cultural alternatives to pesticide use that are currently available include: resistant varieties of crops, crop rotations, innovative tillage practices, cultural controls, timing of planting and harvesting, biological controls of pests, promoting natural enemies of pests, host-plant resistance to attack, water management, fertilizer nutrient management, short-season crops, weather forecasting, pest-forecasting, development of economic thresholds, integrated crop management, increased crop diversity, pest scouting, planting trap crops, and maintaining plant diversity. There is increasing evidence that the use of organic matter in crop production, particularly when it has been composted or vermicomposted, can decrease the incidence of plant diseases and plant parasitic nematodes greatly.

We currently have many well-tested biological pest control measures available, many of which are greatly underutilized. Biological control options that are available for the management of insect pests include: use of pathogens of insects, use of entomopathogenic nematodes that kill insects, release of sterile male insects to interfere with reproduction, release or promotion of parasites and predators, use of genetically modified crops that contain insect control genes such as *Bacillus thuringiensis*, and use of insect sex pheromones or other attractants. Diseases can be controlled through use of mycoherbicides, disease antagonists, allelopathy, and most importantly, resistant varieties. The control of weeds by a broad range of live and dead mulches can be very successful, as can the use of soil cover crops. There is a need for ecological studies on weeds, which have been neglected because of the widespread use of herbicides.

Potential New Energy Resources

Using currently available renewable energy techniques, such as biomass, hydroelectric power, solar energy, and wind power, an estimated 200 quads of renewable energy could be produced worldwide (Pimentel and Pimentel 1996). A self-sustaining renewable energy system producing 200 quads of energy per year for about two to three billion people would provide each person with 5,000 liters of oil equivalents per year (half of America's current consumption per year, but an increase for most people of the world). However, the use of up to 20 percent of global land area for energy production would decrease the amount of land directly available for food production. If more food is to be produced to support a large population, innovative and productive renewable energy technologies are needed, as well as development of those currently available. There is little doubt that the transition from fossil fuel dependency to full adoption of renewable energy technology will have many difficulties. Renewable energy technologies, which require considerable areas of land, will have to compete with agriculture, forestry, and urbanization for available land.

Growing human populations will demand increased electricity supplies and liquid fuels and renewable sources may need high investment costs. Additional complications to use of renewable energies are the relationship between ideal production sites and large population centers, since ideal locations for renewable energy production are remote. Hence, much more extensive networks of distribution lines would be needed (Weeks 1981).

A first priority is for individuals, communities, and industries to reduce consumption of fossil fuels to conserve these resources as long as possible. We hope that new, more efficient, renewable energy technologies may yet be developed, since basically, food production and many other needs depend on energy.

Management of Water Supplies and Irrigation

A critical issue is that in much of the world, drinking water is unsafe. More people die every year from drinking unsafe water than from all forms of violence, including war. More than one in five people on Earth (more than a billion) do not have access to safe drinking water. In Ethiopia, only 18 percent of the population has access to safe drinking water; in Sudan, 45 percent; in Pakistan, 56 percent; in Mexico, 72 percent; and 99 percent in the United States (WQHC 2001).

Currently surface and groundwater is often managed inefficiently and overtapped (Postel 1999). There are many ways of conserving water and increasing the efficiency of its use. These include increasing the capacity for water storage by dams, reservoirs, lakes, and so on; encouraging water development projects, particularly in neighboring countries; developing early warning systems of future water shortages; and by training farmers and professionals in hydrology principles and conservation technology. More efficient use of water by urban water utilities can release additional water for agriculture. There are also many techniques, such as drip irrigation, which can reduce water use for crops by as much as 50 percent. Although the total amount of water made available by the hydrologic cycle is currently adequate to provide the current world population with necessary water, the global regional distribution and intransigence between countries on sharing water creates major problems. The amount of available water is and will be a major constraint to increased food production unless international cooperation can be improved.

Decreases in Global Climatic Changes

It is clear that gaseous emissions are already causing significant changes in mean temperatures and warming and rising levels of the oceans. It seems likely on current evidence that climates will change in the long term. However, with concerted international cooperation the process can certainly be slowed down, although there are considerable doubts whether it can be reversed.

Clearly, there is an international will to implement reductions in gaseous emissions, as was demonstrated in the Kyoto protocol in 1989 and by recent meetings in South America, Amsterdam, and the Netherlands in 2001. However, for such reductions to be effective, the nations with the greatest contribution to emissions, such as United States, European nations, and Eastern European countries, must make significant decreases in their emissions. These are the countries, especially the United States, that seem most reluctant to implement new regulations, mainly from a fear of effects on their national economies.

Currently, developing countries, with the exception of India, make much smaller contributions to emissions, but as their living standards increase, so will their contributions to global gaseous emissions become greater. It is only by example from industrialized nations and by international cooperation that global climate change can be retarded. For instance, the United States is the leading emitter of gaseous emissions, releasing 23 percent of the global total of carbon emissions. The Eastern Bloc countries account for 14 percent of emissions, but their output of carbon emissions fell 32.5 percent between 1990 and 1998 (Brown et al. 1999).

In terms of decreasing carbon emissions, the trading of emissions between countries and clean development technologies have been focuses of climate talks since the Kyoto Protocol in 1989. However, to date, few of these measures or industrial constraints have been implemented. Major thrusts in carbon-decreasing strategies are essential if climate change is to be retarded or reduced to acceptable levels. Additionally, major international efforts are needed to slow the cutting down of tropical forests, which can absorb large quantities of carbon dioxide.

Carbon dioxide emissions from fossil fuel burning have not increased significantly over the last three years and have leveled out at about 6.3 billion tons per year. However, even at this level they still exceed the ability of the environment (soils and plants) to fix carbon and limit CO_2 emissions, and it seems likely that they will continue to increase in the long term.

Conclusions

It seems unlikely that the human population increases projected by the United Nations and others will actually be reached, due to insufficient food production and other factors. Population growth rates tend to fall into three stages. In developing societies, birth rates and death rates are both high with relatively low population growth. As countries industrialize, death rates begin to fall and a second stage is reached, when birth rates remain high, and population growth can be as high as 3 percent per annum. However, as further development continues, countries enter a third demographic stage when the birth rates and death rates balance at relatively low levels so that populations tend to stabilize. The European countries, Germany, Hungary, Sweden, and Italy and 32 other countries, have reached this stage (Brown et al. 1998). About 150 developing countries are still in stage two and 39, including China, are approaching stage three.

Countries with stable populations make less claims on agricultural production. This has happened in most of the countries in the European Union, which have high incomes and grain consumption per capita of about 470 kg per year. This means that European countries have basically stabilized their needs for agricultural production and natural resources. It is the developing countries where this has not occurred, and where major population problems exist. For instance, India, which has reached 1 billion people in 2000 (compared to 1.2 billion in China) is expected to add 600 million people to their population in the next 50 years compared with 300 million for China. Many African countries face a doubling or tripling of their populations in the next half century. Some Asian countries where stage three is close have populations that are multiplying more slowly. The inevitable conclusion is that if those countries that have the greatest rates of multiplication do not act to slow these down they will face falling living standards, which could drive them back to stage one. This may itself slow rates of multiplication.

Clearly if these governments do not face the population issue, their citizens face poor standards of living, increased disease, malnutrition, and starvation. Our thesis is that although populations may increase to as many as eight billion in the shorter term, populations will stabilize to numbers of two to three billion in the next 100 years, which represents global decreases in birth rates. This level could be maintained on a sustainable basis and with a reasonable standard of living for the global population. The alternatives are frightening, involving conflicts for scarce energy, water, or land resources. The challenge for governments is to do everything possible to reach stage three before time runs out. This would coincide with the lower prediction for populations of 7.7 billion by 2050 made by the United Nations and provide time for a sustainable population to resource ratio to be attained to the benefit of all humankind (Brown et al. 1998).

References

Alexandratos, N. 1995. *World Agriculture: Towards 2010*. Rome: Food and Agriculture Organization of the United Nations.

Bartlett, A. A. 1998. "Reflections on Sustainability, Population Growth, and the Environment Revisited." *Renewable Resources Journal* 15, no. 4: 6–23.

Bartlett, A. A., and R. A. Ristinen. 1995. "Breeding for Nutrition." *Journal of the Federation of American Scientists* 15, no. 4: 6–23.

BP. 1994. *British Petroleum Statistical Review of World Energy*. London: British Petroleum Corporate Communications Services.

Brown, L. R. 1995. *Who Will Feed China? Wake-Up Call for a Small Planet*. New York: W. S. Norton and Co.

Brown, L. R. 1997. *The Agricultural Link*. Washington, D.C.: World Watch Institute.

Brown, L. R., G. Gardner, and B. Halwell. 1998. *Beyond Malthus: Sixteen Dimensions of the Population Problem*. Washington, D.C.: World Watch Institute, Paper No. 43: 89.

Brown, L. R., M. Reimer, and B. Halwell. 1999. "Carbon Emissions Dip." Pp. 60–61 in *Vital Signs for 1999*. Washington, D.C.: World Watch Institute.

Buringh, P. 1989. "Availability of Agricultural Land for Crop and Livestock Production." Pp. 69–83 in *Food and Natural Resources*, edited by D. Pimentel and C. W. Hall. San Diego: Academic Press.

Campbell, C. J. 1997. *The Coming Oil Crisis*. New York: Multi-Science Publishing Company & Petroconsultants S.A.

Covich, A. P. 1993. "Water and Ecosystems." Pp. 40–55 in *Water in Crisis*, edited by P. H. Gleick. New York: Oxford University Press.

Crabbé, P., A. Hølland, L. Ryskowski, and L. Westra. 2000. *Implementing Ecological Integrity: Restoring Regional and Global Environmental and Human Health*. NATO Sciences Series IV: Earth and Environmental Sciences, vol. I. Netherlands: Kluwer.

Doeoes, B. R. 1994. "Environmental Degradation, Global Food Production, and Risk for Larger-Scale Migration." *Ambio* 23, no. 2: 124–30.

Duncan, R. C. 1997. "The World Petroleum Life-Cycle: Encircling the Production Peak." *Space Studies Institute* (May 9): 1–8.

Edwards, C. A., and D. Pimentel. 2000. "Global Aspects of Agricultural Sustainability." Pp. 280–90 in *The Future of the Universe and the Future of Our Civilization,* edited by V. Burdyuzha and G. Khozin. Singapore, New Jersey, London: World Scientific.

Elwell, H. A. 1985. "An Assessment of Soil Erosion in Zimbabwe." *Zimbabwe Science News* 19: 27–31.

FAO. 1991. *Food Balance Sheets*. Rome: Food and Agriculture Organization of the United Nations.

FAO. 1992a. *Food and Nutrition: Creating a Well-Fed World.* Rome: Food and Agriculture Organization of the United Nations.

FAO. 1992b. *Nutrition: The Global Challenge*. Rome: FAO Sponsored International Conference on Nutrition.

Flesher, J. 2001. *Supplies of Fresh Water in Trouble Report Says*. A.P.

Gardner, G. 1997. *Recycling Organic Waste: From Urban Pollutant to Farm Resource, World Watch Paper no. 135*. Washington, D.C.: World Watch Institute.

Giampietro, M., and D. Pimentel. 1994. "Energy Utilization." Pp. 73–76 in *Encyclopedia of Agricultural Science*, edited by C. J. Arntzen and E. M. Ritter. San Diego: Academic Press.

Gleick, P. H. 1993. *Water in Crisis*. New York: Oxford University Press.

Hinrichsen, D. 1998. "Feeding a Future World." *People and the Planet* 7: 6–9.

Ivanhoe, L. F. 1995. "Future World Oil Supplies: There Is a Finite Limit." *World Oil* (October): 77–88.

Kapitza, S. P. 2000. "Global Population Growth and the Future of Humankind." Pp. 227–48 in *The Future of the Universe and Our Civilization,* edited by V. Burdyuzha and G. Khozin. London: World Scientific.

Lal, R. 1989. "Land Degradation and Its Impact on Food and Other Resources." Pp. 85–140 in *Food and Natural Resources*, edited by D. Pimentel. San Diego: Academic Press.

Leach, G. 1995. *Global Land and Food in the 21st Century*. Stockholm: International Institute for Environmental Technology and Management.

Maberly, G. F. 1994. "Iodine Deficiency Disorders: Contemporary Scientific Issues." *Journal of Nutrition* 124: 1473–78.

Malthus, Thomas R. 1798. *An Essay on the Principle of Population.* 2 vols. London: J. M. Dent.

McMichael, A. J. 1993. *Planetary Overload: Global Environmental Change and Human Health*. Cambridge: Cambridge University Press.

Nesheim, M. C. 1993. "Human Nutrition Needs and Parasitic Infections," in *Parasitology: Human Nutrition and Parasitic Infection*, edited by D. W. T. Crompton. Cambridge: Cambridge University Press.

OTA. 1982. *Impacts of Technology on U.S. Cropland and Rangeland Productivity*. Washington, D.C.: Office of Technology. U.S. Congress.

Parry, M. 1990. *Climate Change and World Agriculture.* London: Earthscan.

Pimentel, D., and H. Lehman, eds. 1993. *The Pesticide Question: Environment, Economics, and Ethics.* London: Chapman and Hall.

Pimentel, D., and C. A. Edwards. 2000. "Agriculture, Food, Populations, Natural Resources, and Ecological Integrity." Pp. 377–98 in *Implementing Ecological Integrity,* edited by D. Crabbé, A. Hølland, L. Ryszkowski, and L. Westra. Netherlands: Kluwer.

Pimentel, D., C. Harvey, P. Resosudarmo, K. Sinclair, D. Kurz, M. McNair, S. Crist, L. Shpritz, L. Fitton, R. Saffouri, and R. Blair. 1995. "Environmental and Economic Costs of Soil Erosion and Conservation Benefits." *Science* 267: 1117–23.

Pimentel, D., and M. Pimentel. 1996. *Food, Energy and Society*. Boulder, Colo.: Colorado University Press.

Pimentel, D., J. Houser, E. Preiss, O. White, H. Fang, L. Mesnick, T. Barsky, S. Tariche, J. Schreck, and S. Alpert. 1997a. "Water Resources: Agriculture, the Environment, and Society." *Bioscience* 47, no. 2: 97–106.

Pimentel, D., X. Huang, A. Cardova, and M. Pimentel. 1997b. "Impact of Population Growth on Food Supplies and Environment." *Population and Environment* 19, no. 1: 9–14.

Pimentel, D., X. Huang, A. Cardova, and M. Pimentel. 1998. "Impact of a Growing Population on Natural Resources: The Challenge for Environmental Management." Pp. 6–21 in *Environmental Management in Practice*, edited by B. Nath, L. Hens, P. Compton, and D. Devuyst. London: Routledge.

Postel, S. 1994. "Carrying Capacity: Earth's Bottom Line." Pp. 3–21 in *State of the World 1994*. Washington, D.C.: World Watch Institute.

Postel, S. 1997. *Last Oasis: Facing Water Scarcity*. New York: W.W. Norton.

Postel, S. 1999. *Pillar of Sand: Can the Irrigation Miracle Last*. Washington, D.C.: World Watch Institute.

PRB. 1996. *World Population Data Sheet*. Washington, D.C.: Population Bureau.

PRB. 1998. *World Population Data Sheet*. Washington, D.C.: Population Bureau.

Troeh, F. R., J. A. Hobbs, and R. L. Donahue. 1991. *Soil and Water Conservation*. 2nd Ed. Englewood Cliffs, NJ: Prentice Hall.

Troeh, F. R., and L. M. Thompson. 1993. *Soils and Soil Fertility*. New York: Oxford University Press.

U.S. Congressional Record. 1997. "U.S. Foreign Oil Consumption for the Week Ending October 3." *Congressional Record (Senate)* (October): 143.

US DOE. 1991. *Annual Energy Outlook with Projections to 2010*. Washington, D.C.: Energy Information Administration.

US DOE. 1995a. *Annual Energy Outlook with Projections to 2010*. Washington, D.C.: Energy Information Administration.

US DOE. 1995b. *International Energy Annual 1993*. Washington, D.C.: Energy Information Administration.

USWRC. 1979. "The Nation's Water Resources. 1975–2000." *Second National Annual Water Assessment*. Washington, D.C.: U.S. Water Resources Council, Vol 1–4.

Weeks, W. L. 1981. *Transmission and Distribution of Electrical Energy*. New York: Harper and Row.

Wen, D., and D. Pimentel. 1992. "Ecological Resource Management to Achieve a Productive, Sustainable Agricultural System in Northeast China." *Ecosystems and Environment*. 4: 215–30.

WHO. 1992. *Our Planet, Our Health: Report of the WHO Commission on Health and Environment*. Geneva: World Health Organization.

WHO. 1995. *Bridging the Gaps*. Geneva: World Health Organization.

WHO. 1996. *Micronutrient Nutrition: Half the World's Population Affected*. World Health Organization. 78(Nov 13): 1–4.

(WQHC). 2001. Water Quality and Health Council. "Water Is Unsafe in Much of the World." *USA Today*. (May 17).

WRI. 1994. *World Resources 1994–95*. Washington, D.C.: World Resources Institute.

Youngquist, W. 1997. *Geodestinies: The Inevitable Control of Earth Resources over Nations and Individuals*. Portland, Ore.: National Book Company.

Chapter 12

Impacts of Milk and Meat on People and the Planet

Robert Goodland

Introduction

The Earth Charter holds that all living beings, including animals, should be treated with respect and consideration (Earth Charter 2002). The Charter also recognizes that all beings are interdependent. We will see in this chapter that when human beings mass produce animals for the mass consumption of the animals' milk and meat—which sooner or later involves a lack of respect and consideration for the animals—humans will ultimately suffer. We will suffer from unnecessary disease, pain and suffering, and premature mortality; and the ecology of our planet will suffer too.

The poor in developing countries spend up to 80 percent of their incomes on food, yet are often malnourished because of inadequate access to food. Malnutrition also occurs in the Western diet, due to the excess of some harmful nutrients and the deficiency of some essential nutrients. Although an evolving concept, the prototypical "Western" diet presently includes significant amounts of meat and dairy; low intake of unrefined grains, vegetables, and fruits; and high intake of fats, sugars, and processed foods. The world has reached an historic turning point. For the first time the number of malnourished worldwide who are overweight (1.1 billion) equals the number who are underweight.

The main interest of this chapter's author is not to persuade readers to eschew the consumption of animal products. While that may be one result among some readers who were not previously aware of the facts presented here, our main interest is to persuade individuals and agencies presently engaged in promoting the spread of large-scale livestock and dairy production to developing countries to cease such promotion—for health, equity, and environmental reasons.

The general case against large-scale animal production and consumption is well known (Durning and Brough 1991; Goodland 1997, 1998a, 1998b; Goodland and Pimentel 2000). However, that case has not included a specific focus on dairy production and consumption. Therefore, this chapter begins with a summary of the case against livestock production generally, and then focuses on the particular case of dairy.

Livestock Production

Demand for meat in developing countries has been increasing dramatically (Gill 1999). The International Food Policy Research Institute (IFPRI) asserts that a "Livestock Revolution" is now taking place, and projects that by the year 2020, developing countries will consume 100 million metric tons more meat and 223 million metric tons more milk than they did in 1993, dwarfing developed-country increases of 18 million metric tons for both meat and milk (IFPRI 1999).

The demand for these products in developing countries is generated largely by urban, affluent people, or people well along the road to affluence. These products are widely understood not to be part of the package of products consumed in order to meet the basic needs of the urban or rural poor. With rapid population growth, there is a strong tendency for the number of poor to rise; the number of people worldwide living on less than one dollar a day has increased to nearly 1.5 billion. About 800 million people, including 200 million children under the age of five, are malnourished today, in terms of insufficient caloric consumption. It is estimated that in the year 2020, 150 million of these children may remain malnourished (Pinstrup-Andersen et al. 1997).

Most malnutrition among the poor arises from inequitable food access, rather than inadequate food production. Livestock products in developing countries are produced at prices too high for the poor to be able to afford, except in rare cases (e.g., when produced in a pastoral setting). In developing countries, most poor people who are properly fed eat very little or no livestock products, yet their diets—composed of grains, legumes, fruits, vegetables, and other plant products—meet all nutritional requirements. Far more poor people can eat such a diet for the same cost as the number who can eat a diet that includes increased amounts of livestock products. Further, producing livestock and feed, especially on a large scale, is capital intensive rather than labor intensive, whereas the production of legumes, fruits, vegetables, and other plants is usually more labor intensive, thus providing more income for the poor.

Environmental Impacts

In some categories of environmental damage, livestock production now constitutes the largest source of adverse impacts, with the impacts continuing to increase in magnitude. The main categories of environmental damage caused by livestock are (Goodland et al. 1984; Steinfeld et al. 1997; Goodland and Pimentel 2000):

- Deforestation and loss of biodiversity as tropical forests and other relatively intact ecosystems and habitats are converted to cattle ranches, and as arable lands are converted to cattle pasture.
- Overgrazing, accelerated soil erosion, loss of topsoil, soil compaction, decreased percolation rates of rain into soils, depleting water tables, and desertification.
- Feedlot runoff, eutrophication, pollution of rivers and coastal waters (red tides), decrease in fish and other aquatic harvests, and diminished availability of unpolluted water.
- Slaughterhouse and meatpacking factory water use, effluent disposal, and the pollution of soil and air.
- Greenhouse gas production, the use of fossil fuel and other scarce resources for the production, transport and export, processing, waste disposal, and packaging of livestock products.

Public Health Impacts

In the area of nutrition and public health, an epidemiological transition is occurring, whereby the number of people of developing countries afflicted by infectious diseases is being overtaken by the number afflicted by noncommunicable diseases—of which chronic degenerative diseases are the most significant subset (WHO 1996). By 2020, noncommunicable diseases will account for 57 percent of all disability and 70 percent of all deaths in demographically developing countries. Public health specialists are especially concerned about increases in chronic degenerative diseases because the cost of treating each case is, on average, significantly higher than the cost of treating an infectious disease. Therefore, chronic degenerative diseases pose a significant threat to poverty alleviation and to the overall economic development of developing countries.

In a review of epidemiological literature performed for the World Bank, it was found that "higher red meat [defined as beef, pork, and lamb] consumption probably increases risk of coronary heart disease, colon cancer, and prostate cancer, and possibly breast cancer"—all of which are chronic degenerative diseases (Hu and Willett 1998). The China-Oxford-Cornell Diet and Health Project (the world's most comprehensive project ever to study diet and disease) found a strong correlation between a measurable increase in chronic degenerative diseases in China and a relatively small increase in the consumption of livestock products among people who previously had eaten little or none of such products (Chen et al. 1990).

It appears that childhood growth rates and attained adult heights, often considerably lower in developing countries than in developed countries, are best improved by the control of childhood infectious and parasitic diseases, known to cause permanent stunting, rather than by adding livestock products to diets in those countries (Campbell 1997). Studies carried out during the 1980s in 65 counties in China showed that the attained heights of adults were strongly associated with the intake of foods containing plant protein (i.e., plant-based foods), rather than livestock products. From 1950 to 1980, infant mortality in China was reduced by about 80 percent, while childhood growth rates were increasing as rapidly as those observed in Japan during the same period (Piazza 1986). This occurred while diets in China contained, on average, only 3–6 percent of total caloric intake in the form of livestock products. In 1995, the U.S. Department of Agriculture's dietary guidelines stated, for the first time, that livestock products are *not* needed for human nutrition, and that all nutritional requirements can be met from nonlivestock sources, including requirements for protein, Vitamin B_{12}, and iron.

Dairy as a Subset of Animal Products

It is difficult to disaggregate the case against the consumption of animal products from that specifically against dairy. Not enough people have been monitored who consume dairy but not meat, partly because there are relatively few such people. Nevertheless, in the literature, there is a substantial number of studies that do disaggregrate the effects of dairy from those of meat. It turns out that the effects are similar, but with some notable differences, which are outlined below.

Dairy is an animal food, with a nutritional profile similar to that of meat. It has similar amounts of saturated fat and protein as meat. Like meat, dairy completely lacks the fiber and hundreds of phytochemicals that are contained in plant-based foods and that have been found to be protective against degenerative diseases such as coronary heart disease and cancers.

Dairy Production

The environmental impacts of large-scale dairy production generally fall into the categories outlined under "Livestock Production" above. However, there are some impacts that are particular to dairy. The ruminant's extraordinary ability to digest cellulose can be valuable. When dairy cattle are not fed, but rather scavenge for most or all of their food—as in much of India, their impact is lower. In such cases, if cattle recycle what would otherwise not be used, they often have much lower impact, while providing manure that can reduce soil depletion and provide fuel. However, these cattle produce very little milk. In addition, recent evidence suggests that India's dairy herd is exacerbating India's forest loss.

Cattle grazing on natural range produce little milk, and none prior to weaning, albeit possibly more than scavenging cattle. Range cattle are not useful for milking commercially, in part because they are distant from markets for dairy products, although they may supply their herders' families with dairy products, and occasionally adjacent villages. Range cattle usually do not provide attractive opportunities for dairy investments for international development assistance.

The poor in developing countries may, under certain conditions, consume insufficient amounts of fat, so small amounts of fat in limited whole-milk consumption can be beneficial to lactose-tolerant people. As this is a poor choice of fats, this should be an exception only. Small-scale projects promoting the family milch cow, mainly for domestic consumption, thus might be exceptions that could be financed. Selling small amounts of milk from the family cow can generate a small revenue stream that is important to the poor. Development assistance can boost fat or oil consumption for the poor in developing countries at lower financial, social, and environmental cost—and at lower risk—by investments in plant-based oil production, such as soy and corn oil. The use of the family cow for plowing or traction, and the use of its manure for fertilizer, can be useful niche roles. The widespread use of manure for fuel accelerates agricultural and environmental decline.

Dairy Consumption

Nutritional Value

Fat

Adequate amounts of dietary fat are essential for health. The minimum intake consistent with health varies throughout a person's life and among individuals. Adequate intake of dietary fat is particularly important prior to and during pregnancy and lactation. The FAO has recommended that for most adults, dietary fat should supply at least 15 percent of their energy intake (FAO 1993). This amounts to 34g in a diet of 2000 calories per day, which is the recommended daily amount for an average person weighing 150 pounds or 68 kg. The USDA recommends that no more than 30 percent of an adult's calories come from fat, which amounts to 67g in a diet of 2000 calories per day (USDA 2001). The U.S. National Institutes of Health recently lowered the limit of calories to come from saturated fat from 10 percent to 7 percent, which amounts to 16g in a diet of 2000 calories per day (NIH 2001).

Milk is about 87 percent water. Of the solids fraction, about 50 percent of milk's calories come from fat. One cup of whole cow's milk contains about 8g of fat. Around two-thirds of the fat in whole cow's milk is saturated. This means that just one cup of whole cow's milk contains about 5g of saturated fat, or fully one-third of the NIH-recommended limit of daily saturated fat. "Lowfat" milk is not really low fat. It contains from 24 percent to 33 percent of its calories as fat, or 4–6g per cup. (The "2 percent" figure is misleading as it refers to weight, but milk is mainly water.) One cup of "1 percent" milk contains 2–3g of fat, and skim milk about half that. "Nonfat" milk contains 0.4g of fat per cup.

The fat content of most cheeses varies from 7 to 10g per standard serving, and rises to 15g in some varieties. More than half of the fat in most cheeses is saturated. "Lowfat" cheese contains 2–4g of fat per serving. Most cheeses provide 40–70 percent of calories from fat—though in some, the figure is up to 90 percent—of which most is saturated. Butter's calories are 100 percent from fat, which is high in both cholesterol and saturated fat. The USDA's latest dietary guidelines recommend low- and nonfat dairy products (USDA 2001)—but reduced-fat dairy products (e.g., skim milk) are generally not available in poor developing nations.

Protein

Under the Western diet, the average person consumes about double the protein her or his body needs. The Recommended Dietary Allowance (RDA) for protein for the average adult is 8 percent of caloric consumption, or 40g per day in a diet of 2000 calories per day (Muñoz de Chavez and Chavez 1999). Estimates of the minimum required are as low as 4–5 percent, or 20–25g per day in a diet of 2000 calories per day. Protein needs are increased for women who are pregnant or breastfeeding, and for especially active people.

Whole cow's milk contains about 3g of protein per cup. While that is not a large portion of the RDA of protein for an adult, people who consume substantial amounts of dairy are usually consuming a Western diet, which on average includes 15 percent of calories in the form of protein, which is excessive and contributes to the development of coronary heart disease, cancers, and osteoporosis (Barnard et al. 1995). For infants, a diet of cow's milk is unnaturally high in protein, as it contains three times as much protein as breast milk.

The protein of cow's milk is approximately 85 percent casein and 15 percent whey protein (lactalbumin and lactoglobulin). Milk protein is implicated in some cases of diabetes, allergies, migraines, and arthritis (Barnard et al. 1995). Casein has been shown to enhance tumor growth in experimental animals (Youngman and Campbell 1992), and has been shown to increase blood cholesterol levels in experimental animals in many studies (Terpstra et al. 1983). Dairy protein is said to be more effective than saturated fat in enhancing cancers and increasing blood cholesterol (Campbell 2001).

Protein deficiency was thought to be a grave problem worldwide until fairly recently. There are still some pockets of protein deficiency in developing countries, but the cause of it is really inadequate caloric intake. If sufficient calories are consumed, it is almost impossible not to consume enough protein. Even potatoes contain 11 percent of calories in the form of protein, so a person would consume sufficient protein if they ate only potatoes, as long as the amount of potatoes were enough to supply the amount of calories needed. Therefore, assuring sufficient caloric intake, rather than focusing on protein deficiency, should be a priority for development agencies. Because dairy is a relatively expensive way to provide calories, it would not be an efficient investment by development agencies as a means of assuring sufficient caloric intake, and therefore sufficient protein intake. The best solution will vary from place to place, but will generally hinge on legumes and grains. Leafy vegetables, too, are useful sources of protein (2–5 g/serving), without the risks associated with dairy protein.

Vitamins

Vitamin A deficiency is a problem in some developing countries. About 250 million children under five are affected by subclinical deficiency. Vitamin A is required to survive measles, but stores are depleted by chronic diarrhea. Vitamin A deficiency also causes 500,000 new cases of corneal lesions each year. This nutritional component is difficult to acquire from dairy without also ingesting much animal fat. Vitamin A needs are met more healthfully from the carotenoids common in vegetables such as carrots, squash, sweet potato, and tomato. Many carotenoids, such as beta-carotene and lycopene, are antioxidants, which inhibit the oxidation of lipoproteins, thus reducing the risk of heart disease.

Dairy products are relatively rich in riboflavin (vitamin B_2, 0.18mg/100g whole cow's milk). But riboflavin is easily available at low risk from soybeans, green leafy vegetables, and especially sea vegetables. Riboflavin deficiency is rare worldwide, except in the institutionalized elderly.

Only microorganisms—bacteria, fungi, and algae—synthesize Vitamin B_{12}; other plants and animals cannot produce any B_{12}, although plant roots can readily absorb generous levels of B_{12} when grown in organically healthy soils. B_{12} is ingested in animal products if the animal eats foods containing $B_{12,}$ and in plant products contaminated with B_{12}-producing bacteria. Human gut bacteria produce much B_{12}, although it is not clear how much is absorbed. WHO recommends 1.0 µg daily. Because so little B_{12} is needed, B_{12} deficiency due to inadequate intake is rare; 95 percent of today's B_{12} deficiency worldwide occurs in individuals unable to absorb it, typically in old age. Those who do not consume any animal products need to be especially careful to obtain adequate B_{12}. However, one tablespoon of yeast provides 4 µg, while a cup of milk contains 0.9 µg. B_{12} supplements and folate fortification are becoming more available in developing countries.

As vitamin D is manufactured less by dark-skinned people, they need more sun than do light-skinned people. Rickets, a disease associated with Vitamin D deficiency, is now rare except in some highly polluted northern cities where children do not get enough ultraviolet light for their bodies to manufacture enough vitamin D. Many commercial cereals are rich sources. Most of the vitamin D in milk comes from fortifying the milk; soymilk and ricemilk are often fortified too.

Calcium

The science of calcium nutrition is controversial. The USDA's recommended daily allowance (RDA) of 800 milligrams is almost twice that of the WHO's RDA. A curious fact is that bone fractures are highest where animal protein (e.g., milk) intake is highest. Milk, cheese, and yogurt contain relatively rich levels of calcium (119mg/100g in whole cow's milk), yet substantial milk consumption does not seem to reduce bone fracture rates significantly. The Harvard Nurses' Health Study, which followed 75,000 women for 12 years, showed no protective effect of increased milk consumption on fracture risk. In fact, increased intake of dairy calcium was associated with higher fracture risk (Fescanich et al. 1996). This was subsequently corroborated in an Australian study (Cumming and Klineberg 1994). The reason is that most dairy calcium neutralizes the acidity caused by milk and other animal protein (Fescanich et al. 1996). When protein (especially animal protein) metabolizes to acidic products, calcium is needed for buffering. This renders such calcium unavailable for nutrition.

Do milk and dairy consumption tend to weaken bones or to strengthen them? The global problem of osteoporosis suggests answers to this controversy. Calcium in milk may not be as helpful against osteoporosis as calcium in a more available form. Osteoporosis is complicated by the fact that dairy calcium intake and hip fracture rates are directly correlated. A further complication is that calcium may be assimilated only in the presence of magnesium, which is very low in cow's milk. There seems to be no protective effect of dairy calcium on bone (Huang et al. 1999; Cumming and Klineberg 1994).

Exercising more, and reducing animal protein and sodium intakes, reduce calcium loss. Green vegetables are rich in calcium and magnesium in the proportion that enable both to be assimilated. Calcium is obtainable at much lower risk from broccoli, kale and other green leafy vegetables, and especially tofu, than from dairy products. Development assistance can help more people at lower cost by promoting plant foods high in assimilable calcium, and investing in calcium fortification of staples.

A recent study financed by the dairy industry claims that drinking three 8–oz servings of milk a day could improve older adults' skeletal health (Heaney et al. 1999). Nearly half of the 132 women in the milk-drinking group of the study were on conventional menopause therapy to prevent bone loss by taking steroid hormones. But only 31 percent of the control group women—those not drinking milk—were on steroid therapy, so the whole study is questionable (Cohen 1999).

Milk and Children

Traditional maternal nutrition is exceptionally important and influences health throughout their offspring's life. It is possible—but not at all advisable—for newborns to survive on formula. Exclusive breast-feeding for six months or more, followed with complementary feeding to 24 months or more, is the widely recommended start for a healthy life. Breast-feeding is associated with significantly higher scores for cognitive development than is formula-feeding (Anderson et al. 1999; Uauy et al. 1999), although formula-fed and breast-fed infants do not always diverge reliably. Fetal and infant wellness carries throughout adult life.

All infants possess lactase, but it decreases rapidly following infancy in most humans except Caucasians, as they maintain their adaptability to milk with routine consumption. Cow's milk is not necessary for growing healthy children. Today, most children in the world thrive without consuming a drop of cow's milk. Any child can thrive without cow's milk. On the other hand, there is growing evidence that milk can do more harm than good. The American Academy of Pediatrics discourages giving cow's milk to a human baby before its first birthday, because a diet of cow's milk is the leading cause of iron-deficiency anemia in infants (cow's milk is low in iron). Cow's milk may displace human milk, and may contribute to type-1 diabetes in children. Humanitarian aid supplying infant formula causes dependency, and forces families to buy cow's milk when aid infant formula supplies and breast-milk dry up.

Milk allergies are common in children, causing sinusitis, diarrhea, constipation, and fatigue. Cow's milk proteins are the first foreign proteins entering the infant gut, since most infant formulas are cow milk based. Milk allergies are related to chronic ear infections, to behavioral problems, and to childhood asthma. Soymilk and ricemilk cause far fewer problems.

Cow's milk combined with other foods can nourish lactose-tolerant children for a few years. This is useful if breast-feeding is felt to be inadvisable for infants with HIV positive mothers, although some evidence questions this (Coutsoudis 1999; UNICEF 2001).

Milk and Menarche

Dairy consumption appears to accelerate menarche. OECD girls' menarche has fallen from 16.5 years in 1840, to 13 years in 1995, and to 11–12 years today. In Japan, it appears that dairy has helped accelerate menarche from 15.2 years in 1950 to 12.2 years in 1975. Early age at menarche is one of the few established early life predictors of breast cancer risk. In cases of early menarche, changes in diet from animal- to plant-based may reduce breast cancer risks later in life. Late menarche is associated with decreased breast cancer rates later in life, decreased coronary heart disease, fewer teen pregnancies, and later first pregnancy (Rees 1995).

Diseases Correlated with Dairy

Heart Disease

Coronary heart disease (CHD) is the most important public health issue in most OECD nations because of its incidence, cost of treatment, and mortality. It is the leading cause of death in the United States, and is rapidly intensifying in many developing countries. Of the emerging public health priorities in developing countries with enormous long-term consequences, CHD is at or near the top. There is general agreement that the consumption of meat increases the risks of CHD.

Of the dairy risks, part stems from the high levels of saturated fats in most dairy products. The other dairy risk factor contributing to CHD is milk protein. While it is difficult to disaggregate dairy from Western diet epidemiology, the correlations of dairy with CHD appear to be strong warnings. Myocardial infarction patients have elevated levels of antibodies to milk protein compared with healthy people (Davies 1980). Dairy consumption has been correlated positively with blood cholesterol, as well as with coronary mortality (Law and Wald 1994). The contributions of saturated fat and cholesterol (contained in high levels in dairy products) to CHD risk are inescapable. Milk consumption correlates positively with coronary mortality rates in 43 countries, and with myocardial infarction in 19 regions of Europe (Segall 1977, 1994). A synthesis of 428 peer-reviewed scientific papers concluded that milk drinking is a health hazard, "even a threat of death" in later years (Gordon 1999).

Most of the world has become urban and more sedentary than fifty years ago, when the world was primarily rural and active. Because of this change in activity, milk for adults poses an even greater health risk. CHD is not an inevitable consequence of diets high in dairy; other dietary factors (such as antioxidants and omega-3 fatty acids), physical activity, and other factors can lower CHD risk. However, WHO data have shown mortality to be most closely correlated with dairy consumption, second with animal protein, third with animal fat, and fourth with sugar (Seely 1981). For coronary heart disease, liquid cow's milk itself seems to be the main risk of dairy consumption. CHD risk seems to be somewhat reduced in cheese consumption.

Breast Cancer

Breast cancer is the most common cause of cancer death in women, and the third most common cancer overall. The incidence of breast cancer is increasing worldwide; about one million new cases are diagnosed annually. Only half of all diagnosed cases survive more than five years, even with appropriate treatment. Breast cancer is presently much less common in developing countries than in developed countries.

Correlations between breast cancer incidence and dairy consumption are stark (Outwater et al. 1997). There is a significant correlation between breast cancer mortality and milk consumption (R=.55, p=.001). This supports the hypothesis that estrogens and the insulin-like growth factor (IGF-I) in cow's milk stimulate breast cancer. It has also been shown that milk produced with recombinant bovine growth hormone (rBGH), now commonly used in a number of countries, raises IGF-1 levels in human blood (Heaney 1999). This is consistent with other bone mineral acquisition findings (Cadogan et al. 1997). Soy consumption reduces the incidence of breast cancer (Potter 1998).

Carcinogens in Milk

In cancer research, pinpointing a singular mechanism that triggers tumor growth is invariably an elusive quest. Each cell where cancer may develop passes through several precancerous stages; some may have mechanisms in common and yet have other pathways peculiar to one bodily organ—lymph nodes, say, or brain cells. There are likely many mechanisms. In the case of breast cancer, milk protein may be a major factor (as described in the section on protein above). Another major factor may be fat. Milk fat acts as a sink for a wide range of environmental pollutants that contaminate range, pastures, forage, and all other sources of cattle feed. Contaminants include carcinogenic biocides, industrial chemicals, and airborne pollutants such as from coal-fired power plants, or from aerial and other crop spraying (Epstein 1998a, b). Some breast and prostate cancers are linked to the insulin-like growth factor (IGF-1) in cow's milk (Chan et al 1998).

Inequitability of Dairy Products

The oldest major civilization, the Chinese, did not produce or consume any dairy until very recently, partly because of their widespread lactose intolerance. Even now, in China, dairy is consumed mainly in the north. In developing countries generally, the main groups who consume dairy products are rich elites and expatriate Caucasians. In many developing countries, most people are lactose intolerant. Dairy consumption by lactose-intolerant people can cause total incapacitation, extreme discomfort, or gastrointestinal problems including cramps and diarrhea. Most minorities and some of the majorities become lactase deficient in adulthood

Policymakers in the United States are slowly recognizing lactose intolerance. For example, in September 1999, a U.S. Senator called for alternatives to cow's milk in schools because 95 percent of Asian Americans, 56 percent of African Americans, and 50 percent of Hispanic Americans are lactose intolerant. The USDA's Dietary Guidelines, which U.S. federal nutrition programs use for nutritional guidance, still recommend two to three daily servings of dairy products (even though they could by themselves far exceed the NIH-recommended limit of saturated fat consumption). As most U.S. individuals with African,

Asian, Hispanic and Native American backgrounds are lactose intolerant, the Dietary Guidelines and nutrition programs are inconsistent with those individuals' needs, hence are racially biased (Bertron et al. 1999a,b).

Conclusion

The growing demand for milk and meat, especially strong in developing countries, is engendering an inevitable change in the systems in which livestock are raised, from small-scale and integrated mixed farming systems, to large-scale and vertically integrated systems. This is now spreading to developing countries, with the result that the livestock sector has become more environmentally destructive worldwide than any other sector. This is also troublesome in light of the Earth Charter, as animals raised on a large scale are generally treated with less respect and consideration than those raised on a small scale (Warrick 2001).

The impacts of large-scale milk and meat production that are arguably the most directly important to humans are the public health impacts. Diets that include milk and meat are positively correlated with degenerative diseases that are very expensive to treat and cause high levels of mortality.

The precautionary principle is essential in public health. Developing countries will benefit greatly if they are able to forego the Western experience of very expensive morbidity and mortality associated with Western diets. The diet designed to prevent cancer is strikingly similar to the diet designed to prevent CHD—and it resembles the traditional diet eaten in most developing countries. ("Traditional diet" is here used to mean a diet that is mainly plant based, rich in grains, legumes, vegetables, and fruit, with little or no animal product.) Prevention works, especially if adopted from the start. However, for those who have started down the road to a Western diet, research shows that reverting from the Western diet to a traditional diet actually reverses degenerative diseases such as CHD.

Today's burgeoning demand for milk and meat in developing countries is not inevitable; demand follows advertisements, emulation, and subsidies. Education helps reverse such trends. It is clear that animal-based foods contain no essential nutrients that are not better contained in plant-based foods. Most children in the world thrive without consuming dairy products. There are many less costly and healthier alternatives to milk and meat. Soy product labels, such as soymilk, are now permitted by the U.S. Food and Drug Administration to state that soy can reduce heart disease. In addition, soy inhibits blood-clotting mechanisms, maintains bone calcium levels with potentially beneficial effects in the prevention of osteoporosis, prevents menopausal symptoms, and reduces the incidence of breast cancer (Geissler 1999).

The bottom line is: Can developing countries withstand the perilous lure of the Western diet? Or can the Western diet change, to become more like the traditional diet of most developing countries? The challenge is for developing countries to reaffirm their own traditional diets—while the challenge for developed countries is to learn from developing ones.

Acknowledgments

The following people helped generously with drafts of this chapter: Jeff Anhang, Neal Barnard, T. Colin Campbell, Samuel S. Epstein, David Gordon, and William Harris.

References

Anderson, James W. et al. 1999. "Breast Feeding and Cognitive Development: A Meta-Analysis." *American Journal of Clinical Nutrition* 70, no. 4: 525–35.

Barnard, N. D., A. Nicholson, and J. L. Howard, J.L. 1995. "The Medical Costs Attributable to Meat Consumption." *Preventive Medicine* 24: 646–55.

Bertron, P., Neal Barnard, and Milton Mills. 1999a. "Racial Bias in Federal Nutrition Policy, Part I: The Public Health Implications of Variations in Lactase Persistence." *Journal of the National Medical Association* 91, no. 3: 151–57.

Bertron, P., Neal Barnard, and Milton Mills. 1999b. "Racial Bias in Federal Nutrition Policy, Part II: Weak Guidelines Take a Disproportional Toll." *Journal of the National Medical Association* 91, no. 4: 201–8.

Cadogan, Joanna, Richard Eastell, Nicola Jones, and Margo E. Baker. 1997. "Milk Intake and Bone Mineral Acquisition in Adolescent Girls: Randomized, Controlled Intervention Trial." *British Medical Journal* 315, no. 7118: 1255.

Campbell, C. 2001. Personal communication.

Campbell, T. Colin. 1997. "Associations of Diet and Disease: A Comprehensive Study of Health Characteristics in China." Paper presented at the conference on "Social Consequences of Chinese Economic Reform" at the Fairbank Center on East Asian Studies, Harvard University, Cambridge, Mass. May 23–24.

Chan, J. M., M. J. Stampfer, and E. Giovanucci. 1998. "Plasma Insulin-Like Growth Factor-1 and Prostate Cancer Risk." *Science* 279: 553–61.

Chen, Junshi, T. Colin Campbell, J. Li, and Richard Peto. 1990. *Diet, Lifestyle and Mortality in China: A Study of the Characteristics of 65 Chinese Counties*. Oxford: Oxford University Press; Ithaca: Cornell University Press; Beijing: People's Medical Publishing House.

Cohen, Robert. 1999. "The Dairy Industry Self-Destructs." October 3, 1999. <www.notmilk.com/deb/100399.html> (20 May 2001).

Coutsoudis, Anna, et al. 1999. "Influence of Infant-Feeding Patterns on Early Mother-to-Child Transmission of HIV-1 in Durban, South Africa: A Prospective Cohort Study." *Lancet* 354: 471–76.

Cumming, R. G. and R. J. Klineberg. 1994. "Case-Control Study of Risk Factors for Hip Fractures in the Elderly." *American Journal of Epidemiology* 139: 493–505.

Davies, D. F. 1980. "Cow's Milk Antibodies and Coronary Heart Disease." *Lancet* 1, no. 8179: 1190–91.

Durning, Alan, and H. B. Brough. 1991. *Taking Stock: Animal Farming and the Environment*. Washington, D.C.: Worldwatch Institute.

The Earth Charter Initiative. 2002. "The Earth Charter." San José, Costa Rica: Earth Council. <http://www.earthcharter.org/earthcharter/charter.htm> (January 12, 2002).

Epstein, Samuel S. 1998a. *The Politics of Cancer—Revisited.* Fremont Center, N.Y.: East Ridge Press.

Epstein, Samuel S. 1998b. *The Breast Cancer Prevention Program.* 2nd edition. New York: Macmillan.

FAO. 1993. "Fats and Oils in Human Nutrition: Report of a Joint Expert Consultation." < http://www.fao.org/docrep/V4700E/V4700E00.htm>.

Fescanich, Diane, et al. 1996. "Protein Consumption and Bone Fractures in Women." *American Journal of Epidemiology* 143, no. 5: 472–79.

Geissler, Catherine A. 1999. "China: The Soyabean-Pork Dilemma." *Proceedings of the Nutrition Society* 58: 345–53.

Gill, M. 1999. "Meat Production in Developing Countries." *Proceedings of the Nutritional Society* 58, no. 2: 371–76.

Goodland, Robert, et al. 1984. *Environmental Management in Tropical Agriculture.* Boulder, Colo.: Westview Press.

Goodland, Robert. 1997. "Environmental Sustainability in Agriculture: Diet Matters." *Ecological Economics* 23, no. 3: 189–200.

Goodland, Robert. 1998a. "The Case against Consumption of Grain-fed Meat." Pp. 95–115 in *The Ethics of Consumption*, edited by David Crocker and Toby Linden. Lanham, Md.: Rowman & Littlefield.

Goodland, Robert. 1998b. "Environmental Sustainability in Agriculture: The Bioethical and Religious Arguments against Carnivory." Pp. 235–65 in *Ecological Sustainability,* edited by John Lemons, Laura Westra, and Robert Goodland. Dordrecht: Kluwer.

Goodland, Robert. 1999. "Livestock Sector Environmental Assessment." Pp. 239–61 in *Nachhaltigeit in der Landwirtschaft,* edited by M. Hardtlein et al. Berlin: (E. Schmidt) Umwelt Stiftung, Deutsche Bundesstiftung Umwelt.

Goodland, Robert, and David Pimentel. 2000. "Environmental Sustainability in the Agriculture Sector," in *Ecological Integrity: Integrating Environment, Conservation, and Health,* edited by David Pimentel, Laura Westra, and Reed F. Noss. Washington, D.C.: Island Press.

Gordon, David B. 1999. *Milk and Mortality: The Connection between Milk Drinking and Coronary Heart Disease.* Livermore, Calif.: Gordon Books.

Heaney, Robert P., et al. 1999. "Dietary Changes Favorably Affect Bone Remodeling in Older Adults." *Journal of the American Dietetic Association* 99: 1228–33.

Hu, Frank B., and Walter C. Willett. 1998. *The Relationship between Consumption of Animal Products (Beef, Pork, Poultry, Eggs, Fish, and Dairy Products) and Risk of Chronic Diseases: A Critical Review. A Report for World Bank.* Cambridge, Mass.: Harvard School of Public Health.

Huang, J., S. Rozelle, and M. Rosegrant. 1999. "China's Food Economy to the Twenty-First Century: Supply, Demand, and Trade." *Economic Development & Cultural Change* 47, no. 4: 737–66.

IFPRI (International Food Policy Research Institute). 1999. "Where's the Beef? Experts Say 'Livestock Revolution' Is Here to Stay." June 7, 1999. <http://www.ifpri.org/textonly/pressrel/2060799.htm> (20 May 2001).

Law, Malcolm R., and N. J. Wald. 1994 "An Ecological Study of Serum Cholesterol and Ischaemic Heart Disease Between 1850 and 1990." *European Journal of Clinical Nutrition* 48, no. 5: 305–25.

Muñoz de Chavez, M., and A. Chavez. 1999. "Diet that Prevents Cancer: Recommendations from the American Institute for Cancer Research." *International Journal of Cancer Supplement* 11: 85–89.

NIH (National Institutes of Health). 2001. "Third Report of the Expert Panel on Detection, Evaluation, and Treatment of High Blood Cholesterol in Adults (Adult Treatment Panel III)." <http://www.nhlbi.nih.gov/guidelines/cholesterol/index.htm>.

Outwater, J. L., A. Nicholson, and Neal Barnard. 1997. "Dairy Products and Breast Cancer: The IGF-1, Estrogen, and Bgh Hypothesis." *Medical Hypotheses* 48, no. 6: 453–61.

Piazza, Alan. 1986. *Food Consumption and Nutritional Status in the People's Republic of China.* London: Westview Press.

Pinstrup-Andersen, Per, Rajul Pandya-Lorch, and Mark Rosegrant. 1997. *The World Food Situation: Recent Developments, Emerging Issues, and Long-Term Prospects.* Washington, D.C.: International Food Policy Research Institute (IFPRI).

Potter, Susan M. 1998. "Soy Protein and Cardiovascular Disease: The Impact of Bioactive Components in Soy." *Nutrition Reviews* 56: 231–35.

Rees, M. 1995. "The Age of Menarche." *Orgyn* 4: 2–4.

Seely, Stephen. 1981. "Diet and Coronary Disease: A Survey of Mortality Rates and Food Consumption Statistics of 24 Countries." *Medical Hypotheses* 7: 907–18.

Segall, J. J. 1977. "Is Milk a Coronary Health Hazard?" *British Journal of Preventive and Social Medicine* 31: 81–85.

Segall, J. J. 1994. "Dietary Lactose as a Possible Risk Factor for Ischaemic Heart Disease: Review of Epidemiology." *International Journal of Cardiology* 46: 197–207.

Steinfeld, Henning, Cees de Haan, and Harvery Blackburn. 1997. *Livestock-Environment Interactions: Issues and Options.* Rome: FAO and World Bank.

Terpstra, A. H. M., et al. 1983. "Dietary Protein and Cholesterol Metabolism in Rabbits and Rats" Pp. 9–18 in *Animal and Vegetable Proteins in Lipid Metabolism and Atherosclerosis: Current Topics in Nutrition and Disease*, edited by M. J. Gibney, and D. Kritchevsky. New York, Alan R. Liss.

Uauy, Ricardo, and P. Peirano. 1999. "Breast Is Best: Human Milk Is the Optimal Food for Brain Development." *American Journal of Clinical Nutrition* 70: 433–34.

UNICEF. 2001. "Preventing the Spread of HIV through Breastfeeding." December 14, 2001. <http://www.unicef.org/newsline/00breastfeeding.htm> (20 May 2001)

USDA (U.S. Department of Agriculture). *Dietary Guidelines.* 2000. <http://www.health.gov/dietaryguidelines/dga2000/document/frontcover.htm> (20 May 2001).

Warrick, Joby. 2001. "Modern Meat: A Brutal Harvest: 'They Die Piece by Piece'," *Washington Post*, 10 April, 2001. A1.

WHO (World Health Organization). 1996. *Investing in Health Research and Development: Report of the Ad Hoc Committee on Health Research Relating to Future Intervention Options.* Geneva: WHO.

Youngman, L. D., and T. Colin Campbell. 1992. "Inhibition of Aflatoxin B1-Induced Gamma Glutamyl Transpeptidase Positive (GGT+) Hepatic Preneoplastic Foci and Tumors by Low Protein Diets." *Carcinogenesis* 13: 1607–13.

Chapter 13

Integrity and Sustainability of Natural and Man-Made Ecosystems

Lech Ryszkowski

The Quest for Sustainability and Integrity

Worldwide changes of ecosystems and landscapes induced by humans are presently well recognized not only by scientific circles but also by administrators and the general public. The accelerated rate of changes in nature was recently reported in several publications (Collins and Shepherd 1996; Hannah et al. 1994; IUCN 1980; Lubchenco 1998; Mannion 1995 and 1998; Pimentel and Edwards 2000; Postel 1996; Postel et al. 1996; Reaka-Kundla et al. 1997; Ryszkowski 2000; Vitousek et al. 1997 a and b; Watson 1999, and others). Thus, for example, it was shown that almost 75 percent of total habitable terrestrial ecosystems have been affected by humans. About half of the available freshwater resources are consumed and more nitrogen compounds suitable for plant uptake are produced by industry and by introduced leguminous crops than by all natural sources combined. Cycles of carbon, phosphorus, and many other elements are also influenced by humanity. Many natural resources are exploited and quite substantial amounts of new chemicals are released into the environment. Modern means of transportation have increased enormously the opportunities for worldwide spread of organisms. Invention of methods to form transgenic organisms have opened new frontiers for manipulation of biodiversity.

In short, transformations of the environment caused by human activities are overwhelming the globe and for the first time in history the sustainable management of resources is more important than intensification of production. This conclusion relies on observations that increasing anthropogenic pressures on the environment are undermining functions of soil, water, air and living resources on which sustainability of human populations depends. Not all transformations, however, are inherently tied to environmental degradation.

Long ago, when the human populations had low densities, visible impacts on the environment appeared only locally and degraded sites regenerated sooner or later after they were given up, due to nature's overwhelming restorative capacities. Ensuring their prosperity, people subjugated nature in order to gain profits that enabled higher standards of living. Similar to pioneer biotic populations colonizing a new substrate at the first stage of ecological succession, man in pursuit of his anthropocentric goals maximized production and reproduction efforts that increased nature's exploitation. When there were less and less natural ecosystems to subjugate, competition and resources exploitation increased and environmental problems started to be more and more apparent. Present widespread recognition of environmental problems calls for a program of threat control and attempts at elaboration of guidelines for the sustainable development of human society are proposed.

Many of the proposed definitions of sustainable development are of a descriptive kind rather than an operational one. The most popular definition was proposed by the Brundtland Commission (Brundtland 1987) as development that "meets the needs of the present without compromising the ability of future generations to meet their own needs." Appreciating the didactic value of that definition, one needs a more functional approach when discussing integrity of ecosystems. Some hints could be obtained from analysis of ecosystem succession, especially from analysis of the succession of biotic communities when they are approaching a so-called mature or climax stage of development. In transition from pioneer to mature or climax natural communities, there is a switch of a system functioning from maximizing of energy use for production to its more efficient use by recycling of nutrients and elaboration of storing capacities and other functions that support the endurance of the whole ecosystem into which particular populations of organisms are embedded. This is achieved by development of feedback designs in a system that maximizes the flux of energy for internal works useful for system endurance (Lotka 1956; Odum E. 1969; Odum and Odum 1976; Odum H. 1983; Nicols and Prigogine 1989). The feedback designs are a result of the interconnectivity of the system elements that determines its integrity.

Diversity of elements often is assumed as an index of ecosystem stability and by that token its integrity. But this assumption could be misleading. Diversified assembly of noninteracting elements is not integrated. Nevertheless, it is often assumed that the higher the diversity the higher the possibility for various component interactions. Some of them could have formed negative feedback loops creating the resilience of the system to external factors, which in turn creates system sustainability.

In the case of the human population, a change in attitude toward nature—from exploitable use of living and abiotic resources to recognition of the need for reconciliation of human activities with nature protection—developed recently. Despite the warning expressed by scientists some decades ago (e.g.,

Despite the warning expressed by scientists some decades ago (e.g., Hardin 1968), the sustainability concepts of development gained due concern among decision-makers only when environmental degradation had started to influence the health of people and undermine prospects for economic success on an almost worldwide scale. A free-market economy, which could be considered as homologous to competition between species in ecosystem succession, stimulates production efficiency, but is not able to handle the internalization of environmental costs on its own (Anderson et al. 1995). Internalization means that costs of environmental degradation are included in the price of produced goods, which results in decreases in gains if, because of competition, the prices cannot by raised. In this situation, administrative regulations are needed to promote internalization that leads to the invention of more efficient technology of production that safeguards the environment. Thus, in order to develop guidelines for sustainable development of society, besides economic, societal, and political dimensions, the knowledge of ecosystem functioning should be included if environment-friendly technologies of production would be invented. But because effects of human activity are now omnipresent over the Earth, the socioeconomic and ecological processes should be included in analyses of *all* ecosystems, not only in humanly controlled ones, when their integrity properties are studied. Recent developments in studies on ecosystem or landscape ecology can be relied on in attempts at improvement of the means of production.

The attempt to implement such a holistic approach to nature management has been proposed in the Earth Charter. The new opportunities to counteract increasing global deterioration of the environment are sought in pursuit of coherent policy integrating environmental, economic, political, and social aspects of humanity development. The Earth Charter strongly emphasizes that humanity is a part of an evolving universe and the concept of ecological integrity is the leading guideline of development.

Together with increasing recognition of processes sustaining large-area ecological systems is a growing conviction that it is the way in which natural resources have been used, not the fact that they are exploited, which has resulted in environmental degradation. Due to this growing recognition, a new paradigm for nature protection can be advocated. Nature should not be separated from or shielded against socioeconomic activities, as proposed in dominant programs of wildlife conservancy, but those two aspects of integrity should be reconciled (Ryszkowski 2000). The argument that the less an ecosystem is changed by human activity the higher the integrity it shows is challenged by the proposition that people using knowledge of ecosystem functions and socioeconomic processes can enhance or substitute controlling negative feedback loops to such an extent that sustainable systems could be formed. Such an approach facilitates more objective evaluation of alternative technologies of production under objectives that seek to optimize both production and environmental protection and meet social needs at the same time.

This approach requires the following changes in assumptions concerning nature protection:

1. Inventories of conserved objects, e.g., species or their communities, relying on knowledge of their adaptations to environment, should be grounded in understanding life-supporting processes (energy flows, matter cycling, and their control mechanisms). Species conservancy should be changed to protection and management of ecosystems in which the species are living. Such an approach to nature protection is strongly recommended by IUCN (1980), but many conservancy programs do not observe those strategic guidelines. In many conservancy approaches it is still assumed that separating protected objects from direct contact with people can save them from threats. But global changes of matter cycling also induce transformations in objects that are isolated from direct contact, and if protected ecosystems are to be preserved, then management practices counteracting those alterations should be included in the arsenal of protection means.
2. Phenomenal characteristics of conserved objects like rareness, extraordinariness, and beauty should be supplemented by functional characteristics. Biotic communities should be characterized not only by the appearance of rare, endemic or endangered species but also by such categories as guilds or functional groups (trophic, conditioning habitat in a special way, playing a role in matter cycles, etc.) as well as keystone species like those that control, for example, regrowth of trees. Decrease in abundance of key species controlling regrowth of trees in some steppe ecosystems should call for protection measures like those for endemic or rare species.
3. Because diversity of system components could facilitate their functional interconnectivity, one can expect that a heterogenic set of objects will be more resistant to threats than a homogenic one. Thus, increasing heterogeneity (diversity) of areas in which protected objects are present will stimulate higher resistance to threats than a pure stand of protected elements. Unprotected elements that increase the diversity of an ecosystem also have important value for conservancy.
4. Reconciliation with economic activities (tourism, hunting or fishing save for protected targets, herb and mushroom picking, etc.) will raise not only the interest of local population in maintenance of protected areas but could provide also fund for the installation of structures enhancing protection.

The best way to compare ecosystems (whether natural or man-made) is to focus on differences in basic functional processes determining their properties. To those categories one can number the following processes:

- energy flows driving all processes (abiotic, biotic, and man-related activities). The energetic costs of process performance could be used as common denominator for comparison of all dimensions in natural and man-made ecosystems, including human activities;
- recycling of matter (carbon, nitrogen, water, etc.) ensuring formation of new structures and regeneration of those already existing;

- various forms of interactions between components, especially development of negative feedback loops (when a product exerts a controlling effect on input), which determine resilience of the ecosystem to threats and by that token their integrity;
- among feedback mechanisms, the processes of coadaptation of components play an important role in enhancing fluxes of energy for useful work in the system.

In reference to these processes the comparison of natural (forest and grasslands to some extent influenced by man) with agroecosystems will be carried out.

Natural versus Agroecosystems

Agricultural activity focuses on yield, being part of the total net primary production, which is the plant material produced due to photosynthetic plant activity. Because of the immunity of basic photosynthetic processes to human influence to date, the strategy of agriculture is to increase allocation of photoassimilates into yields by manipulation of subsidy energy used for fertilizers, pest control agents, agrotechnology, breeding of more yield-productive kinds of cultivated plants and domesticated animals, protection against harmful microclimatic conditions, and so on. It should be emphasized that the achievements of modern agriculture sprang from channeling solar energy and nutrient fluxes into products useful for man. Thus, from the ecological point of view, agricultural activity is concerned with the change of the pattern of energy fluxes in ecosystem to magnify goals needed by man, but not with an expansion of the interception of solar energy by plants.

In order to achieve that goal, farmers simplify plant cover structure, eliminating other plant species besides the desired cultivar as well as creating large open fields facilitating operation of machines. Field margin, hedges, shelterbelts, small mid-field ponds or wetlands are eradicated (Baldock 1990, Stanners and Bourdeau 1995). Simplification of the plant cover structure as well as direct impacts of agrotechnical procedures (plowing, pest control, harvests, rotation of cultivated plants, etc.) eliminate many species of animals. Among soil animals, for example, large organisms with long development cycles and weak ability to move are eliminated. The mean annual standing biomass of the total set of soil animals in cultivated fields is lower by factor of 5 to 15 in comparison to grasslands and forests (Ryszkowski 1985; Karg and Ryszkowski 1996).

Primary production or production of plant biomass determines the energy flux used by all biota. Net primary production rates for a total vegetation season are convergent in forests, grassland, and in cultivated fields when plants are growing during the whole vegetation season (usually this could be achieved in agroecosystems by combination of fore- or after- crops with main-crops) in a temperate climatic zone without shortage of water. The mean values of annual primary production in those three kinds of ecosystems converge to about 1500 grams of dry weight per square meter (Ryszkowski 1984; 1996). Out of the annual net primary production, from 30 percent to 70 percent of biomass is removed from field as harvest. A balance of organic matter providing regeneration of humus is essential for long-term sustainability of the soil. Thus organic fertilizers become crucial for sustainable agriculture. A decrease in soil organic matter has been observed in many situations where natural systems were converted to agroecosystems (e.g., Ketcheson 1980; Mann 1986; Martel and Mackenzie 1980, and others).

Although the amounts of produced plant biomass are similar in main terrestrial types of ecosystems experiencing the same climate influences, their fates are different. One can distinguish three general trends in organic matter transformations (Ryszkowski 1975). Forests have very high capacities for the storage of organic matter in living forms (cumulation in living standing biomass), which enable construction of very complicated biotic structures and modification of microclimatic conditions. Grasslands have a simpler structure than forests and possess the highest capacities to store energy and nutrients in the form of humus. Cultivated fields are ecosystems artificially maintained by man at an early stage of biotic community succession with a simple structure of plant biomass from which substantial amounts of organic matter are removed in yields. Increasing inputs of organic matter into soil in agroecosystems is one of the factors that augments their sustainability.

Because of the lower diversity in agroecosystems controlled by a farmer, a less complex network of interrelations among the components develops. Observed loss of humus undermines storing capacities of nutrients and water in agroecosystems. As a consequence of these simplifications, relationships among agroecosystem components are altered, so that there is less tie-up in local cycles of matter as well as lower abilities for resilience to external threats. Higher rates of chemical compounds leaching, surface runoff, volatilization, and wind erosion are characteristic for agroecosystems in comparison to forest and grasslands (Haycock et al. 1997; Ryszkowski 1985, 1992a).

Agriculture intensification, simplifying the network of energy fluxes within biotic communities of agroecosystems as well as decreasing their recycling and storing capacities for nutrients, also eliminates some important coadaptation between organisms. For example, presence of high concentrations of mineral nitrogen introduced with fertilizers could inhibit nitrogen fixation by bacteria (Sawicka 1996). In the majority of cultivated fields, the decrease in biomass of soil fungi and increase of bacteria in comparison to other land ecosystems is observed, which indicates intensification of organic matter decomposition (Kaszubiak 1996).

Directions for Agricultural Reform

All those functional changes in agroecosystems, if they are not recognized and counteracted, could decrease integrity of agroecosystems as well as provoke environmental problems. This is well illustrated by the appearance of diffuse pollution problems all over the world. In the 1960s and 1970s, anthropogenic eutrophication of major European water reservoirs was observed and point sources of pollution were considered the main reason for water deterioration (Vollenweider 1968). By the late 1970s, decreases in water pollution occurred in some reservoirs (OECD 1986) such as Lake Constance (Switzerland and Germany), Mjosa (Norway), Malaren and Vattern (Sweden), as a result of efficient control of point sources of pollution. New concerns about water quality arose in the 1980s when high concentrations of nitrates were detected in water reservoirs located far from the point sources of pollution (OECD 1986; Halberg 1989). In the assessment of environmental problems prepared by the European Environment Agency Task Force of the European Commission (EC), diffuse pollution of soils and water reservoirs by nitrates was recognized as the one of the most serious environmental problems in Europe (Stanners and Bourdeau 1995). That situation was confirmed by the second assessment of Europe's environment (European Environment Agency 1998). Environmental considerations became an important element of the new Common Agricultural Policy (CAP) since 1996 and various proposals were issued by the EC in order to control growing threats. In regard to water pollution, the Nitrates Directive was adopted by the EC ministers as an important step for implementation of the "polluter pays" and the "prevention at source" principles. The codes of good agricultural practices are imposed by that Directive on the EC member states. But the success of implementation of the Nitrates Directive so far is low, as 87 percent of agricultural area in Europe has nitrate concentrations above the guide-level of 25 mg l^{-1} and 22 percent surpasses maximum admissible concentrations of 50 mg l^{-1} (Com 1999).

This situation is a good example of elaborating administrative regulations that will lead to creation of negative feedbacks between the intensification of agricultural production and environment protection. First, the widespread threat should be recognized, then some regulations for its control are proposed and imposed. Some dissonances or flaws in regulation appear during implementation and amended mechanisms of control are in turn proposed. It is important to understand that misconceptions and inefficiency of proposed regulations are normal ways of regulating feedback elaborations. Selection of the systems showing higher performance of control mechanisms is achieved by way of trial and error. Thus, the errors in application of proposed regulations are normal phenomena in the evolution of feedback loops forming the integrity of the system, despite the fact that they raise alarming disputes in societies. But the more hotly disputes are carried out, the faster amendments to the regulation are made.

Basing Agricultural Reform on Ecological Knowledge

The better the knowledge of underpinning processes (energy flows, matter cycling and their control mechanisms), the more efficient are the regulations that can be proposed. But because there is little information on recent developments in ecology as well as existing gaps in that knowledge, some administrative bodies try to treat the symptoms instead of introducing protective management of underpinning processes. Quite often environmental discussion is focused on visible degradation rather than on reasons for diminished capacities of the ecosystem to maintain the object in question. In case of pollution the increased recycling of elements should accompany measures for control at source, while reductions at the "end of pipe" often are not as efficient as assumed. Use of knowledge on the cycling of elements in the landscape therefore help to enhance efficiency of pollution control.

There is no doubt that intensive agriculture creates environmental problems. Documentation of the environmental degradation caused by intensive agriculture were presented in many publications (Baldock 1990; European Environment Agency 1998; Mannion 1995; Matson et al. 1997; Ryszkowski 1990, 1992a, 2000; Stanners and Bourdeau 1995; and many others) and here only general categories of the impacts are pointed out. Loss of the organic matter contents in soil is a widespread form of degradation evoked by agriculture intensification, especially when farmers rely only on mineral fertilizers. Because the soil organic matter not only determines storing capacities of agroecosystems for water and nutrients, but also influences soil structure and abundance as well as activity of bacteria, fungi, and invertebrates living in soils, the changes in soil's humus contents influence agroecosystems' integrity. The degradation of soil quality (e.g., accumulation of inhibitors of plant growth) caused by agricultural technologies also have substantial effects therefore on agroecosystem functioning. Loss of the humus contents impair agroecosystem integrity. The organic matter accumulated in ecosystems (live or humus) serves as an operational basis for maintaining resistance to threats in periods of nutrient input shortages, severe meteorological conditions, and so on.

An intensive application of fertilizers, pesticides, and large quantities of liquid manure bring about problems of diffuse pollution that degrades ground and surface water quality. The problem of soil erosion is another widespread environmental threat in rural areas, although its intensity varies greatly between regions. Another serious environmental threat in some regions is an increasing shortage of water due to overdrainage, destruction of plant cover due to intensive animal grazing, and so on. Soil salinization is also a problem when, in regions of high evapotranspiration rates, the plant cover structure is simplified, exposing bare soils, and high inputs of fertilizers are introduced. Simplification of the agricultural landscape structure by eradication of refuge sites leads also to impoverishment of wildlife.

All those forms of degradation are the result of farmers' influences on the pattern of partitioning of solar energy, which drives various processes in ecosystems, induces changes in biogeochemical cycles, or directs eradication or modification of ecosystem structures. For example, the water transport of soluble as well as insoluble materials is one of the main routes of matter cycling between ecosystems. Hence, the recognition of mechanisms modifying water fluxes across landscape is of paramount importance, not only for the management of water resources, but also for development of the strategy for control of diffuse pollution of groundwater and surface water reservoirs (Ryszkowski et al. 1999).

In accord with many published studies (e.g., Haycock et al. 1997; Peterjohn and Correll 1984; Ryszkowski 1992 a and b, 1998; Ryszkowski and Bartoszewicz 1989, 1996; Ryszkowski and Kędziora 1987; Ryszkowski et al. 1999, and many others) reduction of chemicals and especially nitrates is observed when groundwater seeps under shelterbelts or stretches of meadows in an agricultural landscape. All those studies indicate that in an agricultural landscape, with a dense network of afforested areas and grasslands, the diffuse pollution of groundwater can be controlled. Thus in landscapes having a mosaic structure of plant cover, higher doses of fertilizers can be applied than in homogenous ones composed of arable fields only. The lower tying of matter cycles in agroecosystems can be compensated by creation of mosaic agricultural landscapes.

But when restoring landscape integrity by increasing its diversity, one finds a contradiction between economic and ecological approaches. Farm sizes are too small in many countries to provide enough land for efficient systems of biogeochemical barriers (afforestations, shelterbelts, stretches of meadows, small ponds, and wetlands) for control of water and chemical fluxes or modifications of meteorological conditions. From the economic point of view the farm is the basic unit of activity and the free market influences farm performance, therefore. This can interfere with the protection of the environment at the landscape scale, and in turn can undermine the sustainability of agriculture development. It seems that in this case an administration elaborating an environmental protection plan that is really able to increase the integrity of the system should rely to a higher extent on ecological considerations than on economic ones. This does not mean that economic aspects are not important, but indicates that the hierarchy of approaches in the creation of policy for sustainable development should be reversed with respect to what is usually proposed.

Better Farm Practices and a Diversified Landscape Structure

In order to restore integrity of agroecosystems, two mutually supplementary directions of management of rural areas can be proposed.

First, at the farm level, enhancement of ecologically sound technologies should be implemented, including:

- diversified crop rotation and organic fertilizers restoring soil organic matter resources;
- conserving soil moisture;
- application of fertilizers in quantities adjusted to cultivars' needs;
- integration of plant cultivation with animal husbandry within a farm;

- integrated methods of pests and pathogens control;
- control of negative effects of mechanization, e.g., soil compaction.

Those and many other activities are described in the Codes of Good Agricultural Practices, whose implementation will increase sustainability at the farm level.

The second direction connected with restoring agriculture sustainability is diversification of the landscape structure. Promotion of a mosaic rural landscape by introduction of shelterbelts, hedges, stretches of meadows, mid-field water reservoirs and wetlands, and riparian strips of permanent vegetation increases control of diffuse pollution and erosion, provides refuge sites for wildlife, and modifies meteorological conditions, which in turn can influence more efficient use of water for agricultural purposes.

Success of implementation of agricultural policy based on those two directions strongly depends on revenues that farmers receive.

In conclusion, one can state that sustainability of the agroecosystems or rural landscapes as well as all other ecosystems or landscapes can be assured only if all important driving forces are taken into account and systems of negative feedback loops are developed. Economic activities are sustainable only if they are incorporated into an integrated system showing resilience to threats. This can be achieved only if feedback between ecological and socioeconomic processes is controlled by policy regulation imposed on the system.

References

Anderson, T., C. Folke, and S. Nystrom. 1995. *Trading with the Environment*. London: Earthscan Publications.

Baldock, D. 1990. *Agriculture and Habitat Loss in Europe*. London: The Institute for European Environmental Policy.

Brundtland, G. H. 1987. *Our Common Future*. Oxford: Oxford University Press.

Collins, G. B. and R. J. Shephard. 1996. *Engineering Plants for Commercial Products and Applications*. New York: The New York Academy of Sciences.

Com. 1999. *Direction towards Sustainable Agriculture*. Brussels: Commission of the European Communities.

European Environment Agency. 1998. *Europe's Environment: The Second Assessment*. Amsterdam: Elsevier.

Halberg, G. R. 1989. "Nitrate in Ground Water in United States." Pp. 35–74 in *Nitrogen Management and Groundwater Protection*, edited by R. F. Follett. Amsterdam: Elsevier.

Hannah L., D. Lohse, C. Hutchinson, J. Carr, and A. Lankerani. 1994. "A preliminary Inventory of Human Disturbance of World Ecosystems." *Ambio* 23: 246–50.

Hardin, G. 1968. "The Tragedy of the Commons." *Science* 162: 1243–48.

Haycock, N. E., T. P. Burt, K. W. T. Goulding, and G. Pinay, eds. 1997. *Buffer Zones: Their Processes and Potential in Water Protection*. Harpenden, U.K.: Quest Environmental.

IUCN. 1980. *The World Conservation Strategy*. Gland, Switzerland: IUCN-UNEP.

Karg, J., and L. Ryszkowski. 1996. "Animals in Arable Land." Pp. 138–72 in *Dynamics of an Agricultural Landscape*, edited by L. Ryszkowski, N. French, and A. Kędziora. Poznań: Państwowe Wydawnictwo Rolnicze i Leśne.

Kaszubiak, H. 1996. "Microbial Biomass in Agroecosystems." Pp. 185–203 in *Dynamics of an Agricultural Landscape,* edited by L. Ryszkowski, N. French, and A. Kędziora. Poznań: Państwowe Wydawnictwo Rolnicze i Leśne.

Ketcheson, J. W. 1980. "Long-Range Effects of Intensive Cultivation and Monoculture on the Quality of Southern Ohio Soils." *Canadian Journal of Soil Science* 60: 403–10.

Lotka, A. J. 1956. *Elements of Mathematical Biology*. New York: Dover.

Lubchenco, J. 1998. "Entering the Century of the Environment: A New Social Contract for Science." *Science* 279: 491–97.

Mann, L. K. 1986. "Changes in Soil Carbon Storage after Cultivation." *Soil Science* 142: 279–88.

Mannion, A. M. 1995. *Agriculture and Environmental Change*. Chichester: Wiley.

Mannion, A. M. 1998. "Global Environmental Change: The Causes and Consequences of Disruption to Biogeochemical Cycles." *The Geographical Journal* 164: 168–82.

Martel, Y. A., and A. F. Mackenzie. 1980. "Long-Term Effects of Cultivation and Land Use on Soil Quality in Quebec." *Canadian Journal of Soil Science* 60: 411–20.

Matson, P. A., W. J. Parton, A. G. Power, and M. J. Swift. 1997. "Agricultural Intensification and Ecosystem Properties." *Science* 277: 504–09.

Nicolis, G., and I. Prigogine. 1989. *Exploring Complexity*. New York: W. H. Freeman.

Odum, E. P. 1969. "The Strategy of Ecosystem Development." *Science* 164: 262–70.

Odum, H. T. 1983. *Systems Ecology*. New York: Wiley.

Odum, H. T., and E. C. Odum. 1976. *Energy Basis for Man and Nature*. New York: McGraw-Hill.

OECD. 1986. *Water Pollution by Fertilizers and Pesticides*. Paris: OECD Publications.

Peterjohn, W. T., and D. L. Correll. 1984. "Nutrient Dynamics in an Agricultural Watershed: Observations on the Role of Riparian Forests." *Ecology* 65: 1466–75.

Pimentel, D., and C. A. Edwards. 2000. "Agriculture, Food, Populations, Natural Resources and Ecological Integrity." Pp. 337–38 in *Implementing Ecological Integrity,* edited by P. Crabbe, A. Holland, L. Ryszkowski, and L. Westra. Dordrecht: Kluwer.

Postel, S. L. 1996. "Forging a Sustainable Water Strategy." Pp. 40–59 in *State of the World* edited by L. R. Brown. New York: Norton.

Postel, S. L., G. C. Daily, and P. R. Ehrlich. 1996. "Human Appropriation of Renewable Fresh Water." *Science* 271: 785–88.

Reaka-Kundla, M. L., D. E. Wilson, and E. O. Wilson. 1997. *Biodiversity.* Washington: Joseph Henry Press.

Ryszkowski, L. 1975. "Energy and Matter Economy of Ecosystems." Pp. 109–26 in *Unifying Concepts of Ecology,* edited by Van W. H. Dobben and R. McConnel. The Hague, Netherlands: Junk.

Ryszkowski, L. 1984. "Primary Production in Agroecosystems." Pp. 77–94 in *Option Mediterrannennes.* Zaragoza: International Centre for Advanced Mediterranean Agronomic Studies.

Ryszkowski, L. 1985. "Impoverishment of Soil Fauna Due to Agriculture." *Intecol Bulletin* 12: 7–17.

Ryszkowski, L. 1990. "Ecological Guidelines for Management of Agricultural Landscapes." Pp. 249–64 in *Ecological Risks. Perspectives from Poland and United*

States, edited by W. Grodziński, E. B. Cowling, and A. Breymeyer. Washington D.C.: National Academy Press.

Ryszkowski, L. 1992a. "Agriculture and Nonpoint Sources of Pollution" (in Polish). *Postępy Nauk Rolniczych* 39/40: 3–14.

Ryszkowski, L. 1992b. "Energy and Material Flows across Boundaries in Agricultural Landscapes." Pp. 270–84 in *Landscape Boundaries: Consequences for Diversity and Ecological Flows,* edited by A. J. Hansen and F. di Castro. New York: Springer Verlag.

Ryszkowski, L. 1996. "Primary Production." Pp. 79–97 in *Dynamics of an Agricultural Landscape,* edited by L. Ryszkowski, N. R. French, and A. Kędziora. Poznań: Państwowe Wydawnictwo Rolnicze i Leśne.

Ryszkowski, L. 1998. "Ecological Guidelines for the Management of Agricultural Landscapes." Pp. 187–201 in *Modern Trends in Ecology and Environment,* edited by R. S. Ambasht. Leiden: Backhuys Publishers.

Ryszkowski, L. 2000. "The Coming Change in the Environmental Protection Paradigm." Pp. 37–56 in *Implementing Ecological Integrity,* edited by P. Crabbe, A. Holland, L. Ryszkowski, and L. Westra. Dordrecht: Kluwer.

Ryszkowski, L., and A. Bartoszewicz. 1989. "Impact of Agricultural Landscape Structure on Cycling of Inorganic Nutrients." Pp. 241–46 in *Ecology of Arable Land,* edited by M. Clarholm and L. Bergstrom. Dordrecht: Kluwer.

Ryszkowski, L., and A. Bartoszewicz. 1996. "Influence of Shelterbelts and Meadows on the Chemistry of Ground Water." Pp. 98–109 in *Dynamics of an Agricultural Landscape,* edited by L. Ryszkowski, N. French, and A. Kędziora. Poznań: Państwowe Wydawnictwo Rolnicze i Leśne.

Ryszkowski, L., and A. Kędziora. 1987. "Impact of Agricultural Landscape Structure on Energy Flow and Water Cycling." *Landscape Ecology* 1: 85–94.

Ryszkowski, L., A. Bartoszewicz, and A. Kędziora. 1999. "Management of Matter Fluxes by Biogeocyhemical Barriers at the Agricultural Landscape Level." *Landscape Ecology* 14: 479–92.

Sawicka, A. 1996. "Nitrogen Fixation in Soils of the Turew Agricultural Landscape." Pp. 204–12 in *Dynamics of an Agricultural Landscape,* edited by L. Ryszkowski, N. French, and A. Kędziora. Poznań: Państwowe Wydawnictwo Rolnicze i Leśne.

Stanners, D., and P. Bourdeau. 1995. *Europe's Environment.* Copenhagen: European Environment Agency.

Vitousek, P. M., J. D. Aber, R. W. Howarth, G. E. Likens, P. A. Matson, D. W. Schindler, W. H. Schleisinger, and D. G. Tilman. 1997a. "Human Alteration of the Global Nitrogen Cycle: Sources and Consequences." *Ecological Applications* 7: 737–50.

Vitousek, P. M., H. A. Mooney, J. Lubchenco, and J. M. Melillo. 1997b. "Human Domination of Earth's Ecosystems." *Science* 277: 494–99.

Vollenweider, R. A. 1968. *Scientific Fundamentals of the Eutrophication of Lakes and Flowing Water with Particular Reference to Nitrogen and Phosphorus as Factors in Eutrophication.* Technical Report. Paris: OECD.

Watson, R. 1999. "Common Themes for Ecologists in Global Issues." *Journal of Applied Ecology* 36: 1–10.

Addressing the Destruction in Production

Chapter 14

Gold, Cyanide, and Fish in the River of Life and Death

Imre Lázár and Emese Kiss

It is uncertain whether climate change, unsustainable land use and resource management practices, poorly planned and designed infrastructure, or incompetent management skills are responsible for the increased frequency and intensity of natural and man-made disasters in the Carpathian Basin. At the turn of the millennium, however, floods and toxic spills resulting in the dislocation of villages, saturated cultivated lands, significant loss of regional food supply, wildlife, and aquatic habitat were very much a reality in the life of the basin's communities. Intense deforestation has altered the holding capacity and flow within these sensitive hydrological systems. Water quality and aquatic habitat have deteriorated due to increased nonpoint sources of pollution from agricultural and urban runoff as well as from large-scale industrial spills.

In the context of the wide span of prevalent water-related environmental management problems, their direct and indirect impacts, and the institutional responses to compliance and remediation issues, the aim of this article is twofold. Primarily, we wish to outline the events along with the consequences of the greatest man-made ecological disaster in the history of these watersheds since Chernobyl: the large-scale industrial discharge/spill of cyanide and heavy metals into the Tisza River from poorly maintained gold mining waste retention ponds. Secondarily, we shall discuss the actual and potential inter-jurisdictional institutional responses to this event: the multinational integrated assessment and management framework/accountability system for its remediation, monitoring, performance evaluation, and governance.

Background

Unsustainable deforestation practices within the watersheds crowned by the Carpathian Mountains, the Sub-Carpathian regions of the Ukraine, and other neighboring countries, left the hillsides deprived of vegetation, and the wildlife without habitat. Rainwater and melting snow run unimpeded onto developed and cultivated flood plains, carrying the precious topsoil of the eroding forest floor into valley streams. The drainage pattern of the mountain slopes has been distorted with the reduction of wooded areas, which have diminished from the pre-agriculture level of 95 percent (of total area) to 51 percent. Between 1877 and 1933 there were four major floods with an average interval of 18 years, while between 1933 and 1964 their frequency increased to every three to four years. Presently, floods occur every other year, if not every year (Hamar and Sárkány-Kiss 1999). The three greatest floods of the twentieth century within the region have occurred in the last three consecutive years, and they were most likely the result of increased deforestation in the Ukraine.

Another good example of a fairly recent ecological disaster resulting from poor environmental planning and management decisions was the building of the C variant hydro utility station at Bős-Gabcikovo, along the Old-Danube in the western part of Hungary. The requirement for the establishment of this electricity supply facility was the rerouting of the river bed by Slovakia and thus, the changing of the river flow. These hydrological alterations however, have led to the drainage of the Szigetköz wetland, and the significant loss of its flora and fauna.

The most recent event that has attracted widespread international attention was the severe contamination of the Tisza River with cyanide and heavy metals in late January of 2000. A jointly owned and operated Australian-Romanian gold mine was responsible for the spill, considered to be the largest man-made catastrophic event in Europe since the meltdown of the Chernobyl nuclear power plant. This environmental tragedy has had a very significant impact on the river ecosystem and surrounding populated areas and riparian communities, as well as on the entire regional and international watershed it flows into.

All of the above examples clearly demonstrate the lack of institutional coordination, participatory decision making, and effective governance of transboundary environmental issues in terms of harmonizing regional, national, and international environmental regulations, standards, policy, compliance procedures, enforcement, and remediation processes. We are basically dealing with the potential direct and indirect long-term public health effects of environmental problems stemming from the immediate contamination of local drinking water and food supplies. Further, destruction of aquatic habitat, and decline of fish stocks are causing socioeconomic deterioration of subsistence fishing communities. Further research and analysis are needed to illuminate:

- the implications (demographic, psychological, biophysical, socioeconomic, cultural) of deconstructing such complex bioregions as the Tisza River watershed;
- the role of institutions, corporations and the local communities within its boundaries;

- the potential for innovative stewardship activities that prevent further environmental degradation and aim to restore the system to its natural state.

The Tisza River: Ecological Life Support, Cultural and Intrinsic Values, Symbolic Meaning, and Interpretation

The Tisza is not just a geographical feature entrenched in the constantly changing landscape. Society expressed its mourning for the river as a living entity by hanging black flags in their windows after the spill. They demonstrated that the river's importance goes far beyond that of an economic resource to exploit (Karátson 2000, 26). The significance of the river and its people have also been embedded in the distilled oral traditions of poetry, symbolizing human ecological integrity: humanity living in harmony with its environment over the centuries.

From its headwaters to the point of entering the Danube, the Tisza belonged to one administrative jurisdiction until the end of the First World War. After its bioregional and cultural unity was deconstructed as a result of international political decisions, Hungary lost two-thirds of its territory along with one-third of its mother tongue citizens. The Tisza River as a symbol then ceased to represent the former national unity.

The governance of the river basin became more complex as accountability for its management was shared between five countries: Romania, Slovakia, Ukraine, Hungary, and Yugoslavia. Today, the river and its watershed symbolizes a diverse biophysical, socioeconomic, cultural, and political "transboundary eco-systemic kinship." Increased interdependency between stakeholders and resource flows is creating a highly complex and thus more vulnerable and fragile human ecological system, requiring the improved sharing of information and cooperation in the formal and informal institutional decision making processes underlying environmental management performance and governance.

Metaphors of the Spill

Fish, gold, and cyanide are in themselves symbols and metaphors. The fish as a metaphor signifies the "aion" gone by, the Christian epoch of tolerance and agape for each other as socio-ecological standards.

The fish became a symbol of guarding not only spiritual values but the biological life too. Fish are also sensitive biological indicators for toxicity testing. During the days after the spill, peasants living along the Lápos River used fish in their wells to measure the quality and toxicity of their drinking water.

Gold, on one hand, symbolizes life support, the golden rays of the sun. On the other, it symbolizes material wealth and the utilitarian, profit-maximizing, monetary spirit.

Cyanide, as a dangerous man-made chemical poison, is a symbol of death. It suffocates the cells by disabling the function of iron-containing oxidative enzymes, leading to the termination of life. The mining retention ponds containing cyanide became a symbol of the danger of an outdated theoretically and conceptually closed technological system that was forced open by the power of nature.

Environmental Accidents: When? Where? How? Who? What?

There are several gold mining regions and thus accidental spills all over the world, but not even the largest mining operations, found in Australia and North America, have experienced an accident comparable to the extent and severity of the cyanide and heavy metal spill into the Tisza River at Baia-Mare in Romania (O'Connor 2000). Some of the most significant accidental spills of the past few decades are summarized in table 14.1.

Post-communist countries are especially vulnerable to environmental risks and hazards due to outdated infrastructure, technology, and management techniques, both in terms of industrial operations and emergency preparedness and response. The proof of the pudding is the Baia Mare accident discussed in more detail below.

The Baia Mare Case

The picturesque town of Baia Mare is situated in the northeastern part of the Carpathian Basin. It used to be the home of the "plain air" school of postimpressionist Hungarian artists devoting their lives to capturing the essence of nature, the beauty of a sacred landscape filled with mountains, forests, and rushing streams. This Arcadian epoch ended after the First World War, and in the second half of the twentieth century the landscape has been altered by socialist industrialization. More recently, in a quasi post-socialist period, these industrial initiatives became joint ventures between investors of multinational corporations who were hunting for cheap labor, cheap resources, weak or nonexistent environmental standards, and the desperate local companies that were looking for investors to provide monetary support for their business plans.

The Australian transnational mining company Esmeralda found a partner in the Romanian Aurul mining company for the purpose of extracting nonferrous metals from the waste rock piles of the mines in the area. Using metal enrichment technologies, the extraction is carried out with cyanide after grinding the refuse ore. The process requires a lot of water. The wastewater containing high concentrations of cyanide is usually stored behind dams in tailing ponds, recycled, and reused in the process. Most accidents occur as a result of leakage or bursting of dams that are not well-maintained and the discharge of wastewater into the environment. The characteristics of the spill on January 30, 2000, just nine months after Aurul started its operations, were similar at this particular site.

Table 14.1. Significant Mining Related Cyanide Spills

Date	Company	Location	The Event and Its Consequences
1978		Mochikoshi, Japan	Mine tailings flowed 7–8 km downstream killing one person.
1992	Summitville Gold Mine	San Juan Mountains, Colorado	Cyanide & heavy metal leaked into a 27-km stretch of the Alamosa River, killing aquatic life. Cleanup exceeded US$150 million.
1994	Brewer Gold Mine	South Carolina	Cyanide spill along an 80-km stretch of the Lynches River, killing over 11,000 fish.
1994	Harmony Gold Mines	South Africa	Residential housing complex was buried with cyanide-laced mud; 17 people were killed.
1994	Bakofeng	South Africa	Mine shaft inundated by the tailings that flowed 45 km downstream; 12 people were killed.
1995	Omai Gold Mine (65% Canadian, 30% U.S. ownership)	Guyana	Dam collapsed, 3.2 billion liters of cyanide-laden tailings were released into the Essequibo River; all aquatic life along a 4-km stretch was eliminated.
1995	Manilla Mining Corporation	Placer, Philippines	Coastal pollution caused the death of 12 people.
1996	Placer Dome (Canadian-owned)	Marcopper, Philippines	Contaminated silt deposited onto water course; 1,200 residents had to be evacuated.
1997	Gold Quarry Mine	Nevada	Failure of a leach pad structure released 1 million liters of cyanide-laden wastewater into nearby creek.
1998		Zlatna, Romania	43 ha of soil and 200 km of river contaminated by toxic sulphur oxide release from precious metal works.
1998	Homestake Mine	Black Hills, South Dakota	6–7 tons of cyanide-laden tailings spilled into Whitewood Creek resulting in substantial fish kill.
1998	Kumtor Mine	Kyrgysztan	A truck transporting cyanide to the mine plunged off a bridge spilling 1762 kilograms of sodium cyanide into local surface waters; 2 deaths were reported; hundreds of people were checked into local hospitals.
1999	Placer	Surigao del Norte, Phillipines Manila Mining Corp.	Gold tailings spill 700,000 tonnes of cyanide tailings from damaged concrete pipe; 17 homes buried; 51 ha of riceland swamped.
1999		Brad and Baia de Aries, Romania	Thousands of cubic meters of cyanide sludge spilled from two gold mines, causing fish kill.
2000	Esmeralda-Aurul (Joint Australian-Romanian ownership)	Baia Mare, Romania	"The breach in the retention dam was probably caused by a combination of inherent design deficiencies in the process, unforeseen operating conditions and bad weather" (UN report, O'Connor 2000). 100,000 m^3 of wastewater containing 95 tons of cyanide spilled into Zazar and Lápos Creeks. No human deaths, but 1241 tons of fish killed and several native endangered species went extinct.

Sources: World Information Service on Energy 2001; Klochko 2000; "Cyanide Disaster in Romania" 2000.

According to the United Nations' report, "the breach in the retention dam was probably caused by a combination of inherent design deficiencies in the process, unforeseen operating conditions and bad weather" (O'Connor 2000). The heavy rainfall and the rapid snowmelt saturated and destabilized the embankment wall, allowing the flow through of 100,000 m^3 of wastewater containing 95 tons of cyanide into the nearby creeks. The Zazar and Lápos Creeks are within the catchment area of the Szamos River, which drains into the Tisza, the Tisza into the Danube, and the Danube into the Black Sea.

The UN report has criticized the companies and the local authorities about the lack of rudimentary preparations and procedures for coping with emergencies: it took 10 hours for the local environmental agency to inform the local water authority about the spill. Based on this information, the Lapos stream at 14:00 on January 31 contained 19.16 mg/l concentration of cyanide. Other sources have referenced 126 mg/l at the source of the spill, while the general manager of the Romanian Environment Ministry, Liliana Mara, reported that cyanide levels 700 times above standards had been recorded in the nearby river after the spill. The Romanian environmental and water authorities continuously informed the Hungarian authorities about the changing levels of concentrations over time. According to some of the sources, the wastewater treatment pool's earth dam was restored on January 31; according to others it was not restored until February 1. Within a few days almost all signs of life had disappeared from the Tisza.

Monitoring and Reporting

The Baia Mare Task Force has been established for the assessment, evaluation, and reporting of the case to ensure good transboundary cooperation of environmental experts. The Hungarian environmental protection and water management authorities ordered "third level" preparedness including two-hour intervals of sampling and in situ and laboratory analysis to minimize the detrimental effect of the pollution. The defense action plan was prepared on the basis of these measurement data. The appropriate governing of flows, such as closing sluices of outflows and filling the Kisköre Lake–Tisza reservoir with clean river water, helped to restrict and minimize the impact of the pollution wave. The piped drinking water supply was terminated for the period required for the passing of the pollution wave through the city of Szolnok.

The polluted plume crossed into Hungary at Csenger, at approximately 16:00 on 1 February, with a peak cyanide level of 30.4 mg/l (300 times the threshold of the Hungarian "highly polluted" standard). According to Hungarian environmental laboratories, the average contaminant concentration during the 6 hours it took the plume to cross the border was 18 mg/l (180 times the threshold value). This extremely severe water quality problem was escalated by low water levels and ice on the rivers, preventing the fast dilution of cyanide.

In addition to the cyanide contamination, heavy metal concentrations have also increased. Copper concentrations exceeded the "heavily polluted" threshold

9 times greater than acceptable levels. The contaminated flow reached the Tisza at 04: 00 on February 3, with a cyanide concentration peak value of 12.5 mg/l. The municipal water supply at the City of Szolnok was threatened at 18: 00 on February 8, where cyanide concentrations had dropped to 2.85 mg/l. The overall transit of the plume through Hungary took a total of 12 days. It reached the Serbian border early in the morning of February 12 and eventually, at much less threatening concentrations, flowed into the Danube.

From 12 a.m. on February 1 to 12 a.m. on February 12 more than 500 samples were taken from about 30 sampling sites, on an average of every 2 hours. In addition, nearby wells were also regularly monitored. Regional laboratories, aside from cyanide concentrations, measured other important water quality parameters, such as metals from inorganic micro-pollutants accompanying the spill. Furthermore, supplementary chemical, physical, and hydrobiological tests were conducted to provide accurate information on the nature, degree, and effect of the contamination. Sampling and measurement of water quality parameters were based on applicable Hungarian (MSZ) and international (ISO 5667-4) standards. Dissolved metal content was determined by applying the atomic absorption procedure. Most tests were carried out by the laboratories belonging to the regional environmental protection, assessment, and water management directorates, and the national public health and medical officers' services, as well as by water utility labs.

Assessment and Evaluation of Biological Impacts

Both cyanide and metal complexes of cyanide cause direct acute toxicity in living organisms. Thus, it is important to have thorough knowledge of the toxic effects of these substances on certain groups of organisms and on their habitats in order to be able to determine the degree of damage from contamination and the potential for remediation.

The *biological* investigations proved that the cyanide pollution has led to the decay of most of the plankton in the Tisza and Szamos Rivers. Rapid regeneration and reestablishment of the planktonic populations of *Rotatoria* and *Crustacea* started a few days after the passage of the pollution wave, and the natural purification of the river now is the same as it was in the previous years. Unpolluted tributary streams, oxbow-lakes, flood-berm pools, and excavation pits played a crucial role in this process.

The entire population of microscopic zooplankton were immediately destroyed; however *Cladocera* and *Copepoda* reappeared after five to seven days. By the end of March, 1241 tons of dead fish were removed from the rivers: 33.8 percent predatory fish, 13.5 percent carp, 8.1 percent sturgeon, and 44.6 percent herbivorous and other fish. Almost half of the fish population disappeared in the cases of *Gobio albipinnatus, Gymnocephalus schraetzer, Zingel zingel, Zingel streber,* 40 percent of *Sabanejewia aurata,* and 30 percent of *Gobio Kessleri, Cobitis taenia,* and *Gymnocepahlus baloni*. Some native, protected species such as the *Huso huso* (Danube salmon), the *Acipenser güldenstaadti* (a rare Sturgeon as the *Huso huso* (Danube salmon), the *Acipenser güldenstaadti* (a rare Sturgeon species), *Stizostedion lucoperca, Stizostedion volgense, Lota lota,* have been permanantly eliminated by the spill.

Protected vertebrate species such as the Grey Sea (or White-tailed) Eagle and the Fish Otter *(Lutra lutra)* have also suffered as a consequence of the cyanide pollution. Researchers could find some otters in the south near Tataköz after a period of recovery, but none along the Szamos and the Tisza, which may indicate the temporary extirpation of the species from this area (Gera 2000).

The Baia Borsa Case: Heavy Metal Pollution

Another accidental spill a few months later by a subsidiary of Aurul has further deteriorated the water quality situation in the region. On March 10 at 11 a.m. the dam walls of the Novat sedimentation pond, of the state owned Romanian mining company Remin, fell apart as a result of intensive snowmelt. This firm is a 45 percent shareholder of the Aurul gold processing plant. Twenty-five thousand tons of sludge contaminated with toxic heavy metals were discharged into the Vase Creek. The creek flows into the Viseu (Visó) River, which is also a tributary of the Tisza. The high concentrations of lead, copper, and zinc will remain in the sediments for many years to come.

Romica Tomescu, the environment minister, said that the concentration of lead in the water was almost double the highest acceptable levels, and that of zinc about nine times greater than the legal limit. The Romanian authorities reported the spill at 16: 22 on March 10. A water quality sampling and monitoring program was established by the environmental inspectors (KÖFEs) and locally concerned water authorities (VIZIGs).

At Tiszabecs the peak concentration of lead was 2.9mg/l, while the zinc showed 2.9mg/l and the copper 0.86 mg/l peak values compared to the 0.1 mg/l values measured before the pollution. The quantity of the total mass of pollutants crossing this section was about 50 tonnes for lead, 20 tonnes for copper, and 70 tonnes for zinc.

A third wave of pollution reached the Hungarian section of the Tisza River when the dam failed on March 14 around 15:00 and lasted for two to three hours. This pollution wave reached Hungary in the morning of March 15 and passed through the Tiszabecs border station by the evening hours. Ukrainian authorities notified Hungary that the source of the third wave of pollution was the Novat settling pond of the Baia Borsa heavy metal mine. Hungary did not receive any advance notification from Romania. According to visual observation, the pollution seemed smaller than the previous one, as it didn't cover the whole surface of the river; however, its length was reported to be 30 kms.

As the source of pollution was the same as before, it is anticipated that the main pollutants are the same: lead, zinc, copper, aluminium. The pollution wave reached the downstream border station Tiszasziget in eight days, where lead and copper concentrations were below 0.1 mg/l and the zinc concentration was in the range 0.2–0.3, hardly exceeding background levels, due to the effects of deposition, longitudinal dispersion, and to the dilution of the tributary streams.

Table 14.2. Common Problems of the Two Cases

Baia Mare (Nagybánya)	Baia Borsa (Borsabánya)
DESIGN FAULTS	
Use of a closed circuit (TMF) with no specific provision for the emergency discharge/storage of excess water	Use of a TMF with no specific provision for the emergency discharge of excess water
Non-operation of the hydro-cyclones in very low temperatures	Non-operation of pumping equipment
Inadequate dam wall construction due to lack of homogeneity of the tailings	Inadequate provision for the diversion of surface runoff from the surrounding hill slopes
PERMITTING FAULTS	
Original EIA flawed	The facility was operated in absence of an environmental operating permit
Absence of clear responsibility of final decision on safety in a permitting process that is over complex and diffused	
Monitoring requirements were inadequate	
Failure to understand the water balance implications of the design in that location	
OPERATIONAL FAULTS	
Failure to observe the design requirements for tailings, grades for embankment wall construction	Poor maintenance of pipelines and pumping equipment
	There were no emergency plans for contingencies
WEATHER	
A mix of weather conditions that were extreme but not unprecedented	A mix of weather conditions that were extreme but not unprecedented

Source: Report of the Baia Mare International Task Force, December 2000.

Sediment concentrations of lead, copper, and zinc exceeded allowable limits for sediment and for sewage-sludge. Contamination of sediment in the Tisza River at Tiszabecs-Tiszakóród exceeded the limit values at certain locations of both soil and sediment classification systems. One month after the spill no toxic effects could be detected by the bacteria, algae, and daphnia tests.

Nevertheless, the water of the Szamos River indicated toxic effects with the lemna test. Water and sediment samples taken at Tunyogmatolcs, Tiszaadony, and Tiszafüred were inhibiting the growth of *Lemna minor* and thus can be considered toxic to higher aquatic plants. This toxicity could be traced down to the Tisza River until Tiszafüred. The very high heavy metal content and the dissolved metal ions may be responsible for the adverse effect on aquatic plants.

Although the initial death of wildlife was shocking and largely caused by cyanide, the heavy metals in the water and the sediment will have unpredictable long-term food chain effects. In the medium term, they pose significant potential threats to groundwater contamination, and thus to the drinking water supply of riparian communities.

The heavy metal spill at Baia Borsa may cause even more important medium-term impacts on the ecosystem, because the majority of the sediment has remained within 6–10 km downstream of the Novat Dam. This sediment containing heavy metals may migrate slowly downwards, creating further risks.

Table 14.2 compares the contributing problems for the Baia Mare and Baia Borsa spills.

Assessment and Evaluation of Public Health and Human Ecological Impacts

As a result of concerted action by local municipalities and water supply companies, there were no human deaths or measurable direct human health effects stemming from the spill. Indirect effects, such as loss of employment due to the crisis in the fisheries sector and decreased income from tourism, mounted to significant, tangible socioeconomic costs.

During the six month period fishing was prohibited, 114 full-time and 115 part-time fishermen were without employment income, and 50,000 sport fishermen without recreational opportunity. Loss of income from tourism was significant in all three countries impacted by the accident, but Hungary was affected the most. Financial support from the government to those with the greatest loss was a short-term solution that created a temporary sense of security. However, the long-term feeling of insecurity and social instability caused widespread trauma and psychological problems in many communities. The ultimate objective of our research is to study the long-term psychological and somatic consequence of this post-traumatic state.

A wide range of individual and collective coping strategies have emerged during the closure of the fisheries, ranging from changing local subsistence activities to dependence on interfamily social support, and to increased participation in local self-government and NGO activities. Fortunately, the Tisza River came back to life as a result of ecological rehabilitation and remediation activities. It is still a young and fragile ecosystem, but on its way to gaining back the complexity of its natural state, the diverse, rich, and mature web of life it had prior to the accident. In order to flourish, it will need the infinite support, respect, and care of the surrounding communities of people—the demonstration of a collective behavior based on ecological values that recognize the functional transparency of this unique ecosystem, not only in terms of life support, but as a defining feature of our oneness with the spirit of nature; the guidance, inspiration, and motivation it sparks in our every day lives; and even the smiles in the children's eyes as it reflects the rays of the setting sun.

Alternatives to Cyanide-Based Gold Extraction

According to the experts subscribing to the Berlin Declaration on Gold Mining Using Cyanide Process, "Critical scientific analysis (especially, eco-chemistry, bio-geographical, hydrological and geochemical ecosystems [analysis]) emphatically proves that the cyanide process in Gold mining cannot be accepted because of its irreversible damage to the ecosystems" (Müller, Korte, Sauerland 2000).

Marsh (2000) mentions several environmentally friendly alternatives to cyanide-based gold extraction. The safety of the approach using polymers with ion-exchange capabilities to vacuum up cyanide ions from mine waste before the chemical even leaves the processing plant, seems to be obvious. However, these techniques, due to their high costs, are still years away from replacing the cyanide method. Bio-mining, another ecologically friendlier option, is the use of acid-eating bacteria to dissolve gold similarly to the way cyanide does. It is a less toxic method, but also too expensive to be widely used.

According to the recommendations of the Baia Mare Task Force Report, no new Tailing Management Facility (TMF) where cyanide is used should permit the storage of water/slurry containing cyanide in tailing ponds open to the elements. The cyanide should be removed from the tailings "in-plant" so that only cyanide-free water/slurry is pumped into tailing ponds. It is recommended with respect to similar TMFs elsewhere that an evaluation of the viability of such process modification be undertaken on a priority basis.

Once again, we have become keenly aware of the importance of exploring and evaluating the environmental risks caused by abandoned mining sites and tailing ponds. It is clear that proper binding conditions and guidelines must be established for the termination of mining operations and remediation of old mining sites.

Conclusion

The transboundary environmental disasters in Hungary discussed above illustrate how political and historical deconstruction of the multicultural bioregional unity of the Carpathian Basin may lead to loss of ecological integrity of the region. In the absence of effective environmental monitoring and prevention strategies to minimize risks and hazards, ecological degradation will prevail.

On the other hand, the transboundary cooperation between the local environmental authorities and experts dealing with the cyanide spill has proven to be successful. Remediation of the Tisza River watershed and, ultimately, getting on the path towards sustainable development in the basin require continued cooperation and consensus-building between Romania, Slovakia, Ukraine, Hungary and Yugoslavia. In January 2001 the Hungarian Ministry of Environment invited its counterparts from the above countries to a conference to discuss the following issues:

- improvement of quality of life in the Tisza River Basin
- strengthening of environmental safety
- protection of natural and environmental values
- development of sustainable water quality management strategies
- reduction of point and nonpoint sources of pollution.

The recently drafted Danube Restoration Plan 2001 represents a milestone on this path. The declaration, made on May 1, 2001 in Bucharest by the presidents and environmental ministers of the 16 countries in the Carpathian-Danube region, is aimed at reversing decades of pollution and the protection and renewal of natural resources.

Inter-jurisdictional institutional responses to environmental risks and threats require deeper integration and cooperation for the effective remediation of damages and the prevention of future accidents. A multinational integrated assessment and management framework/accountability system for the region's remediation, monitoring, performance evaluation, and governance may be enhanced by the ratification of relevant UN ECE conventions and protocols regarding environmental hazards. The European integration process will require the establishment of more stringent environmental performance and water quality standards compatible with ISO 14000 management practices. The development and implementation of a common assessment, evaluation, monitoring, and reporting framework will be necessary to successfully address the complexities at hand (Kiss 2001). As is emphasized in the Earth Charter: "We must decide to live with a sense of universal responsibility, identifying ourselves with the whole Earth community as well as our local communities. We are at once citizens of different nations and of one world in which the local and global components are linked. The spirit of human solidarity and kinship with all life is strengthened when we live with reverence for the mystery of being, gratitude for the gift of life, and humility regarding the human place in nature" (Earth Charter 2002).

References

BMTFR. 2000. "Report of the International Task Force for Assessing the Baia Mare Accident," December, 2000. <http://europa.eu.int/comm/environment/enlarg/bmtf_report.pdf> (01.12.2000).

"Cyanide Disaster in Romania." 2000. In *These Times* <http://homepage.newschool.edu/~blaynepo/five/cyanide.html> (17.04.2000).

"Danube Restoration Plan Takes Flight at Summit." 2001. *Environment News Service* <http://ens.lycos.com/ens/may2001/2001L-05-01-10.html> May, 2001 (01.05.2001).

The Earth Charter Initiative. 2002. "The Earth Charter." San José, Costa Rica: Earth Council. <http://www.earthcharter.org/earthcharter/charter.htm> (12.01.2002).

Gera, Pál. 2000. "Ciánméreg és vidravédelem" (Cyanide and the Protection of Otters). Budapest: Alapítvány a vidrákért.

Hamar, J., and A. Sárkány-Kiss, eds. 1999. "The Upper Tisza Valley Preparatory Proposal for the Ramsar Site Designation and Its Ecological Background." A Hungarian, Romanian, Slovakian, and Ukranian cooperation, Szeged.

Institute for Water Pollution Control. 2000. "Preliminary Assessment of the Environmental Consequences of the Romanian Cyanide and Heavy Metal Spills on the Hungarian Reaches of the Szamos and Tisza Rivers." Budapest: Water Resources Research Centre (VITUKI).

Karátson, Gábor. 2000. "Haldokló folyó" (Dying River). Pp. 26–27 in *Sír a Tisza (The Tisza is Crying),* edited by Bognár Antal. Budapest: Masszi Kiadó.

Kiss, Emese. 2001. "The Impact of Water Law Enforcement on Corporations: A Comparison of British Columbia's Lower Fraser Basin and Washington State's Puget Sound Area." Masters Thesis, University of British Columbia, Vancouver.

Klochko, Kateryna. 2000. Chronology of Major Tailings Dam Failures <http://matisse.ceu.hu/students/99/Kateryna_Klochko/Chrono.htm> CEU.

Marsh, Virginia. 2000. "Cyanide Tarnishes Gold." *Financial Times,* July 18.

Müller, P., K. Korte, and P. Sauerland. 2000. "Berlin-Declaration on Gold Mining Using Cyanide Process." Expert Meeting on Ecological and Human Rights Consequences of Cyanide-Based Gold Mining <http://www.infu.uni-dortmund.de/korte-goldmining/news3_11.html> Berlin (27.10.00).

O'Connor, Gillian. 2000. "Inquiry Waters Muddied." *Financial Times,* July 18.

World Information Service on Energy. "Chronology of Major Tailings and Dam Failures." <http://www.antenna.nl/wise/uranium/mdaf.html> (19.02.2001).

Chapter 15

The Planetary Life Crisis: Its Systemic Cause and Ground of Resolution

John McMurtry

The Pattern of Planetary Ecological Collapse

Almost one hundred acres of the Earth's mantle of rainforest is cut every minute, while an estimated two hundred species go extinct every day from sea and land habitat destruction, at least 1000 times the background evolutionary rate ("East and South" 1990, 12; McLaren 1996, 3). Accumulating air and atmospheric pollutions increasingly unleash unprecedented floods, mudslides, and windstorms across continents, make the sunlight carcinogenic and unsafe for the world's children to play in, and will by 2002 kill over 700,000 people a year by respiratory diseases (World Resources Institute, cited by *Greenpeace* 2000, 6). Stratospheric ozone depletion by industrial pollutants simultaneously causes both the destruction of amphibian species' capacity to reproduce, and systematic depletion of phytoplankton at the bottom of the planetary food chain. On the Earth's surface, twenty-six billion tons of topsoil are lost to soil erosion every year across 50 percent of the world's remaining arable land (Sandbrook 1994, D7). More than 60,000 square kilometers of land in over 100 countries becomes desert annually, hastened by global warming caused by industrial effluents that have risen 16-fold in the past 30 years (Leslie 1996). The world's coastal waters and coral ecosystems bearing the most biologically rich life-zones of the planet are increasingly destroyed by pesticide and fertilizer runoffs and water-temperature and atmospheric changes—with over three-quarters of the world's coral reefs, which host 25 percent of all fish species, in catastrophic dieback (Smith and Hunton 1998). Dr. Tom Goreau, Director of the Global Coral Reef Alliance, reports that oscillations of water and current temperatures from climatic warming have caused "a climate-induced mass extinction—with one half of the coral reefs of the world experiencing catastrophic mortality in one year alone." It is interesting to note the response of America's business leadership to such reported effects of global warming (emphasis added), "The main problem with Kyoto, however, is that it is a drastic solution to a *problem that may not exist*" (Glassman 2001). The ocean bottoms themselves are strip-mined of fish and aquatic life across vast tracts by factory-trawlers that drag the ocean floors for marketable fish stock, whose take has increased more than fourfold in the last four decades, and which has led to the collapse of 16 of the world's 17 major ocean fisheries (Radford 1996, 19; WRI 1998).

Above the ocean, three-quarters of all bird species are in decline, one of every four mammals is endangered, and one-third of plant species is extinct or threatened with extinction. Water tables and freshwater sources are so depleted and polluted that the United Nations estimates that two-thirds of the world will be short of water by 2025 (Graham 1998, 20–21). The polar icecaps are rapidly melting—40 percent of the Arctic ice has already liquefied—and threaten coastal communities and ecologies with the rising sea levels they cause, dragging more nutrients, organochlorines and heavy metals into rivers, leaching waste-site and sewer toxins, bacteria and viruses into the seas, and destroying wetlands that act as the Earth's natural water-filtering system (*Earth Island Journal* 1996, 13). A continent-sized hole in the stratospheric ozone layer persists and grows, acid and carbon loads stored in polar ice are unlocked, and the United Nations Intergovernmental Panel on Climate Change (IPCC) predicts progressively extreme floods, storms, droughts, and infectious diseases as global temperatures continue to rise from atmospheric gases and industrial emissions (IPCC 2001).

Stripping of the planet's natural resources and life systems by unregulated and deregulated global market activities will persist and increase in the future without effective intervention. Synergistic interrelations of these simultaneously increasing loads will, in addition, compound their destructive toll (M.I.T. Vegetarian Support Group 1996, 1). At the same time, resource-dependent countries of the South continue to be obliged by "the Washington consensus" and International Monetary Fund (IMF) conditions to implement policies of environmentally damaging mono-crop agriculture and overexploitation of natural resources to receive loans to pay approximately half a billion dollars each day in compounding interest payments to foreign banks (George 1993). The world's richest market also simultaneously increases its demands for consumption—with 99 percent of the materials used in the production process ending up as waste within six weeks, and every ton of garbage, in turn, costing five tons of raw materials to produce it, and 25 tons of natural biomass to yield these usable materials (Weizzsacker 1997).

The underlying causal structure of the mounting planetary ecocide, however, remains publicly unrecognized. Ecological and environmental analyses and positions, including the desiderata principles of the 2002 Earth Charter, have failed to link the life-stripping phenomena they discern back to the inner logic of the global market system that propels them. Where the problem *is* recognized as systemic, its cause is typically ambiguated as "growth" with no definition of what is meant. Like "sin" and "godliness," which remain open to any interpretation, "growth" and "sustainability" have become pro-and-con incantations rather than guides of understanding. The "growth" that business and political lobbies demand means more aggregate sales of market commodities. But that this increase of market commodity sales must lead in free market conditions to more depredations of the environment to extract materials for and dispose of wastes of the increased commodities is a connection that is blocked from view. As with other dominant regimes of the past, *causal structures of life destruction borne by relations of economic rule remain taboo to name* (McMurtry 1999a, 1–45). A recent example is the three-year suppression by the European Union and the World Wide Fund for Nature of its own "devastating report about the destruction of tropical rainforests by multinational companies," and "the role of the IMF and the World Bank in forcing African and Caribbean countries to sell their forests for cash to pay back debts [to foreign banks]" (Brown 2000, 3).

This disconnection of structural cause from effect lies at the core of the growing planetary ecological crisis. Yet it is an ideological block that is easily seen through when it is embedded in a social order that we do not presuppose. Not long ago, we were able to understand well that the environmental devastation of the Soviet Union was related to its model of re-engineering nature to suit central command prescriptions. But the Soviet leadership, as market leaderships now, preferred to interpret each disaster as isolated and resolvable, and to dismiss critics as extremists, malcontents, and unscientific.

Academic communities were no exception. They were too busy with specialist careers in well-paying institutional niches to trace such dangerous connections. Wider-lensed critical thinkers, where they existed, were not funded. The situation is again much the same today. Only it is the far more empowered value program of "the global free market" that is at the helm, and unlike the Soviet Union, there is no external alternative to it or internal inhibitors of its leaders' private acquisitiveness. Global market agents profit without national or ownership constraints from the reduced costs and increased revenues of environmental stripping. Accordingly, the technologically empowered capacities to disassemble, pollute, and waste environments and ecosystems have vastly increased in their volumes, velocities, and transnational accesses, without even the social-property and territorial limits of the Soviet system to restrain their "freedom" to do so.

The environmental crisis is therefore greater in reach in this system, although its blinkers of ruling ideology are not less blinding. The corporate global market's organization of environmental usage is virtually *excluded from funded research investigation as a determinant of environmental depletion and destruction.* It is taboo to identify because control of the mass media and partnership control of public research funding rules out its study and exposure. We are increasingly aware of mass media selection against information that contravenes the interests of major advertisers and the general system by which these corporations profit (McMurtry 1998, 178–213). What is less known is that academic-corporate "partnership" funding has become, with government financing, the dominant and, in the natural and medical sciences, increasingly the sole source of funding of research. (See, for example, the lead editorial, "Is Academic Medicine for Sale?" *New England Journal of Medicine,* May 18, 2000). In consequence, the deep structure of cause-effect determination behind environmental catastrophe is selected against as a field of research and silenced in the media and commercial academic texts, even as the planetary ecological crisis deepens. It has become as unspeakable for those funded to inquire into these issues as challenging the Church over its blocks against causal thought in a previous era.

Because of these blocks to understanding the structural determinants of environmental degradation, we need to release investigation from three common dogmas that select against connected thinking about the environment:

1. The standard view of the biological sciences that ecological processes and environments can be understood independently of the economic determinants that systemically select for and against the reproduction and the distribution of the world's natural species by destruction, depletion, and pollution of their habitats;
2. The assumption that environmental or biological sciences are "value neutral," and that "Science" operates in a realm of pure objectivity that is not funded, directed, and implemented in accordance with the private interests of its corporate sponsors;
3. The presupposition that the worth of the environment does not lie in its life-value as such, but only in its resources for monetized market activities in global market competition.

Despite these unexamined blocks against deep-structural environmental research, we can discern a general pattern from which a general hypothesis can be posed. Most simply expressed, this general hypothesis is that a long-term correlation of intensity and extent obtains between large-scale for-profit use of environmental resources *and* their scientifically ascertainable decline. More specifically: *As corporate for-profit use of environmental resources has advanced across global life conditions and elements, these global life conditions and elements—the atmosphere, fresh waters and oceans, topsoils, trees, animal habitats and species, and mineral resources—have degenerated, in direct proportion to this usage, in their capacities of life-carriage and yield.*

I invite counterexamples to this generalization. But before moving to identification and distinction of the for-profit sequences that are at work in this causal correlation—which I will distinguish below from the much misunderstood term "capital"—a clarification is needed. The structural causation defined above is not intended to be conceived as a "law." It denotes, rather, *the expression of an institutionalized decision-structure, which has become closed to question and to recognition of the effects of its operation.* But this regulating structure, unlike a law of nature, is amenable to immediate modification and change should its bearers and presupposers choose to recognize the need (as has been to some extent the case with the international Montreal Protocol to protect the ozone layer).

Recognition of the global cause-effect structure identified above is the primary condition to be fulfilled if we are to respond effectively to the planetary environmental crisis. There is, however, a profound impediment to this recognition. Besides powerful corporate interests that lie in blocking this recognition, there is conventional presupposition of the ruling order within which one lives as the given structure of reality—"the real world" to which we must adapt. We see this social mind-set most virulently at work today in the public acceptance of calls for "reducing cost burdens" of environmental laws, and of new salable rights to pollute in a for-profit corporate market of the air we breathe itself. No such scheme has demonstrably reduced pollution anywhere. Yet the U.S. has refused to ratify the Kyoto Protocol to limit the emission of greenhouse gases unless a market in pollution rights is the mode of regulatory control. That no demonstration exists of the efficacy of such a regime in reducing pollution, and that it may merely provide rights to pollute and handouts of new marketable equities to corporate polluters, are issues that are blocked from public view. For illustration of how such a proposal can be so wrapped in circular reasoning as to be logically unintelligible in even leading environmental textbooks, see Anderson and Leal (1998). As for "voluntary restraints," even Senator Robert Byrd of the "coal state of West Virginia" now acknowledges that "they won't work" ("Utilities May Be Greener than Bush" 2001, 1).

For-Profit Money Sequences and Their Environmental Effects

Corporate for-profit organization of environmental resources admits of crucially different forms not yet recognized by economic or other analysis. These different forms of for-profit use of the environment can only be recognized from the standpoint of value, *life reproduction and growth itself.* In contrast to received theory, we will here adopt as our ground of value *"the life-ground,"* whose ruling principle of all value is that *the more comprehensive the ranges of vital life* of the organism or ecosystem is, *the better.* Conversely, *the more reduced the range of vital life* of the organism or ecosystem is, *the worse.*

Although *biodiversity* qualifies as a sub-principle of the life-ground of value, it is blind to distinctions of value *within* a species, notably the human; and it does not enable us to distinguish between the good of different *types* of species either—for example, the good of cockroaches and rats as distinct from dolphins and humans as bearers of life-value. Here, in contrast, we begin from the premise that life systems of all kinds become better *if and only if, and to the extent that, they bear more comprehensive ranges of thought, felt being, and/or action.* This is a principle I shall return to, and develop more fully in my recent books. But it is enough here to say that this principle entails the affirmation of biodiversity, or clean air and water, or education, as *good;* and just as clearly entails the repudiation of pollution, degraded habitats, extinctions, and so on as *bad:* each to the precise *degree* that each *enables,* or *disables,* vital life ranges. None of these conclusions are controversial, but the unifying principle from which each follows is not yet a yardstick of value understanding.

From this ultimate *ground* of life-value, we can distinguish among different *types* of for-profit sequence which have altogether different long-term ecological consequences, from the benign to the catastrophic.

Life and Money Capital

Capital, in the generic sense, is wealth that is used to produce more wealth. In the generic sense, capital can mean life-value that is used to produce more life-value—what we might call *"life capital"*—or it can mean money inputs of investment that produce more money outputs of profit for private corporate investors. It is important not to narrow the conception of capital to one dominant form of it, or we sustain an equivocation with ecocidal effects.

With "life capital" or the "life sequence of value," we can define its nature by a simple ecological formula (→ = requires/enables):

Life → Means of Life → More Life (L → M of L → L^1).

Such a formula can apply to an *ecosystem* whose species and habitats reproduce, diversify, and grow by virtue of all *the means of life* they require to do so. Or it can apply to a single member of one species. This *life sequence of value* also, conversely, can suffer deterioration or destruction by virtue of its means of reproduction being deprived from it (for example, by degradation of its sunlight or its food source or its water supply). The general principle here applies across all species, members of species and ecosystems, and all of their declining or improving states. It is what I call *"the life code of value."*

Where do *non*living constituents of ecologies fit in this code of value? They are "means of life," whether natural or man-made, insofar as they are required for or enable vital life ranges to be maintained and/or grow through time, as inanimate air, water, the earth-mass itself, and many kinds of minerals do.

In contrast, "money capital" or *"the money sequence of value"* moves from money inputs to more-money outputs with life-value subordinated as a means of this sequence. Money-demand, not life, is the regulating aim and content of economic reproduction and growth. Its middle term is typically a priced commodity, whether useful or harmful to life, which sells for a higher price than the costs of its production (i.e., *Money→ Commodity→ More Money*). But for-profit investment can also become more money with no commodity at all mediating its growth—as in currency speculations, arbitrages, and compound-interest bonds. So there is no single formula of the money-capital sequence, because it varies profoundly in its forms and consequences. This variation of the for-profit sequence is of singular importance in *distinguishing between capitalist sequences that may be consistent with or promote environmental life* (e.g., small-scale farming, sewage lagoons, self-powered transit) *and other money sequences which may destroy life systems by their nature* (e.g., the weapons industry). Unless we adopt a life-value standpoint as our ground of evaluation, we do not have the theoretical resources to discern the global economy-environment causal interface, and the life-and-death distinctions among its diverse types. This repression of distinctions among forms of capital, in turn, leads to a radically misleading disjunction of those who are for or against "capitalism" *simpliciter*.

A money-capital sequence that creates the commodity of nourishing food, for example, and nourishes the environment with new niche clearings at the same time, is very different from a money-capital sequence that produces commodities that destroy human and environmental life, waste natural and human resources, and provide no life-serving good whatever. The military commodity's profitable production and sale is particularly apposite here because it is the most profitable manufactured commodity on the globe, demands the lion's share of the U.S. federal budget, dominates the country's research grant systems, and is the nation's leading polluter of the environment (McMurtry 1989). Yet does anyone know of any environmental text that features an analysis of this economy-ecology linkage?

On the other hand, for-profit activities may also minimally harm or enrich the environment (e.g., biodiverse sustenance-farming whose surplus is sold for profit), promote new biodiversification and ecosystem possibilities by generating habitats and foods for fauna and flora (e.g., the rapidly expanding organic gardening business), or protect the environment from pollution by the reduction or the elimination of industrial toxic loads (e.g., solar-powered heating and transit and pollution-abatement technologies). The capitalist sequence is not *necessarily* life-destructive, but *can* in limited cases be both profitable *and* beneficial to the environment. Such issues cannot arise as issues, however, within the current confusion of capital sequences.

Within the dominant mind-set, which in this way grounds magical thinking, all capitalism is simply assumed as life-enhancing by the operations of the market's invisible hand, and the major for-profit industries of resource extraction, manufacturing, and service delivery competitively cut their cost inputs and increase their scale and velocity of operations at the systematic expense of planetary and regional environments. But here again, we see very little said on this underlying causal structure in increasingly vast libraries of environmental and ecosystem analysis. In this context and undeterred by effective regulatory inhibition in a global field of "free market" ideology, the dominant money-capital sequences are propelled to an increasingly frantic pace of appropriating every life form and natural resource to maximize profits to stockholders in evermore expanded and leveraged capital circuits. Correspondingly, the planetary environment is ever more cumulatively overloaded and stripped by these life-blind money sequences, whose forms and pathological consequences are not distinguished or recognized. Thomas Berry is a distinctively critical environmental thinker because he does not delink environmental problems from for-profit corporate money sequences, but frontally contends that "the profit of the corporation is the deficit of the Earth" (Berry 1987)—a statement that strikingly conceives the problem at a general level, but does not distinguish *which* for-profit corporate activities are a "deficit of the Earth" and which are not, and what are the principles by which we can tell the degrees of both.

By understanding from the standpoint of the life-ground itself, and discriminating among money sequences in accordance with their differently destructive effects on environmental life-hosts, we can identify the following for-profit *types* of use of environmental resources by the following formulae where:

$ = money capital
C = priced commodity
DC = priced commodity that destroys life

Type I: $ → C+ → $1 (C+: to degree that C is *life-enabling commodity with minimum or no life-destruction to people and/or to the environment* by its production and/or consequences, e.g., organic food production, solar-and-wind powered vehicles and energy systems, permanent plastic appliances and pipes). Note the major distinction here from Herman Daly's implied position that *replacement of harvested environmental resources* does not harm the environment (Daly 1996, 194). What Daly ignores, as all macroeconomic theory does, is that replacing a forest with a tree plantation may reproduce the economic resource, but destroy the forest as a life-habitat and biodiverse host. Here we see that even pro-environment economics fails to recognize the crucial distinction between economic sequences that regenerate economic resources, yet strip it of life habitat and species, and economic sequences which do not.

Type II: $ → C- → $1 (C-: to degree that C- is *non-life-enabling commodity with life-reduction to people and/or environment* by its production and/or consequences, e.g., junk food, natural terrain recreational vehicles, throwaway packages, and ad newsprint).

Type III: $ → DC → $1 (DC: a commodity *constituted so as to reduce or to destroy environmental life by its nature,* e.g., anti-resource armaments and environment-razing machineries like bottom-scraping factory trawlers and forest-clearcut systems of bulldozers, grapplers, and chainsaws). Like the weapons industry with which it has developed from the beginning, the machineries to tear natural life-fabrics apart in order to extract their marketable elements—rainforests, ocean bottoms, and earth strata—grow evermore efficient with development of the global free market. These machines to dismantle and to slaughter life-systems develop scientifically alongside armament commodities for killing human beings. With the established sciences as their servant, they rip up soil communities, demolish forest worlds, and strip aquatic ecosystems in minutes so as to ensure the maximum velocity and volume of competitive money-sequence gains.

Type IV: \$ → \$1 → \$n (Money is *transformed into more money with no good or service produced in between,* e.g., transnational currency attacks, which do not directly destroy human or environmental life, but whose effect is to drain public treasuries and the regulatory and life-security infrastructures they fund).

This framework for distinguishing among money-capital sequences with respect to their opposed impacts on environmental life systems is required if we are to understand the complex *causal structure behind the systemic destruction of planetary life-organization.* By my concept of "causal structure," I do not mean a Humean succession of single antecedent and consequent conditions (as in a struck match and a fire), but specifically *instituted decision-structures which select for processes and actions which are indifferent to or violate environmental life-organization in the implementation of their for-profit goal.* While our conceptual framework picks out corporate money-capital sequences as the primary causal mechanism behind this global environmental breakdown, it does not hold these corporate money sequences as *necessarily* destructive of the life environment, or as *always* so destructive, or as *solely* so destructive. It leaves the matter open to various possibilities, depending on: (1) *the money sequence in question;* and, (2) *the absence or presence of effective and overriding regulation of money-sequence pathways that depredate the environment.*

While the evidence of increasing failure of governments to effectively regulate for-profit destruction of the environment seems overwhelming, there can be little question that effective regulation of such behavior is possible and practical. Deeper than the evolution of for-profit activities that destroy the environment to reduce their costs is the longer evolution of the powers of communities to effectively defend and rule against what invades, pollutes, and destroys their conditions of life. As I have argued at length elsewhere, the evolution of humanity itself has been largely defined by this *"social immune system":* from the origins of language itself in life-warning signals, to primitive taboos against harmful substances and practices, to wars of national self-defense against invading enemies, to—more relevantly here—the rule of life-protective law. All of these phenomena are variations of the developing powers of the human mind, a concept that interestingly derives from the root *monere*, "to warn." I provide a fuller discussion of the "social immune system" in *The Cancer Stage of Capitalism* (McMurtry 1999a, 85–132).

Life-Protective Law and the Environment

A recent example indicates the possibility of life-protective law as a significant inhibitor of ecocidal money sequences, even in a jurisdiction whose governments have all but been occupied by dominant corporate agents. Observe here the qualifier *"life-protective"* before "rule of law." A rule of law does not necessarily protect life, but may impose the rule of a privileged caste or class on others *at the expense of their lives*—as slave-holding property law, instituted feudal privileges or, today, transnational corporate trade and investment treaties (the latter by failure to recognize the claims or rights of any life form except corporate investors whose rights are spelled out as overriding) (McMurtry 1999b, 45–57). A *life-protective* law, in contrast, prescribes an effectively enforceable obligation of parties to refrain from doing what harms life, whether human or nonhuman, individual or collective.

A representative example of this kind of law was a set of national regulations prescribed by the federal government of Canada in 1992, with a 1995 deadline for compliance, to radically reduce environmentally destructive emissions of harmful substances or by-products (dioxins, methanol, furans, and so on) by the country's powerful pulp and paper corporations. After dire warnings of being "unable to compete if costly regulatory burdens are imposed by government," and the like, the industry complied. Five years later in 2000, interviewed company representatives acknowledged that "many mills would not have acted as quickly if it wasn't for the government's edict, since upgrading is a very costly undertaking." One major firm had aggressively reduced its emissions by 70 percent, and asserted that it was "proud of what we've done" (McHardie 2000, B9).

Why was a profit-maximizing corporation "proud of what we've done" in reducing its toxic emissions at its own increased cost? It was *able* to so decide because public authority *required* both it and its competitors to do so by the force of law. Corporately dominated governments never advocate a "level playing field of binding environmental regulations." As Earthjustice policy advocate Maria Weidner observes, "[Appointments to the Environmental Protection Agency] are lawyers and lobbyists who built their careers by helping industry get out of environmental regulations" (Seelye 2001, A10). Yet this kind of level playing field achieves effective pollution reduction. Its success is, moreover, practicable on a global scale by inclusion of such regulatory constraints as binding articles in the disciplines of the World Trade Organization (WTO), whose articles now exclusively protect only international investors, not environmental or human life.

But why would profit-maximizing corporations ever accept compliance with such compulsory regulations? The answer is that once the cost of noncompliance is made greater than compliance, and all are bound by the same rules, corporations can afford and enjoy the reputation of not destroying their environmental life-hosts. Only a psychopathic mind-set chooses to systematically harm life. What is missing is the rule of life-protective law, which is quite achievable on the transnational level through its inclusion in transnational trade treaties. Observe that in the national case identified above, success was achieved despite the relatively great power of the corporations involved, and despite the fact that such law did not apply to international competitors. Consider in the light of such examples how often we hear at a near saturating level that "globally competitive conditions demand less government intervention," that only "voluntary compliance by the private sector can work effectively," that "monetary incentives through a market in pollution credits is the only realistic alternative," and so on.

All of these sweeping claims are, in fact, both lawless and false. They are no more compelling than the appeal of wife-batterers to their right of "freedom from heavy-handed government regulation." In truth, the argument is even less compelling because the for-profit destruction of local and global conditions of life violates the lives of the whole of humanity, other species, and the planetary life-ground itself.

The resources for generalizing such life-protective law across national and continental boundaries are now available in the already instituted obligatory regulatory structures of transnational trade and investment agreements. The latter's current system of protection for corporate investors alone is, in truth, ethically bizarre and tyrannical. What is required to redress its extreme imbalance is to admit already existing minimum standards of human and environmental life protection as *binding terms of already effectively enforced international trade agreements*—from the North American Free Trade Agreement (NAFTA) and the Free Trade Area of the Americas (FTAA) to the World Trade Organization (WTO). With schedules of accession to take account of different levels of economic development—which have long regulated the European Union across such national differences—the problem of ecocide has an effective resolution. But it has not been applied because of the blinkers of a dominant ideological program that assumes that regulation of market activities is only justifiable to protect market property and profits.

The price of noncompliance with a transnational discipline of environmental protection would be the same or greater than noncompliance with any other article of these very detailed transnational regulatory systems—a trade penalty that, as with corporate copyright or market access now, would be triggered by evidence before adjudicating expert panels of "failing to honor trade obligations." Astonishingly, no binding environmental obligation exists in 2001 in any transnational trade and investment regime. On the contrary, NAFTA and WTO trade panels, without any environmental regulations governing their decisions, have in various decisions overridden existing government regulations against toxic gas additives, PCB wastes, dolphin-laced tuna, and cigarette campaigns targeting teenage girls. Meanwhile, government trade and finance bureaucracies and the private transnational corporations they have come to represent resist all such accountability to the protection of planetary and human life-organization with misrepresentation, counterattack, and evasion. "We will oppose," says the powerful president of the U.S. Council on International Business, "any and all measures to create or even imply binding obligations for governments or business relating to the environment or labor" (cited by Clarke 1997, 9). "We've allowed a new kind of protectionism to appear in this country," says U.S. President, George Bush Jr., in defending the abandonment of his campaign pledge to honor the Kyoto Protocol to reduce global warming gas emissions. "It talks of the environment, while opposing the wealth-creating policies that will pay for clean air and water in developing nations" ("In Praise of Free Trade" 2001, A14). Dictatorial and life-blind regimes always behave this way, as long as they are permitted to by public and informed opinion.

So far, unfortunately, the elites and practitioners of the biological and ecological sciences and social and environmental ethics have by the record of their course texts and topics also averted their eyes from the structural causes of ecological depredation and collapse, preferring safer or better-funded issues to discuss.

References

Anderson, Terry L., and Donald R. Leal. 1998. "Free Market versus Political Environmentalism." Pp. 364–74 in Michael Zimmerman et al., eds., *Environmental Philosophy: From Animal Rights to Radical Ecology.* Upper Saddle River, N.J.: Prentice-Hall.

Berry, Thomas. 1987. "The Viable Human." *Revision*, Winter/Spring.

Brown, Paul. 2000. "Report on Forests Suppressed." *Guardian Weekly,* June 1–7.

Clarke, Tony. 1997. *The Corporate Rule Treaty.* Ottawa: Canadian Centre for Policy Alternatives.

Daly, Herman. 1996. "Sustainable Development? No Thank You," in *The Case Against the Global Economy.*" San Francisco: Sierra Books.

Earth Island Journal. Spring (Southern Hemisphere), 1996.

"East and South: The Facts." 1990. *New Internationalist*, September 12.

George, Susan. 1993. "The Debt Crisis." International Physicians against Nuclear War XI World Congress, October.

Glassman, James. 2001. "It's No Time to Go Wobbly on Kyoto." *Wall Street Journal*, May 11: A14.

Graham, Colin. 1998. "Will the Public Expect the Global Economy to Self-Destruct?" *The CCPA Monitor*, July–August: 20–21.

Greenpeace Magazine, Winter 2000.

"In Praise of Free Trade." 2001. Editorial. *Wall Street Journal,* May 11: A14.

"Is Academic Medicine For Sale?" 2000. Editorial. *New England Journal of Medicine,* May 18.

Leslie, John. 1996. *The End of the World.* New York: Routledge.

McHardie, Daniel. 2000. "Rules Have Pared Pulp Pollution," *Globe and Mail Business Focus*, June 5: B9.

McLaren, Digby J. 1996. "Reply to Colin Rowat." *Delta Newsletter of the Global Change Program* (Royal Society of Canada) Vol.7, No.3: 3.

McMurtry, John. 1989. *Understanding War.* Toronto: Samuel Stevens and Science for Peace.

McMurtry, John. 1998. *Unequal Freedoms: The Global Market as an Ethical System.* Toronto and Westport, Conn.: Garamond and Kumarian Press.

McMurtry, John. 1999a. *The Cancer Stage of Capitalism.* London, UK; Sterling, Va.: Pluto Press.

McMurtry, John. 1999b. "World Order by Trade and Investment Decree." Pp. 45–57 in Walter Dorn, ed., *World Order for a New Millennium.* New York: St. Martin's Press.

M.I.T. Vegetarian Support Group. 1996. "How Our Food Choices Affect Life on Earth." *World-Wide-Web,* November 22: 1.

Radford, Tim. 1996. "Filled with More Than a Grain of Truth." *Guardian Weekly*, November 17: 19.

Sandbrook, Richard. 1994. "The Planet through Pollyanna's Eyes." *Globe and Mail,* April 16: D7.

Seelye, Katharine Q. 2001. "Bush Is Choosing Insiders to Fill Environmental Positions." *New York Times*, May 12: A10.

Smith, James (researcher) and John Hunton (producer). 1998. *Warnings from the Wild.* KCTS/KYVE documentary film.

United Nations Intergovernmental Panel on Climate Change (IPCC). 2001. Report. February 19.

"Utilities May be Greener Than Bush." 2001. *Wall Street Journal,* May 10: 1.

Weizzsacker, Ernst. 1997. *Factor Four.* London: Earthscan Books.

(WRI) World Resources Institute. 1998. Report. September–October.

Chapter 16

Global Consumption in the New Millennium

Patricia H. Werhane and Mary A. Hamilton

When one is asked to enumerate the most challenging ethical issues business will face in the next century, environmental sustainability is surely near the top of the list. Underlying this and other issues is a serious global phenomenon: the exportation of Western mental models of free enterprise and consumption.

There is a mental model of free enterprise, a model primarily created in the United States, that is being exported, albeit unconsciously, as industrialized nations expand commerce through the globalization of free enterprise. This model is not one of greedy self-interested cowboy capitalists eagerly competing to take advantage of resources, low-priced employment, or offshore regulatory laxity. Rather we are referring to another model, one that has worked and worked well in most of North America and Western Europe for some time. This model contends that industrialized free enterprise in a free trade global economy, where businesses and entrepreneurs can pursue their interests competitively without undue regulations or labor restrictions, will produce growth and well-being, i.e., economic good, in every country or community where this phenomenon is allowed to operate. The results of global free enterprise, if adapting itself to an American style, "can be compared to the strongest hand in poker: the royal flush, of all five of the most valuable cards of the same suit" (Uchitelle 1999, 16).

What is wrong with adapting a model for global commerce out of the highly successful American model for free enterprise? What is wrong with economic growth and improved standards of living, and increased consumption particularly in developing countries? Isn't reduction of poverty and thus the increase of consumption a universally desirable outcome? Is it fair that those of us in developed nations, having exploited most of the planet's resources, would now curtail development in poor parts of the world? The tempting answer is that there is nothing wrong with the Western model, particularly in face of worldwide poverty and unequal distribution of wealth. In this paper we shall suggest that a more thoughtful reply requires some qualifications.

To begin, we explain the notion of mental models. Although the term is not always clearly defined, "mental model" connotes the idea that human beings have mental representations, cognitive frames, or mental pictures of their experiences, representations that model the stimuli or data with which they are interacting, and these are frameworks that set up parameters though which experience or a certain set of experiences, is organized or filtered (Kelly 1955; Senge 1990, chapter 10; Gentner and Whitley 1997, 210–11; Gorman 1992; Werhane 1991, 1998, 1999).

Mental models might be hypothetical constructs of the experience in question or scientific theories; they might be schema that frame the experience, through which individuals process information, conduct experiments, and formulate theories. Mental models function as selective mechanisms and filters for dealing with experience. In focusing, framing, organizing, and ordering what we experience, mental models bracket and leave out data, and emotional and motivational foci taint or color experience. Nevertheless, because schema we employ are socially learned and altered through religion, socialization, culture, educational upbringing, and other experiences, they are shared ways of perceiving, organizing, and learning.

Because of the variety and diversity of mental models, none is complete, and "there are multiple possible framings of any given situation" (Mischel and Shoda 1995; Johnson 1993). By that we mean that each of us can frame any situation, event, or phenomenon in more than one way, and that the same phenomenon can also be socially constructed in a variety of ways. It will turn out that the way one frames a situation is critical to its outcome, because "[t]here are . . . different moral consequences depending on the way we frame the situation" (Johnson 1993).

Let us now illustrate how the notion of mental models is helpful in understanding the problem of exporting a Western model of consumption.

One of the presuppositions of Western free enterprise, a supposition that fueled and made possible the industrial revolution, is that feudalism, at least as it is exhibited through most forms of serfdom, is humiliating. It demeans laborers, and worse, it does not allow serfs, in particular, to create or experience any sense of what it would mean to be free: free to live and work where they please, to own property, and to choose what they consume and how they live. It is commonly, although not universally, argued that individual property ownership is a social good. In agriculturally based economies in particular, owning one's own farmland is considered a necessary step toward freedom and self-reliance. Within the framework of the Western model of consumption, a global industrial revolution coupled with free commerce, wage labor, and property ownership will change the feudal mental model of underdeveloped countries, and, it is commonly argued, will improve the lives for serfs, farm workers, and tenant farmers, in particular.

However, as Akiro Takahashi points out in a recent article in *Business Ethics Quarterly*, even twentieth-century feudal arrangements are complex social institutions. One cannot simply free the serfs or sharecroppers, engage in redistributive land reform, and hope that a new economic arrangement will produce a higher standard of living. Takahashi's example is from a 1960s rice-growing community in Luzon in the Philippines. From as long as anyone can remember until land reforms in the 1970s the village had operated as a fiefdom. There were a few landholders and the rest of the villagers were tenant farmers. In order to work the land, each year the tenant farmers paid rents equal to half the net production of their farms. However, because the tenant farmers were always in debt to the landlords, they usually owed all the net production to the landlords. The tenant farmers in fact were never able to pay their debts, and because of interest rates, as high as 200 percent, their debt increased each year so that in essence they could never leave the property. Since what was owed the landlord was the net produce, each sharecropper was allowed to hire workers to farm the land they rented. So tenant farmers hired workers from other landlords or from other communities to till and harvest the crop. Each sharecropper, in turn, went to work for another landlord's sharecropper. In addition, it was common practice for the harvesters not to do a perfect job, leaving often as much as 20 to 25 percent of the rice unharvested. Gleaning by tenant farmers or their families on the land they rented was not permitted, but there wasn't anything prohibiting the wives of the farm workers and the rest of the community from "gleaning" the rest of the rice for themselves. This form of gleaning was common practice and enabled the tenant farmers to feed their families. The landlords in turn pretended none of this occurred, still demanding the net product from each of its tenant farmers. Essentially, this practice, while appearing inefficient and inappropriate, created a system in which the poor were supported by the landlords (Takahaski 1997, 39–40). According to Takahashi, agrarian reforms designed to break up large land holdings and feudal practices were instituted in the Philippines in the 1970s. However, lax enforcement and political unrest has left villages such as the ones he describes with pretty much the same arrangement.

This example illustrates the obvious fact that land reform and the redistribution of property, apparently worthwhile projects to free tenant farmers from feudal bonds, will only be successful if the new landholders have means to function as economically viable farmers and in ways that do not threaten age-old traditions. The food distribution relationships in the Philippine example are embedded in a complex cultural and social system that cannot be dismantled merely for the sake of independence and private ownership without harming the complex communal relationships that have maintained this system for centuries. Interestingly, the model of consumption operative in that community is also complex and, as this example illustrates, involves a distributive system of sharing so that no one goes without rice. Coupled with this is a fragile but sustainable ecological equilibrium. Because the land is never completely harvested, the remaining rice refurbishes the soil, and the land is reusable each season.

This example alerts us to a simple precaution. Land reform will not be successful in every community without making drastic social changes that alter communal relationships, family traditions, and ancient practices. This is because, as Michael Walzer reminds us, the notion of what is good or a social good is a socially constructed idea that is contextually and culturally relative. Abstract ideas such as autonomy, equality, private property, ownership, community, consumption, and even environmental sustainability create mental models that take on different meanings depending on the social and situational context. Differing notions of community, ownership, property, exchange, competition, equality, and fairness, what Walzer calls social goods, create cultural anomalies that cannot be overcome simply by transferring private free enterprise to global markets (Walzer 1983). The social context affects the way private enterprise is embraced and developed over time. This does not mean that land reform, for example, is wrongheaded. It does, however, suggest that economic development and environmental sustainability must be reconceived in each situation so that what falls under the rubric of "reform" is contextually relevant in a way that change will not destroy the ability of the people to survive or the cultural fabric underlying what is to be changed.

Does this example, and there are thousands of others, point to the conclusion that because of the relativity of custom and culture, we should either abandon the ideal of global environmental well-being or, alternately, simply continue to convert the developing world into economic versions of "Dallas?" Is John Gray correct when he declares in his recent book that "the global economy system [based on Western laissez-faire free enterprise] is immoral, inequitable, unworkable, and unstable" (quoted in Zakaria 1999, 16)? These two alternatives as we have crudely stated them, present us with lose-lose options as if there were only two sorts of responses to problems of Westernized global consumption and conservation. We want to suggest that there are other ways to deal with these issues.

The existence of wide-spread complex cultural, social, community and even religious differences along with differing social goods does not imply that we can neither operate in those settings if they are alien to our own nor merely export Western versions of consumption. To appeal again to Michael Walzer, despite the plurality and incommensurability of cross-cultural social goods, there is a common thread of agreement, across cultures and religious difference, about the "bads," what cannot be tolerated or should not be permitted in any community. Walzer calls these thin threads of agreement "moral minimums" (Walzer 1994). Human suffering, abject poverty, preventable disease, high mortality, the inability to have clean air and water, farming that destroys the soil, and violence are abhorred wherever they occur. This is the reason the practice we described earlier is tolerable. All social systems are not in agreement about the constitution of the "good life," but there is widespread agreement about deficient or despicable living conditions, indecencies, violations of human rights, mistreatments, and other harms.

Given that perspective, almost everyone will agree that disease, high infant mortality, violence, and poverty, however contextually defined, are bads. Alleviating suffering of these sorts is surely a good. Improving economic conditions, in most cases, alleviates poverty and human suffering, if not violence. Then, is not value-added activity in the form of economic growth the proper solution to these evils? And since free enterprise works best, or is the least of the worst, isn't that the model we should export?

We must cautiously consider that conclusion. Economic growth is not a "bad." Indeed, in most cultures it is considered a social good. But the notion cannot be identified without qualification with a Western idea of free enterprise. The model of economic growth in each context has to be framed in terms of each particular culture and its social goods. Moreover, despite strong Julian Simonesque arguments to the contrary, we cannot take the risk that economic development will "turn out all right." While some of the data are unclear (e.g., on whether we will run out of natural resources), acid rain, the greenhouse effect, the depletion of rainforests and the exponential elimination of animal and plant species are real occurring phenomena that we dare not ignore. Laissez-faire consumption, as practiced in some industrialized nations, can no longer be tolerated as a viable option. It is not only the economy that matters. What matters is the planet, just as what also matters are social relationships, family, religious, and community traditions, and values—deeply held values about what is important and treasured—that is, those social goods a community cannot give up without sacrificing more than its lack of material well-being. If endemic poverty is an evil, we must create new ways to engage in free enterprise that take into account, and even celebrates, environmental sustainability and cultural difference.

All of this is rather vague and, one might well contend, has more to do with public policy. What are needed are stiffer regulations worldwide that are enforced unilaterally everywhere. Yet, as Richard Rorty and Cornell West (hardly hearty libertarians) argue, it is not the state, but the multinational corporation (MNC) that is probably the most viable and creative social institution today. Many multinational corporations are more stable than the cultures of many developing countries and, according to Rorty, their leaders often have "a more perspicuous view of globalizing trends" (Rorty 1999, 3) than our political leaders.

If West and Rorty are even half right, we want to conclude, then, that given their economic power and stability, MNCs have moral responsibilities not to produce economic changes that result in negative environmental or cultural harm in any of the countries or cultures in which they operate. But that, too, is overly simplistic and didactic, and we repeat the mistake of exporting mental models by universalizing a negative harm principle without contextualizing the meaning of harms and benefits. Worse, even if West and Rorty are on target, what multinational in its right economic mind would buy into green strategies in areas of the world where they are not required to do so, or would consider contextualizing commodities to coincide with different cultural mores and environmental constraints?

Interestingly, John Gray suggests that attempts at economic colonization of free enterprise will not produce world homogenization and the destruction of indigenous cultures as we have suggested. Rather, he argues, "[w]hen new technologies enter economies from which in the past they were shut out . . . they will interact with indigenous cultures to generate types of consumption that have hitherto not existed anywhere" (Gray 1998, 58). Thus, he claims, cultures culturally reconfigure technologies and products. Whether or not this is true is situational at best.

There is another way to approach these dilemmas that may help to progress the argument. The idea is to develop different mental models of consumption and sustainability and to use what is called a systems approach to economic development. In commerce we talk a great deal about exchanges. An exchange between two rational parties is fair if each party receives what they think is appropriate for what they have traded or given. We might modify this to limit fair exchanges to those that occur between people or organizations of similar power, each of whom share the same mental model of exchange. This modification or proviso is necessary even if each party *thinks* the transaction is fair. Without such agreement of mental models, parties often would agree to exchanges they would otherwise find unfair had they understood the operative mental model for exchange. For example, indigenous people might believe they were agreeing to share land while companies thought they were buying it.

"Consumption" is ordinarily defined as "using up of good or services either by consumers or in the production of other goods" (*Webster's* 1986, 300). What would happen if we rethought consumption not as "using up" but as exchanging—exchanging or trading products, goods, and services? This is a version of William McDonough's model of "waste equals food" (McDonough 2000, 121). According to McDonough, there are three types of consumables: products of consumption are those that are used up when consumed (agriculture); products of service are those that can be reconfigured and reused (glass bottles); and unmarketable products are those that either cannot be reused or create externalities (pollution). The ideal is that every act of consumption that produces by-products creates not waste, but products that are then reusable, compostable, or recyclable. If consumption means "using something up," McDonough's ideal is zero consumption. This model of consumption, however, refers to material items and does not necessarily take into account the largest component of consumption, energy, both as energy used in the compostable and recycling processes and as it dissipates through entropy (McDonough 2000).

Our idea is to appeal to another model. The first element of the model is to redefine material consumption as exchange, so when something is consumed, it is exchanged for something else. When a company uses resources the idea is that it will exchange them, that is utilize resources in its production processes that are either products of consumption or products of service. Fair consumption under that model would be one in which everything was exchanged so that nothing was wasted or used up. So-called waste would be used for something else. That would mean that gas and coal, for example, would have to be exchanged, an impossibility within most normal lifetimes, so these resources would have to be replaced with another commodity, e.g., solar or wind energy.

But, and this introduces the second element of our model, wind or solar energy is not exchangeable in the ordinary sense of that term, since we do not literally give back to, or exchange something with, wind or the sun. Thus, what is neither replaceable nor exchangeable such as most forms of energy, would have to be substituted with a resource that is virtually inexhaustible.

Our reason for suggesting this reformulation of consumption is that the reformulation makes economic sense. It does not ask those of us raised in developed countries to go back to living in straw huts. Rather we need merely to exchange what we use for an equal something else, or replace exhaustible sources with inexhaustible sources. This exchange model, in which material goods are produced and consumed based on natural resource exhaustibility or inexhaustibility and on exchangeability of material goods, gives firms a feasible measurement of environmental sustainability that can be incorporated into global, economic development.

There is another dimension to rethinking consumption. Going back to the Philippine feudal system, we want to suggest that a systems approach or systems thinking helps to envision how economic growth, environmental sustainability, and respect for diverse cultural differences not only is possible, but also competitively advantageous to global corporations.

A system or alliance is "a complex of interacting components together with the relationships among them that permit the identification of a boundary-maintaining entity or process" (Laszlo and Krippner 1998, 51). "A truly systemic approach considers how this set of individuals, institutions, and processes operates in a system involving a complex network of interrelationships, an array of individual and institutional actors, with conflicting interests and goals, and a number of feedback loops" (Wolf 1999).

Systems thinking involves a multiple-perspective analysis of the subject matter (Mitroff and Linstone 1993). Because "the fundamental notion of interconnectedness or nonseparability forms the basis of what has come to be known as the Systems Approach, . . . every problem humans face is complicated [and] must be perceived as such" (Mitroff and Linstone 1993 95). So each system or subsystem, because it is complex and entails a multitude of various individual, empirical, social, and political relationships, needs to be analyzed from technical, social, and individual perspectives, ranking problems, perspectives, and alternate solutions, and evaluating the problem and its possible resolution from these multiple perspectives.

A multiple perspective approach takes into account the fact that each of us individually or as a member of groups, organizations, or alliances creates and frames the world through a series of mental models, each of which, by itself, is incomplete. While it is probably never possible to take into account all networks of relationships, a multiple perspectives approach forces us to think more broadly, and to look at particular situations from different points of view (Mitroff and Linstone 1993, 98). It is also invaluable in trying to understand other points of view, even if, eventually, one agrees to disagree. A multiple perspective approach is essential if, for example, global corporations are to take seriously environmental concerns and/or understand what is at stake when they expand into developing areas of the world. Such an approach suggests that economic development by any global corporation or organization (e.g., a nongovernmental organization) would have to take into account the social, political, cultural, and environmental context in which the development was proposed.

But still, even with its appeal to a more quantitative approach, why would any company buy into this picture? Is this stretching the limits of what we should expect from global corporations or of free enterprise?

We recognize that there may be some obstacles. In a global economy with scarce resources, focus needs to be placed on sustainable economic development (Shrivastava 2000). Technological advances have brought the world closer together and resources that were previously untapped are now available for productive purposes. We need to be careful not to see this global expansion as a way to gain more natural resources simply because they are easier to access than they were in the past. Access to these resources could create a mind-set that this abundance will last forever.

Further, as consumer preferences continue to change, product life cycles become shorter and employee tenure shrinks; businesses are beginning to think in shorter time intervals. The current emphasis on organization adaptation to change could become counterproductive to sustainable economic development. As business processes and products are adapted to indigenous circumstances, it could lead to the disposability rather than the exchangeability of consumables. The challenge for business, then, will be to think in terms of long-term sustainable development in the midst of these short-term pressures.

Moreover, at least some consumers are shifting their focus to environmentally friendly products and strategically ecological variables are being used more frequently by business to create a competitive advantage (Shrivastava, 2000). The focus of business on the stewardship of scarce natural resources is a response to changed consumer preferences resulting from pressure from environmental groups and leading to the development of environmental friendly products and services. This is a legitimate business response; however, it is not enough because the focus is on demand—revenue generation from a shift in consumer values. It does not necessarily address sustainable supply issues—environmentally friendly production inputs or business processes that in the short run could be more costly to the firm while in the long run less harmful to the environment.

Even with these short-term pressures, we propose that it is of strategic significance and in the best interest of business to take a systems approach in sustainable economic development as we evolve as a global economy. It is important to remember that multinational firms are first and foremost economic entities that are responsible for the continuous process of value creation and long-term viability of the business. Thus, when considering both demand and supply factors, business entities need to create enough value so they can continue its business into the future. Given this emphasis, firms operating simultaneously within many different cultures are beginning to understand the impact that unique practices and noneconomic circumstances of local communities have on the production, distribution, and marketing of products and services. In order to continue to create value and operate within multiple cultures, many of these firms are beginning to recognize the importance of and need for environmental sustainability as an essential practice for long-term viability. We propose that sustainable economic development in this context is a way to create more value for firms, for indigenous cultures, and for the environment when the Western model of consumption is redefined as exchange and when firms' mental models about the environment include both supply and demand factors.

Stuart Hart and C. K. Prahalad (2002, forthcoming) contend that it happens to be in the long-term self-interest of global multinational companies to tread cautiously and with respect in alien cultural contexts. This is because, in brief, developing countries represent 80 percent of the population of the world and thus are a yet untapped source of growth and development. If that growth is done carefully through working within indigenous and environmental constraints, the result could be the creation of exciting new products and services that enhance rather than destroy communities while at the same time benefiting the companies in question (Hart and Prahalad 2002, forthcoming). Taking a longer term perspective, Hart argues that if these new developments are not environmentally sustainable as well as "exchange-oriented," environmental problems will escalate more quickly than they have in the West because of lack of local technology to clean up.

The challenge is to create new mental models for global business that achieve the aims Hart and Prahalad propose. There is at least one such attempt by a large transnational corporation to do exactly this. Unilever is a multibillion-dollar global company with over 300,000 employees operating in almost 100 countries. Its main products are foods, fish, chemicals, and household products. Because it was founded in the Netherlands, a country one-third of which is reclaimed from the seas, Unilever has always been concerned with questions of environmental sustainability. In addition, the more recent expansion of its agricultural and fishing operations in remote communities has made Unilever increasingly aware of cultural difference. Beginning in 1993, using a systems approach, Unilever began a process of changing its mental model of what it meant by shareholder value-added. This resulted in a corporate-wide initiative that they call the "triple bottom line" (Vis 1997). The rationale for this initiative is that if Unilever is going to continue to be successful in the next century, its success depends on its worldwide financial, ecological, and social assets. So Unilever changed the definition of "economic value-added" to an expanded triple bottom line that measures economic, ecological and community assets, liabilities, profits (or benefits), and losses. According to Unilever, in its statement of corporate purpose and practice, each of these assets is of equal importance, and its aim is to be able to quantify the corporate contributions to each of these three areas. Each type of asset represents a source of value to the company and its shareholders. The sustained development of each of these sources of value ensures that the overall value accruing to shareholders is built up and sustained over the long term. This is in essence the significance of sustainable development to a company that aims at sustainable profit growth and long-term value creation (Standish et. al. 1999; Vis 1997, 3).

As part of this triple bottom line initiative, Unilever is working with some indigenous cultures that have environmental constraints. Hindustan Lever, one of their subsidiaries in India, has developed a new low-priced soap that can be used the by Indians to clean their clothing in the river. It is less expensive to produce, biodegradable, and gets the clothes cleaner than the standard laundry soap product. Moreover, the firm is also working in a few small villages in remote areas of India to develop small enterprises owned by these Indians and with products specifically designed for their environmental and economic circumstances.

These are micro-development projects, because the products they are supporting require little capital, they are locally produced, and of only indigenous interest. Unilever's goal, however, is to make those villages and their inhabitants economically viable managers, entrepreneurs, and customers as those notions are defined and make sense within a particular village culture and in ways that are not environmentally threatening (Hart and Prahalad 2002). Whether this will be a success story still remains to be seen. There is to date no outcomes data, since the case events are still unfolding, and it will be some years before one can determine whether these projects are successful.

According to Unilever, human flourishing in diverse settings creates needs for a diversity of products and services, products and services that Unilever will be able to provide. At the same time, human and environmental well-being creates long-term value added, both for Unilever and for the cultures and communities in which it operates.

Is this *the* answer, and will all companies be this creative? We don't know, but if this sort of revolution does not occur, not only will we be much worse off for it, firms will also not be able to survive economically in the long run. Without conservation and replenishing from both supply and demand perspectives, environmental resources will be depleted over time. We do know that even firms who have not explicitly adopted the principles of the Earth Charter are interested in sustainable firm value. "To be sustainable," John Browne, CEO of BR/Amoco, points out, "companies need a sustainable world . . . where environmental equilibrium is maintained . . . [and] in which the population can enjoy the heat, light, and mobility that we take for granted." This suggests that environmental and economic value sustainability are mutually compatible and necessary to tackle the global problems we face. We also know what the initiatives of Unilever have done to help us learn about consumption as exchange. We can then take these initiatives into consideration when creating a new mental model of business inclusive of environmental, cultural, and economic considerations that can be incorporated into businesses practices worldwide.

Acknowledgment

©2000. All rights reserved. Parts of this essay were previously printed in "Exporting Mental Models," *Business Ethics Quarterly*10 (2000), 353–362. Reprinted by permission of the journal and the author, Patricia H. Werhane.

References

Gentner, Dedre, and Eric W. Whitley. 1997. Mental Models of Population Growth: A Preliminary Investigation." Pp. 209–33 in *Environment, Ethics and Behavior: The Psychology of Environmental Valuation and Degradation*, edited by Max H. Bazerman and David M. Messick. San Francisco: The New Lexington Press/Jossey-Bass.

Gorman, Michael. 1992. *Simulating Science.* Bloomington: Indiana University Press.

Gray, John. 1998. *False Dawn: The Delusions of Global Consumption.* New York: The New Press.

Hart, Stuart, and C. K. Prahalad. 2002. "Strategies for the Bottom of the Pyramid: Creating Sustainable Development." *Harvard Business Review* (forthcoming).

Johnson, Mark. 1993. *Moral Imagination.* Chicago: University of Chicago Press.

Kelly, George A. 1995. *A Theory of Personality.* New York: W. W. Norton.

Laszlo, Alexander, and Stanley Krippner. 1998. "Systems Theories: Their Origins, Foundations and Development," in *Systems Theories and a Priori Aspects of Perception*, edited by J. Scott Jordan. Amsterdam: Elsevier.

McDonough, William A. 2000. "A Boat for Thoreau." *Environmental Challenges to Business. Second Monograph of the Society for Business Ethics.* Monograph Ruffin Series. Bowling Green: Philosophy Documentation Center: 115–33.

Mischel, Walter, and Yuichi Shoda. April, 1995. "A Cognitive-Affective System Theory of Personality." *Psychological Review* 102, no. 2: 246–68.

Mitroff, Ian I., and Harold Linstone. 1993. *The Unbounded Mind.* New York: Oxford University Press.

Rorty, Richard. 1999. "Can American Egalitarianism Survive a Globalized Economy?" *Business Ethics Quarterly* 8, special issue no. 1: 1–6.

Senge, Peter. 1990. *The Fifth Discipline.* New York: Doubleday.

Shrivastava, Paul. 2000. "Ecocentering Strategic Management." *Environmental Challenges to Business.* Second Monograph of the Society for Business Ethics. *Businesss Ethics Quarterly*: 23–43.

Standish, Miles, Michael E. Gorman, S. Venkataraman, and Patricia H. Werhane. 1999. *Unilever.* Charlottesville, Va: Darden Case Bibliography, UVA-E-0152, 0153.

Takahashi, Akiro. 1997. "Ethics in Developing Economies of Asia" *Business Ethics Quarterly* 7: 33–45.

Uchitelle, Louis. 1999. "The Stronger It Gets, the Sweatier the Palms." *New York Times: Week in Review*, May 21: 1, 16.

Vis, Jan-Kees. 1997. *Unilever: Putting Corporate Purpose into Action.* Unilever.

Walzer, Michael. 1983. *Spheres of Justice*. New York: Basic Books.
———. 1994. *Thick and Thin*. Notre Dame, Ind.: Notre Dame University Press.
Webster's New World Collegiate Dictionary. 1986. Edited by Victoria Newfeldt. New York: Macmillan.
Werhane, Patricia H. 1991. "Engineers and Management: The Challenge of the Challenger Incident." *Journal of Business Ethics* 10: 605–16.
———. 1998. "Moral Imagination and Management Decision-Making." *Business Ethics Quarterly* 8: Special Issue no. 1: 75–98.
———. 1999. *Moral Imagination and Management Decision-Making*. New York: Oxford University Press.
West, Cornel. 1993. *Race Matters*. Boston: Beacon Press.
Wolf, Susan. 1999. "Toward a Systemic Theory of Informed Consent in Managed Care." *Houston Law Review* 35: 1631–81.
Zakaria, Fareed. 1999. "Passing the Bucks [a review of Gray's False Dawn]." *New York Times Book Review* April 25: 16, 18.

Chapter 17

What Practical Difference Would the Adoption of the Earth Charter Mean to the Resolution of Global Warming Issues?

Don Brown

Introduction

This chapter examines the practical effect that adoption of the Earth Charter would have on resolving outstanding global warming issues. It seeks to determine if the Earth Charter were actually adopted by nations and its principles agreed to, how would such agreement resolve important issues that are currently in contention or yet to be faced in international global warming negotiations.

Before the Earth Summit in Rio Janeiro in 1992, an attempt was made to have the world adopt an Earth Charter. However, the time was not right. Instead, the nations assembled in Rio in 1992 adopted the Rio Declaration on Environment and Development (United Nations 1992, Rio Declaration).

The basic idea of the Earth Charter is to develop a universal code of conduct to guide people and nations toward sustainable development. Its proponents hope to have the United Nations adopt the Earth Charter and have it become a soft-law document. A soft-law document is not binding on the nations that adopt it but is recognized as a set of norms that nations should abide by although they are not legally obligated to do so. The agreements reached in soft law often have become the basis for specific provisions in treaties that are legally binding.

If the Earth Charter were so adopted, it would play the same role in guiding nations to adopt sustainable development as has the United Nations Declarations on Human Rights played in making human rights serious national concerns (United Nations 1948). Many NGOs have held nations accountable for noncompliance with the United Nations Declaration on Human Rights and thereby have been successful in changing national policy, although because this document is a soft-law document, legal suit could not be brought against nations for noncompliance.

Supporters of the Earth Charter argue that such a document on sustainable development is now needed, given the immense global environmental threats and social inequities that have been emerging. It is believed that the transition to sustainable development requires basic changes in the attitudes, values, and behavior of all people in order to achieve social, economic, and ecological equity and security in the context of the globe's limited resources.

What practical difference in the world's approach to environmental issues would be entailed if the Earth Charter were adopted? This chapter reviews this issue in the context of the global warming problem.

Global Warming, the Rio Declaration, and the Earth Charter

The Earth Charter is comprised of a preamble and 16 principles. The 16 principles are organized under the following headings:

- Respect and Care for the Community of Life
- Ecological Integrity
- Social and Economic Justice
- Democracy, Non Violence, and Peace

Each of the 16 principles contains a number of sub-principles. In the March 24, 2000 draft there were 61 sub-principles arrayed under the principles. The preamble, principles, and sub-principles establish a set of norms that, if taken seriously, would apply not only to environmental protection but human rights, equitable human development, and peace. Therefore, if the Earth Charter were adopted by the international community, it would establish a set of international norms needed to build a just, sustainable, and peaceful society. Obviously such a society would not sanction the status quo on global warming. This chapter, however, examines a few of the Earth Charter's specific provisions that are directly relevant to controversies in international negotiations on global warming.

Global warming is the subject of the United Nations Framework Convention on Climate Change (UNFCCC) (United Nations 1992, Climate Convention). The UNFCCC was open for signature at the 1992 Rio Earth Summit at the same time as the Rio Declaration on Environment and Development (United Nations 1992, Rio Declaration). There are a number of unresolved global warming issues that have plagued international negotiations over the last decade. These issues have often been used by the United States as an excuse for not taking meaningful action on global warming (Brown 2002). These include the following:

- Whether global warming science is sound enough to support specific policy prescriptions.

- At what level should the world attempt to stabilize greenhouse gases in the atmosphere.
- How should the world think about costs and benefits of global warming programs.
- Whether the developed word should act without commitments from the developing world.

Scientific Uncertainty and Global Warming

Some of the most of important principles and ideas contained in the Earth Charter that are specifically relevant to global warming are also contained in the UNFCCC and the Rio Declaration. For instance, one argument frequently heard in policy debates in the United States in opposition to strong United States action on climate change is that because there remains some scientific uncertainty about the timing and magnitude of global warming impacts, the United States should continue to pursue global warming research but not take strong action (Brown 2002). Relevant to the issue of scientific uncertainty, the UNFCCC, the Rio Declaration, and the Earth Charter contain versions of the "Precautionary Principle." The relevant UNFCCC principle states:

> The Parties should take precautionary measures to anticipate, prevent or minimize the causes of climate change and mitigate its adverse affect. Where they are threats of serious or irreversible damage, lack of full scientific certainty should not be used as a reason for postponing such measures taking into account that policies and measures to deal with climate change should be cost-effective so as to ensure global benefits at their lowest possible costs (United Nations 1992, Climate Convention: Article 3, Paragraph 3).

The relevant Rio Declaration principle provides:

> In order to protect the environment, the precautionary approach shall be widely applied by States according to their capabilities. Where there are threats of serious or irreversible damage, lack of full scientific certainty shall not be used as a reason for postponing cost-effective measures to prevent environmental degradation (United Nations 1992, Rio Declaration: Principle 15).

A very similar provision is contained in the proposed Earth Charter at Principle six:

> Prevent harm as the best method of environmental protection and, when knowledge is limited, apply a precautionary approach.
>
> 1. Take action to avoid the possibility of serious or irreversible environmental harm even when scientific knowledge is incomplete or inconclusive.
>
> 2. Place the burden of proof on those who argue that a proposed activity will not cause significant harm, and make the responsible parties liable for environmental harm.

Although there are important nuances in these provisions, none of these provisions would condone the current use of scientific uncertainty as an excuse for not taking strong action to reduce the threat of global warming. Because the precautionary principle has already been agreed to in the UNFCCC and the Rio Declaration, its is not crucial that an additional document such as the Earth Charter also contain a version of the precautionary principle.

The Need of the Developed World to Take Action

A second frequent excuse for not taking global warming seriously that is heard frequently in the United States is the notion that the United States should not act until the developing world commits to reduce greenhouse gas emissions (Brown 2002). Yet in the UNFCCC, the United States and all signatory parties agreed that the developed nations, including the United States, should take the lead on reducing greenhouse gas emissions and that each nation should reduce its emissions based upon equity (United Nations 1992, Climate Convention: Article 3). Although the Earth Charter's inclusion of many paragraphs relating to the responsibility of all to move toward sustainable development would be helpful in providing an argument for why the developed world must act independently of developing nations, the UNFCCC is already quite specific on this issue and therefore the adoption of the Earth Charter is not crucial to provide new prescriptive guidance on the responsibility of the developed nations to developing countries.

The Level of Stabilization of Carbon in the Atmosphere

The UNFCCC's objective is contained in Article 2, that is, to "stabilize greenhouse gases in the atmosphere at a level that prevents dangerous anthropogenic interference with the climate system" (United Nations 1992, Climate Convention: Article 2). An extremely important issue under the UNFCCC that has yet to be faced is what level of atmospheric stabilization should be targeted and therefore what allocations should be given to nations to stabilize greenhouse gases in the atmosphere at safe levels.

The Kyoto Protocol to the UNFCCC required the developed world to reduce emissions 5 percent on average below 1990 levels. Yet this 5 percent reduction is generally considered to be a drop in the bucket compared to what will be needed to stabilize greenhouse gases in the atmosphere at safe levels. This is so because some of the greenhouse gases last for over a hundred years in the atmosphere, and therefore slowing down emissions moderately will result in atmospheric levels continuing to rise. As a result, huge reductions of between 50 to 80 percent below current emission levels will be required to stabilize greenhouse gases at safe levels. Yet, what the actual atmospheric stabilization target should be has not been considered thus far in international negotiations. Different atmospheric targets will afford different protection levels for human health, ecological systems, and plants and animals. Therefore an extraordinarily important issue that needs to be faced by the international community, but as yet has not been seriously considered, is the level of human-induced atmospheric carbon that should be tolerated. The higher the level that is targeted, the less protection for animals and plants as well as the greater the threat to human health. The UNFCCC contains no prescription on setting the atmospheric target other than the above language on preventing dangerous interference with the climate system.

Here the Earth Charter is quite relevant. It spells out a strong duty to set environmental policy that will give protection not only to humans but also to plants and animals with whom we share the planet. More specifically, the Earth Charter provides:

> Humanity is part of a vast evolving universe. Earth, our home, is alive with a unique community of life. The forces of nature make existence a demanding and uncertain adventure, but Earth has provided the conditions essential to life's evolution. The resilience of the community of life and the well-being of humanity depend upon preserving a healthy biosphere with all its ecological systems, a rich variety of plants and animals, fertile soils, pure waters, and clean air. The global environment with its finite resources is a common concern of all peoples. The protection of Earth's vitality, diversity, and beauty is a sacred trust (Earth Charter 2002, Preamble).

Additionally, one of the Earth Charter's principles provides:

> *Respect Earth and life in all its diversity.*
>
> Recognize that all beings are interdependent and every form of life has value regardless of its worth to human beings (Earth Charter 2002, Principle 1).

Other Earth Charter principles provide:

> Protect and restore the integrity of the Earth's ecological systems, with special concern for biological diversity and the natural processes that sustain life (Earth Charter 2002, Principle 5).
>
> Manage the extraction and use of non-renewable resources such as minerals and fossil fuels in ways that minimize depletion and not cause serious environmental damage (Earth Charter 2002, Principle 5).

From these provisions it is clear that at the heart of the Earth Charter is an ethic that assumes that plants and animals have intrinsic value. For this reason, if the Earth Charter were to be adopted and applied to the global warming problem it would provide a nonanthropocentric focused set of goals to be achieved in implementing the UNFCCC. Clearly the above provisions of the Earth Charter prescribe a nonanthropocentric ethic, although there is some ambiguity about whether the phrase "every form of life has value" is meant to recognize a "biocentric" or "ecocentric" understood obligation. A more "biocentric" interpretation would require that all policy be evaluated on the basis of how it affects all living beings. An "ecocentric" ethic interpretation of the above Earth Charter language would require environmental policy options to be evaluated on the basis of how proposed policy affects species and ecosystems, not every individual living being. Whether one assumes that this Earth Charter is meant to protect all living beings or species and ecosystems, it clearly requires much more protection of plants and animals than if the Earth Charter were assumed to be concerned with human interests alone. In this writer's view, this is the most significant aspect of the Earth Charter for the climate change debate, namely that the Earth Charter requires that public policy protect and recognize the intrinsic value of, at minimum, ecosystems and species of plants and animals.

If the Earth Charter's "biocentric/ecocentric" ethic is read into the UNFCCC's stabilization objective, it would have profound importance for how the UNFCCC's stabilization goal must be interpreted. The reason for this is that, climate stabilization levels could be evaluated solely on the basis on how stabilization might directly affect: (1) human beings, (2) ecosystems or species, or (3) every living being. Clearly the Earth Charter's "biocentric/ecocentric" ethic would require that stabilization goals be set to protect plants and animals and not only human health. The global warming policy implications of these options will now be examined.

Atmospheric Carbon Stabilization to Protect Humans

A recent Intergovernmental Panel on Climate Change (IPCC) report concluded that unless the world takes strong steps to reduce emissions of greenhouse gases, global temperatures could rise 1.4 to 5.8°C by the year 2100. (IPCC 2001b). The projected expected planetary effects of global warming include:

- Higher average global precipitation resulting in some parts of Earth becoming drier and others wetter;
- A rise in sea level of 0.09 to 0.88 meters by 2100;
- Variations in regional climate and vegetation;
- Changes in productivity of agricultural lands;
- Increases in the intensity and severity of tropical storms (IPCC 2001a, 2001b).

Climate change models show that the effects of climate change are not distributed equally throughout the world. Actual temperature differences would likely differ greatly depending upon location, with projected increases in the tropics much smaller than in regions near the poles. The increases in precipitation are expected in some areas, while precipitation is expected to decrease in others. Climate models show that the poorest people around the world are most vulnerable to change. This is so because:

- The ecological systems of many of the poorest nations are most at risk;

- The poorest nations are the most vulnerable to storms, flooding, and sea level rise;
- The health of the poorest worldwide is at greatest risk from global warming;
- The food supplies of the poor at are risk from global warming;
- The poorest nations have the least financial and institutional ability to adapt to climate change (IPCC 2001a).

If the UNFCCC's stabilization target is interpreted to require only protection of human interests, then the atmospheric stabilization level should be determined by examining what atmospheric carbon will harm human health or well-being, including the human dependence on resources such as food.

Some assume that greenhouse gas emissions might rise to a doubling of CO_2 from preindustrial levels, i.e., from 280 to 560 ppm for CO_2, without seriously endangering human health and food supply. If this were the case, policy should be directed at stabilizing greenhouse gases in the atmosphere so as not to exceed this level. This conventional wisdom, however, is not without controversy. For instance, even small rises in sea levels will harm those people already threatened by ocean storms. Increasing the range of disease-carrying mosquitoes, a phenomenon that is already happening, will put some people at risk. Yet many argue that these adverse human impacts can be anticipated and responded to by such adaptative responses as moving people away from rising oceans or initiating public health measures to wipe out vectors. That is, some argue that humans can adapt to the type of climate change that will be seen with a doubling of greenhouse gases.

However, it is also generally recognized that the climate system is capable of surprises, that is, nonlinear responses of the climate system. These climate surprises could mean that if we allow CO_2 to double we could have much more rapid and larger temperature changes than the 1.4 to 5.8°C predicted most recently by IPCC. These rapid changes could be caused by, among other events, sudden changes in ocean circulation patterns, large instantaneous releases of carbon stored in permafrost, or large melting of the Antarctic ice cap. Most scientists believe these surprises are plausible but low-probability events that could happen in the next century even only with a doubling of CO_2. Of course, if a climate surprise were triggered, then human interests would be threatened much more than generally assumed and adaptation would be more difficult. Yet, humans might still be able to adapt to such rapid climate changes, although some of the poorest people would undoubtedly be hurt even in the absence of climate surprises. (IPCC 2001b)

Because great harm could come to some humans and particularly the poorest, even anthropocentric ethical systems would condemn the status quo on global warming (Brown 2002). That is, the world does not need to agree on the biocentric or ecocentric ethical assumptions embedded in the Earth Charter to find the international community's approach to global warming ethically reprehensible. Yet, for as long as human interests alone are at the center of concern, given that many humans could adapt to warmer planet, there is a lack of urgency among many of the need to radically change course on greenhouse gas emissions.

Atmospheric Carbon Stabilization to Protect All Living Beings

A biocentric interpretation of the UNFCCC's atmospheric target would mean that climate-change policy should be implemented in such a way that individual plants and animals are allowed to flourish. Yet, the conventional scientific wisdom about global warming includes the notion that humans have not only already caused some warming but also that even if the international community was able to stabilize greenhouse gases at current levels, that is 370 ppm CO_2, the Earth would continue to warm for a least a hundred years because of thermal lags in oceans (Lazaroff 2000). Without doubt these changes have and will continue to adversely affect individual animals and plants from flourishing. It is therefore already impossible to implement greenhouse gas stabilization objectives in such a way as to accomplish what a biocentric ethic would demand. Therefore, if the UNFCCC's stabilization goal were to be interpreted as a duty to all living beings, it would require immediate and maximum reduction of greenhouse gas emissions to the greatest extent possible. This is so because irreversible damage from global warming to some plants and animals is already unavoidable and a biocentric ethic would require that we protect all the plants and animals to the extent that we are able to do so.

Atmospheric Carbon Stabilization to Protect Ecosystems and Species of Plants and Animals

An ecocentric interpretation of the Earth Charter's ethic applied to the UNFCCC's stabilization target would require that atmospheric greenhouse gas targets be set at levels that would protect species of plants and animals and ecosystems. However, as was the case for the biocentric goal, it is already probably too late to prevent damage to many ecosystems around the world and many species already threatened with extinction will be even more threatened by unavoidable climate change in the next century. For instance, expected unavoidable rising sea levels will undoubtedly destroy some wetlands and marshes and threaten many estuarian ecosystems because of increasing salinity entailed by rising ocean levels. It is also already too late to prevent changes in many terrestrial ecosystems including forests. Even a doubling of CO_2 will entail that forests will be affected. However, if climate change is gradual enough, it is generally believed some ecosystems will have time to adapt without massive dieback. Yet some climate models now predict that massive forest dieback in the middle to the later part of this century is likely (Hadley Centre 2000). It therefore can be said without fear of contradiction that an ecocentric ethic entailed by adoption of the Earth Charter would require, just as a biocentric ethic would, reducing greenhouse gas emissions as soon as possible at the greatest rate possible.

For these reasons, if the Earth Charter were to be adopted and read together with the UNFCCC's atmospheric stabilization goals, it would entail that humans immediately reduce greenhouse gas emissions to the maximum extent possible in the shortest possible time. A more antroprocentric interpretation of the UNFCCC's stabilization goal would require less urgency because many humans could adapt to a changing climate, although even under a more anthropocentric based prescription, the status quo on global warming is ethically reprehensible.

The Limits of Cost-Benefit Analysis in Global Warming Policy Formation

Another frequent excuse for lack of action in the United States is that cost-benefit analyses (CBA) of global warming policy responses do not justify taking strong action (Brown 2002). On this issue, the adoption of the Earth Charter's biocentric or ecocentric ethic would have great practical significance. This is so because standard cost-benefit methodology makes human interests the measure of value. That is, standard approaches to CBA apply "willingness-to-pay" methods of determining the value of benefits of environmental policy options. According to such an approach the value of nature is reduced to what people are willing to pay for environmental entities in market transactions. Yet the Earth Charter's ethic would condemn such an approach in either its biocentric or ecocentric interpretations because both nonanthropocentric approaches would require us to value nature independently of its use to humans. On this issue, the Earth Charter could not be more explicit as it states we must "[r]ecognize that all beings are interdependent and every form of life has value regardless of its worth to human beings" (Earth Charter 2002: Principle 6).

Several other common methods for calculating CBA would also be incompatible with the Earth Charter's ethical prescriptions. For instance, CBA's methods normally discount benefits to be experienced in the future on the assumption that it is the interests of the persons who are making the current investment in a policy response that should be maximized (Brown 2002). Because the Earth Charter's ethic requires decision makers to protect the interests of nonhumans, discounting procedures usually applied in CBAs would be inconsistent with the Earth Charter. The Earth Charter also contains prescriptions on the duties of current generations to protect the interests of future generations that also would be incompatible with CBA discounting methods.

Conclusion

To overcome some of the barriers to serious policy responses to the problem of global warming it is not necessary adopt or otherwise accept the Earth Charter's prescriptions. That is, if we can get the world to implement some provisions of existing agreements that the international community has already agreed to in the UNFCCC, the Rio Declaration, and Agenda 21, we could make important strides in reducing some of the immense threats entailed by global warming. Yet on a few issues, adoption of the Earth Charter's guidance on how we should understand our responsibility to the planet would be practically important. For example, adoption and implementation of the Earth Charter on global warming would mean that the world would have to reduce emissions to the maximum extent possible in the quickest time possible. At the same time, the use of traditional approaches to cost-benefit analysis would be inappropriate as a test for the acceptance of global warming responses. Moreover, if the world would move to the type of society that is the overall vision of the Earth Charter, the status quo on global warming would be seen as ethically reprehensible.

References

Brown, Donald A. 2002. American Heat: Ethical Problems with the United States' Response to Global Warming. Lanham, Md.: Rowman & Littlefield (in press).

The Earth Charter Initiative. 2002. "The Earth Charter." San José, Costa Rica: Earth Council. <http://www.earthcharter.org/earthcharter/charter.htm> (January 12, 2002).

Hadley Centre. 2000. *Climate Effect on Forestation.* <http://www.met-office.gov.uk/research/hadleycentre/pubs/brochures/B2000/climate.html>.

IPCC (Intergovernmental Panel on Climate Change). 2001a. *Summary for Policymakers, Working Group II (Impacts), Third Assessment Report.* <http://www.usgcrp.gov/ipcc/wg2spm.pdf>.

IPCC (Intergovernmental Panel on Climate Change). 2001b. *Summary for Policymakers, Working Group I (Science), Third Assessment Report.* February, 2001. <http://www.ipcc.ch/pub/spm22-01.pdf >.

Larazoff, Cat. 2000. "World's Oceans Heating Up." Environment News Service. <http://www.climateark.org/articles/2000/1st/worocwar.htm>.

United Nations. 1948. *Universal Declaration of Human Rights.* Adopted and proclaimed by General Assembly Resolution 217 A (III). 10 December. <http://www.unhchr.ch/udhr/index.htm>.

United Nations. 1992. *The United Nation Framework Convention on Climate Change.* Rio de Janeiro.

United Nations. 1992. *Agenda 21: The United Nations Programme on Environment and Development.* Rio de Janeiro.

United Nations. 1992. *The Rio Declaration on Environment and Development.* Rio de Janeiro.

Part 3

Justice, Conflict, and the Preservation of Nature

Introduction to Part 3

Justice is a core social ideal prescribing how benefits, burdens, and obligations of coexistence should be allocated. It is both a rallying cry for revolutions and a banner for the "law and order" control of crime and dissidence. In a dispute, each side wants justice on its side. As a major topic of social philosophy since ancient times, what new could possibly be said about justice? Indeed, though, when justice is linked to resource allocations and use and environmental quality, new understandings of global and human ecology are bound to prompt new reflections on justice. The philosophy of sustainability in *Our Common Future* is founded on a notion of intergenerational and global justice (WCED 1987).

We begin part 3 with three approaches to environmental justice and conclude with five case studies that explore concrete issues in implementing Earth Charter ideals. Conflict, risk, diverse interests, competing interpretations, and the mandate to preserve nature together challenge us to discover or negotiate local forms of *just ecological integrity*.

What Is Environmental Justice?

There are enormous barriers to examining justice in ecological context, says Rees (chapter 18), because the expansionist myth, which dominates governments, economies, and consumers today, is sharply disconnected from ecological considerations. The illusion of freedom from ecological constraints is maintained by a combination of wishful thinking and the fact that nations that exceed their own carrying capacity can appropriate it from others through trade until global collapse is nigh. The antidote to the dominant myth is to look at the facts of human ecology, our biological heritage as patch-disturbers, and our expanding ecological footprints, which collectively have already overshot the long-term carrying capacity of Earth. Eco-footprint analysis provides a compelling tool to measure not only sustainability and unsustainability in resource consumption, but also justice and injustice, by reference to a fair Earthshare.

Toth (chapter 19) is struck by the obvious *inequities* of the economic system. People rationalize the status quo by means of myths about the distribution of natural goods. From his critique of these, Toth concludes that justice needs to (1) broaden the scope of goods considered from humanly produced to naturally produced, (2) broaden the relevant interests considered to include future generations and nonhumans, and (3) find new ways for just distributions appropriate to the varied nature of environmental goods.

The development of new justice-promoting principles and institutions requires analysis and dialogue. Louis and Magpili (chapter 20) have devised Geographical Information Systems (GIS)-based Indicators for Collaboration in Environmental Policymaking (ICEP). A GIS-based web platform provides interactive correlated data on regional demographics, health, industries, pollution, and survey data from stakeholders. This common source of data, accessible by all, can support collaborative policy discussions between stakeholders on the distribution of benefits and risks from industrial development.

Case Studies: Conflict, Risk, and the Preservation of Nature

Louis and Magpili's model is designed for industrial North America. The remaining chapters present case studies from Eastern Europe and Latin America, in which issues related to environmental justice are prominent.

Violence

The Earth Charter (section IV) links Democracy, Nonviolence, and Peace as essential conditions for realizing its environmental and social ideals. Camargo and Castillo (chapter 21) demonstrate these connections by examining the unfortunate circumstances in Columbia, a country of superlatives in biodiversity, drugs, poverty, and violence. Environmental protection is impossible to achieve when violence and the drug trade reign. In such conditions, short-term survival supersedes an environmental ethic for long-term sustainability. Consumer nations for drugs must share the blame for these desperate conditions.

Risk

Medical technologies save lives. They also may introduce risks. Ftacnikova (chapter 22) examines risk assessment, mitigation, communication, and compensation associated with the building of a new cyclotron in Slovakia. She asks what a conscientious application of Earth Charter principles requires.

Nature Preservation

The Earth Charter prescribes that we should "establish and safeguard viable nature and biosphere reserves, including wild lands and marine areas, to protect Earth's life support systems, maintain biodiversity, and preserve our natural heritage" (Principle 5b). By excluding ecologically damaging activities, reserves impose restrictions on users who might otherwise have cleared land or exploited resources there. But these restrictions might be particularly hard on local resource users. Chapters 23 to 25 examine the preservation dilemma, when global conservation mandates conflict with local communities.

Poland's Bialowieza Forest Preserve, notes Blavascunas (chapter 23), is viewed from several perspectives: as a primeval forest, as a core conservation area for Poland and Europe, as an area for scientific study, and as a backyard to local inhabitants. A particular challenge is to find constructive solutions that simultaneously protect the integrity of local communities as well as of the forest.

Durbin (chapter 24) and Isla and Turner (chapter 25) address similar issues in Costa Rica. Durbin believes pragmatic environmentalism is the best perspective for understanding how diverse players coalesced to protect Corcovado National Park. Isla and Turner (chapter 25) are more skeptical of international conservation efforts, which they link to male-dominated corporate environmentalism. Debt-for-nature swaps and other corporate, national, and international initiatives end up exploiting unpaid local indigenous "shadow labor," predominantly women who maintain households, reproduce and support the workforce, and engage in an informal economy of subsistence activities.

Reference

WCED (UN World Commission on Environment and Development). 1987. *Our Common Future.* Oxford: Oxford University Press (for the Commission).

What Is Environmental Justice?

Chapter 18

Socially Just Eco-Integrity: Getting Clear on the Concept

William E. Rees

Introduction: Myth and Modernity

One of the most enduring myths of industrial (and even post-industrial) society is that we moderns, products of the enlightenment all, no longer live in the light and shadow of myth. In fact, nothing could be more illusory. True, modern science has purged a virtual library of shadowy beliefs from our own culture and erodes the cosmological underpinnings of every other society with which it comes into contact. But the equation of myth with mere falsehood, superstition, and the unscientific beliefs of "primitive" people belies a shallow and sterile view of myth. Myth is a universal property of human societies and plays a vital role in every culture.

This assertion becomes easier to accept when we consider Colin Grant's conception of myths "not as mistaken views but as comprehensive visions that give shape and direction to life." In this light, myths "move from being dispensable misunderstandings to essential categories that we all take for granted" (Grant 1998, 1). Anyone who has lived through the past few decades and even occasionally reads the newspaper will recognize that, by this definition, the entire world has succumbed to a common myth of uncommon power. Virtually all "official" international agencies and national governments share a comprehensive vision of global development centered on unlimited economic expansion, fueled by more liberalized trade and driven largely by private corporations. At the heart of this vision (also called our "dominant social paradigm") is the belief that human welfare can be all but equated with ever-expanding material well-being. This contemporary myth has been the principal force giving shape and direction to political and civil life in both industrialized and so-called developing countries on every continent at least since the 1970s.

Consistent with this myth, most so-called development policy is aimed at promoting the rapid growth of national economies and gross world product. The doctrinal authority for the expansionist vision is drawn from neoliberal (neoclassical) market economics. Neoliberal models promote the untrammeled marketplace as the most efficient way of increasing production/consumption and global free trade as providing the largest—and most profitable—possible market. This approach naturally diminishes the role of government, elected or otherwise, since any interference in the workings of the market is, by definition, inefficient. It also transfers significant power to international regulatory agencies and transnational corporations, both of which remain unaccountable to the people they supposedly serve (Korten 1995).

Like all abstractions, the market model simplifies reality—for example, it transforms well-rounded citizens into gluttonous consuming machines. *Homo economicus* is defined as a "self-interested utility maximizer with immutable preferences and insatiable material demands" (definitely not the type of person one might invite home to dinner!). You and I are assumed to act as isolated automatons whose sole goal is to maximize our personal consumption through participation in the increasingly global marketplace. The market model cannot accommodate the concept of "family" and relieves our morally diminished *Homo economicus* of any other responsibility to society. (In Margaret Thatcher's ice-cold phrase, "There is no such thing as society.")

Note that the doctrine of unlimited growth conveniently sidelines the irritating ethical arguments for wealth redistribution that might otherwise apply on a finite planet. Convention has it that in an ever-expanding economy even the poorest of the poor will eventually enjoy a materially adequate life. A cleverly picturesque metaphor—"a rising tide raises all boats"—serves to drown the opposition. Significantly, too, expansionists see no fundamental conflict between economic growth and ecological degradation. (This aimed to hearten those interested in biological integrity.) Indeed, they argue that chronic poverty in the developing world is a primary cause of ecological decay and that the only sure way to eliminate poverty and repair the environment is through growth (Beckerman 1992; WCED 1987).

This is a satisfying myth for denizens of the industrial world and the so-called "emerging economies" alike. The popular culture of high-income countries persuades us that greed is good and that we can indulge our wildest materialist fantasies free of social guilt or ecological recrimination. Indeed, theory says that by consuming goods produced or manufactured in the developing world, wealthy northerners contribute to improved welfare—to rising incomes and higher environmental standards—in the impoverished South. Meanwhile, the global ubiquity of television ensures that people everywhere can compare their traditional cultures with the glitz and glitter of Hollywood and find the former wanting. At the dawn of the twenty-first century, virtually the whole world has been drawn into the materialist net—abetted, of course, by a multibillion dollar transnational advertising industry. (The latter concerned with psycho-engineering real humans into behaving as closely as possible to the "self-interested utility maximizers" presupposed by the economists' models.)

Mything out on Integrity

This last point is critically problematic. Those living a myth are the least likely to see it for what it is. As John McMurtry observes:

> [Like] other social value programs, the doctrine of "the global free market" itself does not recognize its ideology as ideology, but rather conceives of its prescriptions as *"post-ideological"* recognition of law-like truth (original emphasis). . . . The truth of the global market order is believed to be final and eternal, "the end of history." Its rule is declared "inevitable." Its axioms are conceived as "iron laws." Societies that dare to evade its stern requirements are threatened with "harsh punishments" and "shock treatments" (McMurtry 1998, 43).

The brand of global absolutism described by McMurtry actually reflects a peculiar characteristic of neoliberal economics. Most disciplines test their models against the real world and then adapt them to better reflect reality. By contrast, the economists' myth is so entrenched that its devotees presume to force reality to conform to their models. If real-world *Homo sapiens* does not behave quite like *Homo economicus*, this "does not make the basic model wrong, as it would in every other discipline. It just means that actions must be taken to bend *Homo sapiens* into conformity with *Homo economicus.* So instead of adjusting theory to reality, reality is adjusted to theory" (Thurow 1983, 22–23).

One can imagine many circumstances in which a living myth would have few negative consequences. For example, throughout most of human history, "the world is flat" and "the Earth is at the center of the universe" were entirely adequate first approximations of reality. People could live out their entire lives unaware that much of their experienced "reality" was actually constructed from many such shared illusions. Of course, there are also circumstances in which popular myths can do real damage. "If a value system is simply presupposed and obeyed as the given structure of the world that all are made to accept and serve, it can become systematically destructive *without our knowing there is a moral choice involved*" (McMurtry 1998, 10, emphasis added).

One purpose of this chapter is to make the case that the global growth agenda is one such destructive value system. It has all the necessary characteristics. "Growth-through-globalization" has become the received developmental doctrine throughout the world (the forces for global economic integration are taken to be as relentless as gravity); any number of international agencies and institutions from the World Bank and International Monetary Fund to the World Trade Organization are now in place to advance the faith and punish remaining heretics; the global marketplace is treated as the major if not sole arena for international relations; and when people suffer or whole economies collapse from the "harsh discipline" of the market's "brutally competitive" (but grossly imbalanced) rules, this is not perceived as a moral issue but rather as the relentless playing out of unspecified natural laws against which "resistance is futile."

In fairness, we should reiterate that all human societies must subscribe to *some* overarching myth(s). Myth-making is how we make collective sense of the world and our place within it. In fact, there is no other way of being and coping. Despite the miraculous advances of science, our dominant social paradigm(s)—the "comprehensive visions that give shape and direction to life"—necessarily remains a disorderly mix of facts and values, beliefs and assumptions. This is the very essence of myth.

It is also the basis for the postmodern rejection of positive science and the extreme views of "radical relativists." Recognizing that there is no absolute truth, some postmodern scholars propose that that one point of view is pretty much as valid as any other, that we have no basis to claim that a given assertion is more accurate than another (see, for example, Gergin 1991). In other words, all perceptions, no matter how widely shared, are mere "social constructions of reality" and as such are inherently untrustworthy.

Does this mean there no grounds for deciding anything? At this point we must side with Neil Postman when he writes: "You may say, if you wish, that all reality is a social construction, but you cannot deny that some constructions are 'truer' than others. They are not 'truer' because they are privileged; they [become] privileged because they are 'truer'" (Postman 1999, 76). Postman's point is that there is system to the intellectual enterprise. The essence of intelligence in humans "is to be able to assess with some accuracy the extent to which words refer to the world of non-words . . . 'More accurate' means 'closer to reality'; that is, 'truer' or 'more objective'" (Postman 1999, 75–76).

The question before us, then, is the extent to which the facts, values and assumptions underpinning our prevailing development myth provide an accurate map of reality. This is not a trivial question. The expansionist vision, like all grand myths before it, is a social construction with the potential for significant harm. The difference is that the mythos of industrial capitalism is spreading virus-like, invading every society on the planet and infecting all dimensions of life. Does the global, corporate, free-enterprise market model really mark the apogee of human cultural evolution (the putative "end of history") or is it a dangerous diversion that threatens nature, destroys community, and diminishes the human prospect?

The empirical evidence is not encouraging. The Earth Charter (2002) sums matters up this way:

> The dominant patterns of production and consumption are causing environmental devastation, the depletion of resources, and a massive extinction of species. Communities are being undermined. The benefits of development are not shared equitably and the gap between rich and poor is widening. Injustice, poverty, ignorance, and violent conflict are widespread and the cause of great suffering. An unprecedented rise in human population has overburdened ecologi-

cal and social systems. The foundations of global security are threatened. These trends are perilous—but not inevitable.

This passage describes the actions of a rogue species bent on destroying its habitat—on consuming the very planet upon which it depends—and then turning upon itself. That this pattern is at least partially the outcome of an explicit program for global sustainability shows that modern world is still "unclear on the concept" of living in social and ecological integrity. Tom Toles captured our confusion with his usual brilliant insight in a wry April 1995 editorial cartoon celebrating the twenty-fifth anniversary of Earth Day (figure 18.1).

 TOM TOLES

Figure 18.1. Still Unclear on the Concept

If the Earth Charter's description is even generally "accurate" (i.e., if it is closer to reality than conventional wisdom would have us believe) then the prevailing development model has led us astray. Clearly something is missing from our operational map of reality. Its internal assumptions plot an erratic course through well-known waters and whole oceans of understanding vital to achieving socially just ecological integrity have scarcely been charted at all. Humanity is certainly on a "perilous" voyage and a disastrous collision may well be "inevitable." The question is, whether the human enterprise (unlike the *Titanic*) has sufficient rudder to avoid the iceberg of reality once we see it for what it is.

Exploring the Gaps

It is not difficult to find significant gaps in the expansionist myth. The problem begins with the basic structure of economists' abstract models. The conceptual starting point for conventional economic analysis is the "circular flow of exchange value" (Daly 1991, 195). Most standard economic textbooks feature a standard circular diagram of economic process as "a pendulum movement between production and consumption within a completely closed system" (Georgescu-Roegen 1971). Value embodied in goods and services flows from firms to households in exchange for spending by households (national product). A supposedly equal value, reincarnated in factors of production, flows back to firms from households in exchange for wages, rents, profits, and so on (national income).

Remarkably, this model is totally abstracted from the "environment" within which the money economy is actually embedded—there are no connections between the money flows and biophysical reality. It is therefore "impossible to study the relation of the economy to the ecosystem in terms of the circular flow model because the circle flow is an isolated, self-renewing system with no inlets or outlets, no possible points of contact with anything outside itself" (Daly 1991, 196). By definition, then, the most fundamental neoliberal model lacks any representation of the materials, energy sources, physical structures and time-dependent processes that are basic to understanding ecosystems' structure and function (Christensen 1991). Worse, the implied simple, reversible, mechanistic behavior of the economy is inconsistent with the connectivity, irreversibility, and positive feedback dynamics of complex energy, information, and ecosystems, the systems with which the economy interacts in the real world.

Standard economic models are scarcely better at representing real market behavior, ostensibly their most legitimate domain. Mainstream market models are based on the concept of "general competitive equilibrium," a prominent distinguishing feature of which is that it bears little relationship to the real economy (Ormerod 1997). Theoretically, a free-market competitive equilibrium is optimally efficient—that is, demand equals supply in every market (markets clear) and all resources are fully utilized. Moreover, at equilibrium, no individual or firm can be made better off by altering the allocation of resources in any way without making someone worse off (Pareto optimality). (Thus, by definition, any government intervention in the marketplace in defense of the public interest would be inefficient.)

However, even this stinted theoretical ideal depends upon the following critical assumptions—

- diminishing marginal returns in consumption and production;
- perfect competition among a hyper-infinite continuum of traders (buyers and sellers) none of whom can individually influence prices;
- all traders have perfect knowledge of all present and future markets;
- an infinite number of future markets

—and none of these necessary conditions obtain in the real world. Ormerod concludes that "there appear to be so many violations of the conditions under which competitive equilibrium exists that it is hard to see why the concept survives, except for the vested interests of the economics profession and the link between prevailing political ideology [the 'myth' again] and the conclusions which the theory of general equilibrium provides" (Ormerod 1997, 66).

James K. Galbraith makes a similar point in a devastating critique of the year 2000 meeting of the American Economics Association. He observed that discussion of the "great issues of economic policy" were missing from the program despite the fact that the empirical evidence "flatly contradicts" each of the five leading ideas of modern economics. Galbraith takes this "disconnect" from the real world as evidence that "modern economics . . . seems to be, mainly, about *itself*" (Galbraith 2000, 1, original emphasis). He goes on: "But self-absorption and consistent policy error are just two of the endemic problems of the leading American economists. The deeper problem is the nearly complete collapse of the prevailing economic theory . . . . It is a collapse so complete, so pervasive, that the profession can only deny it by refusing to discuss theoretical questions in the first place" (Galbraith 2000, 4).

Despite such unqualified condemnations of prevailing economic theory by economists themselves, its pattern of thinking spills over into adjacent social sciences. In political science, for example, it is increasingly the pure elegance and artificial neatness of models, not their relation to real world activities, that reap the greatest rewards for academics. "In short, political science is sanctifying a chalkboard universe inhabited by *'Homo economicus,'* which, in the name of utility maximization, tries to erase all trace of culture, history, personality or any quirky quality that might smudge the one size fits all model" (Jacobsen 2001).

It should now be clear why most economists and other policy analysts do not consider the productivity and growth of the economy to be seriously constrained by nature. Their formal thinking scarcely acknowledges "the environment" except as a source of virtually free inputs to the production process and as a sink for wastes. Even here, economists are confident that money price is a sufficient indicator of scarcity and that marketplace mechanics will prevent any problems arising from it. Theory says that rising prices for scarce resources (or pollution permits) should automatically stimulate both conservation and the search for technological substitutes. Indeed, Julian Simon, the most ebullient proponent of this doctrine of "near-perfect substitution" recently declared: "We have in our hands now . . . the technology to feed, clothe, and supply energy to an ever-growing population for the next seven billion years" (Simon, cited in Bartlett 1996). In contemporary mythology, the cornucopia of human ingenuity has clearly displaced nature as the great provider.

Reality Check: Disintegrity Rules

With Simon's assertion ringing in the background, a reality check seems in order. What is the state of the economy and how goes the ecosphere? As might be expected, the economy seems to be in great shape, at least on the surface. There can be little doubt that globalization and freer trade has been a strong stimulus to production growth and gross world product. The global economy has expanded fivefold in the past half century, threefold since 1980 alone. Average income is therefore surging far ahead of population growth—human numbers grew "only" 30 percent to over six billion in the same 20-year period.

The ecosphere, by contrast, is much diminished. Land clearing and conversion to accommodate human demand has shrunk the world's forests by half and is now proceeding at over 130,000 km^2 per year; similarly, so-called "development" claimed half the world's wetlands in the twentieth century. In all, half the world's landmass has already been transformed for human purposes and more than half of the planet's accessible freshwater is being used by people. Meanwhile, 20 percent of the world's freshwater fish are extinct, endangered or threatened and 70 percent of the world's major fish stocks are being fished at or beyond their sustainable limits. Given the steady erosion of "natural" habitats, it should be no surprise that the rate of biodiversity loss is now 1000 times the "background" rate.

With the ballooning of the economy, some material economic processes have come to rival natural flows, and their impacts are global in scope. More atmospheric nitrogen is fixed and injected into terrestrial ecosystems by humans than by all natural terrestrial processes combined; stratospheric ozone depletion now affects both the Southern and Northern Hemispheres; atmospheric carbon-dioxide has increased by 30 percent in the industrial era and is now higher than at any time in at least the past 160,000 years (or even the past 20 million years). Partially as a result of this last trend, mean global temperature is also a record post-glacial high and the world is threatened by increasingly variable climate and more frequent and violent extreme weather events (Lubchenco 1998; Tuxill 1998; WRI/UNEP 2001; Vitousek et al. 1997).

These trends make clear that the exponential expansion of the economy is being accompanied by the accelerating degradation of the ecosphere. This should not come as a surprise—common sense would suggest such a relationship. As shown, however, standard economic models are structurally alien to nature and can neither predict nor explain the worsening ecological crisis. The best economists can do is to treat the problem as a case of "market-failure." They see resource depletion and pollution as unintended "externalities" (costs not accounted for in market prices). The favored solution, therefore, is to extend the market process through privatization, proper resource pricing, and pollution charges/taxes, with a view toward "internalizing" environmental costs. Unfortunately, market prices merely reflect current availability, not ecological scarcity, and the whole approach remains incompatible with ecosystems behavior. Because of such nontrivial losses of information, commoditizing nature is misleading and potentially dangerous (Rees 1998; Rees and Wackernagel 1999; Vatn and Bromley 1993). Conventional economics is simply no match for the ecological crisis.

It may not be a match for the welfare crisis either. The conventional growth model is not delivering the promised goods even on its own terms. Nor should this come entirely as a surprise. The modern market model eschews moral and ethical considerations; ignores distributive equity; abolishes "the common good"; and undermines intangible values such as loyalty to person and place, community, self-reliance, and local cultural mores. The negative consequences press particularly hard on developing countries. The latter are being integrated into the global economy through unbalanced trade and debt-financed export-led "development." But the land reforms, the introduction of intensive cropping methods, and the economic "structural adjustments" (cutbacks in public heath, education, and like social programs) required as a condition for the development loan, often have devastating impacts on local environments, subsistence production, and local community integrity.

In these circumstances, economic forces ensure that the benefits of GDP growth accrue mainly to the already wealthy. Forty-seven nations still have a per capita GDP of less than $855 and are heavily indebted, their governments owing foreigners the equivalent of at least 18 months of export earnings. Many debtor nations are forced to spend more servicing debts to the world's richest nations than providing social services to their own impoverished citizens (Roodman 2001). Chronic poverty thus prevails in much of the South and the income gap between high-income OECD countries and the South is growing. The absolute gap is widening everywhere and even the relative income gap is increasing for most regions. (East Asia is the major exception—per capita incomes have gone from one-tenth to almost one-fifth of those in the high-income OECD countries since 1960.) In 1970 the richest 10 percent of the worlds citizens earned 19 times as much as the poorest 10 percent. By 1997, the ratio had increased to 27: 1. At that time, the wealthiest 1 percent of the world's people commanded the same income as the poorest 57 percent and just 25 million rich Americans (0.4 percent of the world's people) had a combined income greater than that of the poorest 2 billion of the world's people (43 percent of the total population). (Income ratios reflect purchasing power parity [data from UNDP 2001].) Far from raising all boats, the rising economic tide is stranding the flimsier craft on the reefs of despair. The expansionist myth is not only wrecking the "environment," but is also deepening the misery of millions of impoverished people.

Moreover, these trends are increasingly connected. Recent reports show that it is the world's poor—those most directly dependent on local ecosystems for their livelihoods—who suffer the most when ecosystems are degraded or collapse (WRI/UNEP 2001). For example, in 1998 singular events such as Hurricane Mitch and the El Niño weather phenomenon, plus declining soil fertility and deforestation, killed thousands and drove a record 25 million people from the countryside into crowded, under-serviced shanty-towns around the developing world's fast growing cities. This represents 58 percent of the world's refugees. For the first time, people fleeing violent weather events and ecological decay outnumbered political refugees (IRC 1999). For all such people, achieving a "just integrity" remains a receding dream.

Back to Basics: The Human Ecology of Eco-Integrity

If the principles of the Earth Charter oriented to building a just sustainability (Principle 3) and maintaining the integrity of the Earth's ecosystems (Principle 5) are to be honored, then twenty-first century society must adopt new, more realistic economic models based on a better understanding of humanity's functional role in the scheme of things. Much of the integrity/sustainability problem resides in the fact that industrial "man" does not see himself as part of nature. Our technical-scientific mind-set has succeeded over the past three hundred years in erecting a self-serving psychological barrier between humanity and the rest of the natural world. Dismantling this barrier requires a major transformation of our cultural mythology.

A first step in the transformation is to develop an understanding of ourselves as ecological entities. The biophysical fact of the matter is that, through the technology-driven expansion of the economy, human beings have become the dominant consumer organism in most of the world's major ecosystems. Nothing could be further removed from mainstream thinking. Conventional economists see the growing economy as a separate system, when it is actually an increasingly embedded dependent *subsystem* of the nongrowing ecosphere.

The real-world nested relationship is typical of complex dynamic self-producing systems. Complex systems theory portrays biophysical systems as Self-Organizing Holarchic Open (SOHO) systems (Kay and Regier 2000). These systems exist in loose, nested hierarchies, each component system contained by the next level up and itself comprising a chain of linked subsystems at lower levels. (Think of the ecosphere as a subsystem of the solar system, individual ecosystems and the economy as subsystems of the ecosphere, individual organisms and people as subsystems of their ecosystems and economies, organ systems as subsystems of the individual, and so on, all the way down to organelles as subsystems of individual body cells.)

From this perspective, both the economy and the ecosphere are seen as complex SOHO systems whose behavior is ultimately governed not by the simple mechanics of neoliberal analysis but by evolutionary forces, complex systems dynamics, and thermodynamic laws. The dynamics of the relationships within the hierarchy containing them is a function of positive and negative feedback loops among and within subsystems. The behavior of SOHO subsystems is therefore decidedly nonlinear, even chaotic.

Most importantly, the subsystems function as "dissipative structures." Dissipative structures require continuous supplies of available energy, material, and information—various forms of exergy—which they use to produce themselves and to maintain their adaptive self-organizational capacities. SOHO systems also necessarily generate a continuous stream of degraded energy and waste (entropy) that is rejected back into the "environment." (For example, photosynthesis in the ecosphere dissipates high-intensity solar radiation, which is re-radiated into space as low-intensity infrared radiation; economic production dissipates mainly fossil energy extracted from the ecosphere and injects low-grade heat, water vapor, and carbon dioxide back into the ecosphere.) All such dissipative processes are inherently thermodynamic in character, so the second law of thermodynamics is central to understanding SOHO dynamics.

To summarize, SOHO systems coexist in nested hierarchies sustained by exchanges governed by the second law. Each SOHO subsystem maintains its internal integrity and grows by dissipating available energy and material imported from its host system one level up in the hierarchy. Subsystems also export their metabolic wastes back into their hosts. In effect, then, all highly ordered subsystems develop and grow (increase their internal order) "at the expense of increasing disorder at higher levels in the systems hierarchy" (Schneider and Kay 1994).

Several important insights flow from this understanding of economy-ecosphere relationships. First, it is clear that all economic production is *secondary* production. That is, the production and maintenance of our bodies and all economic goods and services is fundamentally a *consumptive* process that uses up a vastly larger quantity of energy and material first produced by nature. The accumulation of economic capital (the goal of capitalist growth) is *necessarily* at the expense of "natural capital" (which conventional economics rarely sees as capital at all). Second, the entire throughput of energy and matter—even the portion initially embodied in useful products—is eventually degraded and injected back into the ecosphere as waste. Third, the ecologically important flows in the economy are not the circular flows of money but rather the unidirectional and thermodynamically irreversible flows of matter and energy. This linear throughput is what fuels the economy. Fourth, following from the first three points, the hierarchical relationship between the ecosphere and the economy is potentially pathological. The expanding human enterprise is thermodynamically positioned to consume the ecosphere from within. (This fact lends a new literal poignancy to Toles' Earth Day cartoon [figure 18.1].) Unlike the simplistic structure of prevailing economic models, the SOHO model of the economic process structurally embodies the possibility of both resource depletion and pollution should the host-subsystem (ecosphere-economy) relationship become materially imbalanced.

Humans as Patch-Disturbers

SOHO systems theory can help us reinterpret the ecological history of *Homo sapiens.* I have argued elsewhere that humans are a quintessential "patch disturbance" species, a distinction we share with other large mammals (Rees

2000). A patch disturbance species may be defined as *any organism which, usually by central place foraging, degrades a small "central place" greatly and disturbs a much larger area away from the central core to a lesser extent* (definition revised from Logan 1996).

Human patch disturbance is an inevitable consequence of SOHO theory, the second law, and two additional realities: first, humans are big animals with correspondingly large individual energy and material requirements and, second, we are social beings who live in extended groups. These basic facts of human ecology, together with food productivity data for typical terrestrial ecosystems, suggest, *a priori,* that in most of the potential habitats on Earth, the energy and material requirements of even a small group of pre-agricultural humans would sooner or later overwhelm the productive capacity of local ecosystems. Whenever this occurred, the group would be forced to move on. Because they disturb and deplete whatever habitats they exploit, humans are *by nature* nomadic hunters and gatherers. To this extent at least, the potential for pathological unsustainability is encoded in the ancient human genome.

Despite—or perhaps because of—their great material demands, human beings have evolved uniquely successful strategies to master the full range of earthly "environments." Three of these strategies stand out. First, humans have a remarkably variable diet—we have wide-ranging omnivorous tastes and if we cannot consume something directly (such as grass), we domesticate an animal that can and then eat the animal. Second, humans are as behaviorally adaptable as they are catholic in their diets. Together, these two factors make virtually any terrestrial ecosystem, from grassland and forest to desert and tundra, accessible to *Homo sapiens*. Third, we are creatures of language, culture, and cumulative learning. Continuous technological advances have enabled humans continuously to increase the intensity of their exploitation of virtually all the resources and productive habitats on the planet.

This last fact reinforces our shared illusion that the human enterprise can grow forever. Reinforced by the great abundance of commodities on world markets, the prevailing myth insists that technology has freed us from any biophysical constraints on growth. Arguably, however, the main effect of technology has been to accelerate the exploitative depletion of nature's vast warehouse. We humans and our SOHO economy are steadily increasing our indebtedness to nature.

The Cost to Integrity

As might be expected, the ecological dominance of humans comes at great cost to other species. When people invade a previously "stable" ecosystem they cannot help but produce significant changes in established energy and material pathways. Indeed, human appropriations of available energy and materials invariably cause biodiversity losses and other permanent changes in ecosystem structure and function.

Several mechanisms are at work, the effect of which is to increase the impact of human patch disturbance to the global scale (Rees 2001). Growing human demand:

1. Passively displaces other species from their food niches or appropriates their habitats. (Agriculture pushed bison from the Great Plains of North America; commercial fishing displaces sea lions, seals, and orcas from their preferred food sources.)
2. Actively eliminates nonhuman competitors—other species that compete with us for "our" food. (We shoot wolves that hunt ungulates; we poison insects that would devour our crops.)
3. Depletes both self-producing and nonrenewable "natural capital" stocks. (Humans over-exploit wild populations from rhinos to fish and deplete finite stocks of groundwater, soil, and fossil fuels.)

The above processes are all consumption-related. The first two are forms of "competitive exclusion." Technological "man" is simply more effective than other organisms at appropriating nature's bounty for his own use. Since flows of available energy and material (exergy) consumed by people are irreversibly unavailable for other species, the latter decline, even to extinction, at least locally.

The third mechanism, stock depletion, is the product of many things, including confidence in technological substitution, blind ignorance, material greed, sheer desperation, and the relentless working of the so-called "common property problem" on an overcrowded planet. Sometimes it is the result of willful disregard on the part of those who give no moral standing to other creatures or who simply don't care about the state or fate of the world.

The point is that when we understand the human economy as a kind of rogue subsystem within the SOHO hierarchy of the ecosphere, we recognize that, contrary to popular belief, there is a *fundamental* contradiction between continued material economic growth and the maintenance of bio-integrity. Over-harvesting and habitat destruction are driving what some conservation biologists now refer to as "the sixth extinction," the greatest extinction episode since the natural catastrophes at the end of the Paleozoic and Mesozoic eras. The current rate of extirpation is 1000 times pre-human levels inferred from the fossil and palaeontological record. This is a paradoxical record for a species that sees its economy as all but decoupled from nature.

We should also remember that increased energy and material consumption is necessarily accompanied by equivalent increases in waste production (the other half of the "second law"). The resultant pollution imposes an additional toll on biodiversity. It hardly needs mentioning that globalization, the sanctioning of greed, the rise of consumerism, and the spread of energy-intensive technologies have augmented these dissipative processes. The excessive growth of the economy necessarily increases the entropy of the ecosphere, its immediate host in the SOHO hierarchy.

Eco-Footprints, Overshoot, and Social Justice

It should now be clear that, whether or not we perceive it in our bones, humans remain an integral—if increasingly disruptive—part of nature. To date the continuous expansion of the human enterprise has been largely at the expense of nonhuman species, but another problem looms. Evidence is mounting that there are, in fact, real limits to growth—we have run out of ecological space for expansion. At the same time, billions of people have yet to enjoy the bounty of the material age and we expect the human population to balloon by three more billions in the next half century. These circumstances bode ill for global peace and social justice. If the rich and powerful insist on further increasing their personal consumption, it will increasingly be at the expense of the poor and weak within populations and among nations.

Evidence that this trend may actually already be upon us comes from recent "ecological footprint" studies. The ecological footprint of a specified population is defined as the *area of land and water ecosystems required, on a continuous basis, to produce the resources that the population consumes, and to assimilate the wastes that the population produces, wherever on Earth the relevant land/water is located* (Rees 2001). In effect, eco-footprint analysis estimates the size of the modern human patch at whatever material standard the study population currently enjoys.

As might be expected, per capita eco-footprints are positively correlated with income (Rees 1996, 2001; Wackernagel and Rees 1996). The residents of the United States, Canada, many Western European and other high-income countries each require 5 to 10 or even 12 ha (12–30 acres) of productive land/water to support their consumer lifestyles. By contrast, the citizens of the world's poorest countries have average eco-footprints of less than one hectare. Even burgeoning China's per capita eco-footprint is less than two ha. The average human ecological footprint is about 2.8 ha (Wackernagel et al. 1999; WWF 2000).

Because of their large per capita eco-footprints, many densely populated high-income countries have eco-footprints several-fold larger than their domestic land-bases. The citizens of these countries live, in part, on carrying capacity imported from other countries and by imposing on the global commons. In short, the enormous purchasing power of the world's richest nations enables them to finance massive "ecological deficits" by extending their ecological footprints deeply into exporting nations and throughout the ecosphere. Even the apparent productive surpluses of large "under-populated" countries like Canada have been absorbed by the ecological deficits of other countries.

Ecological footprint analysis thus undermines a major sub-theme of the expansionist myth. Trade does not actually increase global carrying capacity—it merely shuffles it around. True, the exchange of factors that would otherwise be limiting enables each trading region/country to exceed its own local carrying capacity. However, this virtually ensures that all countries, their economies happily expanding through trade, breach the biophysical limits to growth simultaneously (ozone depletion and climate change illustrate the point).

Eco-footprinting also provides new insights into the forces of globalization. First, many high-income countries could not maintain their consumer lifestyles if confined to the biophysical output of their domestic land and water ecosystems. The United States, wealthy European countries, and Japan, for example, are dependent on trade and the unsanctioned overuse of common pool life support functions to maintain their economies and to grow. These countries *need* globalization to continue prospering. Second, the same money wealth and trade that enables these rich countries to appropriate so much of the world's economic/ecological output insulates them from the negative effects of ecosystems degradation and resource depletion in their own countries. Imported carrying capacity short-circuits negative feedback from local land that would otherwise limit domestic population and economic growth. Globalization thus helps to sustain the illusion among the rich and powerful that the limits to material growth have been abolished, thus eliminating any reason to question the expansionist myth.

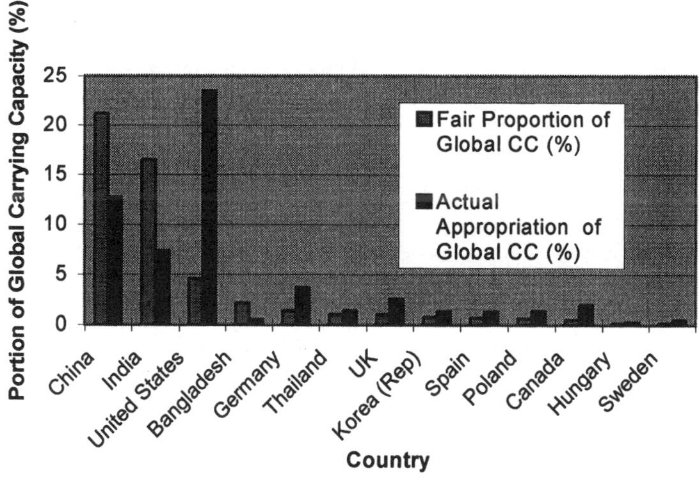

Figure 18.2. Equitable vs. Actual Appropriations of Global Carrying Capacity by Selected Countries

We can highlight the dangers in this situation through international comparison. Figure 18.2 allocates the biophysical output of the planet to a selection of countries in proportion to their 1997 populations. The figure also shows each country's eco-footprint as a proportion of the Earth's total productive land/water area (eco-footprint data from Wackernagel, et al. 1999). This comparison reveals that wealthy market economies like those of the United States, Canada, and Western European countries appropriate two to five times their equitable share of the planet's productive land/water (and 20 times or more per capita than the chronically impoverished). By contrast, low-income countries, like India, Bangladesh, and even China, use only a fraction of their equitable population-based allocation. The prevailing forces of globalization tend to exacerbate rather than level these gross economic inequities. As noted, on a finite planet, such trends can lead only to greater geopolitical instability (Gurr 1985; Homer-Dixon and Blitt 1998; Homer-Dixon et al. 1993)

The possibility of greater scarcity-induced international tension begs the question: just how close are we to global ecological limits? Eco-footprinting enables such an estimate. There are only about nine billion ha of productive cropland, pasture, and forest on Earth and perhaps three billion ha of equivalent shallow ocean, for a total of 12 billion productive ha (two hectares per capita). However, with an estimated average eco-footprint of 2.8 hectares per capita, the present human population already has a total eco-footprint of almost 17 billion ha.

These data suggest we have already "overshot" the long-term human carrying capacity of the Earth by as much as 40 percent. If this seems impossible, remember that a population can live in overshoot—i.e., beyond its ecological means—for a limited period by depleting vital ecosystems and drawing down nonrenewable resource stocks. Empirical evidence in support of this liquidation hypothesis comes in daily newspaper reports on ozone depletion, climate change, deforestation, fisheries collapses, biodiversity loss, and so on. More generally, the Worldwide Fund for Nature recently reported that its "living planet index" is declining in proportion to the increase in humanity's eco-footprint (WWF 2000).

Of course, capital liquidation permanently reduces future carrying capacity—extinction/depletion is forever. Julian Simon's assertion that we have the technology "to feed, clothe, and supply energy to an ever-growing population for the next seven billion years" may well be sorely tested in just the next 50 years! In fact, it is doubtful that we can safely sustain even current gross production/consumption levels for the next few decades using known technologies, let alone the five- to eightfold increase in industrial activity expected over the next half century.

Is a Just Integrity Possible?

> The conquest of the Earth, which mostly means taking it away from those who have a different complexion or slightly flatter noses than ourselves, is not a pretty thing when you look into it too much (Joseph Conrad, *Heart of Darkness*).

Through trade and exploitation of the global commons, the wealthy fifth or so of humanity who consume 80+ percent of global economic output has effectively "appropriated" the entire long-term carrying capacity of Earth. Thus, for all the ebullient optimism of growth-bound globalists, the material excesses of northern consumer lifestyles cannot be extended to the rest of humanity without massively compromising ecological integrity (and ultimately humanity itself). Nature simply cannot provide sufficient "natural income" to support even the present world population at northern material standards while simultaneously maintaining critical life support functions (see also Goodland and Daly 1993; Haavelmo and Hansen 1991).

To provide for today's six billion sustainably, at average Canadian material standards using prevailing technology, we would require three additional Earth-like planets. Such a generous supply of blue-green orbs is unlikely to be forthcoming—as some wag has put it, "good planets are hard to find." Meanwhile, back on the single planet we do have, eroding ecosystems and changing climate are beginning to harm innocent, economically marginalized peoples. Needless to say, the world has yet to acknowledge that one indirect cause of this outrage is excess consumption, the unsustainable lifestyles of the world's wealthy.

Conceivably, some unanticipated technological breakthrough could pull the sustainability rabbit out of the shrinking global hat. Or perhaps governments will finally implement ecologically sound tax policies that force industry to make effective use of existing energy and materially efficient technologies. All to the good—certainly in the absence of such a technological or policy revolution, prospects for a just sustainability (*any* sustainability) look grim indeed.

The only other way to create the ecological space needed for significant material expansion in the impoverished South would be for that space to be vacated by wealthy consumers in the materially bloated North. This is unlikely to happen voluntarily any time soon, given prevailing values of industrial countries and the dominant mind-set of consumer capitalism. The first U.S. President Bush went on record as declaring that "the American Lifestyle is not up for negotiation." And, extending the family tradition, the present Bush administration seems to have rejected serious conservation as a solution to the growing U.S. energy shortage. Instead, it is determined to seek new supplies of petroleum and gas to fuel future growth by extending the U.S. eco-footprint into ecological reserves and into other countries by consolidating a continental energy policy.

Such determined intransigence might be understandable if higher incomes for the already wealthy produced tangible benefits, but this seems not to be the case. World Bank data show that life expectancy and other objective indicators of national population health no longer respond significantly to income growth once it passes a modest $7500–$8000 (international dollars) per person and year. The average per capita incomes of the world's wealthiest countries already exceed this amount by a factor of three or four and the competition to increase the ratio is feverish.

Even more surprising, beyond a certain income level there is little indication of improvement in subjective assessments of well-being. Between 1957 and 1993, U.S. real per capita income more than doubled to $16,000. Compared to 1957, "Americans [had] twice as many cars per person—plus microwave ovens, color TVs, air conditioners, answering machines and $12 billion worth of new brand-name athletic shoes a year" (Myers and Deiner 1995, 13). But were they any happier? Apparently not. In 1957, 35 percent of respondents told the National Opinion Research Center that they were "very happy." With doubled affluence, 32 percent said the same in 1993. Certainly to judge by "soaring rates of depression, a quintupled rate of reported violent crime since 1960, a doubled divorce rate, a slight decline in marital happiness among the marital survivors, and a tripled teen suicide rate, Americans are richer, and no happier" (Myers and Diener 1995, 14). Other studies in the United States and elsewhere report similar results.

All of which begs the question: What compels people so adamantly to defend their right to unlimited income growth when the getting of it apparently sacrifices much of what they value in life, arguably deprives other people of the right to live at all, and demonstrably threatens the ecological integrity of the planet, all for no measurable benefit?

Overcoming Unreason: Can We Rewrite Our Cultural Myth?

> The rise and fall of cultures . . . has always been primarily determined by the tides of human passion, not by the ebb and flow of reason (Morrison 1999).

This chapter began with a description of the prevailing expansionist paradigm, a materially optimistic but narrowly conceived development model based on the abstract assumptions of neoliberal economic theory. I then showed, using the arguments of well-known economists themselves, that the fundamental assumptions of the economic models do not apply to the actual economy. Next, I argued that the structure and behavior of conventional economic models have no parallels whatever in the structure and behavior of real-world biophysical systems (with predictably tragic results).

Given the totality of this "disconnect" between theory and reality, a neutral observer might well express surprise that intelligent people would pay the economic model much heed as a guide to practice. Surprise would justifiably yield to astonishment on discovery that governments everywhere are doing all they can—actually competing with each other—to force their national economies into the conceptually narrow straightjacket of the model. And stunned disbelief would be a reasonable reaction on learning that the official world's response to the implosion of the ecosphere has been to facilitate the global *spread* of the expansionist model. How can we explain such irrational behavior on the part of the self-proclaimed most intelligent species on Earth? Reg Morrison (1999) argues that humans have a genetically enforced predisposition to attach "mystical significance" to their dreams and fantasies, their myths and prejudices, whatever the evidence to the contrary. Apparently the tendency to abandon reason and the deliberate process of rational thought had significant survival value early in human evolution. When early "man" was confronted with fearsome natural forces and events beyond his understanding, his cultural myths conferred intelligibility, social cohesion, and a sense of personal security. (Sociobiologist E. O. Wilson has written that the human mind evolved to believe in gods.) The result today is a species in which only a small fraction of the population is consistently capable of applying the most basic rules of evidence to emotionally loaded information. "For us to maintain our way of living, we must . . . tell lies to each other, and especially to ourselves . . . . The lies act as barriers to truth. These barriers . . . are necessary because without them many deplorable acts would become impossibilities" (Jensen 2000). In short, human beings regularly persuade themselves into believing the unbelievable if they perceive it to enhance their perceived wealth, security, or social status.

This mechanism ensures that those who covet leadership and political prestige, and who actually work their way into positions of power, will act as if unaware of the avalanche of data signaling ecospheric distress (Morrison 1999). This is particularly so if responding rationally would conflict with what they perceive to be the interests of those to whom they feel most beholden—usually the rich and powerful, people with the greatest interest in the *status quo*. Focused on reducing fiscal deficits and national growth, and bound to the interests of capital, even the elected leaders of the major democracies remain blind to the ecological deficit and humanity's cumulative debt to nature. According to Hoyle, "We are traveling in a vehicle that guides itself, just as our species has arisen from an evolutionary process that guided itself throughout past ages. It is my belief that nothing has changed, we are still in the grip of natural processes, we are not in charge of our own destiny" (Hoyle 1964, 61, 67).

If society remains obsessed with the notion of sheer growth at the expense of virtually all other life-values and human concerns, the result is potentially catastrophic. The human enterprise "exhibits all four major characteristics of a malignant process: rapid uncontrolled growth; invasion and destruction of adjacent tissues (ecosystems, in this case); metastasis (colonization and urbanization, in this case); and dedifferentiation (loss of distinctiveness in individual components)" (Hern 1997). Smith and Sauer-Thompson (1998) postulate that the resultant environmental decay, coupled with geopolitical stresses induced by resource scarcity, will inevitably cause industrial society to "self-destruct, producing massive ecological damage, social chaos, and megadeath."

In the final analysis, it seems that both humanity's genetic coding and our current socio-cultural coding (itself partially a product of genetic coding) are prejudiced against sustainability. This suggests that there is only one way out of our dilemma, one chance to rewrite our cultural myth in the spirit of the Earth Charter. Fittingly, the solution harkens back to yet another myth, that humans are rational beings and the prime evidence of intelligent life on Earth.

Very simply, our salvation resides in seeing things for what they are, in "getting clear on the concept." If we are to find effective solutions, we must acknowledge both the distal and proximal causes of our dysfunctional cultural behavior and assert our independence from both genetic control and maladaptive myth. Let us finally seize rational collective control of our destiny. This single act of social intelligence would at last distinguish humankind from species that are still largely slaves to instinct. Indeed, the triumph of reason over scripted determinism, whatever its source, would herald a whole new phase in human evolution.

References

Bartlett, Albert. 1996. "The Exponential Function XI: The New Flat Earth Society." *The Physics Teacher* 34: 342–43.

Beckerman, Wilfred. 1992. "Economic Growth and the Environment: Whose Growth? Whose Environment?" *World Development* 20, no. 4: 481–96.

Christensen, Paul. 1991. "Driving Forces, Increasing Returns, and Ecological Sustainability," in *Ecological Economics: The Science and Management of Sustainability*, edited by Robert Costanza. New York: Columbia University Press.

Daly, Herman E. 1991. "The Circular Flow of Exchange Value and the Linear Throughput of Matter-Energy: A Case of Misplaced Concreteness," in H. E. Daly, *Steady-State Economics,* 2nd edition. Washington, D.C.: Island Press.

The Earth Charter Initiative. 2002. "The Earth Charter." San José, Costa Rica: Earth Council. <http://www.earthcharter.org/earthcharter/charter.htm> (January 12, 2002).

Galbraith, James K. 2000. "How the Economists Got It Wrong." *The American Prospect* 11, no. 7 (February 14).

Georgescu-Roegen, Nicholas. 1971. *The Entropy Law and the Economic Process.* Cambridge, Mass.: Harvard University Press.

Gergin, Kenneth. 1991. *The Saturated Self: Dilemmas of Identity in Contemporary Life.* New York: Basic Books.

Goodland, Robert, and Herman Daly. 1993. "Why Northern Income Growth Is Not the Solution to Southern Poverty." *Ecological Economics* 8: 85–101.

Grant, Colin. 1998. *Myths We Live By.* Ottawa: University of Ottawa Press.

Gurr, Ted. 1985. "On the Political Consequences of Scarcity and Economic Decline," *International Studies Quarterly* 29: 51–75.

Haavelmo, T., and S. Hansen. 1991. "On the Strategy of Trying to Reduce Economic Inequality by Expanding the Scale of Human Activity," in *Environmentally Sustainable Ecological Development: Building on Brundtland*, edited by R. Goodland, H. Daly, S. El Serafy, and B. Von Droste. Paris: UNESCO.

Hern, W. M. 1997. "Is Human Culture Oncogenic for Uncontrolled Population Growth and Ecological Destruction?" *Human Evolution* 12, no 1–2: 97–105.

Homer-Dixon, Thomas, and Jessica Blitt, eds. 1998. *Ecoviolence: Links among Environment, Population, and Security.* Lanham, Md.: Rowman & Littlefield.

Homer-Dixon, Thomas, J. Boutwell, and G. Rathjens. 1993. "Environmental Change and Violent Conflict." *Scientific American* (February): 38–45

Hoyle, Fred. 1964. *Of Men and Galaxies*. Seattle: University of Washington Press.

IRC (International Red Cross). 1999. *World Disasters Report.* Dordrecht: Martinus Nijhoff.

Jacobsen, Kurt. 2001. "Revolt in Political Science." *Post-Autistic Economics Newsletter*, Issue no. 6 (8 May).

Jensen, Derrick. 2000. *A Language Older than Words*. New York: Context Books.

Kay, James J., and Henry A. Regier. 2000. "Uncertainty, Complexity, and Ecological Integrity." Pp. 121–56 in *Implementing Ecological Integrity: Restoring Regional and Global Environment and Human Health,* edited by P. Crabbé, A. Holland, L Ryszkowski, and L. Westra. NATO Science Series IV: Earth and Environmental Sciences, Vol 1. Dortrecht: Kluwer.

Korten, David. 1995. *When Corporations Rule the World.* West Hartfort, Conn.: Kumarian Press; San Francisco: Berrett-Koehler Publishers.

Logan, John. 1996. "Patch Disturbance and the Human Niche," <http: //dieoff.org/page78. htm> (20 May 2001) (also, e-mail exchanges with Logan on patch disturbance, August 1997).

Lubchenco, Jane. 1998. "Entering the Century of the Environment: A New Social Contract for Science." *Science* 297: 491–97.

McMurtry, John. 1989. *Unequal Freedoms: The Global Market as an Ethical System.* Toronto: Garamond Press.

Morrison, Reg. 1999. *The Spirit in the Gene: Humanity's Proud Illusion and the Laws of Nature.* Ithica, N.Y.: Comstock Publishing Associates (Cornell University Press).

Myers, David G., and Ed Diener. 1995. "Who Is Happy." *Psychological Science* 6, no. 1: 10–19.

Ormerod, Paul. 1997. *The Death of Economics.* New York: John Wiley and Sons (originally London: Faber and Faber, 1994).

Postman, Neil. 1999. *Building a Bridge to the Eighteenth Century.* New York: Alfred A. Knopf.

Rees, William E. 1996. "Revisiting Carrying Capacity: Area-Based Indicators of Sustainability." *Population and Environment* 17, no.3: 195–215.

Rees, William E. 1998. "How Should a Parasite Value Its Host?" *Ecological Economics* 25: 49–52.

Rees, William E. 2000. "Patch Disturbance, Eco-Footprints, and Biological Integrity: Revisiting the Limits to Growth (or Why Industrial Society Is Inherently Unsustainable)." In *Ecological Integrity: Integrating Environment, Conservation, and Health,* edited by David Pimentel, Laura Westra, and Reed F. Noss. Washington, D.C.: Island Press.

Rees, William E., 2001. "Ecological Footprint, Concept of." Pp. 229–44 in *Encyclopedia of Biodiversity*, Vol. 2. New York: Academic Press.

Rees, William E., and Mathis Wackernagel. 1999. "Monetary Analysis: Turning a Blind Eye on Sustainability." *Ecological Economics* 29: 47–52.

Roodman, David M. 2001. *Still Waiting for the Jubilee: Pragmatic Solutions for the Third World Debt Crisis* (Worldwatch Paper 155). Washington, D.C.: The Worldwatch Institute.

Schneider, E., and James Kay. 1994. "Life as a Manifestation of the Second Law of Thermodynamics." *Mathematical and Computer Modeling* 19, nos. 6–8: 25–48.

Smith, J. W., and G. Sauer-Thompson. 1998. "Civilization's Wake: Ecology, Economics, and the Roots of Environmental Destruction and Neglect." *Population and Environment* 19: 541–75.

Thurow, Lester. 1983. *Dangerous Currents.* New York: Random House.

Toles, Tom. "Still Unclear on the Concept." Editorial Cartoon. © Universal Press Syndicate, Kansas City, Missouri.

Tuxill, J. 1998. *Losing Strands in the Web of Life: Vertebrate Declines and the Conservation of Biological Diversity* (Worldwatch Paper 141). Washington, D.C.: The Worldwatch Institute.

UNDP (United Nations Development Program). 2001. *Human Development Report 2001.* New York and Oxford: Oxford University Press (for UNDP).

Vatn, Arild, and Daniel W. Bromley. 1993. "Choices without Prices without Apologies." *Journal of Environmental Economics and Management* 26: 129–48.

Vitousek, Peter, H. Mooney, J. Lubchenco, and J. Melillo. 1997. "Human Domination of Earth's Ecosystems." *Science* 277: 494–99.

Wackernagel, Mathis, and William E. Rees. 1996. *Our Ecological Footprint: Reducing Human Impact on Earth.* Gabriola Island, B.C. and Philadelphia, Pa.: New Society Publishers.

Wackernagel, Mathis, L. Onisto, P. Bello, A. C. Linares, I. S. L. Falfán, J. M. Garcia, A. I. S. Guerrero, and M. G. S. Guerrero. 1999. "National Natural Capital Accounting with the Ecological Footprint Concept." *Ecological Economics* 29: 375–90.

WCED (UN World Commission on Environment and Development). 1987. *Our Common Future.* Oxford: Oxford University Press (for the commission).

WRI/UNEP. 2000. *World Resources 2000–2001.* United Nations Development Program, UN Environment Program, World Bank, World Resources Institute. Washington, D.C.: World Resources Institute.

WWF. October 2000. *Living Planet Report 2000,* edited by Jonathan Loh. Gland, Switzerland: Worldwide Fund for Nature (and others).

Chapter 19

The Fair Distribution of Environmental Goods

János I. Tóth

According to the Earth Charter, the fair distribution of wealth is of utmost importance in considering the future of the Earth. At the same time, it emphasizes that we should "promote the equitable distribution of wealth within nations and among nations" (Earth Charter 2002, Principle 10a). According to John Rawls (1971), a fair distribution of material goods need not be a strictly equal one if it results in the improvement of the condition of those who are the least well off. That is clearly not the case in the current global system. If the population of the world is reduced to 100 people—maintaining the currently characteristic ethnic, social, economic features, then 6 of them would possess 59 percent of goods in the world. Eighty of them would live under unsatisfactory conditions. Seventy would not be able to read. Fifty would be underfed. One would be a university graduate and would have his own computer (Community 2000). So the Earth Charter is entitled to say that the present form of distribution is unfair. "The benefits of development are not shared equitably and the gap between rich and poor is widening. Injustice, poverty, ignorance, and violent conflict are widespread and the cause of great suffering" (Earth Charter 2002, Preamble).

Distributive justice *(iustitia distributiva)* means, first of all, the fair distribution of resources and goods of a material nature. Conceptually, distributive justice can be interpreted in a relation made up of three factors: (1) the material resource or good to be distributed, (2) the actors interested in the distribution, (3) the authority performing the distribution. Ever since the development of the welfare society, the model is simplified to the problem of the relationships between the income to be distributed, the persons in competition, and the state performing the distribution (Heller 1987, chapter 4.1). Considerations of justice may also address the distribution of burdens and harms, but in this paper I shall focus on the distribution of environmental goods. So the present form of the distribution is unfair. The false prejudices, misconceptions, and ideologies characteristic of modernity tend to veil this injustice. In this chapter I would like to take a look at these myths in relation to the three basic factors in a distribution in order to reveal what is required for a fair distribution of environmental goods.

Natural Resources to Be Distributed

The problem of the distribution of natural goods makes it necessary to reinterpret the elements of this threefold model in a wider framework. Let us start with the material resource to be distributed. The criteria of justice must be applied only if the goods to be distributed are *important* for the human community and they are available only in *scarcity*.

Myths about the Irrelevance of Natural Goods

The resource to be distributed must be relevant for *change* in individual and social welfare. Some goods might be important for human welfare, but due to their constancy, their permanent presence, they might be irrelevant to *changes* in welfare through social development or economic growth. In the case of social-economic goods, the criterion of relevance to change in welfare applies almost automatically. However, one of the great myths of Western thought is that natural goods are irrelevant for social welfare. This view has many roots.

Naturalism

There are many biological units in nature (genes, organism, populations, races), each of which strives to sustain and extend its existence, while other biological units are successfully and mutually engaged in restricting these expansional efforts. Producers, consumers, decomposers and abiotic factors all construct one ecosystem, where forces and counter-forces level out each other. So the working of the ecological system does not require self-restriction from any of its parts. In the early phase of anthropogenesis, *Homo sapiens* was only a consumer living in the ecosystem. Just like every consumer population, the only concern of the primitive human community was its survival and procreation.

That is the reason why humans can easily disregard their special position and, as László (1994, 69) has put it, can easily develop an illusion originating in the Neolithic Age, in which humanity needs no such self-restriction. But according to Endreffy (1999), this form of naturalism leads to environmental destruction, while environmental protection is the result of self-restrictions derived from reason and morality.

Western religions

Ever since White (1967), many experts have pointed out that Western religious thinking—belief in one God, the everlasting soul, creation, the hierarchy of existence, and so on—is closely linked with the devaluation of nature, which lies at the bottom of the hierarchy. Secularization has even fortified this process, as the place of the Almighty has been occupied by humanity.

Cartesianism

Descartes distinguishes sharply between nature and the human sphere. Consequently, a person, as an independent substance of a higher quality, may disregard the damages caused to nature and, moreover, humanity can become the ruler of the world. The goods and services provided by nature are exterior to the sphere of influence of social practice. Natural goods do not influence the change in human welfare, which is thought to depend exclusively on social factors (Descartes 1636, IV, 2). A later development in this tradition holds that human welfare can be expressed and measured in money, so the development of society and human welfare become identical with economic growth (Tóth 2000). Contrary to Descartes, the Earth Charter underlines the fact that humanity is part of the universe and Earth has provided the conditions essential to life's evolution. The resilience of the community of life and the well-being of humanity depend upon preserving a healthy biosphere with all its ecological systems. (Earth Charter 2002, Preamble).

Liberalism

According to liberal conception, a human being is an atom independent of his environment, who follows his own interests (Heller 1987, chapter 4.1). The most important value is the freedom and autonomy of the person. The principal idea behind the ideal of personal autonomy is that people should have the freedom to create their own lives. The liberal argument for freedom is based on the harm principle. This principle was first formulated by John Stuart Mill (1974, 68): *"The sole end for which mankind are warranted, individually or collectively, in interfering with the liberty of action of any of their member is self-protection. That the only purpose for which power can be rightfully exercised over any member of a civilized community, against his will, is to prevent harm to others."* Since the environment is not another person, Mill's principle has been interpreted to mean that coercion cannot be applied for purposes of environmental protection, as this will harm the freedom and autonomy of the atomic-people subjected to coercion without serving the freedom and autonomy of other people.

However, environmental philosophy rejects the conception of the atomic-person independent of his environment. Our point of view is that the existence of every organism, including human beings, depends on the condition of the environment (See Earth Charter 2002, Principle 1a). Destroying the environment will seriously damage those living there. This is most obvious in the release of toxic environmental contaminants injurious to human health, but the following two examples provided by Raz (1986, chapters 14 and 15) illustrate as well that a free and autonomous human life is impossible in a degraded environment:

The Man in the Pit. A person falls down a pit and remains there for the rest of his life, unable to climb out or to summon help. There is just enough ready food to keep him alive without (after he gets used to it) any suffering. He can do nothing much, not even move much. His choices are confined to whether to eat now or a little later, whether to sleep now or a little later, whether to scratch his left ear or not (Raz 1986, 373).

The Hounded Woman. A person finds herself on a small desert island. She shares the island with a fierce carnivorous animal, which perpetually hunts for her. Her mental stamina, her intellectual ingenuity, her will-power, and her physical resources are taxed to their limits by the struggle to remain alive. She never has a chance to do or even to think of anything other than how to escape from the beast (Raz 1986, 374).

Raz argues that neither the Man in the Pit nor the Hounded Woman leads an autonomous life. The first has only short-term options of trivial worth and consequence. The other has choices with potentially dreadful consequences. According to Raz the conditions of autonomy are complex and consist of three distinct components: appropriate mental abilities, independence, and an adequate range of options. It follows from this that environmental destruction harms the interest of both individuals and local communities, so the logic of the harm principle can be well applied for purposes of environmental protection with a proper view of humankind.

Myths Related to either the Absolute Abundance or Scarcity of Resources

Hume (1966, 187) thought that a fair distribution is possible only in conditions of relative or restricted scarcity. According to Hume, any fair distribution is needless and impossible in the condition of absolute abundance and absolute scarcity. The restrictive scarcity as a prerequisite of fair distribution has been stressed by Rawls (1971, 161) as well.

The Lockian Concept of Nature: The Absolute Abundance in Natural Goods

It was Locke who first defined the features of the world of *abundantly* available natural goods (Locke, §§25–30). It is from this ground that Locke argues in favor of private property, labor-value theory, and economic liberalism. Everybody is free to consume, enjoy, and expropriate these goods available in abundance. According to his theory, the expropriation of natural resources by labor and cultivation multiplies the quantity of goods useful for humankind, while there are goods abundantly left for others as well (Locke, §27). Natural resources are inexhaustible, so there is no need to restrict socially the availability of these goods and there is no need to employ alternative technologies to restrict the use and pollution and to protect nature. Consequently, there is no need for any fair distribution of natural goods.

My point of view is that natural resources are goods available in relative scarcity, so the concept of nature presented above does not apply at all. (See also the Earth Charter, Preamble and Principle 7f) Consequently, Korten (1995, chapter 2) is right to talk about a cowboy economy in relation to the modern economic system. Environmental problems result from the fact that we behave as exploiters of unlimited and open territories, even though we are living in a limited organic space. Our environment-shaping activity is threatening the ecological order, which secures the conditions for our living. This is, first of all, the result of the fact that natural limits do not appear spontaneously at the level of economic actors. Economics does not do anything to restrict the free availability of natural resources. Moreover, the total and merciless competition prevents the necessary brakes from being imposed to the system. The environmental and humanitarian catastrophe is going to occur because the actors do not perform the collective restrictions that the finitude of natural resources make necessary, and they respond to the exhaustion of resources with an increase in competition. As the Earth Charter says, "We stand at a critical moment in Earth's history, a time when humanity must choose its future. . . . The dominant patterns of production and consumption are causing environmental devastation, the depletion of resources, and a massive extinction of species" (Preamble).

The Absolute Scarcity of Natural Resources: "Lifeboat Ethics"

Absolute scarcity is the counterpoint to absolute abundance. In this case, human demand so exceeds the capacity of resources that neither the theory nor the practice of fair distribution can be carried out. Presumably it was Malthus (1978) who first treated the problem of the absolute scarcity of natural goods. According to Malthus, as a result of the excessive reproduction of the lower social classes, any effort or program developed to improve the condition of the poor becomes impossible and meaningless. One of his modern followers, Hardin (1974) also stresses the absolute scarcity of natural goods in relation to which he formulates the so-called "lifeboat ethics." Hardin argues that rich nations ought to refuse to offer any kind of help to poorer nations. He rejects not only supplying food, but any other kinds of help as well, including the acceptance of refugees from misery. The destitute, of course, want to establish themselves in richer countries, but there are simply too many of them, or, what is even more alarming, their rate of reproduction is more than twice that of those who are well off. Consequently, if these more prosperous countries incorporate even a small part of the Third World population, it will cause such an increase in the number of the population that it will ruin their well-being. Hardin agrees that the destitute do not deserve this treatment, but their poverty is only of minor importance and factors of justice are also irrelevant for the environmental crisis.

For illustration, let us suppose that 50 people are sitting in a lifeboat in which there are still 10 places left, so the boat seats 60. People sitting in the boat notice 100 other people swimming towards them, who want to get into the boat as well. If those sitting in the boat help all their fellows, as Christian ethics dictates it, or if they consider human demands, as requested by Marxist theory, they should accept every drowning person into the boat. This way, there will be 150 people in a boat for 60, the ship will sink, and they will all drown. It is perfect fairness and perfect catastrophe, says Hardin.

Humanity lives undoubtedly on a planet of a limited size, with limited natural resources, so the increase in demands and population after a certain limit will lead to environmental and human catastrophe. However, the picture drawn by Hardin is misleadingly schematic. On the one hand, excessive production, the transformation of nature, and consumption are just as responsible as the increase in the number of population. If the excessive production in welfare societies can be reduced, the capacity of Earth as a lifeboat can be considerably increased. On the other hand, with an increase in efficiency, the sustaining capacity can be increased as well. That is, humankind will be able to build a bigger ship. Finally, the excessive reproduction of the periphery is not a natural law. The birthrate will decrease with social-economic development.

Even though the concepts of nature identified with Descartes and Locke and with Malthus and Hardin differ very much theoretically, their practical outcomes are very similar. The fair distribution of natural goods is unnecessary within conditions of absolute abundance and it is impossible within the conditions of absolute scarcity, so both encourage us to preserve the present state of unfair distribution, which is very unfair for the environment. The spread and prevailing of an environment-aware thinking is most significantly obstructed by the fact that in the developed world, the political and economic elite are interested in preserving present economic practice.

Heterogeneity of Natural Goods

Our age interprets ecological services and environmental goods as undifferentiated. However, there are enormous differences among environmental goods. Think, for example, of such essential polarities as scarcity–abundance, private–common goods, natural values–resources, long-term–short-term goods, renewable–nonrenewable goods, and so on. It is accidentally possible that a natural resource is available in abundance (e.g., sand in Sahara, saltwater in oceans), but in most cases both renewable and nonrenewable natural resources are available for humanity only in scarcity. It is obvious that we must relate differently to the natural and environmental goods with different properties. It follows from the differences among natural values, goods, and services that we should strive for different social, legal, and economic methods that reflect the differences among natural resources. For example, a completely different procedure should be applied to renewable than to nonrenewable goods. Use of renewable resources should be restricted to a level where they can endlessly reproduce, while the use of nonrenewable resources should be constantly reduced and should finally be ended.

Actors Interested in the Distribution

Exploiting of the Next Generations

Ethically speaking, justice requires that everyone who is entitled to some sort of resource should have his share of it. This principle, of course, can never be perfectly put into practice. Besides, a certain process of democratization is clearly distinguishable in history, and, as a result of such a process, an ever larger circle of justified agents get their share from the resources in question. The appearance of democratic societies was an important step in this process.

After this, the number of those agents whose interests were taken into consideration at the distribution and who were able to influence the principles related to distribution increased by measures. Many experts think that the historical process of democratization culminated in the emergence of democratic societies, because in this ideal-typical form the interests of all the entitled agents are taken into consideration. However, this is a faulty view.

The present practice considers only the interests of the present generation (and within this generation, only of those with the right to vote), so *future generations*, who are also interested in the problem of distribution, are put into a very disadvantageous situation. The present practice of democratic decision taking legitimates those decisions that will deprive future generations of natural resources and adequate environmental conditions. However, the formal legality of democratic process makes no difference to the fact that such a behavior is unfair from a moral point of view (Earth Charter 2002, Principle 4).

Anthropocentrism

Moreover, not only humankind, but other species are also interested in preserving natural resources and environmental values. Consequently, *eco-centric* justice ought to consider the interests and welfare of subhuman species. In contradiction to the present generation, which always has some capacity to impose their interests, future generations (and subhuman species) can rely only on the sense of justice of the present generation.

Authority Performing the Distribution

The notion of distributive justice first of all refers to a situation in which a main power distributes the goods. Theologically speaking, only God can do this. However, in our secularized world the question emerges: who or what can fulfill this position? Although totalitarian ideologies often attribute such a power to the state, it does not have the necessary capacities and information to carry out directly the fair distribution of goods. So, in the category of distributive justice there is a considerable shift of emphasis from the problem of the direct distribution of goods to the indirect procedural justice realized in the form of distributive principles. In the later case, distribution can be considered fair if its principles are fair. As competition is one of the main forms of organization in modern welfare societies, the prerequisite of a fair distribution is the securing of the necessary conditions for competition in accordance with the spirit of justice. The direct distribution of goods practiced by the state and by other charity organizations is only of secondary importance as a form of compensatory justice.

Conclusion

To sum up, I would like to point out that modern welfare societies concentrate, first of all, on the distribution of private and economic-social goods. Consequently, there emerged enormous injustices to the distribution of environmental, natural goods—through not necessarily consciously and deliberately. We should radically reconsider the three-factor distributive model for the fair distribution of environmental and natural goods. On the one hand, we should recognize that natural goods have a very important role in the change of social welfare and they are available only in a restricted scarcity, so it is possible and necessary to try to distribute these goods fairly. On the other hand, the circle of the actors entitled to natural resources should be acknowledged in a much broader context, reflecting reality. Third, there is a need for new principles and institutions of distribution that will consider the peculiarities and justice in relation to natural resources.

References

Community. 2000. <http://www.webofculture.com/home/community.html>. (30 Nov. 2000).

Descartes, Rene. 1964. *Discourse on the Method of Rightly Conducting Reason and Reaching the Truth in the Sciences*. English translation by L. J. Lafleur. Indianapolis: Bobbs-Merrill.

The Earth Charter Initiative. 2002. "The Earth Charter." San José, Costa Rica: Earth Council. <http://www.earthcharter.org/earthcharter/charter.htm> (January 12, 2002).

Endreffy, Zoltan. 1999. *Hogy mûvelje és õrizze*. Budapest: Liget Mûhely Alapítvány.

Hardin, Garret. 1974. "Lifeboat Ethics." *Psychology Today*. Reprinted in *People, Penguins, and Plastic Trees: Basic Issues in Environmental Ethics*, edited by Donald VanDeVeer and Christine Pierce. Belmont, Calif.: Wadsworth, 1986.

Heller, Ágnes. 1987. *Beyond Justice*. London: Basil Blackwell.

Hume, David. 1966. "An Enquiry Concerning the Principles of Morals." *Enquiries*. London: Oxford University Press.

Korten, David C. 1995. *When Corporations Rule the World*. West Hartford, Conn.: Kumarian Press; San Francisco: Berrett-Koehler.

László, Ervin. 1994. *The Choice: Evolution or Extinction?* New York: Jeremy P. Tarcher/ Putnam.

Locke, J. 1995. *Second Treatise on Government,* edited by Garry Wiersema. <http://www.let.rug.nl/~usa/D/1651-1700/locke/ECCG/govern05.htm> (10 June 2001).

Malthus, Thomas R. 1798. *An Essay on the Principle of Population.* 2 vols. London: J. M. Dent.

Mill, John Stuart. 1974. *On Liberty,* edited by Gertrude Himmelfarb. London: Penguin.

Rawls, John. 1971. *A Theory of Justice.* Cambridge, Mass.: Harvard University Press.

Raz, Joseph. 1986. *The Morality of Freedom.* Oxford: Clarendon Press.

Tóth, János I. 2000. The Conception of Natural Goods in Economics. Pp. 362–63 in *Implementing Ecological Integrity,* edited by P. Crabbé, A. Holland, L. Ryszkowski, and L. Westra. Netherlands: Kluwer, 362–63.

White, L. Jr. 1967. "The Historical Roots of Our Ecological Crisis." *Science* 155: 1203-7.

Chapter 20

A Stakeholder-Based Approach to Environmental Justice Using Geographical Information Systems (GIS)

Garrick E. Louis and Luna M. Magpili

In the post Bretton-Woods era, economic development is characterized by an increased focus on manufacturing and industrialization. These activities are thought to improve the living standards of people by increasing labor productivity, leading to a larger regional gross domestic product (GDP) or per capita income (PCI) and the provision of a broad range of goods and services to consumers. However, GDP or PCI and other aggregate measures of economic performance, do not account for the negative externalities of manufacturing and industrialization, nor do they reflect the distribution of costs and benefits from these activities across different segments of the population. The same processes that drive regional economic development and its related benefits, also consume resources and yield by-products that adversely affect human health and the environment. In the United States alone, industries treat, store, and dispose of 550 million tons of hazardous wastes each year (Center for Env. Res. 1988). In addition, factories annually discharge directly into the air, water, and land 3 million tons of toxic chemicals, almost a quarter of which are chemicals suspected of causing birth defects, and 8 percent of which are suspected of causing cancer (Citizens Fund 1990). To some extent, measures to curb these negative impacts are reflected in the price of goods and services, as relevant, mitigating regulatory costs are passed on to consumers. However, this market-based social equilibrium between benefits and costs can mask pernicious inequities, which consistently ascribe disproportionately lower shares of benefits and higher shares of costs of industrialization to selected segments of the population.

The risk communication and environmental justice literature has begun to address the link between socioeconomic inequality, imbalances of social power, and local environmental quality under various labels such as "environmental justice," "environmental racism," or "environmental cost/risk and distributive equity." This study will employ the term environmental justice. The Environmental Protection Agency (EPA) defines environmental justice as follows:

> Environmental justice is the fair treatment and meaningful involvement of all people regardless of race, ethnicity, income, national origin or educational level with respect to the development, implementation, and enforcement of environmental laws, regulations, and policies. Fair treatment means that no population, due to policy or economic disempowerment, is forced to bear a disproportionate burden of the negative human health or environmental impacts of pollution or other environmental consequences resulting from industrial, municipal, and commercial operations or the execution of federal, state, local, and tribal programs and policies (Environmental Protection Agency 2000).

The environmental justice literature has voiced the concern that environmental hazards, costs, and risks are borne disproportionately by people of color and disadvantaged socioeconomic status. Numerous studies have suggested that the most common victims of environmental pollution are racial minorities (African American, Hispanics, Asian and Pacific Islanders, American Indians, Eskimos, and Aleuts) and the poor (Bullard 1983; Bullard and Wright 1988; Freeman 1971; Lester et. al. 2001; United Church of Christ 1987). People of color and poor people are likely to be exposed to higher levels of pollution than their white or higher-income counterparts and the economic cost of pollution control is borne more heavily by them than by other groups (Bullard 1993). These groups must assume relatively high personal costs that include elevated health risks and reduced property values from the sources of pollution (waste treatment facilities, waste disposal facilities, manufacturing facilities) that are hosted in and around their communities. At the same time, they share less of the benefits that society as a whole derives from these noxious facilities than residents in more affluent communities and those with lower percentages of racial minorities (Bryant and Mohai 1992).

Measuring Environmental Injustice

Several studies have examined the distribution of pollution and the equity of pollution control by measuring the geographical incidence of pollution (United Church of Christ 1987; Goldman 1991; Bullard 1993). By correlating geographical indicators of this incidence, such as the location of dumps or the level of air pollution, with socioeconomic characteristics of surrounding communities, researchers draw conclusions about the extent of environmental discrimination. This is known as the proximity-based approach (Institute of Medicine 1999).

One of the initiating cases in the environmental justice movement began with protests against the establishment of a PCB disposal landfill in Warren County, North Carolina, where there was a predominantly black and poor population (Lee 1993). This event convinced the U.S. General Accounting Office (GAO) to conduct a study in 1983 that examined the racial and socioeconomic makeup of communities surrounding four hazardous waste landfills in the southeastern United States. The key finding of the GAO study was that in three out of the four communities studied, blacks comprised the majority of the population. This GAO conclusion utilized the proximity-based approach.

A larger, more comprehensive study of a nationwide extent was the 1987 study *Toxic Wastes and Race*, commissioned by the United Church of Christ Commission for Racial Justice. The racial composition of a community was found to be the single variable best able to explain the existence or nonexistence of commercial hazardous waste facilities in a given community. Communities, defined by zip code, that hosted a single hazardous waste facility, were found to have twice the percentage of minorities as communities without such a facility (24 percent versus 12 percent). Communities with two or more facilities had more than three times the minority representation than communities without any such sites (38 percent). Again, the proximity-based approach was used, comparing the percentages of minorities in zip codes without facilities to the percentages of minorities in zip codes with facilities. Multiple sources of risk were taken into account, noting not only the presence of hazardous facilities, but the number of such facilities existing in a given community.

Goldman's *The Truth about Where You Live* (Goldman 1991) was another nationwide study that used a variation of the proximity-based approach. He analyzed industrial toxin measures (industrial air emissions from smokestacks, hazardous chemicals, suspected carcinogens, acutely hazardous chemicals, and hazardous waste incinerators); health statistics (such as mortality, birth defect, and cancer rates); and demographic characteristics (such as race and income) of counties. His study concluded that the poor, black, Latino, and Native American communities were consistently hit more severely by pollution and death than other groups in the population (Goldman 1991). In the counties that rank the worst across all of the industrial toxin measures, minorities comprised more than twice the percentage of the population than the average for the rest of the country. The demographics were the same for counties with the worst mortality from diseases such as cancer, heart disease, and acutely hazardous exposures. An added improvement of Goldman's study was his extensive exploitation of geographic maps to highlight the demographic characteristics, toxicity levels of certain substances, and mortality on a per county basis. Goldman's study also conducted correlations between birth defect/mortality and industrial releases of suspected teratogens (drugs, chemicals, and infections that can cause birth defects). It found the top 10 counties for teratogenic pollution having significantly above-average rates of birth defect/mortality. The finding connected health status of county population with industrial pollution/releases in the counties.

A deficiency of the proximity-based approach is the use of a predefined unit of analysis, referring to the partitioning of the study area such as zip codes or census tracts. For example, a 1994 study conducted at the University of Massachusetts found little difference in the minority percentages of areas containing hazardous facilities and those without when census tracts were used instead of the zip code method used by the United Church of Christ study (Anderton et al. 1994). However, it should be noted that along with the difference in choice of unit of analysis, the study also used a different definition of control population and a different selection of independent variables in their correlation analysis (Mohai 1995). As a solution to the unit of analysis issue, some studies have started to use radii of fixed distances to approximate areas of impact. Such an approach has the advantage of standardizing the size and shape of geographic units and of ensuring that the locally unwanted land use or potential source of pollution is always at the center. One of the first studies to use geographic information systems was completed by Theodore Glickman. His study used GIS software to draw the area of concern as concentric circles centered at the facility in question (Glickman 1994).

Still, a study by the Institute of Medicine (1999) cautions against the proximity-based argument as well as correlation studies. The study pointed out that mere proximity to hazardous facilities is an inexact measure of actual contact of affected groups to the source. Quantification of the actual emissions from the source must be examined in order to measure actual human exposure to an environmental hazard. This requires estimating the rate of release and path of the material into and through the environment. Moreover, correlation studies do not explain direct causality. A myriad of other factors/variables have to be accounted for.

Related studies have sprung from the economics field as well. These efforts deal with distributing the costs of pollution, or an index of change in the physical environment, and then calculating the benefits by income and racial category based on willingness to pay (Gelobter 1992). Willingness to pay is a measure of the dollar value that households are willing to pay for an incremental quantity of a good like environmental quality. It is usually derived from surrogate measures such as calculations of how much housing values change when air quality improves. The latter method uses hedonic pricing to capture the value of lost workdays, shortened lifespan, health hazard, other impacts of exposure to pollutants, reduced wildlife diversity, and damage to ecosystems. Calculating these costs to the affected communities and society at large yields their value in economic terms. Society then faces the choice of assigning these costs as direct charges to polluters or trying to equitably distribute an equivalent amount of benefits as compensation to all who bear the costs and risks of pollution. Such a distribution of benefits to offset costs faces formidable hurdles. Environmental taxes attempt to assign the appropriate social costs to polluters (Morganstern 1996). One of the shortcomings of such taxes is that they do not redress social and economic inequities they created through past practices. Compensation schemes that attempt to pay affected communities for the risk of hosting noxious facilities have been attempted and are documented in the literature (Petts 1994). The problem is that there is no consensus approach to quantifying the risks borne by these communities objectively. Furthermore, communities that are economically disadvantaged may be predisposed to accept compensation offers that are below any realistic lower bound on the estimated value of the risks they face. In addition, questions of intergenerational equity arise since the effects of exposure to hazards in host communities may not be manifested for several years and may take the form of chronic long-term and life-threatening illnesses (Bryant and Mohai 1992). Thus, the present generation in the host communities is poorly served by compensation schemes for proposed or existing noxious facilities and future generations in these communities inherit a legacy of risks and costs that they had no voice in negotiating.

A New Approach to Environmental Justice Research

The combination of resource consumption, health risk, and environmental risk may be viewed as the generic costs of economic development and related industrialization (Roseland 1998). Ideally, the benefits of economic development should outweigh the costs to all those affected (Sen 1984). When aggregated at the national, state or county level, as is standard practice, indicators of economic development, such as the gross domestic product (GDP) and per capita income (PCI) may show net gains (Cobb, Halstead, and Rowe 1995). However, these gains are distributed across a region, where some localities may actually suffer net losses. Such nonuniformity is to be expected in any aggregation process. However, questions of equity and ethics arise when the higher costs or lower net benefits are consistently borne by the same groups or areas within a region or across different regions (Sen 1984).

The proposed methodology uses GIS-based Indicators for Collaboration in Environmental Policymaking (ICEP). ICEP advances previous work in the environmental justice and environmental GIS literature in three ways.

First, ICEP takes an initial step toward establishing a standard method of analyzing the coincidence between the siting of noxious facilities and the demographic characteristics of host communities. One might argue that much of the debate about environmental justice claims derives from the absence of a common method of analysis for the claims made by different parties involved in related disputes. ICEP proposes such a standard based on the proximity approach.

Second, ICEP bases its assessment of regional environmental quality on surveys of the main stakeholder groups in the region. These groups are community residents, regional industries, and the government agencies with responsibility for environmental regulation in the region. This method of assessment provides two primary benefits. The first benefit is that it gives each group of stakeholders direct access to the perceptions of environmental quality held by their likely antagonists in any regional environmental dispute. (ICEP will be hosted as an open website that provides regional information on environmental quality based on zip code.) The second benefit is that it provides a ready comparison of the differences in the perceptions and priorities of environmental quality held by residents and industry in a region, and the monitoring and regulatory priorities of the regional environmental agencies. This can serve as a measure of the extent to which the community and industry are informed about actual environmental problems in their region as well as a measure of the extent to which government agencies are responsive to local environmental concerns.

Third, while the database of correlation coefficients does not establish causality between reported environmental concern, demographics, or industry type, it can serve as an indicator of the need for the more detailed transport-fate and risk assessment models that can establish such causality. Thus, the database provides a reference for parties interested in the national context for their regional environmental dispute and a common basis for deciding whether more detailed study is needed to establish causality in the local/regional circumstance.

ICEP Goal and Objectives

The goal of ICEP is to establish a national database of correlation coefficients between types of noxious facilities, reported possible health and environmental impacts, and the demographic characteristics of the communities that host noxious facilities.

The first objective is to develop a standard reference, based on nationwide statistics, against which claims of environmental discrimination may be evaluated. This requires a consistent, analytically rigorous method for assessing pollution incidence and possibly associated human health and environmental effects. Though subject to the critiques of unit of analysis discussed above, this method uses the proximity-based approach with zip codes or metropolitan statistical areas (MSA) as its units. The rationale for this is that most of the pollutant discharge and demographic data on which the method is dependent are reported by zip code or MSA, prevalent standards in agencies such as the Bureau of Census and the EPA.

The second objective of ICEP is to assess the extent of agreement between the three main groups of stakeholders (residents, industry, and regulators) on their respective perceptions of regional environmental quality and the priorities each group assigns to the perceived issues. This is accomplished through surveys of each stakeholder group on their perceptions of air, soil, and water quality as well as issues such as noise, volume of traffic, levels of development, and availability of green areas. GIS is used to add a visual display to these reported statistics and to show how these reports compare to state environmental quality data for the region.

The third objective is to display the relative distribution of benefits as represented by median household income (MHI) across demographic groups in the region and show the corresponding distribution of costs in the form of proximity to noxious facilities with discharges reported to the Toxics Release Inventory (TRI). The distribution of benefits will be displayed as the number of standard deviations away from the median household income for the region. When coupled with an overlay of the proximity to noxious facilities in the region, this method of displaying benefits provides a graphic representation of the relationship between benefits (as approximated by MHI) and costs/risk (as approximated by proximity to noxious facilities) in a region. Admittedly, it is debatable whether median household income is an appropriate measure of social benefit for a community. At this stage in the development of ICEP, it is the most reliable measure available with extensive data at the national level.

The fourth objective is to make ICEP web-based and interactive. This allows residents, industry, or regulators from any zip code to access information on environmental quality and related equity statistics for that zip code as well as to link to resources for supplementary information such as health and regulatory issues. These resources include Environmental Defense Fund's *Scorecard* and EPA's *Envirofacts*. The open access this method provides to information on regional environmental quality greatly reduces the barrier of differential access to information across stakeholder groups and provides each group with a clear display of the perceptions and assigned priorities on environmental quality of their likely adversaries in the region (Ramasubramanian 1999). This feature creates an opportunity for collaboration between the groups on the development of policies and programs to mitigate environmental problems identified through ICEP.

Layered Displays of Environmental Statistics Using GIS

As noted in the previous section, stakeholder reports of environmental quality are displayed on GIS maps for each region in the study. Initially, sites will be selected based on their frequency of mention in the environmental justice literature and on our desire to have three representative sites from each of the ten EPA districts. Based on a review of the reported stakeholder concerns, a set of indicator species will be chosen as markers for air, soil, and water quality as well as for aesthetic concerns in the region. Indicator species will initially be selected based on the availability of state or federal monitoring data on the species in the selected area. However, as the capacity to test and validate issues of environmental quality reported by the community, ICEP will have the full capability to represent validated, stakeholder-reported environmental quality concerns. The individual layers are explained in greater detail below.

Stakeholder-Reported Environmental Layer(s)

A survey is conducted from community residents (by zip code or MSA), regional industries, and environmental regulators to elicit their concerns about environmental quality for air, soil, water, and others issues, such as rate of development, traffic, aesthetics, noise, crime. The aim is to develop a genuinely stakeholder-derived environmental layer where the stakeholders explicitly identify their desired environmental indicator (what is important to them and what to them constitutes a quality environment). The results can be sorted to produce a list of ranked "indicator species" (risk indicators) for the stakeholders. Ranking will depend on the frequency of reference in the surveys. However, the total number of responses is likely to be large. Hence, the Delphi method (Kerzner 1998) can be used with a panel of experts and representatives from each stakeholder group to select the top indicators. The mapping allows each stakeholder to observe the others' environmental quality concerns and their ranking relative to their own perceptions. This is especially valuable to compare a regulatory agency's priority against those of industry and the community.

Furthermore, a risk education component shall be provided, especially for the affected communities. Information such as toxicology reports and health and hazard facts of the releases shall be linked to the map.

Industry Layer

The industry layer provides an aggregate view of the industry as well as details of the facilities that make up the industry characterized by its Standard Industrial Classification Index (SIC). The SIC classifies facilities by their primary type of activity. Aside from displaying the locations of TRI facilities, major SIC codes (first two digits) predominant in each zip code or MSA are also indicated, as well as their environmental performance (whether a particular industry as a whole has striking environmental release rates). This layer is linked to full four digit categories and individual firms, which in turn provide links to publicly available information of firms such as their annual report. This information gives insights into the sources of environmental costs in relation to the benefits they derive (profit information in annual reports).

With a representative sample of communities, a regression is performed to establish correlation between environmental quality concerns/indicator species, SIC code, and demographics. A 95 percent confidence interval is sought.

This can eventually provide flags for correlations concerning SIC codes. Note that these regression results:

- Only address point or stationary sources (not auto emissions, agricultural runoffs, etc.);
- Cannot establish causality (identify a particular SIC code as the source of a particular environmental concern/damage).

However, a high correlation coefficient can be a red flag to indicate the need for more detailed investigation of the SIC/environmental indicator/demographic relationships (perhaps with source-fate-transport models).

A noteworthy limitation for this layer is that it includes only those facilities required to report to TRI. A facility must report to TRI if the facility (1) has 10 or more full-time employees, and (2) manufactures or processes over 25,000 pounds of the approximately 600 designated chemicals or 28 chemical categories specified in the regulations, or uses more than 10,000 pounds of any designated chemical or category, and (3) engages in certain manufacturing operations in the industry groups specified in the U.S. Government Standard Industrial Classification Codes (SIC) 20 through 39, or is a federal facility, which are all now required to report per the August 1995 Executive Order signed by President Clinton. Therefore, a significant group of small polluter facilities and other sources of pollution are excluded from this data layer.

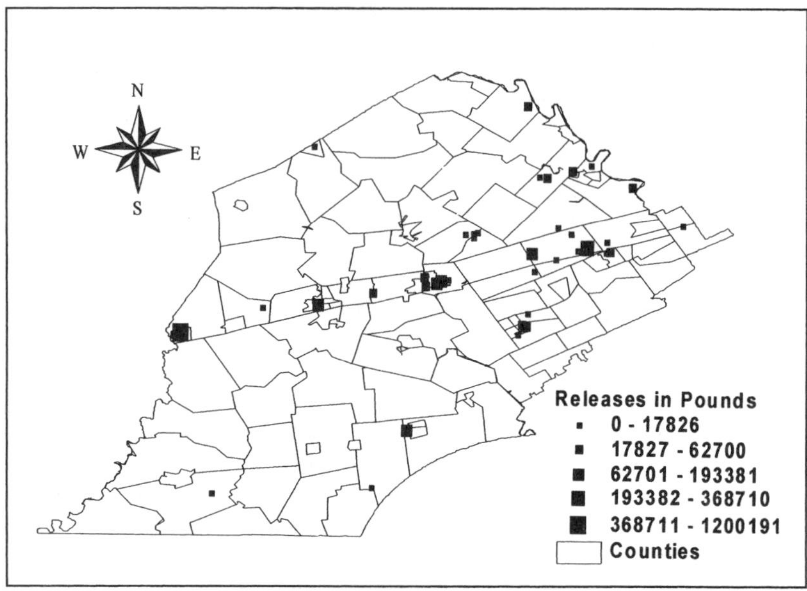

Figure 20.1. Releases per Facility (Environmental Layer)

Demographic Layer(s)

This layer displays demographic indicators such as race, household income, age distribution, and educational attainment, as well as health statistics such as mortality, cancer statistics, infant health and mortality. Demographic data can be extracted from the CensusCD+Maps, developed and distributed by the U.S. Bureau of Census. It is an integrated Windows software package of current and historical demographic data with built-in thematic mapping and reporting tools. CensusCD+Maps includes extensive sets of demographic and geographic boundary data. The core database is comprised of the results of the 1990 U.S. Census Long Form Questionnaire (distributed by the Census Bureau on 67 CD-ROMS titled STF-3-A,B,C, & D) for 16 geographic levels down to the census block group. However, unlike other demographic data, health statistics pose certain limitations. Mortality and other health-related data are summarized down to only the county level. Hence, census tract statistics are not readily available.

The distribution of benefits is displayed for residents using +/- standard deviations from median household income or per capita income (PCI). Other demographic characteristics can be displayed as absolute values or normalized by total population. Links are also made to corporate profits and contribution to the community (jobs to locals, local taxes, other local benefits).

Web-Based Application

The web–based application provides access to the survey-based maps, statistical results, and links to toxicology, public health and other information/resources such as the *Scorecard* and EPA's *Envirofacts*. Chat areas are provided for community residents, industry representatives, and regulators to discuss and negotiate issues. This web-based forum provides a virtual town meeting for stakeholders. Concerned groups, who may not be local to the community, will also have access to these websites.

Case Study of Chester, Pennsylvania

Chester County, Pennsylvania was selected from the environmental justice literature (Liu 2000). The study was based on the 1990 population data from the U.S. Bureau of Census and the 1990 toxic facilities data downloaded from the EPA website.

Stakeholder-Based Environmental Layer(s)

Currently, the environmental layer displays indicators based on the TRI database. The Toxics Release Inventory (TRI) contains information about more than 650 toxic chemicals that are being used, manufactured, treated, transported, or released into the environment. Manufacturers of these chemicals are required to report the locations and quantities of chemicals stored on-site to state and local governments. EPA compiles this data in an on-line, publicly accessible national computerized database. Figure 20.1 shows the map of total chemical releases per facility, based on the 1990 TRI data (*Envirofacts* 2000).

Industry Layer

Locations of TRI facilities are displayed with SIC codes (first two digits) indicated by the different icons (see figure 20.2). This layer is linked to full four-digit categories and individual firm information. Information on the facilities was derived from the TRI database at the EPA website (*Envirofacts* 2000).

Demographic Layer

Demographic indicators selected were household income and race (see figure 20.3). The distribution of benefits is displayed for residents using +/- standard deviation from median household income. The demographic data are based on the 1990 census (U.S. Bureau of Census 1990).

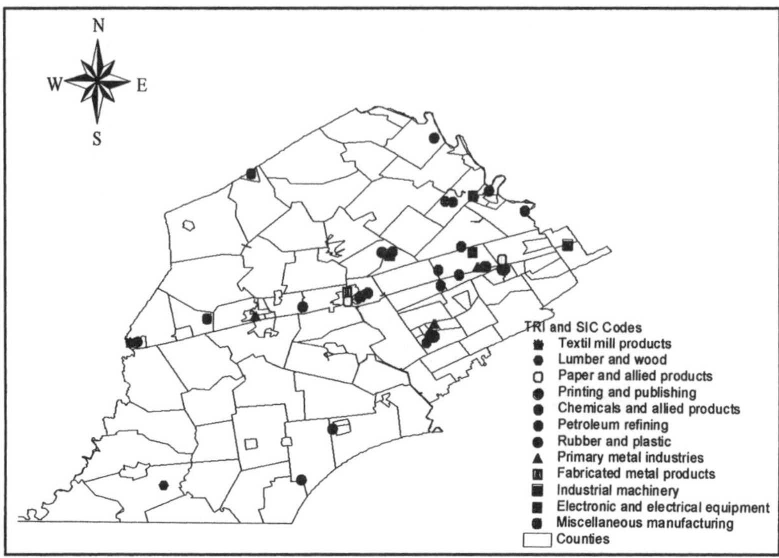

Figure 20.2. Facility SIC Codes (Industry Layer)

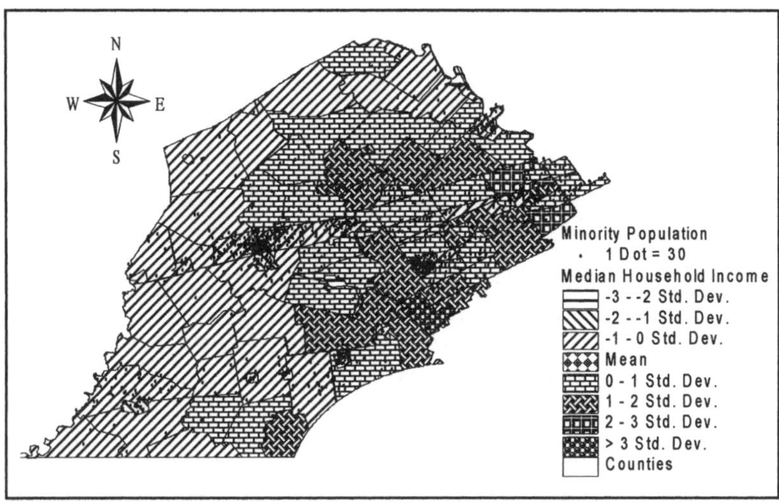

Figure 20.3. Distribution of Median Household Income and Race (Demographic Layer)

The Chester case is only a single data point and thus serves for illustrative purposes only. Figures 20.4a and 20.4b show the resulting map when layers are superimposed over one another. When the environmental layer is superimposed on the demographic layer, the coincidence between race and proximity to facilities with high TRI discharges is evident (see figure 20.4a). The facilities, depicted by squares, seem to follow the race distribution, depicted by black dots. A similar coincidence between median household income and proximity to facilities with high TRI discharges is apparent (see figure 20.4a). Facilities, depicted by squares, for the most part lie in low-income communities.

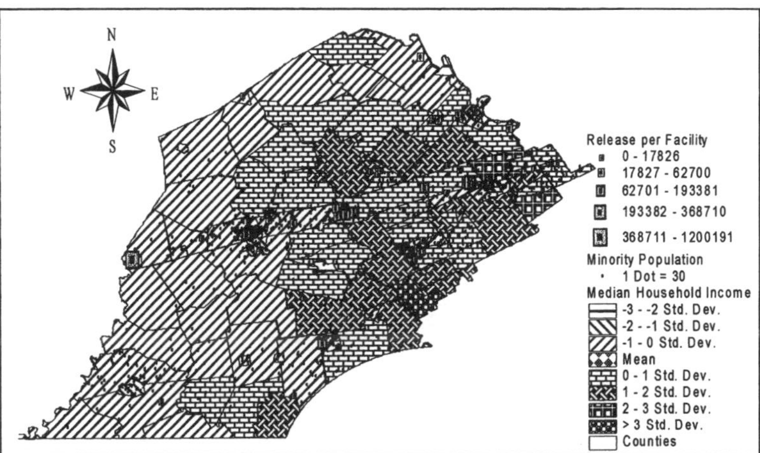

Figure 20.4a. Demographic Layer vs. Environmental Layer

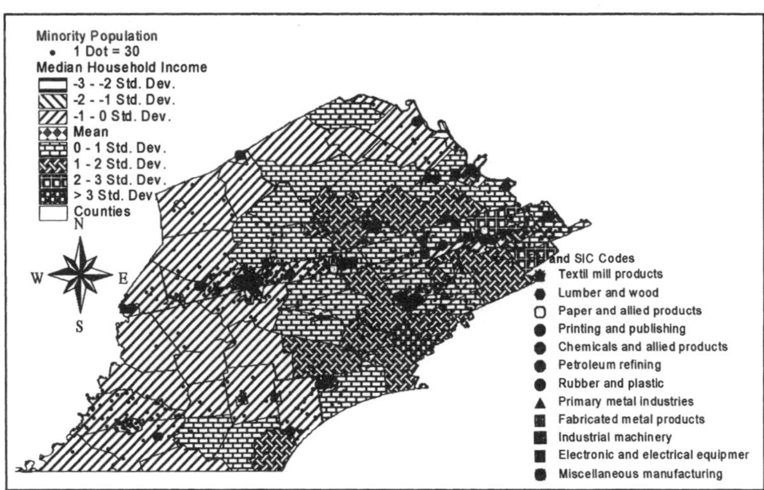

Figure 20.4b. Demographic Layer vs. Industry Layer

No regression is possible with this single example. However, from a simple graphical display of this case, the potential of the multilayering method is apparent. The coincidence between environmental concerns, industry by SIC code, and demographics is immediately apparent from the display. These relationships may also be displayed graphically and interactively by zip code via the Internet. They thus provide a means for stakeholders in any community to perform a quick check on the reported environmental issues in their area. They can follow up the preliminary results from ICEP with a more detailed analysis to either confirm or disprove the causal relationship between the variables from each of the layers in the ICEP map.

Conclusion

The EPA now has an Office of Environmental Justice, and Executive Order 12898 requires federal agencies to consider environmental justice in their decision-making processes. However, claims of environmental injustice continue to be driven by factious disputes between community residents, industry, and government agencies. Industry is accused of imposing disproportionate environmental risk on the community. Government is accused of pandering to industry in noxious facility siting and of denying the community meaningful participation in the decision-making process.

Environmental justice analysis seeks to analyze four main areas of such claims. First, is there a statistical relationship between demographics and the siting of noxious facilities (locally unwanted land use)? Second, is such disproportionate siting the result of discriminatory practices by industry and/or government? Third, what are the relative risks and benefits to communities living close to noxious facilities? How can causality be established from proximity and demographics? Fourth, what are the policy options for mitigating the pernicious effects of environmental injustice?

This paper proposes a standard method for conducting environmental justice analysis and describes a new tool—indicators for collaboration in environmental policy-making (ICEP)—being developed to facilitate collaboration between stakeholders in environmental decision making.

ICEP primarily contributes to the first area of environmental justice analysis: the statistical relationship between locally unwanted land use (LULU) and demographics. ICEP does this by proposing that the zip code be adopted as the standard unit of analysis for preliminary screening for a statistical relationship. ICEP uses surveys of members from the three major stakeholder groups (residents, industry, and government) to determine what are the key indicators of environmental quality for air, soil, water, and aesthetics in a given area. It then tabulates the incidence of these indicators against the standard industrial classification (SIC) codes for industrial facilities, and demographics, such as race, median household income, and education level per household. A database of the correlation coefficients between these variables (environmental quality indicator, industry SIC code, and demographic) is then made for sample zip code areas nationwide. This database is useful for conducting preliminary screening of claims of disproportionate siting against a particular industry (by SIC code) by a particular demographic (e.g., race, income). The results of this preliminary screening could justify more refined analysis, using either census tract or circles of fixed radii about facilities as the unit of analysis and selecting the demographics that are appropriate for the goals of the analysis. Positive results from these refined analyses would indicate the need for detailed studies to establish causality between observed human health and negative environmental effects, and suspected sources of environmental pollution.

ICEP contributes to the area of environmental negotiation through the use of stakeholder-based GIS maps. These maps present the perceptions and priorities about environmental quality of each stakeholder group in a selected area of one or more zip codes. Stakeholders have access to these maps via the Internet. Thus, they can see their own environmental quality concerns and how they prioritize them, along with the concerns and priorities of the other stakeholder groups in the community. The Internet site also provides extensive links to resources and information on the environmental issues at hand. This feature enhances current approaches to environmental negotiation in three ways: (1) it provides a means for stakeholders to have a shared view of the perceptions and priorities of their adversaries in local environmental quality issues; (2) it reduces the differential access to information and decision-makers that plagues the LULU decision-process today; and (3) it provides a means for directly comparing government's environmental priorities against those of industry and of residents. We posit that these three benefits facilitate a more open environmental decision-making process and greater participation of all stakeholders in that process.

ICEP also uses its GIS displays to represent the distribution of benefits in communities under study by the number of standard deviations away from the average median household income for the community. Thus, on a series of multilayered maps, an interested party can assess the distribution of risks, in the form of noxious facility sites, and of benefit, in the form of median household income, against a variety of demographics for the zip code. These results can then be compared to other areas across the nation.

Finally, ICEP enhances the services provided by existing web-based community environmental quality services like *Scorecard* and *Envirofacts*. It does so by mapping the environmental quality perceptions of stakeholders, rather than just the data compiled by the government. This provides stakeholders a means to directly state their environmental quality concerns and compare those to the priorities of government and other communities nationwide.

In summary, this chapter proposes a standard approach to environmental justice analysis based on the use of the zip code as the preliminary unit of analysis and the establishment of a national database of correlation coefficients between stakeholder-supplied indicators of environmental quality, noxious facility types by SIC code, and pertinent demographics. This approach is captured in a web-based GIS tool, ICEP, which gives stakeholders access to the perceptions and priorities of other stakeholders on relevant environmental issues and reduces the problem of differential access to information and decision-makers that plagues the current siting process. It provides a means for comparing the priorities of environmental agencies against those of industry and community residents. It enhances current web-based resources by generating stakeholder-based environmental maps and by displaying the distribution of benefits to the community.

The new method of analysis and the tool for implementing it, ICEP, are small steps in resolving the technical issues facing environmental justice. They also present a way for stakeholders to pursue equity in the distribution of risks and benefits from the siting of noxious facilities. Such equity is a precondition for sustainability in any industrial society.

References

Anderton, Douglas L., A. Anderson, J. M. Oates, and M. Fraser. 1994. "Environmental Equity: The Demographics of Dumping." *Demography* 31 (April): 229–48.

Bryant, Bunyan, and Paul Mohai. 1992. "Introduction," in *Race and the Incidence of Environmental Hazards: A Time for Discourse*, edited by Bunyan Bryant and Paul Mohai. San Fransisco: Westview Press.

Bullard, Robert. 1993. "Introduction," in *Confronting Environmental Racism: Voices from the Grassroots*, edited by Robert Bullard. Boston: South End Press.

Bullard, Robert. 1983. "Solid Waste Sites and the Black Houston Community." *Sociological Inquiry* 53 (Spring): 273–88.

Bullard, Robert, and Beverly Wright. 1988. "Environmentalism and the Politics of Equity: Emergent Trends in the Black Community." *Mid-American Review of Sociology* 12: 21–37.

Center for Environmental Research. 1988. *1986 National Screening Survey of Hazardous Waste Treatment, Storage, Disposal, and Recycling Facilities*. Washington, D.C.: U.S. Environmental Protection Agency (September).

Citizens Fund. 1990. *Poison in Our Neighborhoods: Toxic Pollution in the United States.* Washington, D.C.: Citizens Fund.

Cobb, Clifford, Ted Halstead, and Jonathan Rowe. 1995. *The Genuine Progress Indicator.* San Francisco: Redefining Progress.

Envirofacts. <http://www.epa.gov/enviro/html/tris/tris_query.html> (1 December 2000).

Freeman, Myrick A. 1971. "The Distribution of Environmental Quality," in *Environmental Quality Analysis*, edited by Allen V. Kneese and Blair T. Bower. Baltimore, Md.: Johns Hopkins University Press for Resources for the Future.

Gelobter, Michel. 1992. "Toward a Model of Environmental Discrimination," in *Race and the Incidence of Environmental Hazards: A Time for Discourse*, edited by Bunyan Bryant and Paul Mohai. San Francisco: Westview Press.

Glickman, Theodore S. 1994. "Evaluating Environmental Equity in Allegheny County: A Case Study." Unpublished manuscript, prepared for the Rockefeller University Forum on Environment and Community Health, on file with the *Virginia Environmental Law Journal*, September 20.

Goldman, Benjamin. 1991. *The Truth about Where You Live: An Atlas for Action on Toxins and Mortality*. New York: Random House.

Institute of Medicine. 1999. *Toward Environmental Justice*. Washington, D.C.: National Academy Press.

Kerzner, H. 1998. *Project Management: A Systems Approach to Planning, Scheduling, and Controlling*. New York: Wiley.

Lee, Charles. 1993. "Beyond Toxic Wastes and Race," in *Confronting Environmental Racism: Voices from the Grassroots*, edited by Robert Bullard. Boston: South End Press.

Lester, J. P., D. W. Allen, and K. M. Hill. 2001. *Environmental Injustice in the United States: Myths and Realities*. Boulder, Colo.: Westview Press.

Liu, Feng. 2000. *Environmental Justice Analysis: Theories, Methods, and Practice*. Boca Raton, Fla.: Lewis Publishers.

Mohai, Paul. 1995. "The Demographics of Dumping Revisited: Examining the Impact of Alternate Methodologies in Environmental Justice Research." *Virginia Environmental Law Journal*. 14: 615–53.

Morganstern, R. D. 1996. "Environmental Taxes: Is There a Double Dividend?" *Environment* 38, no. 3 (April): 16–20, 32–34.

Petts, J. 1994. "Effective Waste Management: Understanding and Dealing with Public Concerns." *Waste Management & Research* 12, no. 3 (June): 207-22.

Ramasubramanian, 1999. "Nurturing Community Empowerment: Participatory Decision Making and Community-Based Problem Solving Using GIS," in *Geographic Information Research: Trans-Atlantic Perspectives*. London: Taylor and Francis.

Roseland, Mark. 1998. *Toward Sustainable Communities*. New York: New Society Publishers.

Scorecard. <http://www.scorecard.org> (1 Dec. 2000).

Sen, A. 1984. *Resource, Values, and Development*. Cambridge, Mass.: Harvard Press.

United Church of Christ Commission for Racial Justice. 1987. *Toxic Wastes and Race in the United States: A National Report on the Racial and Socioeconomic Characteristics of Communities with Hazardous Waste Sites*. New York: United Church of Christ.

U.S. Bureau of Census, 1990.

U.S. Environmental Protection Agency (EPA). <http://es.epa.gov/oeca/main/ej/index.html> (20 Dec. 2000).

U.S. General Accounting Office (GAO). 1983. *Siting of Hazardous Waste Landfills and their Correlation with Racial and Economic Status of Surrounding Communities*. Washington, D.C.: U.S. General Accounting Office.

Case Studies: Conflict, Risk, and the Preservation of Nature

Chapter 21

Violence and the Environment in Colombia: Questions Regarding Environmental Ethics

Luis Alberto Camargo and Vicky Castillo

Colombia is a country vastly rich in natural resources. It possesses two of the areas of highest biodiversity of the planet, the Chocó region and the Amazon basin. Its wealth is immense in hydrological resources, forests, fauna and flora. It is, at the same time, a country where a long-standing armed conflict exists within most of its territory. Due to this, the civil population is visibly affected, since displacement, kidnapping, massacres, homicides, and terrorism are becoming daily occurrences. Worsening the situation, drug production and traffic add an additional dimension to the war. This situation of violence produces a great variety of environmental impacts such as deforestation, contamination of water sources and soils with illicit crop by-products, expansion of the agricultural frontier caused by colonization and forced displacement (refugees), increased impacts of mega-projects, and terrorism represented mainly by the blowing up of oil pipelines.

Natural Resources

Colombia is considered one of the countries with mega-diversity. These countries hold 40 percent of all the species in the world. In a territory that is equal to 0.77 percent of the continental surface of the Earth we find 10 to 14 percent of all the species of the world (Aljure 2000). Colombia is the second richest country in diversity, next to Brazil, which possesses more species but in a surface area seven times larger.

Water

Colombia is the fourth world power in hydrological resources. It possesses a hydrological capacity of 2,000 km^3 per year, 34,000 m^3 per habitant, which is five times more than the world average (Aljure 2000).

In spite of this enormous wealth, many Colombians do not have access to potable water, and the distribution of the resource in the territory is not homogeneous. The main causes of water contamination are domestic waste, industrial waste, and the by-products of agricultural activities and mining. It is calculated that 15 percent of the 15,900 daily tons of garbage that the country produces, that is to say, nearly 900 thousand tons, will end up in bodies of water. According to 1990 data, the country has 4,737 industries that pour polluting waste into water sources, representing 85 percent of the total of industrial establishments (Wilches-Chaux 1998, 18).

Air

The greenhouse effect, atmospheric contamination, acid rain, global warming, and the ozone hole are worldwide issues. Colombia is obviously affected by these problems, the main one being atmospheric contamination. In 1999 Colombia released an estimated 113 million tons of carbonic gas to the atmosphere as a direct consequence of logging and burning of forests, placing the country in a disproportionate position with an annual rate per inhabitant of 4 tons a year. Additionally, 2,139 industries pour polluting waste into the atmosphere, representing 38.5 percent of the total (Wilches-Chaux 1998, 18).

Forests

Sixty-nine percent of Colombia's continental surface area of 114.7 million ha has forest potential; forests could cover 78 million ha of land, due to its biological and ecological characteristics. At the present time approximately 40 million ha have forest cover (Ministry of Environment and Department of National Planning Data 1996).

The country possesses tropical forests, savannas, alluvial forests, Andean forests, Amazon forests, and lowland forests. It is estimated that one-third of the country's forest cover has been deforested. The main causes are: expansion of the agricultural frontier and colonization (73.3 percent), timber production (11.7 percent), firewood consumption (11 percent), forest fires (2 percent) and illicit crops (2 percent) (Instituto Von Humboldt 1997a, 134).

According to the national planning department, deforestation in Colombia is in the order of 600 thousand ha per year. In order to break this deterioration of timber resources, the country set aside forest reserves equivalent to 10 percent of the national territory (Official Report 1998–2000). These reserves include forest reserves and areas within the national park system. The park system represents 9 million ha (8 percent of Colombian territory), 45 protected areas distributed in 34 national parks, 7 flora and fauna sanctuaries, 2 natural reserves, and a unique natural area. These areas hold an enormous wealth of biological resources and protect the main watersheds of the country.

Flora

"Colombia possesses between 45,000 and 55,000 species of plants, which make flora the first great wealth of the country. Of those species, approximately one-third are endemic. Orchids stand out, represented by nearly 3,500 species, 15 percent of the total number of species in the world" (Instituto Von Humboldt 2000). In spite of this great wealth, orchids are one of the most threatened families of plants. Around 1,000 species are at risk of extinction due to destruction of their habitats by deforestation and contamination.

Fauna

Colombia is third in the world in regards to terrestrial vertebrates, with 2,890 species. Of these, 1,768 species are birds, constituting 20 percent of the world total (first in biodiversity); 609 species are amphibians, 10 percent of the world total (second in biodiversity); 475 species are reptiles, 6 percent of the world total (sixth in biodiversity); and 467 species are mammals that represent 7 percent of the world total (sixth in biodiversity). Fauna in Colombia are threatened by slash and burning of forests, deforestation, contamination, and the indiscriminate poaching caused by the illegal wildlife trade. Consequently, 89 mammal species, 133 bird species, 20 reptilian species and 8 fish species are in danger of extinction (Aljure 2000; Instituto Von Humboldt 2000).

Besides the other causes mentioned for loss of natural wealth, the persistent violence within the country today generates a vertiginous increase in the negative impacts on the natural environment by humans.

Violence

The situation of violence in Colombia has a history that extends over many years. Violent actions started in the fifties with the partisan violence. From that time until the present day, violent actions, massacres, poverty, delinquency, kidnappings, and so on have not ceased. The situation is so constant that Columbians have almost grown used to it and perceive atrocious acts as part of their daily lives, without overt reaction to daily violent occurrences.

During 1999, 24,081 homicides were registered, 4 percent more than the previous year. This means that the rate ascended from 56.6 in 1998 to 57.9 in 1999 per hundred thousand inhabitants. Rural areas present the largest number of homicides. The estimates of the number of civilian victims of political violence (based on information from various sources) range from 138 to 210 per month. The groups identified as mainly responsible for these crimes are guerrilla and paramilitary organizations. Next to violent deaths, we find kidnapping to be the most frequent crime, followed by extortion and torture. According to País Libre (NGO), in 1999 2,945 cases of kidnapping were reported; according to police there were 2,663. Kidnapping for extortion went from 1,611 in 1998 to 2,020 in 1999 and political extortion from 340 in 1997 to 422 in 1998. Of 3,006 believed kidnappings in 1999, 1,678 are attributed to guerrillas (FARC, ELN, EPL, and ERP). Kidnappings by common criminals have diminished from 406 in 1998 to 273 in 1999, although it is known that this is due to criminals carrying out the kidnapping and "selling them" to the guerrillas who then ask for ransom (Columbian Human Rights Observatory 1999; Colombia Programa Presidencial de los Derechos Humanos y DIH 2000).

We can say that the main causes of violence in Colombia are the drug trade, armed conflict, and poverty. All of these have fateful consequences for the population and generate massive forced displacement of Colombians—particularly those who live in conflict areas.

Poverty as a Form of Violence

High levels of poverty affect all of Colombia, rural and urban. A drastic change for the worse is currently seen in rural Colombia. According to DANE (National Demographics and Statistics Department), of the 40.2 million Colombians, 18 million live under poverty conditions and most of this population reaches levels of homelessness. Of these 18 million people, 8 million live in cities and 10 in rural areas.

Regionally, the departments of Sucre, Chocó, Córdoba, Cesar, Cauca, Guajira, Boyacá, Nariño, Tolima, Bolivar and Santander (see map, figure 21.1) present the lowest UBN (Unsatisfied Basic Necessities) index. Levels of poverty range from 64 percent in the case of Sucre to 33 percent in Santander.

Cities in the the Atlantic Coast and Chocó (Pacific coast) concentrate the largest levels of poverty: Valledupar 66 percent, Sincelejo 64.7 percent, Quibdó 64.2 percent, Barranquilla 63.8 percent, Cúcuta 62.4 percent. Bogotá, the capital city with a population of 7 million, presents the lowest UBN but at the same time presents the largest number of poor people given the high population (Rojas 2000).

The unemployment crisis increased tremendously in the mainly urban environments. In 1998, unemployment surpassed 20 percent in Bogotá while other cities showed similar situations. The current war has forced thousands of persons to move from their places of origin and work in search for safety. Many arrive in cities, generating an increase in urban poverty.

Figure 21.1. Map of Colombia's Bioregions

Some other poverty indicators (Sánchez 1998):

- Poverty level average UBN: 32.2 percent
- Infant mortality rate: 28.1 in every 100 births
- Housing with no services: 10 percent
- Housing with no sanitary services: 15 percent
- Illiteracy rate: 11.1 percent
- Primary schooling rate, urban: 87 percent
- Primary schooling rate, rural: 73 percent

Guerrilla Presence

The origin of Colombia's guerrilla movement is preeminently agrarian; the movement was born during the political violence of the fifties. It found its place in areas of colonization on the mountainsides, and in small rural properties in Córdoba and Sucre. Its political actions were originally present in Cauca, Huila, and Tolima where we can currently find the oldest contingencies. Later on, following the agriculture crisis, guerrilla groups expanded through the territory, arriving into coffee producing areas of Risaralda, Valle del Caldas, and Quindío and in other traditional rural economy areas, such as Cundinamarca, Boyaca, and Santander.

"In areas of economies driven by labor intensive multinational foreign enterprises, guerrillas have found vast economic resources deriving from extortion in exchange for allowing the company to carry on with their business" (Instituto Von Humboldt 1997b, 68). Currently, they are also found in colonization areas such as Caquetá, Guaviare, Macarena, and Putumayo, perfect areas for their criminal operations due to the existence of illegal crops and the lack of government presence. These factors strengthen their political and economic power. The Revolutionary Armed Forces of Colombia—FARC—is the largest guerrilla group in Colombia (tables 21.1 and 21.2).

Guerrilla organizations use drug production and trafficking, robbery, extortion, and kidnapping, among other crimes, as financing methods. It is evident that drugs represent the largest source of their funds, over 40 percent (Presidente de la República 1995, 69). Thus the alliance between guerrilla activities and the illegal drug trade has contributed the most toward the ever increasing intensity and scale of the conflict.

Paramilitary Presence

Paramilitary groups appeared approximately 15 years ago in the Magdalena Medio region. The main purpose of these groups was to defend the cattlemen and landowners of the region from the guerrillas. In many cases, these groups were formed by the landowners themselves as a way to protect their own interests, which brought the name or classification of these groups as "self-defenders" (autodefensas). Initially, they were only devoted to defensive action but with time they became pro-attack groups sponsored by drug dealers, landowners and others with major economic interests (Instituto Von Humboldt 1997b, 70).

It is common knowledge that these groups have been involved with the armed forces due to the fact that they share a common enemy. This is the reason they are labeled paramilitary groups.

In the late eighties, these groups multiplied and attacked the leaders of the Patriotic Union, a leftist party, killing a large number of individuals and bringing this political party to the point of extinction. Paramilitary groups also carried out "social cleansing" against deviates, drug addicts, indigents, and so on. At the same time, mass murders became common in rural areas and several massacres were carried out. The number of paramilitary groups grew to 29, establishing bases of operation in the country's major cities.

During the beginning of the nineties, this problem kept worsening as more paramilitary groups appeared and the total area covered by them multiplied. Over 90 groups covered most regions of the country. "The quick multiplication of self-defense groups shows the lack of control that the Government has, through the . . . armed forces, while justifying them puts in evidence their inability to control public order problems" (*Revista Cambio* 1994, 16).

Table 21.1. Strength and Presence – FARC

Year	1986	1990	1994	1996
Personnel	3,200	5,000	7,000	7,500
Contingencies	32	48	60	62
Arms	2,800	5,000	7,000	7,500
Municipalities	289	393	434	450

Source: *Periódico La Prensa*. 1996 (Inst. Alexander Von Humboldt 1997b, 68).

Table 21.2. Number of Individuals in Guerrilla Groups

Year	FARC	ELN	EPL	Total	Other Sources
1970	740	150	100	990	1,000
1975	820	27	70	917	1,100
1980	980	70	140	1,190	2,300
1985	2,590	700	670	3,960	5,800
1990	5,380	1,600	820	7,800	
1992	5,805	2,080	210	8,095	12,500
1994	6,966	2,710	715	10,391	

Source: Presidencia de la República. Oficina del Alto Comisionado para la Paz; González s.f. (Instituto Von Humboldt 1997b, 69).

Displaced Persons (Refugees)

As displaced populations are forced to leave their places of origin and move towards and among the borders of territories, they become a "shield" for insurgent activities; they are the object of harassment and violations of human rights. According to CODHES (Consultancy for Human Rights and Displacement), "Those displaced are a reflection of the changing geography of war scenarios and a manifestation of contempt for the civil population from those who are in combat, without limits or norms in order to control their territories, impose ideologies, defend minority interests or to preserve institutions." This desire to escape from the conflict forces many Colombians to move toward municipal centers, departmental capitals, or frontier areas (Bennet 2000, 7).

During the last several years, violence in Colombia has worsened. Currently, the country has the biggest number of displaced people in Latin America, occupying the seventh place in the world. During 1999 the situation increased when an estimated 288,127 people, representing 57,625 homes, were forced to leave their residences due to guerrilla, paramilitary, or military actions. Of this number, 11,700 looked for refuge in neighboring countries such as Panama, Venezuela, and Ecuador, making evident the tendency toward internationalization of the conflict. Approximately 1,900,000 people have been displaced from their homes by causes related to the armed conflict (Bennett 2000, 1).

According to Germán Vélez (1998), the causes of forced displacement are:

- Widespread violence related to regional and national political and socioeconomic conflicts.
- Territorial redistribution that obeys an agrarian counter reform, led by drug dealers, paramilitary, and economic groups associated with multinationals.
- The new definition of poles (North-South) and priorities for capital investment in sectors of the economy that involve certain natural resources and the territories where they are found. These priorities are framed in the globalization and liberalization processes of the economy (new economic order, national and international) and in the role the country plays as supplier of raw materials and services in this context.
- The planning and execution of mega-projects in the country: energy (oil tanker, mines, hydroelectric), transportation infrastructure (highways, ports, interoceanic channel), and industrial installations, among others. One can also consider bioprospecting as biodiversity mega-projects led by biotechnology sectors in countries of the North.
- Mandatory displacements generated by pressures and threats of different actors in the conflict. The paramilitaries have been identified as the force that generates the most displacement, although in many cases other political and economic interests move behind them. Areas where the armed conflict is greater show higher displacement rates and at the same time match geographically to areas where mega-projects are being executed.
- Aside from all the previously mentioned factors, widespread acceptance of the internal war without limits is the primordial cause of forced displacement in the country. For such a reason, negotiation and dialogue in search of peace are the roads towards diminishing mass population mobilizations.

Narcotraffic and Illicit Crops

Drug production and traffic has been present in Colombian territory for several decades. This business started in the 1970s with the marihuana hype. The marihuana produced in Colombia was of excellent quality, which created a high demand. Towards the mid-1980s, the United States created hydroponic varieties of marihuana and displaced the Colombian production, becoming the largest producer of marihuana in the world. The 1980s gave birth to the coca explosion. Since then, it has acquired such importance that it is not only cultivated, but also coca paste is made and transformed into cocaine. In the most recent years, Colombia has become not only the largest producer of coca leaf but also the main supplier of cocaine, with more than 75 percent of the world market share (Nyholm 1998, 147). During the 1990s the cultivation of the poppy seed plant *(amapola)* began to spread. Initially, *amapola* appeared as a response to the increased demand for heroine. Soon after, farmers realized that this plant could be cultivated in high Andean ecosystems including the fragile *páramos,* so large areas were cleared and planted with *amapola.*

Drug traffic is one of the most complex elements in the current conflict. All illegal groups are involved in this traffic in one way or another. Many paramilitary groups have illegal crops and are in charge of the traffic, while other groups are involved in protecting the land owned by the traffickers. Drug traffic is the main source of revenue of the FARC. This guerrilla group is involved in the production of the leaves and the processing and movement of the product to the international drug markets. In many cases drugs are exchanged for weapons. People living in the areas where there is production of the raw materials or processing of the drugs are directly involved with the process. Some of the individuals do it voluntarily, while others are forced to participate by the different groups involved.

Drug traffic is a very delicate topic because it generates violence, insecurity, and problems with international relationships. For such reasons the government uses its war against the drug trade as an argument for the implementation of mandatory, forced eradication, holding that such a policy is a necessary national security policy aimed at diminishing violence. At the same time, forced eradication produces more violence, displacement, and negative economic effects, especially for peasants and people linked to working the crops. They plant coca because they do not have any other alternatives for subsistence and the government does not provide other solutions to aid them in satisfying their basic needs (Pineda 2000). It is estimated that there are currently 120,000 ha of coca, 7,000 of poppy, and 5,000 of marihuana planted.

Areas that are used for illegal crops usually lack adequate access roads, which cause legal crops to lack a form of transportation to mainstream markets and increases transportation costs many times over the market value of the products. The option for most people is to plant the illegal crops in their small pieces of land of 0 to 5 ha. Eradication efforts by the government force peasants further into forested areas, recreating the slash, burn, and plant cycle.

As the Institute Von Humboldt (1997c, 47) has indicated, "If social investments are not adapted to satisfying basic needs and don't allow communities to really improve their quality of life, peasants in colonization areas will continue cultivating marihuana, coca and poppy as a source of revenues and guarantee of survival."

As a way to help peasants in these areas the government created PLANTE, a program created to help implement alternative legal crops. Unfortunately its resources are very limited. Furthermore, legal crops do not have a guaranteed market and alternatives such as cattle, which have been supported, are generating critical environmental impacts on rainforest lands of the Amazon region.

Larger crops, 5 ha or more, are considered industrial production. Drug traffickers usually own these crops, which are eradicated by means of air fumigation schemes with Glyphosphate. In a contradictory way, when the supply is diminished, fumigation has contributed to maintaining high prices of the crops, stimulating production because of the guaranteed high return on their investment (Instituto Von Humboldt 1997c, 46). Aerial fumigation has also been linked to environmental damage, health problems in local communities, and damage of legal crops due to its inexact and unpredictable dispersal system.

Drug production is an enormous business. Thanks to its illegality, it generates large amounts of resources and intensifies the war that Colombia lives with, by generating business links with armed groups. Klaus Nyholm notes, "There is a direct relationship between guerilla, paramilitary and drug lords. The guerrillas and paramilitary groups offer protection for crops and drug lords, who in return pay handsome 'taxes' allowing the availability of capital to finance the war. In other words, drug lords are prospering inside the internal conflict, diverting them from an interest in peace. At the same time the armed conflict depends on money from drug production and trade. This means that in order to fight drugs successfully, the country requires peace" (Nyholm 1998, 147).

The many environment-degrading impacts generated by poverty, insurgency, paramilitarism, displacement, and illegal drug production and trafficking affect both the natural component (including water, forests, soils, fauna, and flora), and the human component, namely, the homeless and injured human beings.

Violence and Environment

The natural environment is impacted directly and indirectly by the war, transforming it into the stage for war and for an uncountable number of human- and nonhuman-related deaths. Deforestation for illegal crop cultivation, fumigation of fields and wilderness areas, and oil spills caused by the blowing up of pipelines puts an end to vegetable resources, fish, birds, insects, mammals, and reptiles; displaced people invade new lands and increase population levels in cities. These elements cause further deterioration of the environment, and are intimately related to the situation of violence the country lives with; they are related to each other as well. We will explore three main factors of environmental impact: illegal crops, terrorism, and war.

Illegal Crops

We can enumerate many environmental impacts of illegal crops. Water pollution and ecosystem degradation are a couple of major ones. "It is estimated that more than two metric tons of chemical wastes are generated by the cultivation process of each cultivated hectare" (Proyecto Enlace 2000, 3).

Coca plantations require a warm, humid environment. This means that tropical rainforests are the ideal setting for this plant. Most coca production occurs in the Amazon basin, threatening one of the most important and biodiverse regions of the world. Poppy production, on the contrary, occurs in high altitude Andean forests. These are the ecosystems that are responsible for the production and regulation of most water in the country and are considered strategic areas for conservation by many international organizations. Looking at statistics presented by the PLANTE program in 1995, we can say that approximately 200,000 ha of forest are being deforested each year for planting illegal crops. Deforestation is not only associated with illegal crops; as people are displaced by violence from their homelands, they are forced to colonize and look for new territories, usually settling in frontier lands where mature forests have to be destroyed.

The slash and burn method required to clear land for illegal crops is also destroying the soils. It is estimated that between 850,000 and 1,000,000 ha of natural forests have been destroyed to make room for illegal crops. It is estimated that for one hectare of coca planted, four are destroyed; for one of poppy seed, two-and-a-half hectares of forest are needed; and for one of marihuana, one-and-a-half hectares of forest are destroyed (Pineda 2000).

Eradication techniques used in destroying crops and laboratories are another source of adverse environmental impact.

From another perspective, we find the human component. Illegal crops provoke social and economic processes that are atypical in peasant and indigenous communities, destroying belief systems and cultural traditions. Urban populations are also affected as excessive material wealth is strived for, illegal behaviors become more acceptable, and mass population migrations are generated looking for wealth and over paid hand labor.

"War has forced the displacement of close to one million people who have left their land, their means of production, and have been forced to find refuge in wilderness areas often inside National Parks or Reserves." (Instituto Alexander Von Humboldt 1997c, 48). People that have been displaced but do not go into wilderness areas, end up in the main cities, settling in high-risk unserviced areas, thus increasing the burden on the urban environment even as they suffer a reduction in their own quality of life.

As mentioned earlier, alternatives to illegal crops such as cattle have generated a need to clear Amazon forestland in order to create grazing land, generating catastrophic impacts to the forest and the delicate soils found in these areas.

Terrorism

Linked to controversial environmental issues related to oil extraction and commercialization are issues that evolve around terrorism. Terrorism has caused large oil spills as guerrilla groups, mainly the ELN, blow up pipelines. The FARC in the last few years has also given support to such actions.

Between 1986 and 1999 there were 628 attacks against the Caño Limón–Coveñas pipeline, spilling over two million barrels of crude oil. During this time Ecopetrol, the governmental oil company, has cleaned close to 2,000 km of rivers and 1,516 ha of land that have been affected by the oil spills. Clean-up efforts were suspended in 1997 due to lack of safety guarantees for clean-up crews since these lands are controlled by guerrilla groups, causing a drastic impact on the environment.

War

Military actions know no environmental ethics or respect. As many of the armed groups hide in wilderness areas throughout the country, they create a bull's eye for the destruction of forests and other wilderness ecosystems. Bombings, roads, shelters, camps, and combat scar the land. There is no possibility of addressing this problem unless peace can be achieved.

Given the current conflict one question is repeatedly raised: Is it possible to protect the environment while human rights violations and war are so constantly present that the environment itself ceases to be, and indeed cannot be emforced as, a priority for either the government or the general public?

Conclusions

Colombia's current war situation makes it very difficult for environmental issues to be taken as a priority. A large part of the government's economic resources are concentrated on financing the fight against drug traffic and armed groups at the margin of law. The Colombian population lives fearful of being kidnapped or murdered. Many Colombians prefer to escape to other parts of the country or even outside of it. Sometimes they have no choice; they are simply displaced by force in a mandatory way to leave their homes and their land. Darkening the panorama even more, we must note that an economic and social crisis is evident; poverty affects a vast percentage of the population.

This situation of violence and its reality unchains a series of causal changes that affect human essence. When humans are put under pressure they assume a "survival" and "fight or flight" response; they are forced to use their most primary animal instincts. This is how they are driven to inappropriately exploit and destroy natural resources. They try to satisfy their basic needs of food and well-being, setting aside the conservation of the environment. In Caquetá (Amazon Basin), for example, inhabitants of a region that is mainly rural do not receive support or answers to the petitions made to the government; they lack options for profitable production. There, peasants try to survive, to feed their families any way possible. Clear and overwhelming options do not exist to stop illegal crops. So, the impact generated by these crops on the soil, water sources, forests, flora and fauna are not a priority in the face of hunger and the need to meet basic needs. Environmental repercussions of fumigations and the destruction of laboratories under international pressure for the eradication of illicit crops and drug traffic merely intensify the problem.

It is important to question if such behavior of the population is ethically correct, when putting into practice a form of life where the ethics of survival prevail. Is it pertinent to wonder what it really means to live an environmental ethic? Is it realistic to think that in a territory invaded by violence, environmental ethics can even exist? Next to poverty? Next to hunger? How can basic survival and conservation be balanced out? Does the concept of "Environmental Violence" exist? How are humans involved in, and how can they avoid, this type of violence?

When meditating upon these questions we realize that the solution is neither clear nor easy to find. The survival of humans in the long term depends directly on the health of its environment and its capacity to provide and fulfill human's basic necessities of food, housing, and health. At the same time, as an individual, if one does not have food, he\she will do anything possible to get it, even if this means destroying or notably affecting future capacity for production and health of the natural environment. How can we solve the immediate problem while assuring a long-term solution as well? This is the dilemma facing us. Apparently, if we pretend to provide for the immediate survival necessities of the population, the possibilities of long-term survival are destroyed, and if we want to assure the future possibilities we cannot survive the present.

In order to understand the situation that Colombia lives in, a country invaded by violence and poverty, which also, at the same time, has immense natural wealth, it is important to define what wealth is. When we speak of wealth do we speak of capital accumulation, money, or do we speak of potential for life, natural system diversity, and quality of life for all beings?

In searching for an answer to these questions, we always return to the same principle: as long as humans consider themselves a separate element from natural systems, there will never be a clear integral definition of wealth, much less a solution to our paradigm of survival. Unfortunately, our culture and development history during the last one hundred years have erased from our individual and collective memory the necessary knowledge of how to live as harmonic and natural elements within natural environments on the planet Earth. We have also lost much of our capacity to return easily to harmonic ways of life such as those practiced by some aboriginal and indigenous groups hundreds of years ago. This is clearly seen throughout the country. Because of the imposition of a traditional development model based on extractive practices, local indigenous and African American communities are losing their ancestral knowledge and culture, and they have modified their production methods and accepted the environment-degrading realities that come with "development."

Another question arises: Is the violence that Colombia lives an exclusively Colombian problem? When Colombians, in their desire to survive, negatively impact natural areas such as the Chocó or the Amazon regions, they are affecting small spaces that represent a large percentage of the planet's natural wealth. With these actions they affect and involve all the planet's inhabitants in the problem!

Let us think about several factors feeding the Colombian internal conflict. Illegal drug and weapon markets that feed violence (by making money available for the tools of war) are dominated mainly by outside countries and driven by a supply and demand economy. Therefore the responsibility is not Colombia's alone, but also belongs to countries consuming illegal drugs and countries supplying weapons. In modern economics it is well known that if demand ceases to exist, supply for that product diminishes and can potentially disappear. In the case of Colombia, it is seen how drugs are financing weapons and armed groups. If drug profitability were to be reduced significantly, the war would lose its main financial source. Is it worth asking yourselves how and where the largest consumers of drugs in the world are distributed? What is their responsibility? What are they doing to reduce demand? What are they doing to reduce their impact? Finally, is legalizing drugs worldwide an option that would eliminate part of the violence and profitability generated by illegality? Is it worth considering?

In conclusion, the violence that Colombia lives with, and the environmental impacts that it produces, are clear examples that in our (human) rush and desire to survive, to generate economic "wealth" and to satisfy our secondary or recreational needs (drugs, products of mass consumption, etc.), we are directly responsible, not only for the destruction of natural systems that provide us with raw materials and food, but also for the social and economic conditions that lead to poverty and violence, thus creating a never-ending downward spiral. This cycle can only be broken when we humans assume our responsibility for changing our attitudes globally—subscribing to well-defined environmental and personal ethics that keep in mind the long-term well-being of *all* the planet's inhabitants.

A set of principles such as the ones presented by the Earth Charter represent guidelines to our behavior and ethics that would generate a marked change for the better, not only for present generations but inevitably for those still to come. It is up to individuals, in Colombia and around the world, to commit personally and become agents of change through their daily actions. Countries of the North, such as the United States, have to assume this responsibility immediately, showing real leadership to other, less "wealthy" countries.

Acknowledgment

The authors thank OpEPA (Organización para la Educación y Protección Ambiental—Colombia) and Camilo Camargo for his editorial assistance <http://www.opepa.org>.

References

Aljure, Luis Carlos. 2000. "Colombia y el día de la tierra. Diagnóstico reservado." *Revista Diners*, Bogotá. April.

Bennet, Jon. 2000. "1999: Desplazamiento sin tregua." *Boletín* 28 (February 22). Bogotá: CODHES.

Colombia Programa Presidencial de los Derechos Humanos y DIH <http://www.rdh.gov.co> (May 10, 2000).

Colombian Human Rights Observatory. 1999. *The Colombian Situation.*

Instituto Alexander Von Humboldt. 1997a. *Informe nacional sobre el estado de la biodiversidad.* Volume II. Bogotá.

Instituto Alexander Von Humboldt. 1997b. *Informe nacional sobre el estado de la biodiversidad.* Anexo 2.4 Actores del conflicto armado en Colombia. La guerrilla. Bogotá.

Instituto Alexander Von Humboldt. 1997c. *Informe nacional sobre el estado de la biodiversidad.* Cultivos ilícitos. Bogotá.

Instituto Alexander Von Humboldt. 2000. <http://www.humboldt.org.co/c-biodiversidad.htm> (May 10, 2000).

Ministry of Environment and Department of National Planning Data, 1996.

Nyholm, Klaus. 1998. "Narcotráfico, medio ambiente y paz." Paper presented in Ambiente para la paz—National Environmental Congres, Bogotá, Colombia.

Official Colombian Report to the UNDP (1998–2000).

Pineda, Diego. 2000. Ministry of Environment. Taken from a personal interview. May 2000.

Presidente de la República. 1995. "Consejería para la Defensa y Seguridad Nacional" (DNP).

Proyecto Enlace. 2000. "Los efectos ambientales de los cultivos ilícitos: Un problema de ecología humana?" *Red* 33, Año 9 (January).

Revista Cambio. 1994. "Tabla de presencia paramilitar."

Rojas, Jorge E. 2000. "Un pais que huye. Conflicto armado y desplazamiento forzado interno en Colombia." <http://www.codhes.org> (May 10, 2000).

Sánchez, Enrique. 1998. "Los territorios colectivos de las comunidades negras y la conservación de la biodiversidad en la región del Pacífico." (Paper presented in Ambiente para la paz—National Environmental Congres, Bogotá, Colombia.)

Velez, German. 1998. "Biodiversidad y derechos colectivos de los pueblos indígenas y locales en Colombia." Paper presented in Ambiente para la paz—National Environmental Congres, Bogotá, Colombia.

Wilches-Chaux, Gustavo. 1998. *Nuestro compromiso político con el Cosmos.* Bogotá, Colombia: Corporación Viva la Ciudadanía (August 28).

Chapter 22

Ethics and Risks in Building a Cyclotron

Sonia Ftacnikova

In Slovakia we have a great opportunity to build our first cyclotron, which is planned mostly (80 percent) for medical uses. A cyclotron producing 72 MeV protons will allow us to introduce new diagnostic techniques, using positron emission tomography by producing short-lived radionuclides. It also will give new hope to some cancer patients who cannot be treated with sufficient effectiveness by gamma rays or by electrons. There are plans for introducing eye proton therapy, boron neutron capture therapy, and possibly fast neutron therapy. The remaining 20 percent of cyclotron time will be devoted to research activities and educational purposes by nuclear physicists, chemists, environmental specialists, and so on.

Besides all the technical documents and feasibility studies, there is a strong need for risk assessment study and for the development of a risk communication plan. This is also stressed in the Earth Charter in Principle 13a: "Uphold the right of everyone to receive clear and timely information on environmental matters and all development plans and activities which are likely to affect them or in which they have an interest" and in Principle 13f: "Strengthen local communities, enabling them to care for their environments, and assign environmental responsibilities to the level of government where they can be carried out most effectively." The risk assessment study includes risks to the population and also to the environment from all kinds of pollution produced by the cyclotron during both normal and emergency situations. Now we have to develop a plan for providing answers to very sensitive questions. We have just built an information center, which will coordinate all needed activities.

People living in the neighborhood are naturally asking questions like: What will be the influence of the cyclotron on my everyday life? Is it dangerous for me, my family, and the environment? Is it really necessary to build such a facility in Slovakia? Why exactly here, in my neighborhood? This is a typical case of NIMBYism (Not in My Backyard). We have to develop a communication plan and strategy that confronts these issues and that enables us to look at them from an ethical point of view.

First, there is a strong need for public education that incorporates explanations concerning (1) why such facilities are necessary to build and (2) the risk associated with such a facility.

Second, there is an ethical question about potential compensation to the affected population. Is it right to offer some kind of compensation? When the answer is "yes," what kind of compensation would be appropriate?

The main purpose of this contribution is to discuss all these questions with the aim (important for those of us who are not yet very experienced in this field), of acquiring the help needed for discovering the best solutions to these sensitive issues together with the methods needed to apply them in the ethically best way.

Why Is This Project Necessary?

Is It Necessary to Build Such a Complex At All?

Cancer diseases increase by 20,000 new cases each year and are, along with cardiovascular diseases (Plesko et al. 1997), the main lethal factor in Slovak Republic. The incidence of these diseases is continuously growing, their rate of increase being higher in Slovakia than in the rest of Europe and the world. Early diagnosis and more efficient treatment are vital for suppression of cancer-related mortality.

In Slovokia at the present time, the possibilities for early tumor diagnosis and for early diagnosis of cardiovascular and neurological diseases are not satisfactory in several respects. In Slovakia there isn't any nuclear medicine facility equipped with modern *positron emission tomography* (PET); this technological option has become an essential diagnostic technique in Europe (e.g., in Germany about 50 of such devices are being used). Introduction of this method requires an accelerator operating within 200 km so that short-lived isotopes produced in it can be delivered to the examined patient with precise quantity and timing. The PET examination provides really early diagnosis; it can identify some diseases as much as two years earlier than other techniques (Chiti et al. 1999).

The situation in *cancer treatment* is similar; in Slovakia there is no oncological facility equipped with a proton and neutron source, whose availability increases the patient's chance to be cured even when common treatment doesn't work. With such equipment some patients would live much longer; also the range of treatment possibilities with many tumors would be broadened. Moreover, through the provision of this equipment new ways of controlling and checking the treatment, e.g., for relapsing tumors, would be introduced. Thus the chance to survive would further increase for the oncological as well as the cardiovascular patients.

In addition to the initial problem created by the lack of a nuclear facility, Slovakia confronts a second major problem—this with regard to *the training of the top experts in nuclear physics, environmental science, dosimetry,* and other disciplines. Our economy is tied to the electrical energy produced in nuclear plants, which contribute about 60 percent of our total electrical supply. For the safe operation of such plants, experts are needed in nuclear physics, chemistry, and related technical disciplines. The need for such experts is emphasized by the fact that all major accidents in nuclear power plants have been due to a human failure. Yet the equipment of the nuclear physics and science laboratories and technical departments at our universities, colleges, and the Slovak Academy of Science is obsolete and frequently worn out. It is thus not suitable for educational and research purposes on the cutting edge of science. A new cyclotron could be used for training and experimental purposes and would thus enable more up-to-date training and research.

For all the reasons given above, a new cyclotron is critical to the well-being of Slovakians.

Is It Necessary to Build Such a Complex in Their Neighborhood?

In 1996 the Slovak government, by its Resolution 434/96, approved the project of building the cyclotron and related technological equipment within the Slovak Institute of Metrology in Bratislava - Karlova Ves. Why in Bratislava? Bratislava has a very good geographical position. It has very good international connections (it is close to Vienna, Budapest, Prague), which enables transportation of short-lived radiopharmaceuticals to the hospitals in Austria, Hungary, and Czech Republic.

Why in the Karlova Ves location, within the Slovak Institute of Metrology? The site was chosen due to the existing infrastructure, space, and location. This location is also excellent because of very good conditions for emission dispersion and one of the lowest densities of settlement.

How Should We Discuss Risk Associated with the Cyclotron Complex?

Our answer to this question is (1) explain the effect of ionizing radiation on human beings, (2) explain the levels of exposure from the facility, (3) compare these levels to the legislated limits of exposure, (4) compare expected exposures to other natural human-enhanced and human-made sources of radiation exposure, (5) relate levels of exposure to carcinogenic effects, and (6) compare the radiation exposure risks to common nonradiation risks that people experience.

Explain the Effect of Ionizing Radiation on Human Beings

Deterministic effects are those for which the severity of the effect varies with the dose, and for which a threshold may therefore occur. Stochastic effects are those for which the probability that the effect will occur, rather than the severity of the effect, is regarded as a function of the dose, without threshold. Deterministic effects are generally associated with acute exposures involving doses in the range of tens of Sievert (Sv) delivered to the part or all of the body over a short period. Deterministic effects include cataracts, sterility, tissue damage, organ atrophy, and death, and are basically degenerative. Most stochastic effects are the result of chronic exposures (in the workplace and ambient environment) involving repeated low doses to all or part of the body over a period of years. Stochastic effects include cancers (such as leukemia and solid tumors) and genetic damage, manifested in blood abnormalities, metabolic diseases, and physical abnormalities in the exposed person's descendants.

Explain the Estimated Levels of Exposure

Assessment of human exposure requires estimation of the number of people exposed and the magnitude, duration, and timing of their exposure. In case of external exposure, the resulting injury from ionizing radiation will depend on the total dose, the dose rate, and the percentage and region of body exposed. Internal exposures result from the presence or deposition of radioactive material in the body through ingestion or inhalation. The potential for harm depends on the types and quantities of material taken in and how long they remain in the body (on effective half-life).

External Neutron and Gamma Radiation

Table 22.1 identifies radiation exposures at various distances from the cyclotron center expressed in μSv (microSevert) per year. (One million μSv equal one Sievert.) In the worst scenario (highly unlikely) when the inhabitant spends all his time only 100 m from the cyclotron center the effective dose per year from external (neutron + gamma rays) irradiation will be 41.14 μSv.

Table 22.1. Effective Dose Rate [μSv/year]

Distance[m]	Neutrons	Gamma rays
100	41	0.14
200	7.2	0.024
300	2.3	0.0076
400	0.92	0.00031
500	0.42	0.00014

Radioactive Aerosols

In our case, the radionuclides in question would be 15-oxygen, 13-nitrogen, and 41-argon. The first two are short-lived biogenic elements, which are able to be incorporated into the human body and cause the radiation burden from internal irradiation. But because of very short half-lives (15-oxygen 2 minutes and 13-nitrogem 10 minutes) the radiation burden in this case can be neglected. Calculated effective dose rate from 41-argon during the radionuclide production in the cyclotron center is about 1.1 μSv per year.

Thus the total individual effective dose per year from external radiation and aerosols combined for someone living 100 m away from Cyclotron center is about 42.24 μSv, which is 4.2 percent of the annual limit for the population, which is one mSv. (One mSv [milliSievert] equals 1,000 μSv [microSievert] and 1/1000 of a Sv [Sievert].)

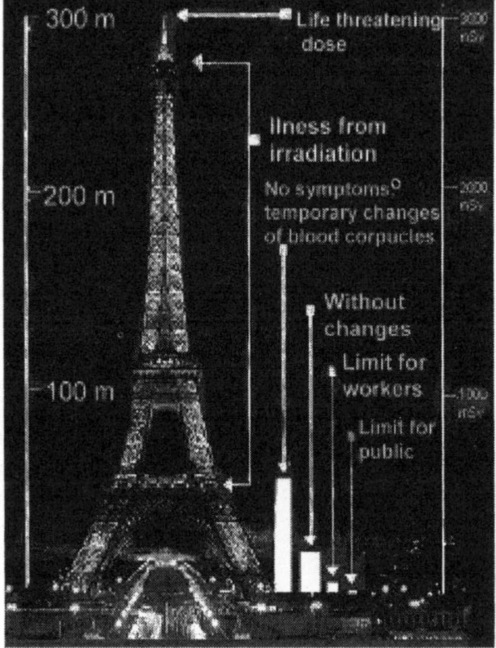

Figure 22.1. The effects of a range of effective doses of ionizing radiation on human health

Compare to Legislated Limits

The acceptance by society of risk associated with radiation is conditional on the benefits to be gained from the use made of radiation. Nonetheless, the risks must be restricted and protected against by the application of radiation safety standards that include three basic principles: justification, optimization, and limitation. The dose limits apply to the exposure attributable to controlled practices, with the exception of medical exposures and of exposures from natural sources.

There are two different dose limits: for occupational exposure, 20 mSv/year, and for public exposure, the average effective dose to the relevant *critical groups* among the public that are attributable to the running cyclotron shall not exceed *1 mSv per year*. (According to the International Committee for Radiation Protection [ICRP] definition, the critical group is a group of members of the public that is reasonably homogeneous with respect to its exposure for a given radiation source and given exposure pathway, and is typical of individuals receiving the highest effective dose by the given exposure pathway from the given sources.)

Figure 22.1 schematically illustrates the effect of ionizing radiation on human beings and compares them with the occupational and public limits. Here the doses are shown that cause the deterministic effect: doses above 3 Sv cause early lethal effect cerebrovascular, gastrointestinal, hematopoietic syndrome; lower doses of 2–3 Sv cause illness from irradiation (cataract, temporal anemia from platelet and red blood cells depression).

The legislated limit for a worker in a radiation facility is about his height (20 mSv/year) and the limit for the public is about the thickness of a brick (1 mSv/year).

Compare to Other Sources of Radiation

All human beings are inevitably exposed to ionizing radiation. The sources involved are of three general types: unperturbed natural sources, enhanced natural sources, where human activity has increased the level of individual exposure, and finally man-made sources. The third group includes exposure from x-rays and radiopharmaceuticals in medicine and also consumer products containing radioactive materials, atmospheric testing of nuclear weapons and accidents in nuclear power plants. These exposures are identified in table 22.2.

Natural sources of ionizing radiation pervade the environment and cause exposures to all human beings. There are four main components of these exposures: cosmic rays, terrestrial gamma rays, ingested or inhaled long-lived radionuclides, and inhaled radon isotopes. The first three may be said to form basic natural radiation background because of the relative constancy of exposure. According to the United Nations Scientific Committee on the Effects of Atomic Radiation (UNSCEAR 1993), the worldwide annual effective dose is about 1.1 mSv.

The source of natural radiation ignored until recently is *radon gas*, which leads to the irradiation in the surface of lungs when the gas and its daughter products are inhaled. Radon levels in houses vary enormously, but the average effective dose from indoor radon exposure in Slovakia is 2.0 mSv and from outdoor about 0.2 mSv (Vicanova et al. 1997).

The extra dose for *smokers* comes from naturally occurring radionuclides in tobacco products. The annual effective dose for the average smoker is about 13 mSv (Hall 1988, 485).

Table 22.2. Radiation Exposure to the Slovak Population

Sources	Number of Exposed Persons	E* to Exposed Person [mSv]	E*/caput [mSv]	S_E ** [person Sv]
Natural sources				
Radon	5,367,790	2.2	2.2	11,809
Other	5,367,790	1.1	1.1	5,904
Sum			3.3	17,713
Occupational	6,323	0.49	0.0005	2
Nuclear Fuel Cycle	2,856	1.11	0.0006	3
Sum	9,179		0.0011	5
Medical (diagnostic)				
X – ray (5)	5,749,869	0.9	0.96	5,176
Nuclear Medicine	27,855	2.37	0.012	66.1
Sum			0.97	5,242
Consumer Products				
Tobacco	1,063,732	13	2.6	31,828
Other	5,367,790	0.12	0.12	644
Miscellaneous				
Environ. Sources	350,000	0.015	0.001	5
Sum			2.72	14,477
TOTAL	**5,367,790**		**7.0**	**37,437**
Nonsmokers	4,304,058		4.4	18,938
Smokers	1,060,732		17.4	18,457

*E - effective dose, **S_E - collective dose

The data in table 22.2 indicate that the greatest contribution to the effective dose for nonsmokers in the Slovak population comes from natural sources, from inhaled radon-daughter products (2.2 mSv).

Among *human-made* or *human-enhanced sources* of radiation, medical exposures represent the largest contribution. These are different in character from inadvertent exposures, since they contribute directly to the benefit of the individuals receiving them.

Most other human-made or human-enhanced sources of radiation are minor. It is of interest to view doses from other man-made sources in the context of medical exposures. The doses for fallout from 1959–1962, when above ground testing of nuclear weapons was at its peak, never reached more than a small fraction of those from medical diagnosis. The radiation dose to the general population from nuclear power stations is also very small.

A significantly higher contribution, especially to younger age groups who travel a good deal, comes from flying in commercial jetliners. The transatlantic flight from United States to Europe involves doses of about 50 μSv from cosmic radiation (Hall 1988, 484).

Risk of Carcinogenesis

There is no direct evidence that small doses of radiation, similar to those used in medical exposure, cause harmful effects in the individuals who are exposed. The problem is the estimation of the biological effects that might occur when large numbers of people are exposed to small doses of radiation, based on extrapolation from the known deleterious effects observed when small numbers of individuals (either human or animal) are exposed to much larger doses of radiation.

A risk estimate is usually expressed as an absolute risk, which is the excess risk from radiation. In practice this is the difference between the fatal cancer risk in the irradiated population and the corresponding risk in the unirradiated control population. According to ICRP (1990), the fatal probability coefficient for all kinds of cancer is 5.0×10^{-2} Sv^{-1}. Adjusted, the fatal cancer probability coefficient, which takes into account not only the death itself but also the other mortality effects (as reflected by the years of productive life lost) among individuals who died, as well as morbidity effects of cancers that were not fatal (as reflected in the reduced quality of life for the victim, associated health care cost, and emotional impacts on family and friends) is $7.25 \times 10^{-2} Sv^{-1}$. The effective dose estimated in the previous section is about 40 μSv/ person and the number of exposed persons in the critical group (which were defined as persons living in circle 500 m around the cyclotron) is 2970. The resulting collective dose is calculated as $2970 \times 40 \times 10^{-6} = 118.8$ mSv. This means that the extra cases of cancer induced by radiation connected with running the cyclotron will be $118.8 \times 10^{-3} \times 5 \times 10^{-2} = 0.006$. Every year more than 20,000 new cancer cases are reported in the Slovak Republic (Plesko et al. 1997).

Low levels of exposure, in the range of 10 mSv, can be contrasted with some natural exposures. For example, living in high elevation areas (Kerala, India, for 1 year; Guangdong Province, China, for 5 years; or Denver for 12 years) exposes one to the radiation of this magnitude. In those instances where epidemiological studies have been performed, they have failed to show any increase in cancer incidence over the general variability seen in disease from region to region (Hall 1988, 482).

Compare to Non-Radiation Risk

In an attempt to put into perspective the risk of cancer associated with radiation from the cyclotron, it is instructive to make comparison with other risks to which individuals are subjected in our society, for instance smoking cigarettes, driving an automobile, or accidents.

- Approximately 2,000 people a year die of lung cancer in Slovak Republic (Plesko et al. 1997), almost all of whom are smokers. The risk connected with the average dose about 1 mSv is the equivalent to 20 days of smoking .
- Statistics from United States indicate that there is one fatality on the road for every 18 million miles driven, i.e., 5.6 x 10^{-8} deaths per mile driven (Hall 1988, 498). Similarly, a radiation dose of 1 mSv is equivalent to 1,400 km on American highways.
- If one assumes an average fatal accident rate of 6 per 10,000 per year, over a 50-year period this risk is approximately 3 percent, which is equivalent to an exposure to 600 mSv or 160 average nuclear medical procedures. Accidents also provide a useful spectrum of risks: on an annual basis, motor vehicle accidents account for 3 deaths per 10,000; drowning for 3 per 100,000; air travel for 9 per million and lightning causes 5 deaths per 10 million. The analogy, however, can be faulted, as these accidents are generally immediately fatal in comparison with the long-term consequences of radiation exposure. In contrast, the frightening aspects of radiation risk are the uncertainty of outcome and relatively long period of latency.

Potential Compensation

There is an ethical question about potential compensation to the affected population. Is it right to offer some kind of recompense? If our answer here is "yes," what kind would be appropriate? We are thinking of suggesting at least two kinds of compensation:

1. to offer to the population living in the neighborhood the opportunity to be examined preferentially (if they need it);
2. to offer some amount of money to help with the solving of some of the most urgent environmental problems being experienced in the region.

The first possibility is ethically suspect beceause it would not appear fair to other patients whose cases may be more urgent, and, moreover, of questionable merit as compensation for all, since many in the exposed neighborhood population will not be patients in the future. The second possiblity seems clearly fair; it would improve life both for the neighborhood's immediate residents and eventually for the entire nation.

References

Chiti, A., F. A. G. Schreiner, F. Crippa, K. J. Pauwels, and E. Bombardieri. 1999. "Nuclear Medicine Procedures in Lung Cancer," *European Journal of Nuclear Medicine,* 226: 533–55.

Hall, E. J. 1988. *Radiobiology for the Radiologist.* Philadelphia: J. B. Lippincott Company.

ICRP (International Committee for Radiation Protection). 1990. *ICRP Recommendations.* ICRP Publication 60. Oxford: Pergamon Press.

Plesko, I., A. Obsitnikova, V. Vlasak. 1997. "Registration of the Incidence of the Cancer in Slovakia." *Medicinsky Monitor* 2 (February): 1–7.

UNSCEAR (United Nations Scientific Committee on the Effects of Atomic Radiation). 1993. *Report to the General Assembly: Sources and Effects of Ionizing Radiation.* New York: United Nations.

Vicanova, M., M. Durcik, D. Nikodemova. 1997. "Indoor Radon Exposure of Slovak Population." Pp. 284–88 in *Proceedings of the European Conference on Protection against Radon at Home and at Work, Part II.* Prague (June 2–6, 1997).

Chapter 23

The Tactics of Forest Preservation: Authenticity and Rhetoric in Poland's Bialowieza Forest Preserve

Eunice Blavascunas

With an ever-decreasing number of natural forests left on the planet, preserving the few that remain takes on critical importance. Safeguarding their integrity depends upon traditions of perception on the part of local inhabitants and of national and international conservation groups committed to their preservation. It is not uncommon for the intricacies of these forests to be lost to simple rhetoric about pristine natural environments when the goal of preservation is tied to a single, best form of land management, such as a national park. Nature rhetoric often leads institutions to promote nature in that ideal and thus overlooks other interpretations of what the forest means for various stakeholders.

Among goals espoused in the Earth Charter Initiative is a call to promote more responsible communities that can forge inclusive solutions to environmental problems. The Earth Charter also links environmental and social histories that have served to marginalize people in the past. Thus, in speaking to the international environmental community, this paper's major purpose is to advance our understanding of the way human agency constructs nature, making conservation policy more self-reflective and critical in order to address the responsibility environmentalists have for promoting the integrity of natural places. Specifically, I will be discussing the ways in which the Bialowieza Forest Preserve in northeastern Poland is represented by those working to expand the boundaries of the Bialowieza National Park. The organization of this chapter is based on four views of the Bialowieza forest and its inhabitants: (1) The history of Bialowieza as a primeval forest; (2) Bialowieza's image as a forest belonging to Poland and Europe; (3) The Bialowieza forest as a subject for scientific study; and finally (4) Bialowieza's inhabitants as authentic dwellers on the outskirts of the forest.

Situated on both sides of the Polish-Belarusian border, the Bialowieza Forest Preserve is an area of 150,000 ha, with special biological importance. As one of the last remnants of native lowland forest in Europe, it is the habitat for a relict population of free-ranging European bison. For hundreds of years, local gentry and landowners stocked the forest with game mammals and used it as their exclusive hunting preserve. Thus the woodland was spared from conversion into agricultural land. At present the forest is divided into three forms of management: The Beleveza National Park, Belarus (87,000 ha), the Bialowieza National Park, Poland (10,500 ha), and the Polish state-owned commercial forest (98,000 ha) (Okolow 1999).

Bialowieza as a Primeval Forest

According to the landscape vision of conservationists, Bialowieza has been coined the Bialowieza primeval forest. This environmental imagery draws attention to the forest's archaic character. Standing water, the color of rust, stagnates in swampy terrain where roots of alders grow above the inundated soils. Dead wood accumulates variably upon the forest floor, and giant dead oaks and spruce create perches and cavities for the many rare birds, among them all eight European woodpecker species. Such a forest once extended all the way from the Atlantic Ocean to the Ural Mountains.

In this evocative remnant of European landscape, conservationists use the term "primeval" to infer an absence of humans in natural cycles. Bialowieza's primeval characteristics are said to be the direct benefit of 500 years of efficient and royal protection. This nature narrative begins with King Jagiello, who, in 1409, set off on an eight-day hunt to the forested Lithuanian swamplands, situated just outside the most important trade route from Krakow to Vilnius. While killing moose, bear, boar, roe deer, and bison, Jagiello planned the strategy for the battle of Grundwald to save his peasants from being enslaved by the Teutonic knights. He and his men overwintered in Bialowieza to capture and tame tarpan horses for the Polish Lithuanian army and to ensure a handsome reserve of salted, dried game for his retinue. Jagiello's men defeated the Teutons in 1410 and the beasts of these uncleared lands earned the King's gratitude. Upon claiming Bialowieza as his private hunting ground, formal protection of the Bialowieza forest began (Hedemann 1939).

Royal protection halted uncontrolled colonization of the forested lands. But humans transformed the character of the forest. Land management throughout most of the forest's history favored game animals of the royal hunt. Local people scythed the wet meadows along the rivers for hay, a practice that prevented the encroachment of trees and improved grazing conditions for both the wild ungulates and the livestock belonging to the crown.

Over the course of World War I, German forces exploited the forest and cut 5 million m cubed of timber from 6,500 ha without any replanting. Up until this time only small timber operations had extracted wood resources. Unregulated hunting also killed off game mammals, including the European bison in 1919. The Germans built networks of narrow gauge rail lines to transport timber out. They set up 24 sawmills and a chemical wood-processing factory in what became the twentieth-century city of Hajnowka at the westernmost edge of the forest (Hedemann 1939).

In the aftermath of World War I, April 1919, Polish scientists surveyed what the forest had suffered as a result of combat and exploitation. Moved by the unprecedented damage, they gathered support for protecting a very small 50 sq. km as a strict reserve, Poland's first national park, set aside primarily for scientists. At this time European bison were reintroduced from seven genetically distinct individuals found in zoos around Europe (Okolow 1991).

Following World War II, the geopolitical configurations of the Yalta Agreement drew a national border through the middle of the forest, separating Poland from the Soviet Union. This leads up to the triple management scheme of today; two separate national parks and a state-owned commercial forest.

Due to the input of ecologists, the commercial forest began to be managed with consideration to its ecological uniqueness in the 1970s. Today, the forester must adjust species composition of tree stands to match soil type, harvest timber by considering protective needs of certain species, reconstruct bodies of water, leave standing and dead trees after harvest, and never fell more than 50 percent of the annual growth increment (personal interviews with state forestry officials).

The managed forest consists primarily of spruce and pine. Half of the stands are secondary in origin, but conservation literature lumps the old growth and managed forest together as "primeval." Incidentally, bison prefer the young and managed forests to the old-growth strict reserve. An examination of Bialowieza's history illustrates that both the managed forest and the national park have been transformed significantly by humans, both in their heavy usage as a hunting preserve, and through twentieth-century logging operations. Hence the designation as "primeval" says more about the imaginations of those who seek out pristine nature as such, than it does about the biological composition of the ecosystem.

Bialowieza as Myth and Politic

Expanding the boundaries of the national park has drawn attention to the importance of Bialowieza in the Polish and European consciousness. Poles refer to the classic Polish literature about this region, which regards the forest as an idealized portrait of Polish national identity. Bialowieza is part of an old Poland with feudal rights of gentry. It is a place of romantic attachment to primeval wood, fen, and open space. Poland's poet laureate, Czeslaw Milosz, an active proponent of the national park expansion, reminds Poles that their national history can be redeemed through natural history if Bialowieza is saved from further logging (Milosz 1996).

Aside from its mythic value, the nation of Poland views Bialowieza as strategically important to defining its own identity to foreigners. European Union aspirations make Poland want to shed its long-held image as heavily industrialized and ecologically degraded. Successful conservation intends to make Poland look progressive and reliable in the scope of international agreements. For example, since 1989, Poland has set up 8 new national parks, bringing the total to 22 (Parki Narodowe w Polsce 1999). Poland is working with the World Conservation Union and Council of Europe to design a national ecological network by 2005 linking core protection areas through ecological corridors. And the region in which Bialowieza lies is being promoted as the "green lungs of Poland."

Across Europe, there is widespread recognition that natural forests and important wildlife habitat have been irreparably damaged: 15 percent of European bird species are threatened, 30 percent of Europe's amphibians, 42 percent of reptiles, and 52 percent of freshwater fish *(State of the World's Forests 1997)*. In this European dimension, Bialowieza assumes utmost importance as a protected area. There is a sense of moral duty behind its care, where Western Europeans feel shame and despair at the loss of nature and countryside in their own homelands. For these reasons their organizations come to Bialowieza to transfer technologies and exchange information. The new Europe emphasizes the sum of the diversity of its peoples and landscapes, inviting Bialowieza into the fold.

In one European led effort, World Wildlife Fund designated Bialowieza as the "Yellowstone of Europe," in its newly created Pan Parks Program. Pan Park's vision promotes nature as the kind that humans abstain from using. Nature must be marketed in order to bring tourist jobs to local communities that may be opposed to conservation *(Pan Parks* 1998).

Pan Parks literature speaks in terms of gateway communities, implying that there is a barrier between where the humans live and where the humans may only go as visitors. They boast that the nature within Bialowieza National Park is subject to strict protection. In this way, Pan Parks promotes the values of an urban society that wants to visit nature detached and separate from production activities in the forest. The promoters emphasize that Bialowieza will have to provide the tourist with high quality nature and high quality accommodations where they can see wildlife unafraid of humans and come back to the bed and breakfast for a hot shower and clean toilet.

Scientific Perspectives on Bialowieza

The research of Polish and international biologists living and working in Bialowieza is particularly resonant for conservationists, who need hard factual evidence to convince administrators to save Bialowieza forest as a national park. They direct their research toward how the land can be discovered rather than how the land has been constructed by humans, articulating a language and methodology that view nature as a phenomenon separate from humankind. The deceptively complex world of plants and animals is objectified to observe whether or not organisms will operate in the same way from season to season. First and foremost, these scientists want to know how ecological processes work without human intervention.

Their studies have defined Bialowieza National Park (and remnants of the managed forest) as a forest established through natural self-regeneration. It has a complex structure with an array of multistoried mixed species with uneven ages. Three phases of forest growth operate: there is an initial growth period, where a dense single layer of young trees gradually prevents light from reaching the forest floor; an "optimal" period, when 60–200 year old trees make up a healthy stand; and a third, or terminal, stage when sick and dying trees dominate, leaving a great amount of woody debris on the floor.

Scientists' political activities on behalf of the natural world infer and suggest that the place for humans in Bialowieza lies in observing and watching nature with the least possible interference in its natural cycles. Their expertise is amplified at the cost of overlooking other interpretations of the forest landscape, such as Bialowieza as a rich cultural site with spiritual and practical significance to the local inhabitants. In a scientific search for pure nature, the forest becomes first and foremost a narrative of ecology, where humans can only become restored to nature by uncovering its mechanisms. The scientific narrative makes Bialowieza intelligible to conservationists and outsiders, but not necessarily to the local inhabitants, who view scientists as performing irrelevant science, that is, research that doesn't benefit their community or daily lives.

Bialowieza as Home and Neighborhood

In the scientists' vision for local inhabitants, typified by the agenda of international conservation groups, archetypal households could be turned into a living museum of sustainability for tourists. Residents of Bialowieza could be viewed with curiosity by tourists, as they possess distinct regional traditions that differentiate them from other Poles. Residents of Bialowieza are primarily Orthodox Catholic and have dialects close to Belarusian. They subsist on a mixed economy of small, unmechanized farms, utilizing products of the forest through gathering mushrooms, medicinal herbs, keeping bees, and by cutting trees for commercial purposes and firewood. In all, 25,000 people live in small hamlets scattered on the outskirts of the forest (with an additional 25,000 in the wood-processing town of Hajnowka). Residents emphasize pragmatic uses of the forest and the pattern of seasonal activities transforms the forest into a workaday character.

There are also spiritual and social values in the forest for local inhabitants. The longevity of forest use is told by the presence of graves. People today bury their dead in village cemeteries, but graves and memorials dot the forest, including a number of mass execution sites from World War II. Medieval burial mounds dating from the fifth to the thirteenth century AD inspire a few residents to visit them on day of the dead. Not to be mistaken for natural irregularities the earthen mounds swell three to six feet high in distinctive loaf shapes and run for up to seven feet. People argue that they go back to a pre-Christian presence, possibly one from which they themselves descended.

In naming the landscape, inhabitants ascribe their own implicit understanding of Bialowieza's history. The local people divide the forest by a vernacular inconsistent with the designations of scientists, foresters, and tourists. For example in 1710, the black plague decimated the population by the hundreds. Prohibited from burying their dead in the usual cemetery, inhabitants dropped their diseased corpses along the side of the road where an undertaker burned the bodies in a pit, known today as *Za Krzyzami* (beyond hallowed ground). Despite resident discrepancies over name origins other locations continue to be called by their local referent, *dubowa kaloda* (oak board), *szopa* (the place for storing hay), *cialacza dalina* (calves valley), *czyrwona hara* (the red hill), *srodkowa budka* (the middle building).

Still other places might refer to the animals that live in their worlds. In the local Belarusian dialect, lapwings, or green plovers sing *knihiniawka*. The shorebird nests in the wet meadows next to a forest area residents endowed with that name. The very name of *Kamannoje Bahno* (the rock swamp) warned people from going there. It refers to a meadow where quicksand created unfavorable grazing conditions, and the stones sank.

There are also religious and spiritual aspects to the forest. Krynoczka, a sacred spring, attracts regional Orthodox Catholics on annual pilgrimage. Water from the spring has reportedly cured countless faithful. For hundreds of years, inhabitants have traveled into the forest to dip their handkerchiefs in the waters, which they hang from shrubs in order to cure their ills and alleviate worries. Reportedly it is the one place in the forest where the mosquitoes leave people alone. Miraculously, sufferers of ailing stomachs and cancer find relief there.

Residents possess a living memory of places and identify more with Polish state-owned logging operations than with any ancestral role in guarding the forest as a nature preserve. In fact, local inhabitants by and large refrain from entering the national park unless they work for the park or one of the scientific institutes. Residents must pay approximately $15 for entry to cover the cost of a guided tour. It is currently illegal to enter the park without a guide. But more than the cost, inhabitants lack purpose in the strict reserve. They feel that resources waste, for example wood that could heat or repair their houses rots on the ground. Residents are likely to assert that the forest, even as a national park, ought to give them more. If their subsistence needs are not met, then the government should step in with financial rewards in the form of schools, new roads, and sewage canals.

From discussion about the future for Bialowieza forest arises the specter of what it means to be original. Promoters of eco-tourism view the original inhabitants and their dwelling as the only way to have both the authentic villages and the authentic primeval forest. The living museum concept looks for economic incentives to offer people who will continue to live in subsistence fashion. On the one hand, conservationists and scientists would like to see residents grow more sophisticated and modern, as attested to by their promotion of ecological infrastructure for the villages, such as a switch from wood heating to gas, and the development of a sanitary landfill with the promise of internal plumbing for all. Scientists wish to see humans have less impact upon this forest, to stop cutting trees for firewood, trample less ground in search of mushrooms, and to continue traditional farming over more industrialized ventures.

With Poland's rapid transition to a Western economy, new technologies are necessary to keep people living in the forest hamlets. Maintaining archetypal forms of dwelling frightens local inhabitants and erodes their optimism for the future, as attested to by the out-migration of young people in the last few years. In the current atmosphere there is no structured format for local inhabitants to ask or understand what is valuable in the preexisting archetypes, before they fall into the potential trap of becoming fetishized as authentic. In a sense, local people would be cocooned into representations of themselves.

In a move to commodify and thereby retain the authentic, the scientists and conservationists assume the power to designate what is authentic. Thus, the archetypal dwelling in Bialowieza becomes independent of the activities of everyday life that gave them their character in the first place.

It is not uncommon that *purist* conservation initiatives promote an environmental perception that excludes the creative role of local communities in the forest landscape. Participating in the local imagination gives conservationists a better chance at dovetailing the multiple perceptions of Bialowieza and conserving it as a landscape with both natural and human integrity.

References

Bajko, Piotr. 1997a. "Nazwy Meijscowe Polany Bialowieskiej." *Bialoruskie Zeszyty Historyczne,* no. 7: 100–15.

Bajko, Piotr. 1997b. "Obiekty Geograficzne Polany Bialowieskiej." *Bialowiezanim* 5, no. 2: 1–7.

Biela, Adam, and Bohdan Roznowski. 1995. "Public Perception of Nature Conservation Forms in Inhabitants of the Bialowieza Forest Region." Pp. 257–72 in *Protection of Forest Ecosystems Biodiversity,* edited by Piotr Paschalis. Warsaw: Rozwoj SGGW.

Bobiec, Andrzej. 1998. "Gospodarka Lesna jako Zrodlo Zagrozenia Naturalnych Zbiorowsk Puszczy Bialowieskiej." *Chronmy Przyrode Ojczysta* 54, no. 6, 58–65.

Bobiec, Andrzej. 1996. "Las Naturalny Przyjazny Ludzkosci." *Kosmos* 45, no. 1: 223–27.

Bobiec, Andrzej. 1996. "The Mosaic Diversity of Field Layer Vegetation in the Natural and Exploited Forest of Bialowieza." *Plant Ecology,* no. 136: 175–87.

Cabon-Raczynska, Krystyna, and Malgorzata Krasinka. 1993. "Behaviours and Daily Activity Rhythm of European Bison in Winter." *Acta Theriologica* 28, no. 18: 273–99.

The Contract for Bialowieza. 1998. Warsaw: Minister of the Environment.

Falinski, Janusz. 1996. "Bialowieski Park Narodowy (1921–1996)," *Phytocoenosis* 8, no. 4: 3–160.

Falinski, Janusz. 1986. *Vegetation Dynamics in Temperate Lowland Primeval Forest.* Dordrecht: Dr. W. Junk Publishers.

Falinski, Janusz. 1968. *The National Park in Bialowieza Primeval Forest.* Warsaw: Panstwowe Wydawnictwo Rolnicze & Lesne.

"Forests in Europe: Proceedings." 1994. Warsaw.

Gebczynska, Zosia, and Marek Gebczynski. 1991. "Food Eaten by the Free-Living European Bison in Bialowieza Forest." *Acta Theriologica* 36, no. 3–4: 307–13.

Hartman, Wiktor. 1938. "Jak Exploatowano Puszcze Bialowieska w latach 1798–1833." *Echa Lesna* 15, no 26: 591–92.

Hedemann, Otto. 1939. "Dzieje Puszczy Bialowieskiej w Polsce Przedrozbiorowej (w okresie do 1779)." Warsaw: Ksiegarnia sw. Wojciecha.

Hoedeman, Frederik. 1999. *The Bialowieza National Park in Poland: Directions of Sustainable Development in the Local Community of the Bialowieza Forest Region 1994–1998.* Copenhagen: Aage V. Jensen Foundation (for by the Polish Ministry of Environment and Energy).

Hoosen, David. 1994. *Geography and National Identity.* Oxford: Blackwell.

Karcov, G. 1903. *Belovezshkaya Pushcha.* St. Petersburg: A. Marks.

Karpinski, Jan. 1972. *Puszcza Bialowieska.* Warsaw: Wiedza Powszechna.

Kawecka, Amelia. 1994. "Strict Nature Reserve of the Bialowieza National Park." Bialowieza, Poland: Bialowieza National Park.

Kolbuszewski, Jacek. 1995. *Kresy.* Wroclaw: Wydawnictwo Dolnoslaskie.

Kurcza, Zbigniewa. 1997. *Mniejszoszci Narodowe w Polsce.* Wroclaw: University of Wroclaw.

Lewis, Pierce. 1979. "Axioms for Reading the Landscape." Pp. 11–32 in *The Interpretation of Ordinary Landscapes,* edited by D. W. Meinig. New York: Oxford University Press.

Massey, Doreen. 1994. *Space, Place and Gender.* Minneapolis: University of Minnesota Press.

Massey, Doreen. 1993. "Questions of Locality." *Geography.* 78 no. 339: 142–49.

Mickiewicz, Adam. 1964. *Pan Tadeusz,* edited by Kenneth Mackenzie. London: Polish Cultural Foundation.

Milosz, Czeslaw. 1996. "Rozebrac Wawel na Cegle?" *Katolickie Pismo Spoleczno-Kulturowe.* (18 February).

Mironowicz, Eugeniusz. 1993. *Bialorusini w Polsce 1944–1949.* Warszawa Wydawnictwo Naukowe PWN.

Moroz-Keczynska, Ewa. 1996. "Bialowieza: Percepcja Srodowiska Naturalnego przez Mieszkancow Osadny na Podstawie Badan Terenowych." Master's thesis, University of Warsaw.

Okolow, Czeslaw. 1999. "Krolewska Puszcza." *Lowiec Polski,* no. 4: 60–61.

Okolow, Czeslaw. 1992. "Bialowieza National Park and Science." Bialowieza, Poland: Bialowieza National Park.

Okolow, Czeslaw. 1991. *Bialowieza National Park.* Warsaw: Sport and Tourism.

The Pan-European Ecological Network. 1998. Strasbourg.

Pan Parks: Investing in Europe's Future. 1998. Haarlem, Netherlands: World Wide Fund for Nature.

Parki Narodowe w Polsce. 1999. Bialowieza, Poland: Krajowy Zarzad Parkow Narodowych and Bialowiejski Park Narodowy: 1–111.

Paschalis, Piotr. 1995. *Biodiversity Protection of Bialowieza Primeval Forest: Selected Papers*. Warsaw: Rozwoj SGGW.

Pucek, Zdzyslaw. 1991. "Conservation Strategy for European Bison." *Ungulates* 43: 589–94.

Puszcza Bialowieska: Dosc Przerabianna na Deski. 1997. Hajnowka, Poland: Towarzystwo Ochrony Puszczy Bialowieskiej.

Sadowski, Andrzej. 1995. *Pogrznicze Polsko-Bialoruskie: Tozsamosc Mieszkancow*. Bialystok: Transhumana.

Schama, Simon. 1996. *Landscape and Memory*. New York: Alfred A. Knopf.

Sokolowski, Aleksander. 1995. "The Influence of Artificial Regeneration of Clear Cuttings on Species Composition of Plant Associations in the Reserve of the Bialowieza Forest." In *Protection of Forest Ecosystems Biodiversity*, edited by Piotr Paschalis. Warsaw: Rozwoj SGGW.

State of the World's Forests 1997. Rome: Food and Agriculture Organization, United Nations (FAO).

"Ustawa Okresla Zasady Ochrony Przyrody." *Bialowieski Park Narodowy*, no. 114 (1991): 492.

Woolhiser, Curt. 1999. "Constructing National Identities in the Polish-Belarusian Borderlands" (paper presented at the fourth annual convention of the Association for the Study of Nationalities, Columbia University, New York, April 15).

Chapter 24

Can Corcovado National Park in Costa Rica Be Saved? How to Apply the Principles of the Earth Charter

Paul T. Durbin

> If we allow a "biotic holocaust" to take place, . . . this will be far and away the biggest "decision" ever made by one generation for future generations . . . and we will be regarded as perhaps the most irresponsible generation in the history of this planet. If we are wise enough to seize the opportunities presented by the hotspots strategy and a handful of others, we will be regarded by future generations as true giants of the human condition . . . . [We must] create a value system that recognizes maintenance of the full range of life on Earth as simply "the right thing to do" (Mittermeier et al. 2000, 67).

It is in this context that the Earth Charter seems important. Its principles—to respect and care for the community of life; protect and restore the integrity of Earth's ecological systems; and eradicate poverty as an ethical, social, and environmental imperative—seem ideally suited to provide a justification for "the right thing to do" that Mittermeier and his colleagues call for.

In this paper, I put this thesis to the test, and I do so by contrasting this high-sounding rhetoric with the real-world reality of what will be required to put the Earth Charter and similar proposals into effect. My thesis is slightly different from that of the Earth Charter: *Important as are broad statements of principle, we still need to roll up our sleeves and get to work if we want to see the principles put into practice.*

I share this approach to environmental ethics with philosopher of technology Larry Hickman, whose "Green Pragmatism" echoes John Dewey's claim that it is possible to be too idealistic in our environmentalism (Hickman 1999). Statements of high principle must be treated instrumentally, as guidelines in social problem solving; and, in the practical activism that is required to solve such urgent problems as biodiversity destruction worldwide, we must often work with people who do not share high principles—often with people who in fact oppose such principles.

For my exemplification of this thesis at work, I have chosen a limited portion of just one of Mittermeier's hotspots: Costa Rica, and in particular one of Costa Rica's most biodiverse—and most threatened—regions, Corcovado National Park and its surrounding Golfo Dulce Forest Reserve. Mittermeier and his colleagues acknowledge Costa Rica as the most conservation-oriented country in the "Mesoamerican Hotspot," which they categorize as one of the most biologically rich locations on Earth but also as a region that is seriously threatened. Efforts to save it, they say, have one primary focus:

> Conservation action to counter the ongoing threats to the Mesoamerican Hotspot concentrates on the creation and maintenance of the Mesoamerican Biological Corridor. Adopted by a host of donors, the region's governments, and all four major international conservation groups—Conservational International, the World Wildlife Fund, the Nature Conservancy, and the Wildlife Conservation Society— . . . [the corridor would create] a continuous gallery of habitat for species between Panama and Mexico (Mittermeier 2000).

Of all of Costa Rica's biodiverse areas, why choose the Osa Peninsula and Corcovado National Park? Another major conservation study, supported by the Nature Conservancy and entitled *Parks in Peril,* justifies such a focus this way:

> Corcovado National Park and the surrounding conservation areas in the Osa Peninsula represent the largest remaining lowland rainforest on the Pacific coast of Central America. The park is located in one of the wettest and most remote areas left in Costa Rica. There are over 1,500 species of trees identified thus far in Corcovado, and one estimate placed the overall number of tree species in the park and surrounding areas at 3,000. The park contains over one-quarter of all the tree species known to exist in the country, including some of the largest trees in the country's tropical forests, towering fifty meters above the ground. The fauna are also incredibly rich; to date 375 species of birds, 18 of which are endemic; 124 species of mammals, 46 species of amphibians, 71 species of reptiles, 61 freshwater fish species, and approximately 8,000 insect species have been recorded. The park also protects many endangered tropical species, especially cats and reptiles (Brandon et al. 1998, 143–44).

Corcovado National Park is largely surrounded by the Golfo Dulce Forest Reserve. This reserve, as well as other protected areas on the Osa, is of substantial ecological importance, since the park alone is not sufficiently large to protect many of the species inside its boundaries. Despite the fact that nearly 80 percent of the peninsula is legally protected in some form, rapid land-use changes and forest clearing threaten the biological integrity of the peninsula.

Here I take up two examples, one in which Corcovado National Park was saved from devastation; the other in which its biological corridor escaped destruction—for now.

Corcovado Saved from a Gold Rush in the 1980s

As David Rains Wallace, in *The Quetzal and the Macaw* (1992, chapter 14), tells the story, Corcovado National Park was saved from desecration by gold miners (roughly 1980–1986) by a relatively small number of actors—supported occasionally by a fickle public opinion.

The most famous activist in the effort was the tropical biologist, Daniel Janzen, who had already become world famous for his work on the dry forests of Santa Rosa in the far northwest of Costa Rica. Janzen was asked by leaders of the World Wildlife Fund to do a report on the environmental impact of gold mining on the Osa Peninsula, in and around Corcovado. Janzen's report found that there were up to 2,000 miners doing incredible damage: "Agoutis, pacas, armadillos, tapirs, brocket deer, peccaries, monkeys, guans, curassows, [and] tinamous" had been "practically eliminated," and there was an "almost complete absence of fish, crabs, crayfish, aquatic mammals, insects, and birds in all the rivers affected" (Wallace 1992, 134). Janzen said that "the Park Service . . . should recognize that this is the most dangerous crisis it has undergone in its history." Wallace concludes: "The Janzen report recommended complete removal of miners from the park as the only way to stop the damage" (136).

Implicit here, as a secondary actor, is the World Wildlife Fund. Later in the story, other international environmental organizations—for example, the Nature Conservancy and the Caribbean Conservation Corporation—will show up as funders of the National Parks Foundation, and that money will support the ultimate resolution of the mining problem.

The second primary actor was Alvaro Ugalde, one of the two founders of Costa Rica's national park system and at the time head of the National Park Service. According to Wallace, Ugalde appealed to "virtually every government ministry" and ultimately to President Luis Monge, elected in 1982 under the Liberationist Party banner. Ugalde also mounted a public relations campaign in leading newspapers. When the government agencies waffled, and seemed as concerned about the plight of the miners as about stopping devastation of the park, Ugalde took the matter into his own hands. Claiming authority as head of the Park Service, he used National Parks foundation money, and filed legal proceedings against 100 miners, threatening them with expulsion by the Civil Guard. (It should be recalled that Costa Rica has no army.) And the Judge of Instruction, Gerardo Madrigal in Golfito, granted the requested court order in January 1986 (137–39).

This implicates another secondary actor, the judge, as well as the miners and the general public to whom Ugalde made his appeals for support. The judge gets no mention in Wallace's account beyond his granting of the court order; the Costa Rican public, on the other hand, are depicted by Wallace as being easily swayed, from outrage over the desecration of the park to sympathy for the plight of the miners to amusement when, later, the miners marched on the national capital for redress of their grievances over being deprived of a livelihood (141–44).

The miners themselves are a party to be taken into account in the story. Wallace traces the history of some of them to the pullout of the United Fruit Company from banana plantations just north of the Osa Peninsula; part of the problem seems to have been socialist labor organizing among banana workers, and some of this attitude must have carried over as some of the unemployed turned to gold mining. For his part, Janzen found in his report that a high percentage of the small miners actually had other sources of income in small farms they had carved out of the forest. Large, multinational mining companies seem not to have been a big factor; Wallace says that they were involved, but their operations were mostly outside, though on the edge of, the park—and they seem to have moved out entirely after the hullabaloo (130).

Eventually, most of the small miners moved out of the park, established a cooperative, got involved in limited tourist activities, and received compensation from the government. Wallace concludes, as do others, that illegal gold mining continues, sporadically, in and around the park. But no massive gold rush ever ensued that would have totally destroyed the biodiversity of Corcovado National Park (Wallace 1992, 144; Brandon 1998, 187).

Now it is time to ask whether general principles such as those of the Earth Charter either were or could have been a factor in saving Corcovado from a gold rush. We can ask the question actor by actor.

Daniel Janzen is certainly a high-minded man, passionately devoted to the preservation of biodiversity—but primarily as a scientist wanting to study it.

The leaders of the World Wildlife Fund—and other international environmental agencies indirectly involved—almost certainly would endorse the Earth Charter and all its principles.

Alvaro Ugalde, like Janzen, clearly approached the crisis with high-minded principles, and his decisive actions—undoubtedly supported by other unnamed actors—seem in the end to have made the difference.

President Monge and various government officials seem to have been ambivalent: as worried about fairness to the miners as they were about the fate of the park. (It should, of course, be recalled that the third section of the Earth Charter, under the heading, Social and Economic Justice, does call for "a sustainable livelihood . . . and social security and safety nets for those unable to support themselves.")

The miners were clearly not motivated by high-minded principles, and Wallace reports one of them as replying to Janzen, when he complained about the loss of fish, "Well, Señor, there are a lot of shrimp in the ocean" (134). But no one should denigrate the legitimacy of small actors' concerns for their families in such controversies—even if, as Wallace indicates in this case, many of them were opportunists.

The Costa Rican public? Wallace's picture of them is unflattering—easily swayed from depicting miners as tourist attractions, to outrage over the park's devastation, to amusement over the miners' march on the capital. Perhaps defenders of Earth Charter principles would say the public needs to be educated—and if, in this case, they had been, the favorable outcome would have come sooner.

Osa's Biological Corridor Saved from a Wood Chip Mill in the 1990s

Our second case study focuses on saving Osa's biodiversity corridor, linking two national parks, rather than on Corcovado National Park itself. And again there is an excellent study that tells the story, Helena van den Hombergh's (1999) *Guerreros del Golfo Dulce*.

Van den Hombergh's cast of characters is much larger and more diverse than Wallace's. The struggle she focuses on is the campaign to prevent Ston Forestal, S.A., the Costa Rican subsidiary of the multinational paper company, Stone Container Corporation (based in Chicago), from building a wood chip mill—for exportation—in the northwest corner of the Golfo Dulce, which separates the Osa Peninsula from the mainland. The mill would have impacted a proposed biological diversity corridor intended to link Corcovado National Park with Piedras Blancas National Park (originally a separate section of Corcovado) in one of two ways. One path of the corridor would have run right past the mill. The other, a few kilometers farther north, would have been impacted by road building and the moving of large trucks and construction equipment. Either way, the corridor would have been effectively breached, and Corcovado would eventually have become an ecological island. (That may still happen.)

Van den Hombergh's story centers around the activities of the Asociación Ecologista Costarricense (AECO, ecological association of Costa Rica), aided by the Asociación para la Defensa de los Recursos Naturales y el Desarrollo Sostenible de la Peninsula de Osa (Pro Defensa for short: association to defend the natural resources of and sustainable development in Osa) and various international environmental organizations—Dutch and German, especially, but also including Greenpeace. AECO was a radical environmentalist organization that had already waged several environmental and anti-pollution battles in Costa Rica before this one; its ideology, van den Hombergh says, was overtly socialist and opposed to corporate capitalist depradations of the environment (and impoverishment of workers). Leaders of AECO in the Osa campaign included Maria del Mar Cordero Fernández and Emile Rojas—who were killed in a suspicious fire in San José just days after the limited victory over Ston Forestal.

Pro Defensa was a committee of locals promoted by AECO in 1993 to help carry on the public campaign.

Numerous international environmental organizations got involved, including Greenpeace—which sent one of its ships into the Golfo Dulce at the height of the anti-Ston campaign.

Several government agencies were directly involved. Principal among these was the leadership of the Area de Conservacion de Osa (ACOSA), the branch of the Sistema Nacional de Areas de Conservación (SINAC), under the Ministerio del Ambiente y Energía (MINAE), which had conservation responsibilities for the Osa Peninsula, including Corcovado, Piedras Blancas National Park, and the Golfo Dulce Forest Reserve. (The Reserve included the area where the biological corridor was planned.) The safest thing to say about ACOSA's role is that it was ambivalent; the leaders clearly supported the creation of the corridor—and hence blocking the chip mill—but they were hamstrung by government policy, which favored development in the area. The political parties, including the Liberationist administration of the famed Nobel Peace Prize winner Oscar Arias, straddled the fence between development and conservation.

In the end, it was other government bodies, the Controlaría (an agency overseeing public works) and the Defensoría (the government ombudsman), that tipped the scales against Ston Forestal.

Scientists were active on both sides of the debate, with the renowned biologist Gerardo Budowski championing Ston Forestal's plans for reforestation—although, in this case, that meant large plantations of gmelina, a fast-growing nonnative species. Even Daniel Janzen, mentioned earlier as one of the saviors of Corcovado from the gold miners, at first sided with the reforestation plans, though he later came around to defend the biodiversity corridor idea.

Among quasi-scientific groups, the most important champion of the corridor was the Programa Bosques de Osa (BOSCOSA) of the Fundación Neotropica, which produced a valuable report spelling out the merits of the corridor idea. (Unfortunately, according to van den Hombergh, the authors hid behind a mask of scientific objectivity and would not go public, officially, against Ston Forestal. Still, the BOSCOSA report turned out to be decisive in a way.)

The most important scientist in this case was Hans Hartmann of the University Blaise Pascal in France, who was called in to do an in-depth study of the biological impact of a chip mill on the Golfo Dulce. He proved beyond doubt that the impact would be devastating, not least on a coral reef in the middle of the gulf. More generally, the mill would have devastated mangrove forests on the banks of the gulf, all sorts of fish species, marine birds and mammals (including whales and dolphins), reptiles, and so on. The report, "Golfo Dulce 2000," produced by Hartmann and his team, turned out to be *the* decisive scientific report.

The locals who became involved covered a broad range, from AECO's Pro Defensa supporters to fishermen in the gulf, to local farmers and others lulled by the promise of jobs.

And of course, Ston Forestal cannot be left out of the story. In the early days, the company seems to have been committed simply to profit; later, it took on a "green" image, both in terms of idealistic depictions of the advantages of reforestation over further tree cutting for farms and an explicit company plan of environmental protection.

In the end, Ston Forestal lost and the mill plans were scrapped—leaving the biodiversity corridor still unofficial but a dream for the future. Or rather, Ston was merely slowed down: it was given permission for a mill on the mainland side of the gulf, near Golfito, where its operations were supposed to be less damaging—and would not directly impact the corridor. (At the moment, the chip mill is still not operating, and wood pulp is not being exported from Golfito, though another company is making pencils using Ston Forestal wood.)

What can be said about Earth Charter-type principles and their impact on this struggle?

Clearly the international environmental organizations were motivated by the highest principles—as was the case with AECO, the group of radical activists leading the campaign. On the other hand, Pro Defensa locals supported AECO as much to preserve jobs as to preserve the forest.

Government agencies, from the top down, remained ambivalent—torn between the promise of development for Costa Rica's poorest region and conservation ideals—right up to the point when the Controlaría and the Defensoría agencies acted decisively against Ston's plans. Probably ACOSA's local leaders were, at heart, against the chip mill plan, and to that extent supported conservation ideals; but they were hamstrung by government policies. And the two major political parties were, as usual, ambivalent.

The BOSCOSA project authors probably expressed the highest ideals of biodiversity—and they were backed up by Hartmann's devastatingly negative assessment of the impact on the biodiversity of the gulf. But, perhaps because of the Fundación Neotropica's quasi-governmental status, they remained "scientifically neutral" to the end. And, as mentioned, other scientists took stands on both sides of the development/conservation divide.

In this case, Ston Forestal is perhaps the most intriguing actor. The company was, from the beginning, painted as the "heavy" by the AECO activists and their international environmentalist supporting groups. But Costa Rican officials, supported by scientists, always presented the company and its plans as environment-friendly. And, by the end of the campaign, Ston was promoting itself as a truly green corporation.

As in the first case, Earth Charter-type principles were clearly important, and AECO's defenders might even say they were decisive. But many other actors were involved, and their motives were decidedly mixed.

Conclusion

One week after the Integrity conference in Costa Rica for which this paper was prepared, Costa Rican officials with responsibility for their country's contribution to the Central American biological corridor held a meeting not far from the site of the conference. Fully a third of the presentations at their meeting focused on the corridor linking Corcovado with Piedras Blancas and on to connect with the main corridor. The Costa Rican officials concluded that, to save the Osa corridor, not only will major international environmental groups have to contribute large sums of money, but much work will have to be done at the local level. A Corcovado Foundation has been established to lead this effort, and the effort will clearly need to involve all the actors in the chip mill case, and more. And that means that there will continue to be an incredible diversity of motivations of the various actors; many levels of government will get involved, often with conflicting and competing jurisdictions; there will always be scientific uncertainty—and of course public opinion will be as fickle as ever. Most important, we have to recognize that the outcome may turn out to be as equivocal as in the Ston Forestal chip mill case.

So I take these case studies to be emblematic. Wherever in the world people undertake the "hotspots" strategy to protect Earth's biodiversity, or wherever they take up other environmental crusades, under the banner of the Earth Charter or any other statement of high principle, the practical reality will be the same. As important as it is to invoke high principles of the sort proposed in the Earth Charter, it is just as important to become political activists. And it is never assured that the outcome of a struggle to make any particular development project sustainable (whatever that means, concretely) will be what defenders of Earth Charter-type principles hope for. High-sounding principles are good, possibly even necessary. But blood, sweat, and tears are also needed to get any worthwhile environmental goal accomplished.

References

Brandon, Katrina, et al. 1998. *Parks in Peril: People, Politics, and Protected Areas.* Washington, D.C.: The Nature Conservancy and Island Press.

The Earth Charter Initiative. 2002. "The Earth Charter." San José, Costa Rica: Earth Council. <http://www.earthcharter.org/earthcharter/charter.htm> (January 12, 2002).

Hickman, Larry A. 1999. "Green Pragmatism: Reals without Realism, Ideals without Idealism." Pp. 39–56 in C. Mitcham et al., eds., *Research in Philosophy and Technology*, vol. 18: Philosophies of the Environment and Technology. Stamford, Conn: JAI Press.

Mittermeier, Russell, et al. 2000. *Hotspots: Earth's Biologically Richest and Most Endangered Terrestrial Ecoregions*. Chicago: Conservation International and University of Chicago Press.

Van den Hombergh, Helena. 1999. *Guerreros del Golfo Dulce: Industria Forestal y Conflicto en la Peninsula de Osa, Costa Rica.* San José, Costa Rica: Editorial Departamento Ecumenico de Investigaciones.

Wallace, David Rains. 1992. *The Quetzal and the Macaw: The Story of Costa Rica's National Parks*. San Francisco: Sierra Club Books.

Chapter 25

Gendered Resistance to Corporate Environmentalism and Debt-for-Nature Swaps in Costa Rica

Ana Isla and Terisa E. Turner

In 1984, Lovejoy of the World Wildlife Fund proposed a new approach to Third World debt management called debt-for-nature swaps (DFNs). Such swaps involve government agencies and nongovernmental organizations (NGOs) purchasing part of a country's foreign debt for conservation-related projects. After the Earth Summit in 1992, several governments embraced debt-for-nature swaps as a multi-purpose bilateral mechanism to generate profits for private capital under a complex new ideological formulation purporting to "solve" problems of debt, the environment, poverty and gender equity.

The corporate NGOs' enthusiasm for debt-for-nature swaps was not shared by peasants or by Indigenous Peoples. According to Santos Adam Afsua, of the Inter-Ethnic Association for the Development of the Peruvian Jungle:

> We believe, first of all, that the debt has been created by a total mismanagement of foreign loans, of foreign capital. . . . This is one of the reasons we have met with the banks and the environmental organizations: to make them understand that the debt-for-nature swaps cannot take place with our land because that debt is not ours (*Multinational Monitor*, December 1989: 29–30).

Debt-for-nature swaps are here examined in the context of the specific gendered-class interests of restructured global capital. The promotion of debt-for-nature swaps reflects the convergence of three groups of gendered-class actors within or aligned to international capital. These are first, the owners of some of the largest, most globalized transnational corporations; second, those members of the Third World capitalist class who became major investors in transnational capital; and third, the expanding predominantly male managerial class that both runs the transnationals and dominates the largest international environmental organizations. This strategic bloc within capital is elaborating a discourse and practice of corporate environmentalism, which includes projects for "sustainable development," "women in development," and debt-for-nature swaps using "the global commons" and "natural capital" for the further commodification of biodiversity and unpaid work (or what we call "shadow labor") in the interests of transnational accumulation.

Shadow Work and the Male Deal

Our gendered and ethnicized class analysis centres on three distinctive conceptualizations. First, we emphasize as global agents the majority of unwaged as opposed to the minority of waged workers as simultaneously (1) the source of capital's renewed accumulation in the post 1980 period of restructuring and (2) the source of most of the effective resistance and "counterplanning from the commons" against capital. Second, we recognize that the unwaged majority are predominantly women, peasants, indigenous peoples, students, children, and others outside of the classic Marxian category of the waged proletariat. The unwaged's intensified exploitation by globalizing capital is effected, in important part, through "male deals" that are cross-class and often cross-race arrangements between men from the exploited and the exploiting classes. For instance, the new strategic capitalist bloc includes (mainly European) men who manage environmental NGOs as intermediaries effecting the commodification of nature, subsistence labor, indigenous knowledge, and what McMurtry (2001) calls the "civil commons." Third, social movements in which women and indigenous peoples predominate are at the forefront of gendered, ethnicized class resistance to corporate enclosures and heightened exploitation, not by chance but because such unwaged peoples (1) are central to contemporary global forms of exploitation and (2) are more autonomous from capital than are waged workers, due to their claim to common resources and community. Turner and Brownhill (2001) have characterized this contemporary process of anti-corporate globalization from below as a struggle between commodified and subsistence political economies. In this struggle, the new "globalized" unwaged workers (Dyer-Witheford 1999) exercise their special capacities to draw into ever more powerful alliances all sections of the dispossessed in movements enforcing reparations and the re-appropriation of land and other capital, which have been enclosed and alienated. Some elements of what we call gendered class analysis warrant further elaboration.

We use the term "shadow work" to refer to the hidden character of the work of producing labor power within capitalist relations of production. If labor power is the human capacity to work, then its production underlies all other work. Women produce children. Women, men, and the social institutions they have built over generations, such as educational and health facilities, further develop in the child the capacity to labor. The value of public facilities is quantified, for instance, when they are privatized and purchased. But the value capital gives to shadow labor and the essential facilities for its actualization is a gross underestimate because it does not consider the value such labor and facilities have for past and future generations. Capital makes static and commodifies shadow work. We should be clear, however, that shadow work is not a constant set of specific work activities, but rather a particular relationship both among workers and between workers and capital. These relationships operate in the home or the community, where women perform the greater part of the unwaged labor of producing people and producing labor power, along with cheap wage goods. For example, the Canada/Costa Rica DFNs financed a medicinal plant exporting project incorporating some of the women in the town of Abanico. The women are working at below survival income producing cheap wage goods for industrialized country markets. Their long workday forces their daughters to take over domestic duties. Daughters thereby contribute to the production of the labor power their mothers are expending in the Abanico project. Through corporate environmentalism, two female generations have been transformed from being members of relatively autonomous subsistence communities to being shadow workers.

In most instances, unwaged labor performed in the home and in the community is organized by a gendered division of labor that is part of capitalist relations of production (James 1976; Cox and Federici 1975). Unwaged work may be "captured" directly or through male deals and used for capital's profits. Or, depending on the situation and balance of forces, noncommodified work may enhance the vitality of the noncorporate, noncapitalist, subsistence political economy (Bennholt-Thomsen and Mies 2000).

Individuals and groups who directly produce the majority of the goods and services needed for the production of their own labor power and the labor power of others, have a direct interest in preventing capitalist commodification of communal relationships, the environment and public space (Turner and Benjamin 1995). Furthermore, those individuals and groups whose relationship with capital is primarily defined by "reproductive labor," especially women, have a unique social power to appropriate and abolish the technical/structural divisions of the working class in the struggle against capitalist "enclosure" or the privatization of common resources.

The relationship between capital and shadow labor is prone to crisis and struggle in two ways. First, capital depends on the capacities of women in general, as well as women among groups of peasants, indigenous peoples, and migrant workers, to perform most of the work of producing the commodity labor power. Because capital does not negotiate a wage contract with its shadow laborers, it relies on intermediaries such as male wage laborers, to discipline the shadow workers' labor. This intermediary relationship between capital and largely male waged workers we call the "male deal." This organization of reproductive labor also conveys varying degrees of social power to shadow workers as they use their relationship to the natural environment and other areas of noncommodified production to struggle against their exploitation by rebelling against the male dealers and against capital.

Second, precisely because capital does not pay a market price for the production of labor power and the natural and built environments, in periods of crisis capital will tend to exhaust these conditions of production by intensifying exploitation while at the same time reducing its support for their production (Cleaver 1989). The exhaustion of these "free-to-capital" conditions of production constitutes a direct attack on women and other unwaged peoples who nurture people (labor power), nature (the "global commons"), and public space (public services largely staffed by and serving women). The threatened exhaustion of the social and ecological fabric of production and human life establishes new opportunities for the strengthening of solidarity among the various elements of the dispossessed class.

Debt-for-Nature Swaps: Critical Issues

The rise of corporate environmentalism reconstructs nature conservation (1) as a key element in the process of building and maintaining consensus within the strategic power bloc composed of the owners of the largest, most globalized transnationals, the managers who run these corporations, and the Third World capitalists who have invested in them; (2) as an opportunity to employ the interlocking crises of debt and nature to organize and build support for new strategies of accumulation based on biodiversity in the interest of these specific gendered-class actors; and (3) as a strategy of counter-insurgency aimed directly at those popular organizations most effective in opposing capitalist restructuring.

Among the key criticisms of DFNs as articulated by grassroots organizations and activists are, first, that DFNs have done nothing to "solve" the debt crisis. The few hundred million U.S. dollars in southern debt that has been written off is of limited significance relative to the trillions in debt held by private and multilateral banks. DFNs are also criticized as undermining calls for a debt moratorium (IBASE 1992, 15, 27–8). Second, DFNs are an inappropriate and ineffective method of promoting nature conservation. They allow foreign NGOs and government agencies to manage nature through controlling new regimes of investment, and through the extension of the price system across space and time. Among other things, this has meant the entrenchment of a North American "ringed fence" approach to conservation through conservation areas that has generally failed to prevent land colonization and corporate resource extraction, much less address the underlying issue of land rights. Indeed, such approaches may actually encourage or legitimize the uprooting of local peoples, including indigenous and peasant communities. In addition to the violation of human rights evident in such displacement, dispossession of local communities may destroy patterns of stewardship essential to preserving the ecosystem that the conservation area system is intended to protect. Finally, even when the creation of conservation areas does not directly displace local peoples, the process may undermine efforts to establish local control of resource management or to establish indigenous land title and demarcate indigenous territory.

In sum, DFNs are, in part, public relations and conflict management interventions of value to the leading sectors of international capital, which promote them through their home governments, NGOs, and multilateral agencies. Nature swaps are also mechanisms for genetic engineering firms and the pharmaceutic industry to secure access to research sites in the world's most biodiverse regions. Of crucial importance is the fact that debt-for-nature investments destroy subsistence relations while incorporating indigenous peoples and peasants, notably women, into corporate market relations on highly exploitative terms. We now turn to a case history of debt-for-nature investments involving Canada and Costa Rica.

Canada–Costa Rica Debt-for-Nature Swap Investments

The rest of this chapter focuses on three communities (Fortuna, Z-Trece, and Abanico), which were subject from 1991 to "new enclosures" by Canada–Costa Rica debt-for-nature swap investments.

The two dimensions of the debt-for-nature swap considered here are the Arenal Conservation Area-Tilaran (ACA-Tilaran) Land Plan and a women's micro-enterprise. The World Wildlife Fund-Canada (WWF-C) enclosed and commodified territory of the villages of Fortuna and Z-Trece and, in partnership with Asociacion ANDAR, organized a women's medicinal plant and organic agriculture micro-enterprise in Abanico.

The ACA–Tilaran Land Plan

In ACA–Tilaran the World Wild Life Fund-Canada (WWF-C) and the Costa Rican Ministry of Environment and Energy, (MINAE) organized the Arenal Project. It involved the development of a Land Plan for "sustainable development" covering 250,561.5 ha and affecting 108 communities in the area that were neither informed of nor included in the decision making that dramatically and drastically changed their lives and livelihood. The Land Plan redefined biodiversity as natural capital, appropriated land and wildlife as resources for scientific research for the exclusive use of researchers, undermined local livelihood, and transformed communities from agricultural producers to service providers.

The Land Plan has redefined biodiversity. From being a relational category, which was ecologically, socially, and culturally embedded in local communities, nature has become "natural capital." This embraces the entire environmental heritage of a country, including agricultural lands, pasturelands, timber resources, and non-timber forest, as well as protected areas' biological diversity, water, and non-renewable resources such as metals, minerals, oil, coal, and gas.

All these elements, as "natural capital," must have market prices. The Land Plan has commodified biodiversity by selling oxygen produced by the trees. The Forestry Incentive Program sells pollution credits as "environmental services" (oxygen) to Canada, Norway, Germany, Holland, Mexico and Japan (*El Estado de la Nacion* 1997, 129). The project is marketing biological diversity. Bioprospecting researchers appropriate local knowledge of the attributes of the native plants and animals by hiring the daughters and sons of the rural communities as parataxonomists who initiate the collection. The Land Plan appropriated land and wildlife as resources for scientific research for the exclusive use of authorized researchers. Land that once belonged to the community to be shared among its members now belongs to the Ministry of Environment and Energy (MINAE). Finally the Arenal Project is privatizing the water of the community.

The Land Plan undermined local livelihoods in three ways. First, the land enclosure of the nucleus area eliminated the rights of the communities to their territory and resources and transformed community members into criminal intruders. When the police find community members breaking regulations stipulated in the Land Plan (that is, not paying fees or intruding on designated research areas), they confiscate anything the individual may have obtained on the land (e.g., fish or game) and whatever tools were used, and then report the offence to the office of the public prosecutor.

Among the settlers in the area, natural resources (wild or cultivated) were considered the property of the landowner. However, a significant number of community members traditionally hunted in the jungle surrounding the forest reserves and national parks, or fished in the numerous rivers that now are closed to them as part of the conservation area. MINAE's offices are taxing the free gifts of nature by selling permits to anyone who wants to fish, hunt, or cut forests. Villagers found their immemorial rights to the forest and its products circumscribed. Community members, whose source of sustenance and livelihood is still nature, are turned into criminals.

Second, the Land Plan undermined local livelihoods by violently evicting entire communities. While the majority of the land around the volcano is not arable, or adequate for cattle ranching, small farms had existed in the area. In 1994, this land was bought or expropriated by MINAE to create the Arenal Conservation National Park. Peasants who had organized their lives by clearing land for agricultural production and pasture around the Arenal Basin were thrown off the land. Only 54 percent of the landowners were paid. They lost land, pasture, houses, dairies, and roads. Former property owners have become hut renters *(ranchos)* or slum inhabitants *(tugurios)*. The personal effects of the *campesinas/os*, such as cars and small electrical appliances, were taken by the commercial banks when they could not afford to repay their loans acquired for development (Monestel Arce 1999). When, in desperation, some of them returned to their land to plant yucca, beans, maize, and other subsistence foods, they were declared to have broken the law and some of them were thrown in jail (Siete Dias de Teletica 1999).

Third, the Land Plan transformed communities from agricultural producers to service providers. It deliberately reproduced the social division of labor of the world-system and made some communities specialized areas for eco-tourism. Eco-tourism is described as environmentally friendly, sustainable, and nature-based. It is promoted as an alternative activity that generates income while protecting the environment. This activity promotes visits to relatively undisturbed natural areas with the aim of studying, admiring, resting, and enjoying the Arenal Volcano scenery, wild plants and animals, as well as any existing cultural aspects. But tourism disturbs the areas. For instance, in Fortuna, until recently, farming accounted for an important part of local people's activity. But around 1996 Fortuna's rural areas became less agricultural and more service oriented. Eco-tourism produced changes not only in the production structure, but also in employment. In 1999 the commerce sector, which includes hotels, rental cabins, restaurants, and tourist attractions, became the number one activity in Fortuna Centro (Fortuna City) and Z-Trece. It employed some 240 workers, representing the majority of waged workers in any single sector.

Women's Micro-Enterprise

The Abanico Project is defined as a *campesina* small family business development alternative that will foster community economic welfare in a sustainable environment with gender equality (Asociacion ANDAR 1996). However, the subsistence economy and the seven members of the Abanico Project have suffered serious negative consequences from their involvement.

As natural capital, medicinal plants produced for the market in micro-enterprises changed from being a use value for *campesinas/os* family consumption to being an exchange value. Traditionally rural women were the keepers of medicinal knowledge and plants. In the past, most rural women grew medicinal plants around their homes because they used the plants to cure their families' ailments. Thus medicinal plants represented support for their own health. Plants produced for the market lose their biological, social, ethical, and cultural value to become mainly an economic value. In the commodification process, medicinal plants lose their potency as the loss of wild surroundings and different sunlight exposures change their chemical properties. A plant in its natural ecosystem is interacting with other plants and its biotic resources (soil, water, light). Therefore the plant conserves its properties as a natural defence. Its genetic strength is more active and dynamic against its predators (Alvarado 1998). As medicinal plants become commodified, women become the commodity producers. When carried to markets, medicinal plants change from being a source of women's power (as it was women who provided *cocimientos*, which is a combination of plants for healing purposes), to being a source of women's exploitation. The pharmaceutical companies in particular have exploited the plants and the labor of those who stewarded the land where the plants grew. These plants are sometimes stolen by bio-prospectors, but are often delivered by local women such as in Abanico, where the work is organized by international NGOs.

Each stage of the Abanico Project was built on loans from both NGOs (WWF-C and Asociacion ANDAR) at between 20 percent and 33 percent interest for which the women remain liable (Grupo GEMA 1998). Thus their micro-enterprise activity was a source of deep personal and collective debt for Abanico Project members. To develop a micro-enterprise, families had to transfer an important part of their land from food production to the production of an export-oriented commodity. Yet the financial return to women involved is so small that it does not cover the survival of even one family member. Women involved in the project earned an average of 11 U.S. cents an hour in 1998, or one-ninth of the Costa Rican minimum agricultural wage of 97 U.S. cents per hour. The women's work is time and labor intensive. In the face of inadequate income the legal working day in those micro-enterprises has disappeared. Working for less than the minimum wage, small rural groups such as this will eventually collapse from the exhaustion of a never-ending competitive spiral of reducing real wages (Isla 2000).

Since 1999, on Friday afternoons, these women have spent additional working time preparing food to sell in *la feria* (local market) in order to pay their debts to the NGOs. Women's working time has increased with the closing of the health center and the elimination of one teacher in the elementary school as a result of the structural adjustment programs, imposed by the IMF and World Bank. The increased workload for women contributes to the intergenerational transference of poverty, as household duties are passed to their daughters, decreasing education possibilities.

The Abanico Project was designed in such a way that the group provided medicinal plants to the NGO for resale on the world market at prices that are below their production cost. The marketing activity permits the imposition of extreme pressure and the exercise of a high degree of social control over the women's group by ANDAR, which is the sole buyer of the produce. In the income generating project the members and their families' work is not only cheapened but also controlled because the producers are isolated and unorganized. This process is part of what Mies (1993), von werlhof (1988), and Turner (1994) have called the "housewifization of labor," whereby women's autonomous subsistence work on their own account is eliminated in favor of their unpaid or poorly paid exploitation as shadow workers within capitalist market relations. The housewifization is facilitated by the fact that the medicinal plant project work is "invisibilized" as a prolongation of women's domestic duties at home, and women in this micro-enterprise are not seen as workers.

In practice, in their attempts to generate income, the members of the Abanico women's group have become more dependent on forces over which they have no control, namely the international markets and interest rates. NGOs, by defining women as small entrepreneurs, have advanced the commodification of women's work and ensured the availability on the world market of local produce, local biomass, and unpaid labor. NGOs have not enhanced women's income and independence. In the Abanico case, the market is subsidized by women's labor on the plot, in the household, and in the community.

Resistance and Counterplanning from the Commons

Costa Rican communities have been significantly disempowered by the dismantling in 1948 of the political and union movements and the sell-out by the political class, which, overwhelmed by debt in the 1980s, accepted USAID funds, thereby reinforcing a colonial relationship with the United States (Sojo 1992). Despite this repressive reestablishment of male deals, localities resist through "everyday practices" such as humor, pilfering, slander, foot dragging, false compliance, feigned ignorance, and sabotage to defy the political and economic dominance of rulers (Scott 1990). Local communities use "weapons of the weak" but they also pursue organized, systematic, and cooperative forms of resistance.

Indigenous people refuse to commodify land, trees and other biodiversity. For example, the Canada–Costa Rica debt-for-nature initiative organized a 1998 conference that offered indigenous people help in defending themselves and benefiting from biodiversity negotiations. A spokesperson for the Talamanca indigenous people told Isla that "We do not want to know about making business with biodiversity; we are happy living like we are. What we want is just to keep and use the land, with the knowledge our ancestors handed down to us." Indigenous peoples tend to see biodiversity as priceless and, therefore, non-negotiable. Biodiversity is their pharmacy, their supermarket, and the source of their myths and traditions. Selling biodiversity is comparable to selling their culture and their souls.

Peasants impacted by the DFNs have participated in countrywide resistance to government efforts to privatize state services. In March 2000 a three-week national strike succeeded in forcing the government to reverse its compliance with IMF-dictates to privatize ICE, the publicly owned electricity and telephone company. Women from many small-scale enterprises joined together in 1999 to refuse the DFN-NGOs' exploitative interest rates and marketing monopoly. They participated in a nationwide refusal organized through the Coordinadora Anti-Petrolera to cede territory to foreign petroleum exploration and exploitation. Indigenous people in Costa Rica have successfully defied oil company drilling on reservations, and seek extensions of the no-go zones for big oil to the Caribbean Sea. This expansion of territorial claims underlies an alliance that indigenous peoples have forged with fishing peoples, many of whom are former dockworkers who have been laid off by structural adjustment, which dictates that the state-owned port facilities be privatized. Women are at the forefront of all components of the alliance. The stakes increased with the signing in April 2001 of the Canada–Costa Rica free trade agreement and the strength evident in

Quebec City from April 20–22, 2001, of a hemispheric social alliance and new democracy movement against the Free Trade Area of the Americas.

These and other forms of resistance demonstrate the capacities of "shadow workers," including women, peasants and indigenous peoples, to unite different factions of the dispossessed class in a double-edged mobilization. On the one hand, the new enclosures are rejected and blocked. On the other, democratic self-valorization and service-provision are affirmed through defense of public state capacities and local subsistence political economies.

Conclusion: The Limits of Capitalist Ecology

There is, then, a fundamental gap between the goals of popular movements in relation to the debt-nature crisis and the solutions that capital would impose. This gap is the terrain of gendered class struggle.

This chapter has delineated three dynamics of class composition, economic restructuring, and gendered-class struggle, which are reflected in the promotion of DFNs as a component of the corporate solution to the debt-nature crisis. The first of these dynamics is the recomposition of capital itself. On the one hand, the owners, investors and managers of global capital have the potential to form a strategic alliance or power bloc within capital. This is based on their mutual interests in restoring the rate of profit and the hegemony of a global system of capitalist accumulation badly battered by the popular uprisings of the 1960s. The politicized linking of profit-making activities and conservation projects adopted by most environmental NGOs throws into question their commitment to nature's conservation, given the evidence that shows that profit-making activities have depleted nature more quickly than any other human force in history. On the other hand, the Third World investors and the managerial class find themselves increasingly on the front line of social struggle, as this economic restructuring threatens to exhaust the ecological and social basis of capitalist production and human life. Corporate environmentalism is part of the new male deal holding this strategic alliance together.

The second dynamic is capital's efforts to restructure the relations and conditions in which work is performed. Through a sequence of economic restructuring measures initiated with the oil crisis of the early 1970s, capital has reduced workers' access to relatively high-paying and secure waged work as a means of increasing the exploitation of various forms of low-paid or unwaged, casual or invisible labor typically performed by women in general, as well as by women and men in the urban informal sector and among peasant and indigenous societies.

The third dynamic is the growth in popular insurgency led by precisely those workers whom capital has targeted to pay the price of economic restructuring. These subject groups not only have the power to resist capitalist restructuring, but more significantly the power to transform the social relations of capitalist production through their struggles. This potential has repeatedly forced capital to redouble its efforts to carry out the restructuring of labor relations and to do so by directly attacking the very basis of insurgent social power, namely access to arable land, non-commodified social environments, and public services.

Thus on the one hand capitalist restructuring of labor relations, the enclosure of natural resources, and the debt-imposed assault on state spending, have brought on a reproduction crisis for the urban and rural poor. Capital has enclosed and eroded the natural and social infrastructure through which the poor reproduce their own labor power on a daily and a generational basis. On the other hand, it is precisely in the face of such enclosures that broad-based movements of women and men are struggling to retain or reappropriate popular control over the means of subsistence, and to exert locally defined values, meanings, and forms of social relations in defense of the commons.

References

Alvarado, Celso. 1998. MINAE biologist. Personal Interview.

Asociacion ANDAR. 1996. "Resumen Ejecutivo." *La Educacion Participativa y el Enfoque de genero para fortalecer las capacidades de organizacion de Mujeres y Hombres Campesinos de la Region Huetar Norte.* Unpublished paper. San José, Costa Rica.

Benjamin, Craig S., and Terisa E. Turner. 1993. "Counter-Planning from the Commons: Labor, Capital and the 'New Social Movements,'" *LABOUR, Capital and Society*, 26 (April): 1.

Bennholdt-Thomsen, Veronika, and Maria Mies. 2000. *The Subsistence Perspective: Beyond the Globalised Economy.* London: Zed Books.

Cleaver, Harry. 1989. "Close the IMF, Abolish Debt and End Development: A Class Analysis of the International Debt Crisis," *Capital & Class* 39: 17–50.

Cox, Nicole, and Silvia Federici. 1975. *Counterplanning from the Kitchen - Wages for Housework: A Perspective on Capital and the Left.* Bristol, England: Falling Wall Press.

Dyer-Witheford, Nick. 1999. *Cyber-Marx: Circuits and Cycles of Struggle in High Technology Capitalism.* Chicago: University of Illinois Press.

El Estado de la Nacion en Desarrollo Humano Sostenible (1996). 1997. Primera Edicion. San José, Costa Rica.

Grupo GEMA. 1998. Abanico's Ecological Women's Group that runs the Abanico Medicinal Plant and Organic Agriculture Project (the Abanico Project), Personal interview.

IBASE. 1992. *Debt Swaps, Development and Environment.* Rio de Janeiro: Instituto Brasileiro do Análises Socials e Econômica.

Isla, Ana. 2000. *An Environmental Feminist Analysis of Canada/Costa Rica Debt-for-Nature Investment: A Case Study of Intensifying Commodification.* Doctoral Dissertation, Ontario Institute for Studies in Education, University of Toronto, Canada.

James, Selma. 1976. *Women, the Unions and Work.* Bristol: Falling Wall Press.

Laclau, Ernesto, and Chantal Mouffe. 1987. "Post-Marxist without Apologies." *New Left Review* 166: 79–106.

McMurtry, John. 2001. *Value Wars.* London: Pluto.

Mies, Maria, and Vandana Shiva. 1993. *Ecofeminism*. London: Zed Books.

Monestel Arce, Yehudi. 1999. "Campesinos Precaristas en su Propia Tierra." *Eco Catolico* (January 17): 11.

Multinational Monitor. 1989. Washington, D.C. (December).

Scott, James. 1990. *Domination and the Arts of Resistance*. New Haven: Yale University Press.

Siete Dias de Teletica. 1999. Channel 7, San José, Costa Rica (January).

Sojo, Carlos. 1992. *La Mano Visible del Mercado*. Coordinadora Regional de Investigacion Economicas y Sociales (CRIES).

Turner, Terisa E. 1994. "Rastafari and the New Society: East African and Caribbean Feminist Roots of a Popular Movement to Reclaim the Earthly Commons." Pp. 9–58 in *Arise Ye Mighty People! Gender, Class and Race in Popular Struggles*, edited by Terisa E. Turner. Trenton, N. J.: Africa World Press.

Turner, Terisa E., and Craig S. Benjamin. 1995. "Not in Our Nature: The Male Deal and Corporate Solutions to the Debt-Nature Crisis." *Review: Journal of the Fernand Braudel Center*, State University of New York, Binghamton, N.Y. 17 no. 2 (Spring): 209–58.

Turner, Terisa E., and Leigh Brownhill. 2001. "Fight for Fertility." In *There Is an Alternative,* edited by Veronika Bennholdt-Thomsen and Claudia von Werlhof. London: Zed Books.

Von Werlhof, Claudia. 1988. "The Proletarian Is Dead: Long Live the Housewife!" Pp. 168–81 in *Women: The Last Colony*, edited by Maria Mies, Veronika Bennholdt-Thomsen, and Claudia von Werlhof. London and New Jersey: Zed Books.

"Whose common Future?" 1992. Special issue of *The Ecologist*. 22: 4 (July/August). Cambridge, Mass.: MIT Press.

About the Contributors

Mark Anielski is Director, Sustainability Measurement, Pembina Institute for Appropriate Development, Edmonton, Alberta, Canada, and a Senior Fellow with Redefining Progress (Oakland, California) and Occasional Lecturer at the School of Business, University of Alberta.

Julia J. Bartkowiak is Professor of Philosophy, with a specialization in Ethics, at Clarion University of Pennsylvania.

Eunice Blavascunas is a graduate student in cultural anthropology at the University of California, Santa Cruz.

Rubye Howard Braye is a facilitator with the Greenleaf Center for Servant-Leadership, Indianapolis, Indiana, and the Founder of JIL Group, specializing in business consulting, training, and personal coaching, Wilmington, North Carolina.

Abelardo Brenes is Senior Advisor in Education at the University for Peace and Professor of Psychology at the University of Costa Rica and the National University, Costa Rica. He served on the Earth Charter drafting committee.

Donald A. Brown is Senior Counsel for Sustainable Development for the Commonwealth of Pennsylvania Department of Environmental Protection. He is also director of the Pennsylvania Consortium for Interdisciplinary Environmental Policy, an organization comprised of 43 colleges and universities and the Commonwealth of Pennsylvania devoted to integrating environmental science, law, economics, and ethics in environmental decision making.

Luis Alberto Camargo is Founder and Executive Director of the Organization for Environmental Education and Protection (OpEPA) in Colombia, South America (http://www.opepa. org).

Maria Victoria (Vicky) Castillo is the National Program Assistant for the UN-IPEC-ILO Prevention and Elimination of Child Domestic Labour in South America Project and an Independent consultant in Colombia.

Victoria Davion is Professor of Philosophy at the University of Georgia. She is the founding editor of *Ethics and the Environment*, an interdisciplinary journal focusing on all aspects of environmental ethics.

Paul T. Durbin is Professor of Philosophy at the University of Delaware, where he also works with the Medical Scholars Program and the Center for Energy and Environmental Policy.

Clive A. Edwards is Professor of Entomology and Environmental Science, and Coordinator of the Soil Ecology Program, at the Ohio State University in Columbus, Ohio.

J. Ronald Engel is Research Professor in Environmental and Social Ethics at Meadville/Lombard Theological School affiliated with the University of Chicago, and Co-Director of The Hastings Center project on Nature/Polis/Ethics. He served on the Earth Charter drafting committee.

Fayen d'Evie is Deputy Executive Director of the Earth Council National Councils for Sustainable Development Programme, based in Costa Rica and New York.

Sonia Ftacnikova is a senior research worker at the Department of Radiation Protection in the Institute of Preventive and Clinical Medicine in Bratislava, Slovakia.

Steven M. Glass is Program Coordinator for the Earth Charter Secretariat located in San Jose, Costa Rica.

Robert Goodland is a tropical ecologist, the World Bank Group's environmental advisor in Washington, D.C. (RbtGoodland@aol.com), and author of 22 books on environmental assessment. He served as elected Metro Chair of the Ecological Society of America, and President of the International Association of Impact Assessment.

Mary A. Hamilton is at the University of Virginia, Darden School of Business. Her research in international management focuses on the effects that integrated strategic solutions inclusive of social, political, and environmental issues have on the firm value and the development of global capitalism.

Ana Isla, PhD, teaches at York University and the Ontario Institute for Studies in Education—The Transformative Learning Centre at the University of Toronto. She is an activist with Toronto Women for a Just and Healthy Planet.

James R. Karr is Professor of Fisheries and Zoology at the University of Washington, Seattle, Washington.

Emese Kiss, born and raised in Transylvania, is a poet, painter, and MSc student at the Institute for Resources and Environment at the University of British Columbia in Vancouver. Her thesis is a comparative analysis of the impacts of water law enforcement on corporations in B.C.'s Lower Fraser Basin and Washington State's Puget Sound Area.

Imre Lázár, MD, PhD, MSc, is head of the Centre of Environmental Anthropology and Behavioral Ecology at the Apor Vilmos Teachers Training College and Deputy Head of the Department of Medical Anthropology in the Institute of Behavioral Sciences at the Semmelweis University, Budapest, Hungary.

Garrick E. Louis is Assistant Professor of Environmental Systems in the Systems Engineering Department of the University of Virginia in the United States.

Ruth Miller Lucier is Professor of Philosophy and Religion, and Director of Interdisciplinary Studies, at Bennett College in Greensboro, N.C. She currently serves as Vice President of the International Society for Value Inquiry.

Luna M. Magpili is a PhD student in the Department of Systems and Information Engineering and the Environmental Systems Unit at the University of Virginia.

John McMurtry is Professor of Philosophy at the University of Guelph, a Fellow of the Royal Society of Canada, and author of numerous books and articles.

Peter Miller is senior scholar in the Department of Philosophy and the Centre for Forest Interdisciplinary Research at the University of Winnipeg, Canada.

David Pimentel is Professor of Ecology and Agricultural Science at Cornell University, Ithaca, New York. He has published more than 500 scientific papers and 20 books and has served on many national and government organizations.

William E. Rees received his PhD in population ecology and is currently a professor in the University of British Columbia's School of Community and Regional Planning. He is best known for pioneering the "ecological footprint" concept and is a founding member and past-president of the Canadian Society for Ecological Economics.

Steven C. Rockefeller is Professor Emeritus of Religion at Middlebury College, Vermont. From 1997 to 2000 he chaired the international Earth Charter drafting committee. He serves as a member of the Earth Charter Commission and of the Council of the UN University for Peace in Costa Rica. Active in the field of philanthropy, he is chairman of the Rockefeller Brothers Fund.

Lech Ryszkowski is Professor of Natural Sciences and Director of the Research Centre for Agricultural and Forest Environment of the Polish Academy of Sciences in Poznań, Poland. His major scientific interests are agroecology and protection of agricultural landscapes based on energy flow and matter cycling principles.

Colin L. Soskolne is Professor of Epidemiology and Graduate Coordinator in the Department of Public Health Sciences at the University of Alberta in Edmonton, Alberta, Canada.

János I. Tóth, PhD, is Associate Professor of Philosophy at the University of Szeged in Hungary.

Terisa E. Turner is Associate Professor of Sociology and Anthropology at the University of Guelph, Canada. She has written on gender, class, race, debt, resource conflict, international political economy, the environment, petroleum issues in Nigeria and Costa Rica, and oral histories of Mau Mau women in Kenya.

Patricia H. Werhane is the Peter and Adeline Ruffin Chair in Business Ethics and Senior Fellow at the Olsson Center for Applied Ethics at the Darden Graduate School of Business Administration, University of Virginia.

Laura Westra was principal investigator of the *Global Ecological Integrity Project* (SSHRC 1992–1999). She is Emerita Professor of Philosophy at the University of Windsor and a Doctor of Jurisprudence candidate at Osgoode Hall, York University. She is author or co-editor of 12 books and over 65 articles and chapters in books.

Naomi Zack is Professor of Philosophy at the University of Oregon, Eugene. Her most recent book is *Philosophy of Science and Race.*